PENGUIN BOOKS

The Schweinfurt–Regensburg Mission

On a visit to France and Belgium in 1967 Martin Middlebrook was so impressed by the military cemeteries on the 1914–18 battlefields that he decided to write a book describing just one day in that war through the eyes of the ordinary men who took part. This book, *The First Day on the Somme*, was published by Allen Lane in 1971 and received international acclaim. Martin Middlebrook has since written several other books which deal with important turning-points in the two world wars; these are *The Kaiser's Battle*, *The Nuremburg Raid*, *Convoy*, *The Peenemünde Raid*, *The Battle of Hamburg* and, with Patrick Mahoney, *Battleship*. A reference book, *The Bomber Command Diaries* (with Chris Everitt), and a book on the experiences of those involved in the 1982 Falklands War, entitled *Operation Corporate*, are being published in 1985. Most of Martin Middlebrook's books are published in Penguin.

Martin Middlebrook

The Schweinfurt–Regensburg Mission

American Raids on 17 August 1943

Penguin Books

Penguin Books Ltd, Harmondsworth, Middlesex, England
Viking Penguin Inc., 40 West 23rd Street, New York, New York 10010, U.S.A.
Penguin Books Australia Ltd, Ringwood, Victoria, Australia
Penguin Books Canada Ltd, 2801 John Street, Markham, Ontario, Canada L3R 1B4
Penguin Books (N.Z.) Ltd, 182–190 Wairau Road, Auckland 10, New Zealand

First published by Allen Lane 1983
Published in Penguin Books 1985

Made and printed in Great Britain by
Richard Clay (The Chaucer Press) Ltd, Bungay, Suffolk
Set in Times

This book is dedicated to the memory of those American airmen who lost their lives while flying from England during the Second World War.

Contents

List of Plates 9
List of Maps and Diagrams 10
Introduction 11

1 A Dream Delayed 15
2 The Targets 29
3 Chain of Command 41
4 Briefings 65
5 Revised Plans 74
6 The Luftwaffe 89
7 Going In 105
8 On Their Own 121
9 Over Regensburg 144
10 Under the Bombs 153
11 The Diversions 166
12 Up at Last 174
13 The Dream Fades 193
14 Over Schweinfurt 221
15 In Schweinfurt 233
16 The Cripples 241
17 *'Herr Gott Sakrament!'* 248
18 Distant Action 269
19 The Reckoning 279
20 The Aftermath 299

Appendix 1 American and Allied Operational Performance 318
Appendix 2 Luftwaffe Operational Performance 332
Appendix 3 Regensburg Briefing Notes 338
Appendix 4 The 'Wheels-Down' B-17 Crew 341
Appendix 5 A Gunner's Letter 346

Acknowledgements 347
Bibliography 353
Index 355

List of Plates

1, 2 Messerschmitt factory at Regensburg (M. Ettinger)
3 A briefing (U.S.A.F.)
4 Crew preparations (U.S.A.F.)
5 Out to the aircraft (U.S.A.F.)
6, 7 German pilots waiting (A. Grislawski and W. Mössner)
8 Alarm at Schweinfurt (W. Bach)
9 First bombs at Regensburg (U.S.A.F.)
10 Over Regensburg (U.S.A.F.)
11–13 Bomb damage at Regensburg (Alscher via Konsbrück)
14 Post-raid aerial view of Regensburg (U.S.A.F.)
15 B-17 gunner (U.S.A.F.)
16 Combat wing in flight (U.S.A.F.)
17 Messerschmitt 109 being re-armed (A. Grislawski)
18 Focke-Wulf 190 crash-landing (H. Schliephake)
19 Crashed B-17 (Imperial War Museum)
20 Wounded B-17 crew member (U.S.A.F.)
21 B-17s over Schweinfurt (U.S.A.F.)
22 B-17 crew back from Africa (U.S.A.F.)
23 Margraten Military Cemetery (American Battle Monuments Commission)

List of Maps and Diagrams

Maps

1–3 Development of the Schweinfurt–Regensburg Plan 25
4 The Schweinfurt–Regensburg Plan, 17 August 1943 45
5 *Jafü Holland–Ruhr*'s Standard Response 97
6 Aircraft Casualties to Regensburg 142
7 The Luftwaffe Gathers 180
8 Aircraft Casualties to Schweinfurt 218
9 Schweinfurt Bombing Results 225
10 Aircraft Casualties from Schweinfurt 262

Diagrams

1 The Schweinfurt Force (1st Bombardment Wing) 51
2 The Regensburg Force (4th Bombardment Wing) 52
3 Head-on View of B-17 Group Formation 103
4 Regensburg Missing Aircraft Chart 320
5 Schweinfurt Missing Aircraft Chart 324

Maps by Reg Piggott from preliminary drawings by Mary Middlebrook

Introduction

Schweinfurt and Regensburg, 17 August 1943. Those German names and the date of a famous American bomber operation are well known. It was a day whose events generated immediate and enduring interest. I first heard of them more than ten years ago when I was preparing a book on the greatest disaster suffered by R.A.F. Bomber Command during the Second World War, the raid on the German city of Nuremberg on the night of 30/31 March 1944. By chance, a part of the R.A.F. force attacked Schweinfurt in error that night and my research took me to this town. Schweinfurt had been attacked by American bombers earlier in the war and, out of interest, I followed up that earlier American involvement and found many similarities between their first raid on Schweinfurt and the British raid on Nuremberg. The forces involved in both raids suffered harrowing losses in the culmination of their leaders' pursuance of long-held hopes. The raids to both places were flown over the same parts of Belgium and Western Germany; B-17 Fortress and R.A.F. Lancaster had sometimes fallen into the same parish. By chance, the same Luftwaffe general guided the German defence on both occasions, even though one raid was flown by day and the other by night. Both operations turned out to have been notable turning points in the air war.

Years later, I wrote a second book about R.A.F. Bomber Command to balance the disaster of Nuremberg. This was *The Battle of Hamburg*, which described the series of raids which produced the terrible 'firestorm' and a German death-roll exceeding 40,000. American bombers played a small part in the Battle of Hamburg, twice being sent in small forces to carry out standard daylight bombing attacks on targets in the city. The researching of these American operations and a short interviewing visit to the United States stimulated me. I determined that one day I would return and devote a complete book to an Eighth Air Force operation.

My interest remained with that first American raid on Schweinfurt; the 'shuttle' raid to Regensburg on the same day was an added bonus. I studied all preceding works on the subject to see if there was scope for a book written in the manner in which I like to work. I found that such a gap did exist. The American side of the operation had been covered before, but only using a proportion of the documents available and only through the eyes of a handful of available American participants. Of the 'European dimension' in particular, little investigation had been carried out. Germany had been a vague, shadowy, sinister area for most Americans during the war and, when the earlier Schweinfurt–Regensburg books were written, research and interviewing in distant Europe was still difficult. I was lucky. My contacts in Germany and my helpers with the more difficult parts of its strange language were already well established. The stories of the people of Schweinfurt and Regensburg and of the Luftwaffe men, together with supporting documents where available, were duly gathered in without too much difficulty.

For me, the barrier might have been the expense of working properly in the United States and an attitude I feared I might find among former Eighth Air Force men of 'why do we need an Englishman to write our history when we already have American books on this subject?' I need not have worried. The men who flew to Schweinfurt and Regensburg welcomed this further study almost without exception. More sensible trans-Atlantic air fares and generous, open-hearted American hospitality softened the financial blow. Two visits – one basically for documentary research and a much longer one for interviewing – became a sheer pleasure.

I would like to add a comment about the sources which will be used. I have, as always, attempted to work only from primary material – original documents and the personal accounts of participants – although the personal accounts will be used only with the greatest of care and against as firm a background of documentary evidence as possible. I admire the diligence with which some earlier published works have been compiled but can see no point in the rehashing of old accounts which often occurs and I will not be using such material; there is an abundance of fresh material available.

I must add one more word. A wartime operation such as this one can be described both through its strategic background and through its tactical application. Any book which tried to pursue both of these aims with equal emphasis would probably fail somewhere between the two. Of course the strategic scene and implications must be included, but these will only be given in sufficient detail to provide a backcloth to the main subject. I must tell the reader that my primary interest is in the actual carrying out of the air operations over Europe on 17 August 1943 and their immediate effects on the people under the bombs.

Martin Middlebrook
Boston, England

CHAPTER 1

A Dream Delayed

It was soon after ten in the morning. The formation of B-17s flew steadily south-eastwards towards their target; they had just crossed into Belgium. The first German fighters attacked. One B-17 fell away from its formation and exploded over the Belgian countryside. Four airmen descended slowly by parachute but Lieutenant Bernard Nayovitz of Brooklyn, New York, and more recently of the 94th Bomb Group, and five other members of his crew were killed. Why were Bernard Nayovitz and so many other young Americans risking their lives so far from home? By what process had they reached this distant war, to be flying in these aeroplanes built for nothing except the carrying of bombs? Why were they, on this day, flying to two beautiful towns in Southern Germany? Into what plan did their efforts fit and, if they were successful, how would their efforts change the course of history?

In previous books I have called it 'the bomber dream' – that heartfelt hope of air force commanders that their bomber aircraft would be the main instruments of winning future wars. The seeds had been sown in the First World War, in the very same skies of Western Europe through which the B-17s flew to Schweinfurt and Regensburg. The armies were stalemated; the slaughter incurred in vain attempts to break through the trenches was appalling. There were no flanks to turn on land but a third flank, the air, was wide open. Air commanders had taken planes away from the direct support of the field armies and sent them deep behind the enemy lines, where the pioneer bomber crews flew their hazardous missions. The Germans crossed the English Channel and the North Sea to raid London and other parts of England. The French and the British flew mostly from bases in France to those German cities which were within their range. They were called strategic bombers because they could strike at the heart of the enemy's war effort or at the morale of its civilians and, it was hoped, directly affect the outcome of the war.

A few leaders embraced the idea that the most effective use of the bomber might be an all-out attack on civilian morale but the majority supported the attack on enemy industry. In particular it was felt that a sustained attack against one especially vital industry would be more fruitful than attacking a spread of industries. Thus was born the theory of the 'bottleneck' target. In that first bombing war it was the German chemical industry which was selected for attention. Stop the production of German chemicals, it was said, and the flow of shells to the Western Front would also stop and the German armies would be unable to continue the fight. There is one more aspect of First World War bombing that is relevant to the air operations which will be covered in this book. Initially, to fly by night was an alien and dangerous practice, but it was soon found that bombers flying by day could not defend themselves against the attacks of defending fighters unless strongly escorted by their own fighters. The long-range bomber had to turn to night flying, gaining the protection of darkness but losing much of its ability to find targets and bomb accurately.

The First World War ended before the theory of the bomber dream could be proved. The German collapse caused by relentless pressure on the Western Front, by naval blockade and by America's growing influence on the war occurred before the full strength of the planned Allied bomber fleets could be put into the air to give this new weapon a true test. But every major feature of the Second World War's strategic bombing campaigns had its origin in that earlier war: the general idea that strategic bombing could starve the land armies of materials and cause their collapse; the particular idea that concentration on industrial bottlenecks could hasten that process; the argument that it was better to attack, instead, the spirit of the civilian population until they demanded that their leaders end the war; the desirability of carrying out the bombing by day and the dangers inherent in that course.

There followed twenty years of disarmament and of hopes that the world had seen enough of war. But it was a period during which the bomber dream persisted, fed by memories of the slaughter of soldiers on the Western Front and the desire to avoid a repetition of that slaughter if there had to be another war. In that event the strategic bomber would certainly be given full opportunity to show what effect it could have upon man's age-old habit of trying to impose his will on others by force of arms.

When America found itself at war with Germany in December 1941, its strategic bomber commanders were faced with a dilemma. They passionately believed in and had planned for a policy based on the purest methods of strategic bombing. They intended to commit their forces only to the attack on industry, never onto civilian populations; the accuracy of daylight would never be sacrificed to the concealment of darkness. Yet all the evidence of the European war to that time indicated that the daylight bomber could only operate safely under the cover of overwhelming fighter protection. With poor fighter cover or no cover at all, neither German nor British bombers had survived by day. When the American heavy bomber forces started preliminary operations in late 1942, neither the R.A.F. nor the U.S.A.A.F. had a single fighter in Western Europe which could even reach the German frontier! The R.A.F. begged American commanders not to risk their aircraft by day but to join in the night campaign to which the British had turned and which they were now convinced would win the war. The Americans refused. They believed that their own bombers, more heavily armed with defensive firepower than the R.A.F. bombers and flying in massed formations, could win through to the important industrial targets which lay deep in Germany.

It was this American philosophy for which Lieutenant Nayovitz died. 17 August 1943 was the day when, after a long delay, that philosophy was put to its true test.

The Americans had sent a complete air force to operate from Britain – the famous Eighth Air Force. Their first medium bomber raids took place in midsummer 1942, only seven months after Pearl Harbor; the first heavy bomber raid was carried out on 17 August 1942. The medium bombers will play only a small part in this story but the fortunes of the heavies are all-important and a brief résumé of their first year's operations will be useful.

That first year can be split roughly into three periods. The first of these lasted five months – five months of late autumn and European winter during which the Eighth Air Force could carry out no more than a preparatory campaign because of the slow build-up of its strength. Thirty raids were flown to targets in Holland, Belgium and Northern France. The bombers had the benefit of fighter escort for most of these raids and only forty-six planes were lost out of the 1,369 sorties dispatched. This represented a casualty rate of 3·4 per cent. The targets for these raids were usually railway yards, Luftwaffe airfields and U-boat bases; these were useful targets but the effort of the small forces involved resulted in no more than a small dent in the German war effort: they were certainly not yet striking at the heart of the German war machine. Many people were disappointed at this slow start but it had been a valuable period. The techniques of bombing and of flying defensive formations against fighter attack had been developed and future commanders had gained valuable battle experience.

On 27 January 1943 the American commanders felt strong enough to raid Germany for the first time. Their bombers attacked a U-boat construction yard at Wilhelmshaven and for the next six months the heavies went regularly to targets in Germany, but only to the fringes of that heavily defended country. The raids on France and the Low Countries also continued. A total of 5,958 sorties were flown in this period and 217 bombers were lost. This missing rate of 3·6 per cent was still a reasonable one when it is considered that many of the raids in this period were made without fighter escort. There were several reasons for the German failure to inflict heavier losses. The Germans were sometimes confused by the diversionary raids of other forces; the Luftwaffe's strength in the West was still weak and the American raids, being of only shallow penetration, gave the Germans little time to assemble a large force of fighters.

Again the gradual American build-up disappointed many people but the pace was now gathering. There was still no sign of a long-range fighter escort aircraft but it had been decided that a minimum strength of 300 heavy bombers should be sufficient to defend itself on deeper raids into Germany. The next phase commenced on 25 July 1943 when 323 bombers were sent to attack Hamburg and other targets in Northern Germany. This Hamburg raid was the first time there had been a direct attempt to cooperate with R.A.F. Bomber Command. The British had carried out a heavy raid on the city the night before, dropping over 2,000 tons of bombs, and the Americans followed in this first example of 'round-the-clock bombing' on the same German city. The experiment was not a success. The smoke from the fires still burning after the R.A.F. raid covered the planned American targets and spoiled much of their bombing. One American airman could not believe that the huge black pall over Hamburg was smoke and he reported it as 'a thunderstorm'. A valuable lesson had been learned. If it was to be required in future that both air forces concentrate on the same city, it would have to be the Americans who went first.

The American raid on Hamburg marked the opening of a dramatic six-day period which was later called 'Blitz Week'. Ten major targets in Germany were attacked in five days of intensive operations. But the cost was a heavy one; eighty-seven bombers and crews were lost (6·4 per cent of those dispatched) and a large number of the returning aircraft were damaged. The Eighth Air Force retired to lick its wounds and draw breath. Not many men knew it, but the American units were almost on the eve of an even greater test – the raids to Schweinfurt and Regensburg.

The American strategic heavy bomber in Europe now stood at a crossroads. To perform its true function it had to tackle targets situated even deeper in the German homeland, and yet the casualty rate in Blitz Week had exceeded that at which operations could be maintained. There seemed to be no prospect for many months of a long-range fighter being supplied which would be able to escort the heavy bombers for more than a fraction of their flight to the desired targets. The Luftwaffe was forming new fighter units in the West and bringing back battle-hardened units from other fronts. It is significant that at the beginning of Blitz Week the newly appointed commander of the American heavy bombers in England had taken himself off, in some secrecy, from his headquarters and flown as a passenger in an R.A.F. bomber on two night raids, to the heavily defended targets of Essen and Hamburg. He had been a witness to the awe-inspiring firestorm which had developed at Hamburg. There is no doubt that Brigadier-General Fred Anderson was quietly considering whether his force – or at least part of his force – might be better employed flying by night as the R.A.F. did. If such a change had to be made, it would be a terrible blow to American plans and to their deeply felt convictions on how the heavy bomber should go to war.

Brigadier-General Anderson's superiors, who knew nothing of his two night flights with the R.A.F., had no doubts over the future use of their heavy bombers, and the process by which orders were formulated and passed down to Anderson had been advancing steadily. The orders that Schweinfurt and Regensburg were to be bombed are obviously important to this story and their background should be described.

The efforts of the Allied strategic bomber forces fighting against Germany were, in theory at least, coordinated after discussion and decision at the highest level. When President Roosevelt and Prime Minister Churchill and their top military advisers, the Joint Chiefs of Staff, met regularly to decide upon the future strategy of the war, the direction of their bomber forces in England and North Africa was included in those discussions. Written directives were then dispatched from time to time to the commanders of the United States Eighth and Ninth Air Forces and to R.A.F. Bomber Command, giving quite specific orders on which targets were to be attacked in their respective future operations.

In any study of the major directives issued in the first half of 1943, one aspect of their content becomes clear. The bomber commanders were constantly being told that their main aim was to secure 'the progressive destruction and dislocation of the German military, industrial and economic system, and the undermining of the morale of the German people [the 'morale' was the R.A.F. target] to a point where their capacity for armed resistance is fatally weakened'.* Thus had read the famous Casablanca Directive of January 1943. But the bomber commanders were not yet to be allowed to concentrate on the true core of Germany's war industry. The Allies were in danger of losing the Battle of the Atlantic and the bomber forces based in England had to give priority to U-boat construction yards in Germany and U-boat operating bases in France. A considerable effort was devoted to these targets and many casualties were sustained in the process of attacking them. It is only a side issue here that, although the bombing of construction yards did reduce the number of U-boats available to the Germans, the Atlantic lifeline was really saved by the destruction of U-boats at sea. This victory was achieved partly by naval escorts but mainly by the grudgingly increased use of four-engine bomber aircraft in the maritime patrol role. The aerial victory against the U-boats at sea was achieved by a minute force of long-range aircraft compared to the large numbers being used in the strategic bombing offensive. The historical judgement must be that, in the offensive against U-boats, those who were responsible for the allocation of resources had erred gravely by backing the strategic bomber campaign at

* The directives of 21 January and 10 June 1943, referred to both here and later, are from Public Record Office, London, AIR 14/777 and 779.

the expense of the maritime air forces. The bombing of U-boat bases in France had been particularly unproductive; the Germans had completed the protection of their vital installations with massive bomb-proof shelters before the raids started and the attacks on these shelters must, with the benefit of hindsight, be judged a classic misuse of air power. This subject has been dealt with in some detail here because many of the American airmen who were soon to fly to Schweinfurt and Regensburg had taken part in the raids of the U-boat campaign and because this was also the last phase before the period in which Schweinfurt and Regensburg became prominent names in the target lists.

The worst was over in the North Atlantic by the middle of the summer of 1943 but the planners were now distracted from their main aim by another potential danger. It had come as an unpleasant surprise to find that the Luftwaffe fighter force was becoming more effective despite the constant pressure of the Allied air forces in the West and the attrition suffered in Russia and North Africa. The one lesson learnt by everyone earlier in this war had been that no military operation succeeded without air superiority over the battlefield and the approaches to the battlefield. It would be necessary to break the Luftwaffe fighter arm before the proposed Allied invasion of Europe could be launched with confidence in 1944. The so-called Pointblank Directive of early June 1943 thus contained the following passage:

> The increasing scale of destruction which is being inflicted by our night bomber forces and the development of the day bombing offensive by the Eighth Air Force have forced the enemy to deploy day and night fighters in increasing numbers on the Western Front. Unless this increase in fighter strength is checked we may find our bomber forces unable to fulfil the tasks allotted to them by the Combined Chiefs of Staff.
>
> In these circumstances it has become essential to check the growth and to reduce the strength of the day and night fighter forces which the enemy can concentrate against us in this theatre. To this end the Combined Chiefs of Staff have decided that first priority in the operation of British and American bombers based in the United Kingdom shall be accorded to the attack of German fighter forces and the industry upon which they depend.

The Eighth Air Force was now allocated 'German fighter strength' as its first priority. Although this was hardly, yet, the true core of German industry, the bombing of aircraft and aero-engine factories did not clash with the 'progressive destruction . . . of the German military . . . system' given as the priority six months earlier and it was certainly more profitable than bombing concrete-covered U-boat pens on the French coast. The largest German fighter aircraft factories were at Regensburg, deep in Bavaria, and Wiener Neustadt, south of Vienna in Austria. These two plants were estimated to be manufacturing no less than 500 of the 650 Messerschmitt 109s being produced in German aircraft factories each month. Messerschmitt 109s were the most numerous of the German front line day fighters.

In a temporarily lower category of priority were grouped submarine yards and bases, the rest of the German aircraft industry, ball-bearings and oil. Those studying this second group immediately concentrated on ball-bearings. Here was not only a superb example of the true industrial bottleneck but one which also had a direct link with that first priority, fighter production. How many moving parts in a modern fighter aircraft only moved with the help of ball-bearings! The German ball-bearing industry was conveniently concentrated in the town of Schweinfurt, also in Bavaria but not as distant as Regensburg.

Schweinfurt and Regensburg were both within range of the Eighth Air Force's heavy bombers stationed in England but Wiener Neustadt could only be reached from bases in North Africa. The U.S. Ninth Air Force in North Africa was ordered to attack Wiener Neustadt as well as the vital oil refinery at Ploesti in Rumania. This refinery served the only major oilfield the Germans had under their direct control. Ploesti was an oil bottleneck; destroy this and the Germans would have to rely upon synthetic oil or the capture of oilfields in the Caucasus or the Middle East.

So was drawn up that list of four towns in Europe – Schweinfurt, Regensburg, Ploesti and Wiener Neustadt – whose names were almost unknown to ordinary Americans but three of which were due to become notorious in their history.

Schweinfurt and Regensburg are firmly linked together in aviation history as two targets which were attacked on the same day and in a jointly planned operation, but the attack on these targets had originally been the subject of two quite separate plans. It is believed that active planning for the attack on Regensburg started first, probably at the Washington Conference attended by Roosevelt, Churchill and the Joint Chiefs of Staff in May 1943. The Allied leaders were trying to coordinate the attacks on Ploesti, Wiener Neustadt and Regensburg. There was to be a joint operation on the same day against the Messerschmitt aircraft factories at Regensburg and Wiener Neustadt and a separate raid to Ploesti on another day. To strengthen the bomber force in North Africa – the United States Ninth Air Force – three groups of B-24 Liberators were transferred from England, making a force of nearly 200 bombers available for the operations to be mounted from North Africa. It was initially decided to tackle the joint operation to Regensburg and Wiener Neustadt first, because of the known heavier defences at Ploesti, but Generals Marshall and Arnold in Washington decided to reverse this order. All these operations would be entirely American. The gallant raid on Ploesti duly took place on 1 August 1943. The target was seriously but not critically damaged; fifty-four out of the 177 B-24s involved were lost.

It was then intended that the joint operation to Regensburg and Wiener Neustadt would take place a week later, on 7 August, or as soon as weather conditions were suitable after that date. The detailed tactical orders had been received by the units concerned two weeks earlier. The B-24 units in North Africa, which would have rested after their ordeal at Ploesti, would attack Wiener Neustadt against the expected light opposition there. The Regensburg force, composed of a longer-range version of the B-17 Flying Fortress, could expect to face fierce opposition from the strong Luftwaffe forces which stood between the coast of Europe and the target, 430 miles away in Southern Germany, but it was hoped that the interior of Germany, never before visited by American daylight bombers, would be almost empty of operational German day fighters. R.A.F. and American medium bombers, fighter-bombers and fighters would all give maximum support by providing escorts and carrying out diversionary and harassing raids on German fighter airfields on either side of the penetration route, but only as far as their limited range would allow. The standard B-17 units in England would, however, make a further major diversionary contribution by attacking an industrial target in or near the Ruhr. A bold innovation was introduced to the Regensburg plan. After the bomber force had bombed its target it was not to return to England but would withdraw to the south and fly to bases in North Africa, returning to England at a later date by a comparatively safe route over the Atlantic.

The planners were certainly busy in that month of July 1943 because, alongside the operation to Regensburg and Wiener Neustadt, a further important operation, almost as ambitious, was in preparation at the same time. This was a plan to use the entire B-17 force available in England – both standard and long-range versions – in a combined raid on the ball-bearing factories at Schweinfurt. This Schweinfurt plan had started its active life later than the Regensburg one, having been born in the Combined Operational Planning Committee which had recently been set up in England to coordinate the efforts of the U.S.A.A.F. and the R.A.F. forces based there following the Pointblank Directive. But various supporters of plans to attack Schweinfurt had undoubtedly been active on both sides of the Atlantic for a much longer period. The Air Ministry in London had been urging R.A.F. Bomber Command to raid the town at least since early 1942 and there had long been people in Washington who thought Schweinfurt an equally desirable target for the Eighth Air Force.

The first draft of the Schweinfurt plan was issued in July 1943 and the final draft was ready on 2 August.* The sixteen B-17 groups available were each to dispatch a standard combat formation of eighteen aircraft to Schweinfurt in three task forces totalling 288 aircraft. Two more 'composite groups' were to be formed from spare B-17s and sent in a diversionary attack against the big Luftwaffe fighter airfield at Lille, and the customary smaller diversions by medium and light bombers were also planned. To support the main attack on the ball-bearing factory, R.A.F. Bomber Command was asked to follow up the following night with one of their standard 'area attacks' on the general town area of Schweinfurt. Air Marshal Sir Robert Saundby, the deputy commander at Bomber Command Headquarters and the officer responsible for the detailed planning there, later wrote confirming the R.A.F.'s part in this plan. 'Arrangements were made for Bomber Command to attack Schweinfurt the same night and, if possible, for several subsequent nights. It was hoped that the American attack would have started fires which might still be burning and thus indicate the target to the night bombers.'†

It is quite certain that both the plan for the combined attack on Regensburg and Wiener Neustadt and the plan for the heavy raid on Schweinfurt were current at the same period; both opera-

* Unless otherwise stated, all American documents referred to are from the Mission Report Folders of VIII Bomber Command, the 1st and 4th Bombardment Wings and the relevant bomb groups. These are located at the National Archives at Suitland, Maryland, and are also on microfilm at the Albert F. Simpson Historical Research Center, Maxwell Air Force Base, Alabama.

† Sir Robert Saundby, *Air Bombardment*, Chatto & Windus, 1961, p. 159.

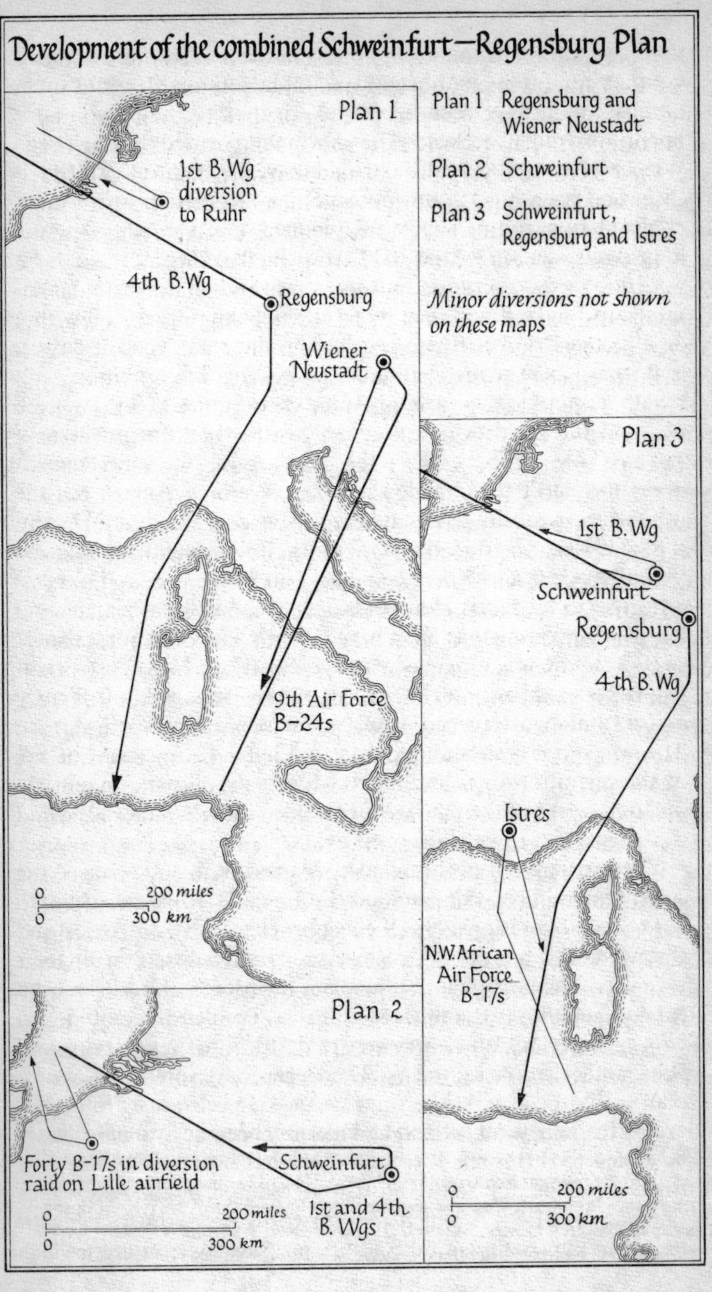
Development of the combined Schweinfurt—Regensburg Plan
Plan 1
1st B. Wg
diversion
to Ruhr
4th B. Wg
Regensburg
Wiener
Neustadt
9th Air Force
B-24s
0
200 miles
0
300 km
Plan 1 Regensburg and Wiener Neustadt
Plan 2 Schweinfurt
Plan 3 Schweinfurt, Regensburg and Istres
Minor diversions not shown on these maps
Plan 3
1st B. Wg
Schweinfurt
Regensburg
4th B. Wg
Istres
N.W. African
Air Force
B-17s
0
200 miles
0
300 km
Plan 2
Forty B-17s in diversion
raid on Lille airfield
Schweinfurt
1st and 4th
B. Wgs
0
200 miles
0
300 km

tions could have been put into effect in the first part of August if weather conditions had been favourable, although careful time-tabling would have been needed to ensure that these two major operations did not clash. The more complicated Regensburg–Wiener Neustadt operation would have been given priority if there had been a clash of opportunities. If both operations had taken place early in August, as planned, the men who flew the long-range version of the B-17 from England would have been forced to fly the operation to Regensburg and on to North Africa, return to England and then fly to attack Schweinfurt – all within an extremely short period, possibly on three consecutive days.

Both of these plans were most interesting and ambitious and would undoubtedly have provided fine subjects for separate books if the vagaries of European weather had not intervened. As has been stated earlier, the Regensburg–Wiener Neustadt operation had been intended to take place on 7 August but the weather between England and Regensburg was not suitable and the raids were postponed several times. It was eventually realized that other operations were being held up by the need to hold two air forces in readiness at airfields well over 1,000 miles apart and the joint operation was abandoned. The Wiener Neustadt end of the operation thus took place independently on 13 August. Sixty-five B-24s made a successful attack on the Messerschmitt factory and all but two returned safely to their bases in North Africa. The same poor weather conditions in England also caused delays to the operation to Schweinfurt. This nearly did get under way on 10 August but the fine weather needed did not materialize and the attack had to be postponed again.

The carrying out of the Wiener Neustadt raid had released the American bomber commanders in England from the need to coordinate operations with their colleagues in North Africa and they were now free to tackle Regensburg and Schweinfurt in their own way. The next phase of the planning process must have been carried out with incredible speed. It was decided to combine the two ageing plans and carry out raids to both Regensburg and Schweinfurt on the same day. The Regensburg force and tactical plan would be exactly the same as the one previously intended, except that a new unit which had recently become available would be added to this force; it would now be 146 aircraft strong. The forces available for Schweinfurt were reduced by the removal of the long-range B-17s which were to go to Regensburg, but partially built up again with the addition of the spare aircraft which would have been sent to Lille as a diversion in the old Schweinfurt plan, and other spare B-17s. The force would now be 230 aircraft strong as against the originally intended 288 aircraft.

The one major diversion that could now be provided could help only the Regensburg force, and only during its potentially less dangerous withdrawal flight to Africa. There existed in Algeria the small American Northwest African Strategic Air Force (later the Fifteenth Air Force), commanded by the famous Major-General 'Jimmy' Doolittle. Doolittle had four groups of B-17s and he arranged that these should attack two German airfields in the Istres area, near Marseilles, at the same time as the Regensburg force would be flying away from its target to Africa, thus splitting whatever German fighter strength there might be in the western end of the Mediterranean. In theory, R.A.F. Bomber Command was still intended to follow up the attack on Schweinfurt with its own raid the following night but there had always been doubts whether the R.A.F. commander, Sir Arthur Harris, would carry out this part of the plan – he was violently opposed to his force being used against this type of target – and, because the R.A.F. normally only flew to distant targets on moonless nights, their most favourable part of the month was fast receding.

The detailed tactical planning for the combined raids was swiftly completed by Brigadier-General Anderson's staff at VIII Bomber Command Headquarters. It was swiftly done because very little in the plan was new; most of its elements had been contained in the two earlier plans. There was not even a new code-name; operational documents merely refer to 'ALABAMA and/or HAYMAKER'. ALABAMA had been the code-name for the original Schweinfurt operation, HAYMAKER for the Regensburg part of the old joint Regensburg–Wiener Neustadt operation. The revised plan was approved by Anderson and also by Major-General Ira Eaker, his superior at Eighth Air Force Headquarters. No doubt the news that these two oft-mentioned targets were at last about to be raided also found its way to Washington. How exciting the prospect must have been to those air leaders who had waited, not always patiently, for the fruition of their plans to use the American heavy bomber arm in its true rule at last! The destruction of the targets at Schweinfurt and Regensburg, together with the recent attacks on Ploesti and Wiener Neustadt, would represent the start of the campaign of truly, purely strategic bombing which it was hoped would lead to the successful invasion of Europe and ultimately to the end of the war in Europe. The men who were to fly to Schweinfurt and Regensburg were certainly pioneering the realization of a long-held dream. Whether the raids would be successful, with their long flights into Germany without fighter escort, and whether the choice of targets was correct were questions which could only be answered by time.

For the men closely connected with the endeavour the prospect was not, however, so immediately appealing. General Eaker definitely felt that his superiors in Washington had pressed him too hard to undertake this type of operation. Eaker says, 'There was always someone who wanted to do something facile to get a quick result. We were pushed into it before we were ready. I protested it bitterly.'* At a lower level, Colonel Maurice A. Preston would have to lead the bomb group he commanded, the 379th, to Schweinfurt:

> It was like lining up the cavalry, shooting your way in and then shooting your way out again. This was definitely the concept of the early Air Corps leaders – also the concept of the design of the aircraft. The Flying Fortress was simply an aircraft with a lot of guns hung on it. There was this idea of massing aircraft together to mass the firepower. If it didn't work, the answer was to get still more aircraft up and even more firepower. The fellows who had to do it weren't too keen but we had to get on with it. But we did get a bit charged up about this particular mission because we were told that ball-bearings were critical and it was felt that, by knocking these out, we would shorten the war. That made it a little exciting.

* Quotations from American, British and German participants are either from personal interviews (mostly) or from correspondence (less often) unless otherwise stated. Ranks held at that time are used throughout.

CHAPTER 2
The Targets

It is unlikely that more than a handful of the American airmen who set out to bomb Schweinfurt and Regensburg on 17 August 1943 had ever heard of either of those names before they were briefed for the raids. These towns were not among the batch of well-known German industrial targets which the Americans knew they might one day have to tackle. It would truly be a venture to an unknown part of Germany. Regensburg was only forty miles from Czechoslovakia!

Of the two towns, Schweinfurt was the more modest in size and historical background. It was an ancient town on the broad River Main, with the beautiful old centre which so many German towns had before the bombers came, but it had not become deeply involved with the wars of the Middle Ages which had so often dominated life in this part of Europe. This lack of importance had continued until the mid 1920s. The 1922 census had shown Schweinfurt as containing a mere 15,000 people. The town was technically in Bavaria but its people were not real Bavarians; they were Franconians, a much quieter and more reserved people than the exuberant Bavarians, and they looked more to the nearby city of Nuremberg than to distant Munich, the capital of Bavaria. Schweinfurt was just a lovely little town in a lovely area of soft countryside.

Germany's runaway inflation in the late 1920s had affected Schweinfurt severely. The town had little defence against the economic storm then blowing and many people had departed; in particular, there had been much emigration to the United States. But the improving conditions of the 1930s gave Schweinfurt a boost which almost reached boom proportions. Schweinfurt had become the centre of Germany's ball-bearing industry, and the world economic recovery – particularly in the motor-car industry – and Germany's own rebirth under Hitler brought real prosperity. The move to rearmament and then to war brought even greater demand for ball-bearings and set the seal upon Schweinfurt's economic recovery. But Schweinfurt never lost its pleasant market-town character and its beautiful centre was not spoiled. New suburbs grew to house the workers attracted by the expansion, although many of the less skilled workers came in daily from surrounding villages. The population more than doubled in size between the depression years and the outbreak of war and had nearly tripled by 1943. (The number of German civilian ration cards on issue the day before the first American raid was 43,480.) Of course, the town was now ruled by the National Socialist Party. A young local businessman, Ludwig Pösl, had become the Bürgermeister. The Nazi rule in Schweinfurt is reputed to have been more tolerant than in many similar towns and Herr Pösl is credited with having prevented some of his party members from burning down the local synagogue.

Schweinfurt's ball-bearing industry had been born in 1906; the area had been purely agricultural until then. Moritz Fischer, son of a mechanic, had started the small ball-bearing manufacturing firm which eventually grew to become the giant Kugelfischer concern (the German noun '*Kugel*' covers anything spherical), although another man, Georg Schäfer, had come into the picture at a later date and the firm was now Kugelfischer, Georg Schäfer. It was producing more than half of the town's ball-bearings by August 1943. The other big firm which had become established was the Swedish-owned Vereinigte Kugellagerfabriken A.G., which had two factories in Schweinfurt. These three major ball-bearing factories were commonly known as K.G.F., and V.K.F. No. 1 and V.K.F. No. 2. But the efforts of the three factories in Schweinfurt had now been rationalized. They no longer produced in competition with each other but in collaboration. Nearly 17,000 people were employed, many of them key technical men.

In trying to assess Schweinfurt's importance to Germany's wartime ball-bearing industry, one can soon become confused by the array of figures available. The post-war United States Strategic Bombing Survey* of German ball-bearing production lists the numbers of bearings produced and the value produced, goes on to express those figures as percentages both of Germany's own production and of the total production available to her from Italy and occupied France and finally calculates the amount of bearings available through German contracts with Sweden. All

* United States Strategic Bombing Survey, No. 53, p. 21.

these figures have been reprinted many times. It is sufficient here to say that Schweinfurt produced just less than half of Germany's total war requirements in terms of the number of bearings but more than half in terms of value. It is reasonable to assume from these figures that Schweinfurt produced the more sophisticated, valuable and therefore important ball-bearings needed by the German war effort.

There were a few other factories in Schweinfurt, the most important being Fichtel & Sachs, a firm which had become established in the boom years before the war as makers of a light two-stroke motor-cycle engine. This firm was now carrying out a variety of important war work unconnected with the ball-bearing industry. Schweinfurt also became a garrison town and there were two large barrack areas, the older Hindenburg Kaserne and the new Adolf Hitler Kaserne. It is believed that the former was the home of an infantry training unit; the latter was certainly the training and replacement depot of the 36th Panzer Regiment.

Every one of the factories and military establishments mentioned above will be relevant to this story. There was one important aspect of their location which was to pose great difficulties to the American airmen and great danger to the civilians of Schweinfurt. All of the factories and the barracks were on the western side of the town, but they were not separated from the town by open ground. Nor were the three ball-bearing factories which would be the American targets situated together in one compact group. All three had residential areas near by. The V.K.F. No. 1 works in particular were situated deep in the town, less than half a mile from the centre. The American bombardiers would have to seek out these small targets from among the rest of the buildings – mostly residential – on that side of Schweinfurt.

By contrast with the small, quiet and recently affluent Schweinfurt, Regensburg was a famous city which had been a centre of civilization and culture for nearly 2,000 years. As Castra Regina it had been a major Roman provincial capital and base of the Third Legion. After the collapse of Roman rule, the city became the first capital of Bavaria until given the privileged status of an independent city under the German emperors. It was the most important city in Southern Germany. Regensburg survived both the Thirty Years War, which was fought in this area, and the subsequent Protestant rule, even though it had been and would remain a predominantly Catholic city. Napoleon's forces came in 1809 and renamed the city Ratisbon, but when the brief period of French rule ended so too did Regensburg's days of greatness. It ceased to be a seat of political power; it was not touched by the Industrial Revolution. The city did not decline; it just stagnated, became a backwater in a remote part of the new united Germany. Nuremberg and Munich, each sixty miles away, attracted all the attention now. Regensburg was left with a famous 800-year-old arched stone bridge over the Danube, a beautiful medieval centre, a cathedral and numerous other reminders of its past. It was a fine place for the discerning tourist to visit. Its pre-war population was approximately 80,000, more than three quarters of whom were still Catholics. Unlike Schweinfurt, the people were truly Bavarian in character.

Although Bavaria became the birthplace of National Socialism, the people of Regensburg were politically very conservative and the city consistently produced voting figures well below both the Bavarian and national averages for Hitler's party until 1933, after which there were no more elections and no way of testing public opinion. The Catholic church was the real leader of opinion in Regensburg. The church did not preach too hard against Hitler's rule; their real fear was Communism. The Nazi leader was Oberbürgermeister Otto Schottenheim, a local doctor who also had a reputation as a humanitarian. There was still one tangible link with the years of glory. The princely family of Thurn and Taxis had made its home in Regensburg since 1748. This was the family which had held the Imperial monopoly for postal services and for the post carriages which carried all road passengers in Germany for nearly three centuries; the modern 'taxi' was probably named after them. This wealthy and influential family continued to live in an elegant *Residenz* in Regensburg. The current head of the family, Prince Albert Lamoral, was not keen on the new politics and was too old for military service, but one of his sons had died at Stalingrad.

Regensburg had gained an even greater economic benefit than Schweinfurt from Hitler's rule. Because this area had also suffered severely from the depression, Regensburg was chosen as a suitable place for the establishment of the large new aircraft factory which the American bombers were now planning to attack. When originally built, between 1936 and 1938, the factory was owned by a firm called the Bayerische Flugzeugwerke but this was no more than a cover for the state Air Ministry which provided all the finance for its building. The Air Ministry had an agreement with the famous designer and manufacturer Professor Willi Messerschmitt, who had his own factory at Augsburg, whereby Messerschmitt could buy all the shares of the new factory, and he did so in 1939. The factory thus became part of Messerschmitt GmbH. The entire Regensburg output was always purchased by the Luftwaffe. The first model to be produced had been the Messerschmitt 108, the *Taifun*, but the factory soon settled down to mass-producing the famous Messerschmitt 109 single-engined fighter – often called the Bf 109 because of the company's earlier name, Bayerische Flugzeugwerke.

The new factory had been constructed in open farmland outside the city and adjacent to the local racecourse which was owned by the Prince of Thurn and Taxis. It was one of those prestigious, showpiece constructions of which Germany produced many in the late 1930s. It was really a factory estate with a multi-storey office block, wide roads and dispersed workshops separated from each other by lawns and trees. There was an apprentices' school for entry to which there was keen competition among the boys of Regensburg and the surrounding villages. The city of Regensburg was exceedingly pleased with the employment benefits and proud of the prestige of the new factory. The facilities for the workers were quite outstanding. There were canteens, showers and changing rooms beneath each workshop, social clubs, a sports field and a swimming pool. When the architects had been drawing up the original plans for submission to Berlin, they had marked the swimming pool as the 'reserve water supply' which would be needed as part of the factory's fire-fighting requirements. It was a case of '*zwei Fliegen mit einem Streich*' – literally, 'two flies with one swipe'. Berlin had agreed.

August 1943 found the factory in full war production, still under the Luftwaffe–civilian partnership; Albert Speer's War Armaments Ministry would not take over and shake things up until 1944. The first director had died early in the war and the Luftwaffe had sent its former chief engineer, Generalstabsingenieur Roluf Lucht, to be his successor. More than 10,000 people now worked in two shifts; production was still concentrated on the Messerschmitt 109 day fighter. The engines – mainly from the Daimler-Benz factory at Neubrandenburg near Berlin – guns and wireless sets all arrived ready-made from elsewhere but the Regensburg factory produced most of the body sections and carried out the final assembly. The resident body of test pilots air-tested the finished planes. The large racecourse alongside the factory would have made an ideal take-off and landing area but it ran north to south across the prevailing wind, so a smaller meadow alongside the Danube was used instead. When the planes were ready for acceptance by the Luftwaffe, Junkers 52 transport planes brought in ferry pilots who took the new fighters off to replacement units.

It is difficult to say exactly what level of production had been reached before the American raid. Allied estimates at that time gave figures of 200–220 planes per month but this was probably too low. Craven and Cate, the American official historians with access to post-war figures, say 380 per month, and this figure tends to be confirmed by three men who worked on the assembly-line and could thus count the number of planes which came past them each day, and by a group of senior men from the factory – an architect, an accountant and a senior test pilot among them – who still live in Regensburg and who put the figure at about 400 per month. It was certainly the leading Messerschmitt 109 factory at that time. Small quantities of parts for other Messerschmitt types were also made at Regensburg but the factory mainly existed and was justly famous for the mass production of that standard Luftwaffe day fighter. It is believed that the bulk of the planes being produced immediately before the American raid were going to the Luftwaffe units in the Mediterranean which had recently been subject to such fierce attrition.

As a target for air attack, the aircraft factory at Regensburg had little in common with the ball-bearing factories at Schweinfurt, where the bombers would have to find three separate locations in or on the edge of a built-up area. The Regensburg Messerschmitt factory stood alone and easily visible on one compact site, separated from the city by nearly a mile of open fields and distinctively situated in a prominent bend of the River Danube. There was only one potentially dangerous aspect of the Messerschmitt factory's location. The site on which it had been built was adjacent to the city's main civilian hospital. This was staffed by a Catholic religious order, the Barmherzigebrüder. There were two modern hospital blocks – one each for male and female patients – each situated only 200 yards from the nearest building in the Messerschmitt factory.

There was one thing that the people of Schweinfurt and Regensburg shared – their attitude to the danger of air attack. They were nearly all living in a dream world. The comments of Alfons

Kuhn, a foreman in one of Schweinfurt's ball-bearing factories, and Martin Ettinger, an apprentice in the Messerschmitt factory at Regensburg, sum up the general outlook.

> I was one of the many who had never even thought that one day a force of bombers would appear out of the sky and bomb the hell out of the factory. We just went on day after day, turning up for work and carrying on with our normal life.
>
> Regensburg was a beautiful town and everyone here was healthy and happy – until noon of 17 August 1943.

There was reasonable cause for this euphoria. No Allied bomber had flown by day into this part of Germany since 17 April 1942 when a force of twelve R.A.F. Lancasters had attacked a factory making U-boat engines at Augsburg. Seven of the Lancasters had been shot down and the R.A.F. had not ventured this way by daylight again except for the occasional flight of a fast photo reconnaissance aircraft. Small places like Schweinfurt and Regensburg did not seem to be on the list of targets for R.A.F. night raids. The more recently arrived American bombers had so far only reached as far as Kassel, 100 miles away from Schweinfurt and 200 from Regensburg. The sounding of air-raid sirens whether by day or by night was largely ignored.

Of the two places – Schweinfurt and Regensburg – the official attitude towards the danger of attack was more realistic in Schweinfurt. Both the town and the factories had some very good air-raid shelters. Protection for the workers at Regensburg had been one of the points borne in mind when the new aircraft factory had been designed just before the war. Again 'to swat two flies with one swipe', the architects had provided each of the six major workshops and the apprentices' school with a canteen built alongside, complete with a set of underground rooms which were to serve both as washing and changing rooms for the workers and as shelters in what had then seemed the unlikely event of an air raid. This system had recently been supplemented by the construction of many *Splittergraben* – splinter-proof shelters. These were zig-zag trenches dug into the ground alongside the factory buildings and protected with a light head cover of earth, and were mainly for the use of the many foreign workers now present. Neither the original shelters under the canteen floors nor the new earth trenches would stand up to the 500-pound high-explosive bombs which the Americans would soon be delivering to Regensburg. The only real air-raid shelter in the Messerschmitt works was one of the small *Zuckerhut* (sugar-loaf) type of conical, reinforced concrete shelter which housed the control centre of the works' air-raid precautions service. This would protect no more than twenty people.

Early in August 1943, the management of the Messerschmitt factory had reconsidered the possibility of air attack. General Lucht, the director, had given as his opinion that the worst that could be expected was a small raid by light, fast aircraft of the R.A.F. Mosquito type; it was his belief that the present shelters would be adequate protection against such an attack. A surviving member of his management team says, 'Those of us who ever thought about it agreed with him but no one thought much about the possibility of attack at all really.' It was probably the recent attack by B-24s from North Africa against their sister Messerschmitt factory at Wiener Neustadt on 13 August which caused the Regensburg factory to hold its first air-raid practice on 16 August, the day before the Americans came. The test worked perfectly. Every worker went to his or her allotted shelter place. The management was pleased. The workers enjoyed the change in routine and the time spent away from their noisy workshops.

It is certain that few officials at either Schweinfurt or Regensburg had any conception of what was about to befall them. A few experts from the Ruhr or Hamburg would have quickly pointed out the deficiencies. It is just as certain that Berlin had little idea that either town was about to be subject to serious attack and scarce resources were not to be diverted to places not thought to be in urgent need. Above all, the morale of the populations of those places should not be disturbed in any way. The German people were being carefully led back to optimism and confidence in Hitler's leadership after the shock of the Stalingrad defeat six months earlier; the closer-to-home shock of the recent destruction of Hamburg had been mostly confined to the north. The official policy was, undoubtedly, not to upset in any way the happy, carefree people making ball-bearings and fighter planes deep in sunny Bavaria.

The ordinary people happily embraced the delusion that their towns were safe. The feeling was even fed by the most unrealistic of rumours. In Regensburg, it was felt that the influential Thurn and Taxis family had so many friends in England that Regensburg would be spared, and that the hospital near the aircraft factory had some link with the United States. Some people in Schweinfurt believed that the Protestant Bishop of nearby Würzburg was friendly with the Archbishop of Canterbury and was using his influence to keep Schweinfurt safe.

And so the people about to be bombed lived out those last few days before the raid. Johannes Rust was a worker at Schweinfurt.

> We were terribly complacent. One alarm was just like another until then. Ordinary people didn't realize at that time that our ball-bearing industry was of any great importance. Those in authority who did realize it kept their mouths shut so as not to alarm us. With hindsight, you can see where we went wrong.

Hans Jordan was a schoolboy gunner with a Regensburg Flak battery.

> We never believed that the bombers would ever come to Regensburg. We were too far into Germany and, for myself, I didn't think the Messerschmitt factory was all that important to be the target for a bombing raid. If the enemy had thought Regensburg important enough to bomb they would have come before now. That Flak business was all a bit of a nuisance, a disturbance to my normal life. I would much rather have had my time free for sport and other pastimes. It wasn't what boys of our age should be doing.

Rose Poschenrieder worked in the Messerschmitt factory at Regensburg.

> That raid came out of a clear blue sky, not only physically out of the sky above but out of 'the clear sky of optimism' in which we were living.

The people who were about to be bombed in Schweinfurt and Regensburg were not all Germans. It had become a feature of everyday German life that the workforce of any industrial concern now contained a substantial proportion of foreigners. Early attempts to attract genuine volunteers from the German-occupied countries had produced only negligible results; the majority of the foreign men and women now working in German factories had been forcibly removed from their own countries. These people could form up to a third of the total labour force in some factories. They lived in harsh conditions, were forced to make weapons of war for their enemies, were not protected by any aspect of international law and sustained heavy casualties in bombing raids. It would be easy to ignore the experiences of these people. The survivors are mostly people of humble background, scattered across Europe, many now old and in poor health. The inclusion of their part in the Schweinfurt–Regensburg story will bring little financial gain, but these men, and some women, make pathetic pleas that the deaths of their friends and their own sufferings be not forgotten.

The Germans often delivered a complete trainload of forced workers to one town in Germany and groups of labourers who had left home together often remained together at their new place of work; it is thus possible to identify the main groups in the foreign workforces at both Schweinfurt and Regensburg. In Schweinfurt there may have been as many as 3,000 foreign men and 2,000 women – about thirty per cent of the total workforce. Large numbers of both were Russians. There were some Polish women but few men. The biggest group from the West in Schweinfurt was a batch of Frenchmen who arrived in the spring of 1943. These men were from Vichy France, the area not occupied by the Germans in 1940, but they were now being sent to Germany in large numbers under a recent agreement with Pétain's government, possibly involving the exchange from Germany of similar numbers of 1940 prisoners of war. A Frenchman sent to Schweinfurt writes bitterly of 'those slave-traders of Vichy'.

The proportion of foreigners in the Messerschmitt factory at Regensburg was far lower. From the East there were Russians – there were Russians everywhere in Germany – and a smaller number of Poles, but the largest foreign group was Belgian; two trainloads had arrived in December 1942, 'to be welcomed by fifteen centimetres of snow and Siberian cold'. Most of these men had come from the industrial province of Hainault, from the towns of La Louvière, Tournai, Leuze and Ath, though a few more had joined from Brussels. One Belgian, a tramways ticket collector, travelled to Regensburg in his smart Brussels Tramways uniform and was always pleased to note the way his uniform attracted German glances when he wore it on his Sunday walks into Regensburg. A smaller transport of men from Vichy France had also arrived at Regensburg recently.

The life-style of the forced workers at Schweinfurt and Regensburg was like that of many thousands of men and women taken to Germany in those years. Accommodation and food at their camps were poor, work-hours were long and monotonous, although the foreigners at Regensburg often speak with admiration of the workers' facilities at the Messerschmitt factory, 'all of an exemplary cleanliness'. Leisure conditions were more relaxed at Regensburg than at Schweinfurt. The foreigners were allowed to walk along the Danube and into Regensburg on Sundays, the French and some Belgians remembering the French occupation of the city 130 years earlier and that this was the only place where Napoleon was wounded in his entire military career. The younger men tried to chase the local girls but with little success; 'the Gestapo were keeping a close eye on the goods [*au grain*]'.

Present-day Germans are understandably embarrassed about their wartime use of forced labour. They often use the euphemisms '*Gastarbeiter*' or '*Fremdarbeiter*' – 'guest workers'. Occasionally a Frenchman or a Belgian will be seen in Schweinfurt or Regensburg today, showing his family where he lived and worked in 1943; the Germans will take such visits as proof that the man concerned had actually enjoyed his time in their town. Unfortunately for German feelings, the French, Belgians and Poles all stress that they hated the forced work for their enemy and the seemingly unending separation from their families. In defence of the Germans it should be said that no one in Schweinfurt or Regensburg had any say in the matter. When Berlin pressed for greater production of ball-bearings or fighter planes, it was forced labour that was provided by Berlin. At least neither industry had started using concentration-camp labour in 1943 and at neither Schweinfurt nor Regensburg was there any deliberate starvation, but there are stories of harsh treatment for Russians at both places. Labour from the East always had the hardest time in Germany. One must never forget the attitude of bitterness and fear which the Germans had towards the countries to her east, that area into which Hitler had ventured in 1939 and 1941 and which was now proving to be Germany's undoing. The local weekly newspaper which appeared in Regensburg immediately after the American air raid contains two items which are relevant to this attitude. On one page there is a short report about a Regensburg woman, Hildegard — (her surname is mentioned), who was sentenced to a long period in a concentration camp for 'sleeping in a vile manner [*in ehrvergessener Weise*] with Poles'. On a nearby page there are private death notices for thirty-four local men who had been reported as killed in action in one week. Thirty-one of these had died on the Russian Front; the locations of the deaths of the other three men were not recorded.*

Many individuals were as kind as they could be to the strangers with whom they worked, but genuine warmth and close contact were rare. A Frenchman says that 'at first we were treated like old enemies in Regensburg and the official propaganda tried to keep up this old spirit, especially with the young people, who, as early as ten or twelve years of age, were put into uniform and became masters of the streets [*maîtres de la rue*] and forced us to get off the pavements to let them pass'. But the same man goes on to say, 'On the whole, with a bit of caution and a lot of tact, we managed to live an almost normal life with the civilians.'

It is possible that the amount of space devoted to this description of the foreign workers at the places about to be bombed by the Americans is greater than is warranted by their actual numbers. But I make no apology for the emphasis given to this subject. The foreigners were an integral part of the societies living around these targets, and their story is rarely heard. They will be met again when the bombs start to fall.

* *Regensburger Kurier*, 24 August 1943.

CHAPTER 3

Chain of Command

Brigadier-General Frederick L. Anderson, Jr, commanding general of VIII Bomber Command, needed just one day of fine weather for the ambitious mission on which he was waiting to dispatch his entire force. Once the combined Schweinfurt–Regensburg plan had been approved by his superior at Eighth Air Force, Major-General Eaker, all Anderson had to do was choose the right day and then allow his staff to add the final details to the plan and issue the necessary operation orders to the subordinate formations.

It was a heavy responsibility which rested on the shoulders of Anderson, who was only thirty-seven years old and who had arrived in England less than four months earlier. His previous appointment had been that of Director of Bombardment at the newly built Pentagon in Washington. He was an energetic officer, described by one of his contemporaries as 'one of Hap Arnold's "wonder boys", a group of five or so very promising professional Air Corps officers – one of that small group of pilots who had grown up as long-range strategic bomber enthusiasts'. Anderson had commanded the 4th Bombardment Wing, part of VIII Bomber Command, for a mere two months before being moved up to head the whole of that organization. Such swift promotion was not uncommon in those heady days. The U.S.A.A.F. was expanding so dramatically that promising young career officers like Anderson were shooting up the ladder of advancement all over the world. There was no doubt about Anderson's bravery; it was he who had recently made two flights with R.A.F. Bomber Command to the heavily defended targets of Hamburg and Essen to study British night bombing methods. He was a popular and well respected figure at both his own headquarters and that of the nearby Eighth Air Force, but he was virtually unknown to the men who actually had to fly the operations he ordered and his experience of handling large-scale bomber operations was limited.

It is probable that the Schweinfurt–Regensburg plan had been ready for execution since 13 August but the Americans had long since learned to be patient with the frequently cloudy European weather. Because of the early-morning take-offs required for this operation, the decision to mount it needed to be made during the morning of the previous day. German and British weather records show that a familiar weather process existed. A low-pressure system (down to 985 millibars) was passing over Denmark and then running north-eastwards up the Baltic. An associated cold front was swinging eastwards like a long chain right across England, France, the Low Countries and Germany. It is possible that Anderson had decided on the 13th to carry out the operation on the 14th when the front was over France and the Low Countries with clear weather on either side of it. Several junior commanders and operations officers say that preliminary orders were received to prepare for the Schweinfurt–Regensburg operation on that date but the operation was cancelled before the ordinary crews were briefed. (It should be recalled that the Schweinfurt-only operation had probably got as far as the crew-briefing stage on 10 August. Unfortunately there are no documents to confirm the dates of these cancelled operations.) While Anderson waited again, the front moved through Europe and was followed by an extensive high-pressure area of fine weather. France, the Low Countries and Germany were all clear by the 16th, and this would undoubtedly have been the best day for the big operation. Unfortunately, when the operation was considered on the morning of the 15th, Anderson's meteorological adviser could not be sure that the front would clear the two targets so quickly. The front moved 1,000 miles in twenty-four hours!

Anderson had not wasted the waiting period. He sent his bombers to German operational fighter airfields in France and Belgium on 15 August, and to depots where reserve aircraft and crews were believed to be located on the 16th. The operations of this second day included a raid on the Paris airfield of Le Bourget, a place of interest to the American airmen involved because their pioneering countryman, Charles Lindbergh, had landed at Le Bourget after his record-breaking solo Atlantic flight in 1927. A total of 581 B-17 sorties were flown in these two days; 528 aircraft bombed their targets and only six were lost. The raids must have caused some attrition to the Luftwaffe crews, aircraft and airfields in the area through which the Schweinfurt–Regensburg operation would eventually fly, and the morale of the American crews was raised by these 'milk runs', escorted by friendly fighters all the way and of only short duration. Of particular importance was the effect of the raids upon American aircraft availability. The biggest problem for the American units – after the European weather – was the repair of the large number of B-17s which returned damaged after each raid. The cause of most of the damage was German Flak. None of these airfield targets raided on 15 and 16 August was heavily defended and the American ground repair organizations were able to use these days to tackle a backlog of repairs without having further problems pushed onto them. It was hoped that as a result of all these operations the German fighter force would face the main American raid, when it did come, in a weakened condition, while the American force would be in a fresher and stronger condition.

On the morning of Monday 16 August, while his B-17s were attacking Le Bourget, Poix and Abbeville airfields, General Anderson and his staff held their daily operational conference at their headquarters at Wycombe Abbey in Buckinghamshire, west of London. The schoolgirls who had formerly lived in this boarding school had been evacuated for fear of bombing earlier in the war. If he had followed his normal custom, Anderson had earlier attended Sir Arthur Harris's R.A.F. Bomber Command conference at nearby High Wycombe. It was the moon period and, because the R.A.F. did not normally fly to Germany in the full moon, Harris had decided to send 154 bombers to attack Turin in Northern Italy in the coming night, that of 16/17 August. Anderson already knew that there was little chance of Harris following up the American attack on Schweinfurt. The poor weather which had delayed American operations earlier in the moon had also robbed the Schweinfurt part of the coming operation of the proposed R.A.F. participation. The 154 R.A.F. bombers being sent to Turin represented less than a quarter of Harris's available strength; the British commander was also conserving his force for a special operation – the raid on the German V-2 rocket research establishment at Peenemünde.

Anderson proceeded with his own decision-making. No record was made, but the known weather conditions and the orders eventually issued clearly reveal what happened at that fateful meeting. The weather men were now satisfied that the frontal cloud had cleared from Germany and the weather in North Africa posed no problem. Unfortunately the next weather system – a warm front – was coming up from the south-west and bringing to England variable cloud; this might reach and cover the American bases before take-off time the next morning. And so all the doubts about cloud over the distant German targets were now replaced by anxiety about the possibility of bad weather over the bases in England. The frustrated Anderson decided he had to make a move. He ordered that the basic plan for the attack on Schweinfurt and Regensburg which had been prepared nearly a week earlier was to be put in hand, with the intention of a take-off immediately after dawn of the following day, 17 August. If the weather over his bases proved to be unfavourable in the morning, then there would be a little time – two hours at most – for a limited postponement. If at the end of that time there was no improvement in take-off conditions, then the whole raid could be cancelled for that day and Anderson would have to start all over again and wait for better conditions.

No essential part of the plan needed to be changed; only minor navigational and bombing details needed to be calculated on the basis of the latest weather forecasts. This work was carried out in the next few hours and then the 'field orders' were sent out over teleprinters to the next level of the chain of command. The raid, when flown the next day, would be Mission No. 84 for the 1st Bombardment Wing but only No. 30 for the newer 4th Bombardment Wing. By no more than a coincidence, the Schweinfurt–Regensburg mission would now take place exactly one year after the first VIII Bomber Command mission when General Eaker had flown with twelve B-17s to bomb a railway marshalling yard at Rouen. The anniversary of this event would provide a useful morale-boosting point at crew briefings in the morning.

It would not be useful to go into too much detail about the plan sent out over the teleprinter that Monday afternoon because circumstances which would be encountered the following morning would force many changes. It is sufficient to state here that the leading unit of the Regensburg force was planned to cross the coast of Holland at 8.30 a.m.; this time would be designated as Zero Hour for the whole operation. The Schweinfurt force would follow fifteen minutes later. The Regensburg force was expected to attract most of the German opposition on the flight to the targets. It was planned that the two targets would be attacked almost simultaneously; the orders actually called for the first bombs to go down on Schweinfurt at 10.12 a.m. and those at

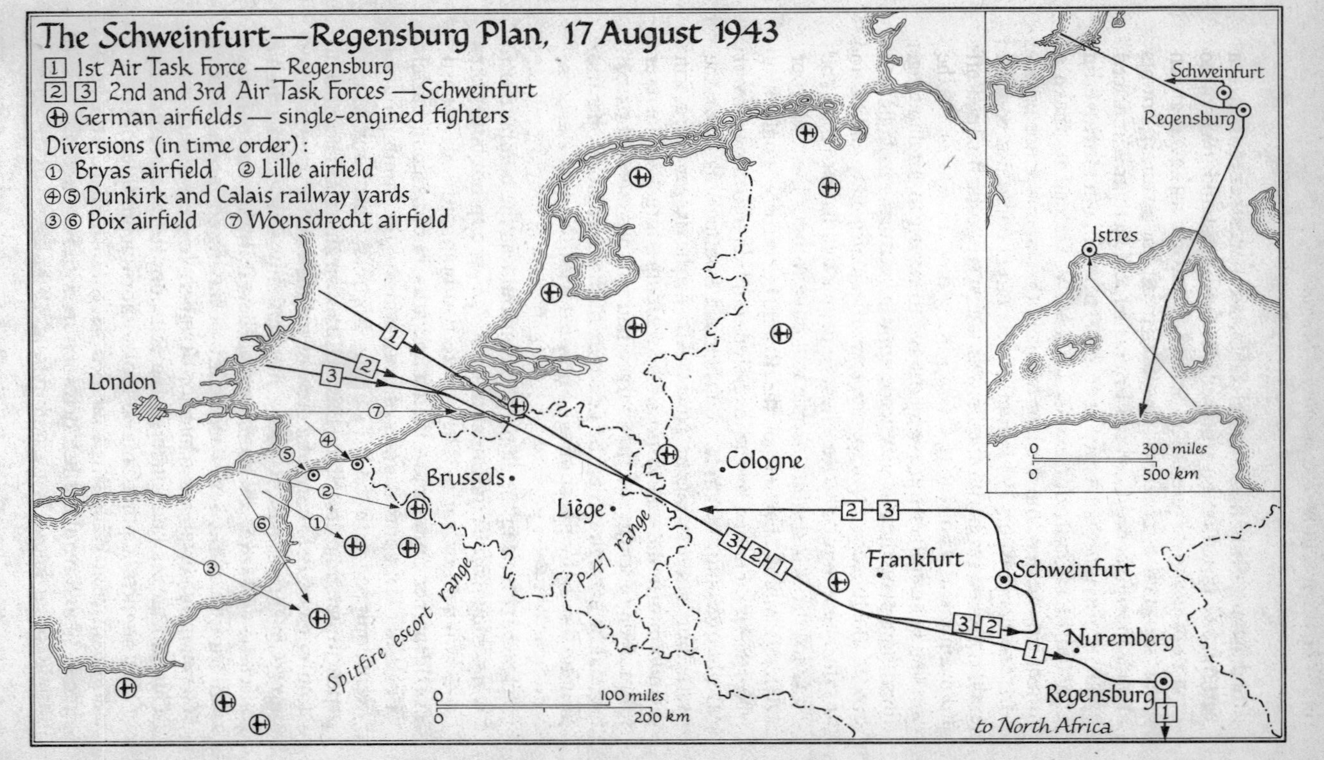
The Schweinfurt—Regensburg Plan, 17 August 1943
1 1st Air Task Force — Regensburg
2 3 2nd and 3rd Air Task Forces — Schweinfurt
German airfields — single-engined fighters
Diversions (in time order):
① Bryas airfield ② Lille airfield
④⑤ Dunkirk and Calais railway yards
③⑥ Poix airfield ⑦ Woensdrecht airfield
London
Brussels
Liège
Cologne
Frankfurt
Schweinfurt
Nuremberg
Regensburg
to North Africa
Spitfire escort range
P-47 range
0 100 miles
0 200 km
Schweinfurt
Regensburg
Istres
0 300 miles
0 500 km

Regensburg one minute later. Elaborate orders were issued for alternative targets to be attacked if either of the main ones turned out to be cloud-covered. The Schweinfurt force was given no less than six such alternatives, the first three, in order of priority, being an engineering works at Frankfurt, railway yards at Aachen and an instruments factory at Bonn. The main alternative target for the Regensburg force was the B.M.W. factory at Allach on the north-western outskirts of Munich; this factory made engines for the Focke-Wulf 190 fighter. If this target could not be found and attacked properly, the bomb loads were to be dumped into the centre of Munich city.

The Schweinfurt force would have to return to England after bombing and could expect fierce opposition during its flight back to the Belgian coast. As so many American airmen would be told at their briefings, 'The Regensburg people will have to fight their way in; the Schweinfurt people will have to fight their way out.' After bombing their target the Regensburg force would fly to North Africa, aided by the diversionary raids to be flown by 180 B-17s from North Africa to airfields in Southern France. After refuelling and resting in North Africa, the Regensburg force would return to England, possibly attacking a target on the return flight. The identity of that target had not yet been chosen; it would be enough to get the first part of this ambitious operation under way before becoming concerned with the next stage.

The next level in the chain of command was the bombardment wing, roughly the equivalent of an R.A.F. group but larger than a German *Geschwader*. There were two bombardment wings in VIII Bomber Command – the 1st and 4th – both based in Eastern England. The combat units of both wings – the bomb groups – were equipped with the B-17 Flying Fortress. This book will not spend much time describing this well-known aircraft. The graceful four-engined B-17 carried a crew of ten men and a bomb load of up to 5,000 pounds. It was a mechanically sound and reliable aircraft, well loved by the men who flew it, but it was currently suffering from the severe disability of having to face a form of German fighter attack which its designers had never envisaged. German tactics had rendered the B-17 obsolete before its time. (This important point will be looked at in detail later.) The 1st Bombardment Wing was equipped with the standard version of the B-17 and would attack Schweinfurt with it. The B-17s of the 4th Bombardment Wing had extra fuel tanks – Tokyo tanks –

fitted in their wing-tips, which gave them the extra range to reach more distant Regensburg and fly on to Africa. (It should be stated that the 1st and 4th Bombardment Wings were in the process of being renamed the 1st and 3rd Air Divisions and many books describing actions of this period use those later terms. While both forms are equally valid, the official change did not take place until 13 September 1943 and the original 1st and 4th Bombardment Wing designations are preferred here.)

The commanders of the two bombardment wings which were to carry out the operations of 17 August 1943 are important to this story, not because they had any influence on the overall plan, but because of the way they had prepared their units for the operation and because both of them actually flew on the raid. Brigadier-General Robert B. Williams was in command of the 1st Bombardment Wing. This officer had more experience of conditions in England than anyone else in the Eighth Air Force, for he had been in London as part of an American liaison team well before Pearl Harbor. He had lost an eye in a German air raid on London, but was allowed to continue flying because of his experience with B-17s in their earliest experimental days. It was said that Bob Williams could land a B-17 with one eye better than most pilots could with two. He was a sound, conventional, well-respected commander; the description of him by one of his subordinates as 'a good, patient manager' probably sums up his style of leadership well, and very few men in the 1st Bombardment Wing even knew the name of their commander.

By contrast, the much smaller 4th Bombardment Wing had the most able and dynamic of commanders; every man in that organization knew of Colonel Curtis LeMay. My interviews resulted in numerous notes describing LeMay: 'that tough, cigar-smoking disciplinarian'; 'old ironpants, a real meanie, but that's what you want when you're fighting a war'; 'part of military's awesomeness'; 'not really the tough old son of a bitch he was made out to be'. LeMay had commanded one of the early bomb groups to arrive in England – the 305th – for nearly a year, during which time he had personally pioneered many of the basic defensive formation features and bombing tactics which would serve the Eighth Air Force for the remainder of the war. Members of the 305th were always proud of the earlier association of LeMay with their unit and the unofficial 'Can-Do Group' subtitle he inspired. LeMay had moved to the command of the relatively new 4th Bombardment Wing in June 1943; his promotion to one-star general was still on the way from Washington. Although not a West Pointer, many around him felt they were watching the rise of a commander of the highest potential. He was an unsmiling man with no time for small talk; his words of criticism could be cutting 'even in his typical brevity'. He was reputed to be as expert in gunnery, navigation and bomb aiming as most of the specialist officers under his command and he was a qualified pilot.

LeMay's whole attitude to command at that time was that the rapid expansion of the U.S.A.A.F. had produced a situation in which most of the men below him, staff officers, subordinate commanders and combat crews alike, though willing enough, were without depth of skill and experience. He relentlessly strove to establish effective but simple operating procedures and then to ensure that his units were fully practised in those procedures. In any study of the operations of 17 August 1943, when the 1st and 4th Bombardment Wings were both tested to the full, the performance of LeMay's command consistently shows a slight edge on that of its sister wing.

The wing commanders and their staffs had been able to make some advance preparations for this major operation. An outline plan for Schweinfurt had been sent to the headquarters of both wings at least three weeks earlier – this was at the time of the old plan that the whole of VIII Bomber Command should attack Schweinfurt – and the Regensburg plan had been with the 4th Bombardment Wing for two weeks. Of the two targets, Schweinfurt had always received more attention because of the potential difficulty of finding its three factories, semi-hidden as they were in and on the edge of a built-up area, in contrast to the Messerschmitt factory's easily identifiable location. It is ironical that the 4th Bombardment Wing had probably devoted more effort to preparing for an attack on Schweinfurt than for Regensburg; in fact the original shuttle plan to fly on to North Africa was to have been linked with the bombing of Schweinfurt, not Regensburg. Colonel LeMay had flown to North Africa in mid July to check the arrangements there for the landing of his units.

The early preparations for the Schweinfurt operation had been conducted at two levels. The first was the selection by every bomb group of a 'lead crew' for an important and difficult operation. The core of the lead crew was its bombardier, because it was the practice of the whole group of eighteen or more B-17s to release their bombs when the lead aircraft dropped. A competent, steady pilot and a reliable navigator made up the rest of the lead team; the remaining members of the crew had only to carry out their normal tasks, although the crew's regular co-pilot would usually finish up in the tail turret, advising the pilot on the formation-keeping of the remaining aircraft of the group. The pilots, bombardiers and navigators of the lead crews had been sent to their respective wing headquarters – the 1st at Brampton Grange, near Huntingdon, and the 4th at Elveden Hall, a country house deep in Suffolk – and briefed by officers of their own wing and from VIII Bomber Command. In locked and guarded rooms they were told that they had been chosen to lead their groups on the most important mission of the war to date, which, if successful, would shorten the war. They were then shown a model and a series of photographs of Schweinfurt and its surroundings and told to study these from every possible angle of approach. The town and the three factories were not identified but only referred to as 'Target A'. All present were told to maintain strict secrecy about what they had seen. The entire crews to which these officers belonged were then relieved of all operations until the day of the raid. The intervening time was devoted to further studies of the model and photographs and much practice flying and bombing.

The waiting period was a strange time for the officers who had been chosen for this duty. Several of them spent many hours poring over maps of Germany trying to find the 'three-target town near a river' which they had been shown on the model and photographs; little Schweinfurt, so far away in Southern Germany, did not reveal itself to many of them. It was an even stranger time for those members of the lead crews who had not yet been briefed and so did not know why they were not to fly on operations for such a long period; three weeks on an operational base was almost an eternity. Captain Everett Blakely was the pilot of the 100th Bomb Group's lead crew.

> The enlisted men in the crew couldn't understand why they had been singled out for all these repeated training flights; they were quite anxious about it. What was going to come down the road? But our men were pretty stable, with a sense of humor, and they sweated it out well enough. There were a few gripes but they gave no trouble. One of the waist gunners, Saunders from Chicago, was a little older than the others. He had a particularly good sense of humor and he helped me out a lot.

One bombardier says, 'Whatever it was that was coming, it seemed big and I was dreading that target coming up, but, when it did come, we would be ready.' Second Lieutenant Johnny Butler, lead pilot of the 384th Bomb Group, says that 'the security was so important that I lived in torment that I would talk in my sleep'. When the 'big one' did come up, the 4th Bombardment Wing lead bombardiers would be amazed to find that they would not be bombing the three-factory town they had been studying for so long but would be raiding a completely different factory in a different town and after being given no more than the normal preparation time – a few hours – to study the Regensburg area.

At some stage during the preparation period, the group commanders were also called to wing conferences. (There is some doubt about the timing of these; it is possible that they took place in two stages, with a preliminary one at which group commanders were only told of a big operation coming up and ordered to select their lead crews, and the main briefing conference much later.) When the 1st Bombardment Wing disclosed the identity of the target to its group commanders, one commander who was present says 'there was much interest, much excitement, at the prospect of "the decisive blow" ', but Major Clinton Ball, whose squadron would be forming part of a composite group, writes, 'The curtain was pulled back to reveal the objective as Schweinfurt. The route ribbon seemed to be twice as long or deep into Germany as any I had seen before and I recall that during the route briefing – point D to point E, for example – a deep voice at the back of the room kept booming out, "them what's left".'

The ability of the groups to take off and assemble in bad weather was to be a critical factor on the morning of 17 August and it is sometimes stated that the groups of the 4th Bombardment Wing carried out special training for this during the preparatory period. This is only partly correct. Colonel LeMay had always insisted upon extensive practice flights to improve the all-round efficiency of his groups. He merely stepped up the intensity of this training with a particular emphasis on instrument take-offs. He ordered that, even in clear conditions, his pilots were always to take off on instruments with the co-pilot checking visually. The 1st Bombardment Wing units also continued routine training flights but, unfortunately, not as intensively as LeMay's units.

The staffs of both bombardment wings had completed most of

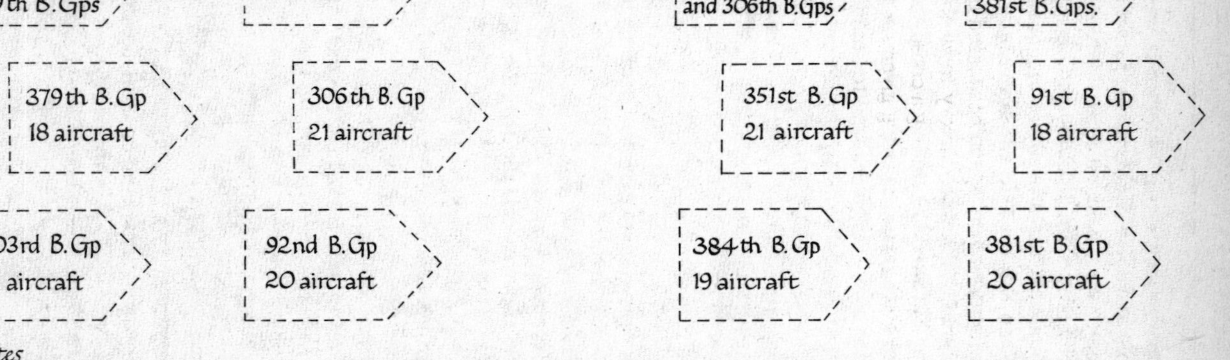

Notes

1. There was an interval of twelve minutes' flying time between the two task forces and of five minutes between the two wings of each task force although the intervals would all become smaller under combat conditions.
2. The 384th B. Gp was one aircraft short on take-off.

THE REGENSBURG FORCE (4th BOMBARDMENT WING)

Commander: Col Curtis E. LeMay

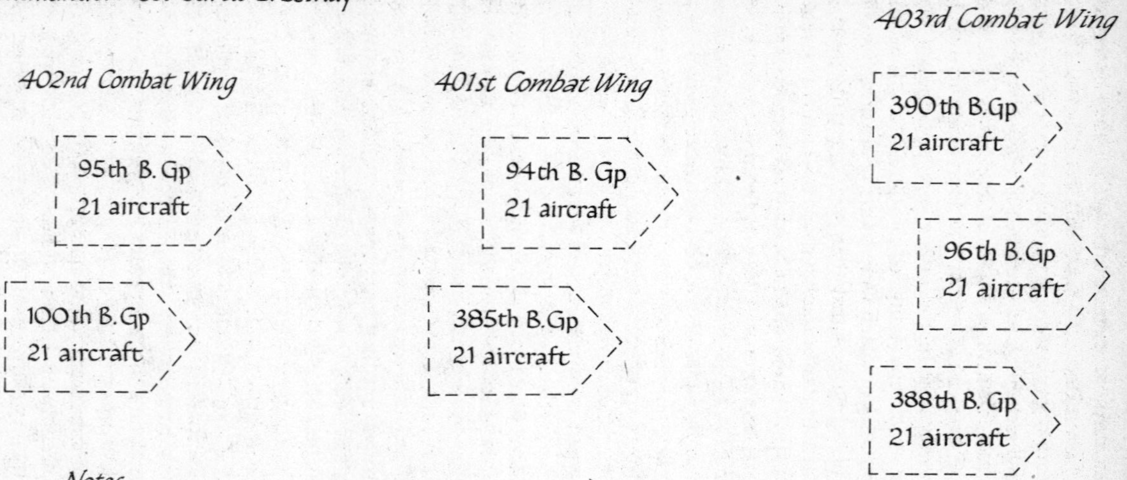

402nd Combat Wing

95th B. Gp
21 aircraft

100th B. Gp
21 aircraft

401st Combat Wing

94th B. Gp
21 aircraft

385th B. Gp
21 aircraft

403rd Combat Wing

390th B. Gp
21 aircraft

96th B. Gp
21 aircraft

388th B. Gp
21 aircraft

Notes

1. The Regensburg force was designated '1st Air Task Force' in VIII Bomber Command's Field Order.
2. There were intervals of three minutes' flying time between combat wings.
3. The 390th B. Gp was one aircraft short on take-off.

their planning days or even weeks before they received their formal orders from Bomber Command in the early afternoon of 16 August. Both organizations had selected experienced groups – the 91st for Schweinfurt and the 96th for Regensburg – to lead their task forces. The disposition of the other groups would normally have been a matter of routine rotation, with groups taking their turn in the high, lead and low positions of the standard three-group combat-wing formation. But there were exceptional factors present in each wing on this occasion. The original Schweinfurt plan had assumed that both the 1st and 4th Wings would be allocated to the attack on the ball-bearing factories but, now that the 4th Bombardment Wing had been withdrawn for the Regensburg operation, the 1st was faced with the problem of carrying a realistic tonnage to the three Schweinfurt factories. In that original Schweinfurt plan, two 'composite groups', made up of reserve aircraft not needed in the regular formations, had been intended to provide a major diversionary attack on the Luftwaffe airfield at Lille. These two composite groups were now added to the main Schweinfurt force, together with a third composite group provided by a further gathering of spare aircraft. Brigadier-General Williams now had twelve groups which he could dispose neatly into four standard combat wings, which were in turn divided between two air task forces. Even after the formation of the composite groups, the 1st Bombardment Wing still ordered a 'maximum effort'. The true 'maximum effort' was a very rare event, and this was probably the first time it had been used. The result was that individual extra planes were added to formations wherever possible. The 'availability status' of the 1st Bombardment Wing for the evening of 16 August shows that 238 B-17s were operational and capable of being prepared for the raid next morning. The groups planned to dispatch 231 of these, while several more were to be sent up as 'air spares' to replace aircraft which had to turn back because of mechanical difficulty. (Appendix 1 gives details of the operational effort of all Allied units involved on 17 August 1943.)

The 4th Bombardment Wing had no problem over providing the number of aircraft required to bomb the Messerschmitt factory. Its availability status was 189 aircraft but it would use only 147 of these. Composite groups to strengthen the Regensburg force had been considered but Colonel LeMay did not like such departures from routine procedure and it was judged that the single factory at Regensburg did not require such extreme measures. LeMay did order each of his groups to take three extra aircraft, not as normal air spares but as a form of long-distance reserve; these aircraft would initially fly as a third flight in each group's high squadron. The main purpose of this unusual move was to prevent the group defensive fire power being unduly weakened by the inevitable loss of B-17s. A secondary purpose was to ensure that the required tonnage of bombs could be delivered to Regensburg. The main problem for LeMay was that of how to dispose of his force. A new unit from the United States, the 390th Bomb Group, had recently become operational and LeMay decided that it would fly to Regensburg, although it would only be the group's third operation. This would be the layout of LeMay's awkward seven-group force.

There remained the selection of officers to command the various elements of the two forces in the air. It is probable that General Eaker personally asked both Brigadier-General Williams and Colonel LeMay to lead their respective forces; LeMay was certainly asked. Both officers would fly on the operation. This disappointed Colonel Russell A. Wilson, one of the officers who often led the 4th Bombardment Wing in the air; LeMay consoled Wilson by promising him that he could definitely lead the first attack on Berlin when that even more prestigious target was tackled. Wilson had to wait until 6 March 1944 for his Berlin flight and would be killed over the city that day. The two air task forces into which the Schweinfurt force was split had Colonels William M. Gross and Howard M. Turner as their air commanders. The role of these officers in the air and their sometimes ill-defined relationship with the lead pilots who flew combat missions more regularly will be discussed later.

The staff officers at the two bombardment wing headquarters finished their work. Brigadier-General Williams had a more experienced staff than LeMay's more recently formed organization. Curtis LeMay, the perfectionist, says that he virtually acted as his own senior operations officer throughout the whole process that day to ensure that nothing would go wrong. Preliminary orders, with bomb and fuel loading instructions, went out to the groups in the early evening but final orders were not ready until much later. The records of the 305th Bomb Group conveniently note that their loading orders were received at 6.45 p.m. and their final orders half an hour before midnight.

Much planning was also being carried out in other places where every effort was being made to provide both direct protection and indirect support to the B-17 units. There was a considerable amount and variety of air power available for these tasks.

R.A.F. Fighter Command had been fighting the Luftwaffe since 1939. It had the advantage of having in England a large force of operational squadrons whose pilots knew every yard of the ground 'on the other side' and most of the tricks of the German fighter pilots. Its unit commanders in particular were outstanding tactical leaders; most were veterans of the Battle of Britain and many were now on their third or fourth tour of operations in this area. The morale of their units was superb. The R.A.F. squadrons now contained not only men from the long-embattled United Kingdom but men of spirit from right across the British Empire and German-occupied Europe and even a few Americans from before Pearl Harbor who still preferred not to transfer to the U.S.A.A.F. Twenty-two R.A.F. fighter squadrons – all flying the famous Spitfire – would be giving direct escort support either to the B-17s or to medium-bomber diversionary operations the next day, and a further ten Typhoon fighter-bomber squadrons would be sent to attack German fighter airfields. Of these squadrons, seven were Canadian, two each were made up of men from New Zealand, Norway and Poland, and there was a Free French squadron which would have the privilege of flying and fighting over its own country. Even the nominally British squadrons were now made up of a high proportion of Empire and Allied pilots and it is safe to say that more than half of the men who would be flying in the next day's operations had come to England from other countries. Hitler had provoked too many people in the world.

The R.A.F. pilots only had one complaint: they did not see enough of the Luftwaffe – and therein was to be found the crippling disability under which the R.A.F. squadrons fought. The Spitfire had been designed for defensive action over England and it had only a limited range. It was an extremely effective fighter when it did meet the Luftwaffe, but the Luftwaffe could afford to stand off and ignore the Spitfires if they wished and they only engaged when they could see an advantage in doing so. The Spitfires would be out in force to help the B-17s the next morning but, on past experience, it was likely that the Luftwaffe would try to avoid action with them.

The Americans had done little better in the provision of fighter escorts which had any useful range. It was a simple but tragic matter. The U.S.A.A.F. had earlier convinced itself that the self-defending long-range bomber concept was valid and had neglected the development of long-range fighter escorts. U.S.A.A.F. commanders all over the world were now competing for what few long-range fighters were available. The P-38 Lightning had been the best early prospect and some had arrived in England in 1942 but, sadly for the Eighth Air Force, they had been sent on to North Africa. More P-38 groups had recently arrived in England but these would not be ready for operations until October. Had they been available in quantity in August 1943, the Schweinfurt-bound B-17s could have had escort all the way to the target – just – and the Regensburg force for most of their way.

The American fighter provided as a partial stop-gap for the Eighth Air Force was the P-47 Thunderbolt. This was a heavy but powerful fighter, named 'the Jug' by its crews from its slightly ridiculous milk-jug-like shape. The P-47 certainly did not look like an effective modern fighter and the pilots of the early units flying it in England had been very doubtful about its prospects against the Luftwaffe. Lieutenant Paul Conger of the 56th Fighter Group was one of these early pilots; the 'damned Eagle Squadron men' he refers to were the American pilots who had flown with the R.A.F. earlier in the war.

> We started with an inferiority complex. Those damned Eagle Squadron men were our downfall with their pessimism over the P-47, talking about those heavy Thunderbolts and the Luftwaffe with their four years of experience. It had taken the Eagle Squadron with their two-ton Spits all their time to cope with the Luftwaffe. 'You'll die in five missions with those seven-ton birds,' they told us. We believed them.
>
> The first few missions, we spent all our time concentrating on flying this big new aircraft in combat but we soon learned the P-47's one big advantage – power. In any trouble, pour on the gas, dive, and that huge powerful engine got us out it. We soon gained confidence, specially when we met the Germans at altitude.

The P-47 actually weighed six and a half tons and it was indeed a powerful plane; few other aircraft could catch it in the dive and its firepower, of eight ·5-inch machine-guns, was extremely effective.

But the problem, yet again, was range. Even with the drop tanks now being fitted – very often unsatisfactory ones – the P-47 could only fight at a range of 250 miles from its bases, half the range of the P-38 and a mere sixty miles beyond the range of the Spitfire. Even within their limited range, there were not enough P-47s in England to provide complete protection for a full-scale B-17 operation. There were only four groups – twelve squadrons – available for the next day's flying and one of the four groups had only been operational for one week. But the American pilots were keen, aggressive and skilful. Some of their commanders were exceptionally good and were well on the way to covering themselves with glory. The German pilots had learnt to treat these peculiarly shaped American planes with respect and intercepted radio conversations showed that they were most anxious to know whether they were likely to meet the P-47 when ordered into action. The Americans were learning to gain a little extra range each time they flew and the Germans never knew exactly how far into an area of operations the P-47s would fly. The fact remained, however, that the B-17 bombers would have hundreds of miles to fly beyond the deepest possible P-47 range and the Germans, if they judged the situation correctly, would still be able to afford to stand off and wait until the fighters left.

The only other element in the support plan for the main operation was the medium bombers which would fly under heavy R.A.F. fighter escort in four diversionary raids. Five bomber units would be involved. Three of these were American B-26 Marauder bomb groups and two were R.A.F. Mitchell squadrons (the Mitchell was the American-built B-25). This was the total Allied air effort planned for 17 August 1943:

Schweinfurt force	231 B-17s
Regensburg force	146 B-17s
Escorts to B-17s	183 P-47s and 97 Spitfires
Medium bomber diversions	108 B-26s and 13 Mitchells
Escorts to mediums	152 Spitfires
Fighter-bombers	78 Typhoons
Total	1,007 aircraft
	(667 American, 340 R.A.F.)

These figures do not include the second sorties to be flown by 211 of the Spitfires and ninety-three of the P-47s, nor do they include those B-17s which would take off as spares to replace early aborts, one R.A.F. Whirlwind squadron and its escort of four Spitfire squadrons which would fly to Brittany early on the 17th with the intention of pinning down Luftwaffe units there, and the 180 B-17s from North Africa which were to raid airfields in Southern France when the Regensburg force was flying across the Mediterranean. If these further operations are added in, 1,566 Allied air sorties were to be flown into German-defended air space the following day. A total of 7,000 Allied airmen would be involved, of whom over 6,500 were Americans. All of these extensive operations were subordinate to one purpose – to enable 376 American-crewed heavy bombers to reach and bomb their targets at Schweinfurt and Regensburg and to return with as little loss to themselves as possible.

As the evening of 16 August wore on, the headquarters of the wings became quieter, with paperwork being completed and staff officers going to bed. The scene of action now moved to the airfields of the combat units which within a few hours would be sending their men out yet again to risk their lives in support of the Allied cause.

The receipt by the bomb groups of the loading orders had allowed much of their outside work to be completed during the evening. There is no need to spend much time on this aspect; most of this work was routine. The balmy evening of early autumn allowed the men of the various ground sections to carry out their work under reasonable conditions. Outside working conditions could be vile in the winter months. A total of 787 tons of bombs were loaded into the B-17s that evening – 480 tons for Schweinfurt, 307 for Regensburg. Machine-gun ammunition would be loaded in the morning. Fuel tanks were filled to the maximum and nearly 1½ million gallons of fuel were required for the B-17 force which would take off in the morning.

The group commanders had known for several hours that the raid to be flown the next morning was 'the big one' which had been talked about for several weeks. Groups normally operated a roster of seven officers who took it in turns to act as air commander of the group. These seven were the group commander, his deputy, the group operations officer and the four squadron commanders. The purpose of the roster system was to ensure that 'rough missions' and the easier 'milk runs' would eventually be shared out evenly. There is every evidence, however, that there was fierce competition among these officers for the privilege of leading the groups on this occasion. For a keen professional officer, a mission such as this could prove to be one of the most important of the war, indeed of a whole career. There was much pulling of rank and invoking of old promises; coins were even tossed for the choice. In the end, nine out of sixteen group commanders decided they would lead their units. Many of those subordinates who were disappointed managed to claim a position elsewhere in the group formation although there was no need for them to fly.

Several ground-duty officers were permitted to take part in this interesting operation. The intelligence and engineering officers of the 385th Bomb Group both flew to Regensburg in this way, and the wing armourer officer of the 4th Bombardment Wing also flew with the 385th as a waist gunner. Two more of these 'tourists', as they were called by the regular fliers, turned up at Thorpe Abbots, the home of the 100th Bomb Group. One was Colonel William L. Kennedy, the commander of an aerial gunnery school in the United States, who had been touring the bases of the groups in England to gain more information on combat gunnery conditions. Kennedy was on the eve of returning to the United States when he heard that this deep penetration raid was being prepared and was given permission to take part. He would fly as a waist gunner in a crew whose original gunner had been sent in disgrace to a gunnery school in England for retraining when he had failed to clear his gun properly after a raid and let off a round which went through his plane's tail. The second visitor to Thorpe Abbots was Lieutenant-Colonel Beirne Lay, a pilot who had been occupying a staff position at Eighth Air Force Headquarters in recent months. Lay would later publish an excellent account in the *Saturday Evening Post* of his experiences during the Regensburg operation, an account which would be heavily quoted by other writers in subsequent years. There was every chance that both of these officers would see plenty of action; the 100th would be flying in the tail-end group position of the Regensburg force. Colonel Kennedy was even flying in the poorest aircraft of the group; it was named *Oh Nausea* and was reputed to have aborted every mission on which it had so far flown and never to have dropped a bomb on a target.

There was much activity in the various section offices at the operations block of each group after the main orders arrived. Again, most of this was routine paperwork but more than usual care was devoted to the preparation of navigation plans, the route of the Regensburg force to North Africa receiving particular attention. Some of the officers preparing these plans would get little or no sleep that night and would have to fly the mission themselves the next day. Did they become tired? 'No,' says one. 'You were getting all pumped up with adrenalin by then.'

Squadron commanders and their operations officers were also busy but their main task was to find the required number of crews for the coming operation. At this stage the squadrons were unlikely even to know the identity of the target, although they probably had a good idea of the length and importance of the operation. The routine in 'squadron ops' was to get the crew lists prepared as quickly as possible and then get everyone to bed. There is evidence that many units had foreseen the unusual nature of this operation and had been carefully conserving their more seasoned crews for it. Leave and courses had been postponed and the deliberately short and easy operations of recent days had helped most squadrons to accumulate plenty of crews.

This chapter can end with a brief look at some of the bomb groups and their preparedness for the coming test. A group contained four squadrons, each of which was expected to be able to provide six aircraft and crews for any operation. But groups varied considerably not only in their strengths of crews and aircraft but in the collective ability of the group to face a difficult mission. I asked each man I met about the condition of his unit at that time. There was surprising unanimity among the answers from the men in each group. The views recorded here are intended to cover only the period immediately before the Schweinfurt–Regensburg operation. The situation within a group changed many times during the war.

The groups had usually arrived in England with high morale and full complements, keen to prove themselves. The dominant factor affecting morale and ability in the ensuing period of operations was always the rate of loss. Groups with a good run of luck could build up great experience and confidence, with new crews being easily and gradually introduced to combat. Heavy casualties over a prolonged period could crush the spirit of any unit. Casualties could be reduced by good training and wise leadership but luck remained an important factor. Leadership was vital. One pilot says that it was important to have 'a group commander who was good on his feet at briefing and also a good pilot, and that's what we had'. That man's commander was Lieutenant-Colonel Clemens L. Wurzback of the 91st Bomb Group at Bassingbourn, a long-established group whose members all spoke well of it. Another 91st man, who would be shot down on the way to Schweinfurt, says, 'If I had to do it all again, I'd do it with that group.' Members of the 379th Bomb Group at Kimbolton also speak well of their commander: Technical Sergeant Johannes Johnson, another man to be shot down on the way to Schweinfurt, has this to say about Colonel Maurice Preston.

> He was a tough man, a strict disciplinarian – not on whether you wore your uniform properly or had shined your shoes but strict on your flying, on whether you knew your job. After the group's first mission he had said, 'Is anyone scared? If not, there's something wrong with you. I'll give you a little clue how to fight this war – make believe you're dead already; the rest comes easy.' I've never forgotten that. We were fortunate to have a man like that for a leader. He seemed that he knew what he was doing all the time.

The 305th Bomb Group, based at Chelveston, was Curtis LeMay's old command and had recently emerged from a period of heavy loss. The resulting shortage of both crews and aircraft had caused a heavy strain on the surviving crews but, as one officer says, 'LeMay's old influence was still strong. I hate to use such a tired old phrase but there was a real "can-do" spirit about the group.' All these groups were in the 1st Bombardment Wing. Two of its other groups in particularly good condition were the 303rd and the 306th, each of which would manage to send no less than thirty planes and crews to Schweinfurt, the best group efforts of the day.

Three groups in the 1st Bombardment Wing can be identified as having difficulties at that time. The basic cause in two of these – the 381st and 384th Bomb Groups – was heavy casualties. Both groups had only been operating since June but had had a bad run of losses. The results were not unexpected – strain among surviving crews being asked to fly too many raids, a big turnover in new crews, poor formation-keeping and bombing results, men refusing to fly or cracking up and being unable to continue flying. Most Eighth Air Force units experienced these difficulties at some time during the war.

The 384th Bomb Group at Grafton Underwood was perhaps the unhappiest group of all. Not one of its members, when asked about the unit's morale, claimed that it was good. An impression was gained that this was a unit run too informally, with a big gulf between the remaining originals and the replacement crews. Men from happier units say that the 'bringing on' of new crews was one of the most important factors in a unit's wellbeing. One original member of the 384th agrees that there was a failure in this respect, claiming that new crews came and went so fast that there was neither time nor inclination to make new friendships with them. It was as though the original crews had come across the Atlantic thinking they were invincible and the replacement crews were the visible evidence that they were not. The same officer, Second Lieutenant Wayne Wentworth, goes on to talk of the fatigue experienced by senior crews in a short-handed group.

> We had known of something big coming up but I had no great desire by this time to be in on it. We were tired; we'd been imposed upon – the whole Air Force was imposed upon. I don't think the powers that be ever considered crew fatigue in their calculations. We were really dragging our ass.

Second Lieutenant Joseph Baggs, another original officer in the 384th, says:

> We were still dedicated to the job we'd come over to do but none of us thought we would complete our tours. If shot down we hoped that at least we would hit the ground alive. The best that any of us hoped for was that we could get down into Switzerland or Sweden or get in with the Resistance.
>
> Our squadron navigator had been a college mathematics teacher in Pennsylvania and he calculated on a slide-rule the odds against completing our tour. The odds were so phenomenal that he threw the ruler away and said there was no chance. A few of us originals did get through, mainly because the replacements took most of the casualties. The older crews took the lead ships; the new ones got the lower and more vulnerable positions.

The hard-pressed 384th was to provide the smallest number of planes – eighteen – for the next day's raid, plus a further crew for which no plane was available and who would fly with the 303rd Bomb Group, which had a plane but no crew – a good example of the maximum effort.

The third group under pressure in the 1st Bombardment Wing was the 92nd at Alconbury, but the cause of the trouble here was not heavy casualties. This was the oldest B-17 group in England but, after flying only four missions in 1942, it had been withdrawn and used as an operational training and replacement unit. It had recently returned to full combat status with one of its squadrons equipped with the YB-40 version of the B-17. This was a plane which carried no bombs but extra machine-gun positions and was designed to reinforce the defensive firepower of standard B-17 formations. The YB-40s had not been successful and were now being phased out; none would fly to Schweinfurt, although one YB-40 had flown with each of the last two days' raids. The various activities of the 92nd had left it with a severe shortage of crews. One crew arrived at Alconbury on 14 August and flew together on a raid on the 15th; the six enlisted men then flew with strange officers on the 16th and would do so again on the 17th and be shot down without having spent one complete day at their base.

None of the groups in the 4th Bombardment Wing had been operating for more than four months. Only the 95th Bomb Group at Horham had suffered serious casualties and the morale of some of its crews was shaky, with a regularly higher-than-average rate of 'early returns'. The rest of the 4th Bombardment Wing groups had been nursed along carefully and most now had that useful combination of lingering freshness and growing experience. The perkiest group in the whole Eighth Air Force was undoubtedly the recently arrived 390th Bomb Group, which had only been in England for one month. It had brought over a pet bear cub, Roscoe Ann, chained to the radio operator's table in one of the unit's B-17s. This fresh, well-trained group had just commenced operations with two easy missions and only one aircraft lost, and its members were now anxious to extend themselves. Staff Sergeant William Adamson, a tail gunner in the group, says, 'We were there to do a job but really we still needed to find out what it was all about. It was like being a small town baseball team and playing in the World League. We were anxious to get started but it was like walking into a dark room – you didn't know what was going to happen.' Another 390th man says, 'We were keen to get going, real gung-ho. We couldn't wait to see what it was like.'

Readers may have been looking for some reference to the 100th Bomb Group at Thorpe Abbots, a unit whose experiences will feature prominently in the story of the Regensburg raid. This was a group which, because of its heavy losses, would soon pick up such unofficial titles as 'The Bloody Hundredth' and 'The Vanishing Americans', a group around which the legend would grow that, because of the behaviour of one of its crews on the Regensburg mission, the Luftwaffe later searched out and concentrated their attacks on its formation. Much of this is in the future, but it is true that the 100th had been a slightly unusual group for most of its career to date. It had been ready to leave the United States for England early in 1943 but had been held back and its crews dispersed to assist in the training of newer crews at training airfields in several locations. This had tended to make the 100th men more individualistic and less unit-minded. Then, after arrival in England in May, the group had been commanded by three different officers in rapid succession. The present commander was in poor health and did not fly often; his influence was weaker than it should have been. By contrast, it is generally agreed that the core of squadron commanders and other senior pilots contained some 'very strong-willed characters'. The group had flown eighteen missions, including some to difficult targets, but its losses had not so far been heavy. Some said the 100th was poor at formation-keeping; members of the group violently deny this, saying it was something that came later after heavy casualties. They do agree, however, that the original crews had an informal, sometimes casual, attitude to flying discipline.

There was certainly nothing wrong with the morale of the 100th Bomb Group on the eve of their flight to Regensburg. One pilot says, 'We were the cockiest bunch of Yankees that ever came down the road. We thought we were hot stuff.' The group had no difficulty in finding the twenty-one aircraft and three spares required for Regensburg. The Group Operations Officer, Major John Kidd, would fly as air commander, but no less than three of those forceful squadron commanders would also fly, although it was not normal procedure for them to do so when another officer was leading the group. But that was how the 100th Bomb Group did things, always in their own way.

CHAPTER 4
Briefings

The big question on the mind of every American bomber-crew member was: 'Will we be out tomorrow?' Most of the men who were to fly on the raid in the morning already knew the answer. There was a variety of signs – the favourable weather conditions, the late activity at 'Ops', the sound of engines being run up at the dispersals, the sight of petrol bowsers and bomb trolleys on the move. In some places the indications were more specific. Many crews were quietly approached with remarks such as, 'Okay fellows, hit the sack early tonight.' The 388th had red lights switched on in the huts of the enlisted men who would be flying and even displayed crew lists the night before their operations. The 390th Bomb Group ran up a red flag. The tension mounted; one man says, 'It was kind of brutal – that long, slow build-up which started the evening before a raid.' Another says, 'You wonder whether this is going to be it. Maybe you'd better write that last letter or pay your buddy that money you owe him.' But Second Lieutenant John Dytman of the 351st Bomb Group, on his last evening in England, says:

> We were on stand-by, that is expected to be sober and flyable next morning at five. We would have a couple of beers, absolutely no more – that warm English beer which we Americans never got used to. Then we would go to bed about ten, not knowing whether we would be on a mission in the morning or not. That uncertainty, whether we would be flying or not, didn't worry us. We had lived with it for a year of training and combat flying. We were carefree, brash youth and we preferred not to give it much sober thought. Those of us who couldn't manage that attitude had been eliminated in training.

The men of some of the groups which were going to North Africa were ordered to pack their toilet articles, a blanket and a change of clothes and told they would be away from their bases for a few days. There was much speculation about their destination – another base in England? North Africa? Russia via Africa? Turkey? The most pessimistic suggestion among the four officers of one crew was 'bombing Berlin and on to Russia; if that was it, what's the use of packing. No one would reach Russia'. The most specific information was given at Bury St Edmunds, home of the 94th Bomb Group, where the radio operators were called together and given details of the radio frequencies they would need the next afternoon when approaching North Africa. 'After the briefing we got on our bikes and rode slowly back to the barracks, everyone keeping pretty silent. The rest of the crews were waiting when I came in and I just said, "Africa". There were a lot of comments but in the end someone said, "Oh well, what the hell! Let's get some sleep; we'll need it".'

All too soon the flying crews were being woken; few men got more than four hours sleep. That 'brutally slow build-up' required the crews to be awake up to five hours before take-off. This was the timetable of the 94th Bomb Group:

Breakfast	1.00 a.m.
Briefing	2.00 a.m.
Stations	5.00 a.m.
Alert	5.25 a.m.
Taxi	5.35 a.m.
Take-off	5.50 a.m.

But the records of other groups show that the 94th was being unduly careful and had provided more time for the earlier parts of the process than most groups, although the men of nearly every unit flying to Schweinfurt and Regensburg that day would be awake by 2 a.m. or very soon afterwards. There was the usual verbal and sometimes physical abuse of the orderlies whose duty it was to wake up the flying crews. Staff Sergeant Raymond Elias, a gunner in a 95th Group crew, was one of many who had recently been listening to Axis Sally, who presented the German radio broadcast aimed directly at the American airmen in England. 'She had said that they knew there was a big one coming up and their fighters would be waiting for us. She was usually pretty accurate so when we were called that morning I said, "Come on you guys, get up; we're going to make history for the Fatherland." When we were prisoners of war the crew teased me about that remark a million times.'

The men were given a good breakfast; it would be many hours before they ate properly again. The provision of fresh eggs instead of the wartime powdered variety was yet another indication that a major raid was in prospect. The enlisted men of the 388th Bomb Group at Knettishall noted the obvious effort made by their cooks to prepare each flying man's eggs according to his individual wish, and that every cook was on duty instead of the normal handful. It was the first time such attention had been provided. Many men remember their meal that morning; there was continuing speculation over their destination, and a mounting tension. There was surprise over the number of crews present, more than for a normal mission. There was 'a quiet undercurrent of concern', 'a definite air of premonition', 'an air of something big about it'. The dread name of Berlin was mentioned again; one officer remembers, 'All summer there had been talk of Berlin; that would have been one of the pinnacles of the war. There was half an air of excitement about it, half a fearful one.'

The men went directly to briefing after breakfast.

> When it was going to be a tough mission, Major Faulkerson always stood at the doorway of the briefing tent handing out cigars. He was a popular officer who didn't hold himself aloof from the enlisted men. The map itself was covered but he tipped you off with that cigar. There you were, sitting, looking at that big sheet, worrying about where you were going, and it was as though he'd given us our piece of candy – a pacifier. (Staff Sergeant Fred P. Weiser, 379th Bomb Group)

> We were seated at the front. The map was covered, as usual, and a red ball of yarn dropped straight down from behind the cover and rested on the floor where Africa would be. Our bombardier, the comedian, remarked, 'Wouldn't it be funny if we went to the end of the ball of string?' This brought a large laugh from the assembled crews. (Lieutenant Paul R. Schulz, 385th Bomb Group)

The briefings opened and the depth of the raids was revealed.

> Everybody had been chatting away and horsing about a little as usual, but when they pulled that curtain back and revealed that route with the line going out so deep into Germany and then not coming back to England, we took one look and said, 'Good God!' There was dead silence for a moment

after that and then we started to ask each other – 'What are we going in there for? What's so important there? How are we going to manage so far without fighter escort?' All the experienced men among us knew it was going to be a tough go. We all knew there were going to be a few of us who were not going to be coming back. (Lieutenant Charles B. Cruikshank, 100th Bomb Group)

When the sheet over the chart was removed, a moan went up. Some men stood up and cursed and expressed their bitter dissatisfaction – too deep, so many miles without fighter protection! It was sheer fear which gripped us – me too. (Staff Sergeant John P. Thompson, 384th Bomb Group)

I thought to myself, 'What idiot at Eighth Air Force Headquarters dreamed this one up!' (Second Lieutenant Darrell D. Gust, 303rd Bomb Group)

They just exploded. It took five minutes to get everyone settled down again. (Major Preston Piper, 385th Bomb Group)

It should be stated that the Schweinfurt-bound groups had been briefed to attack this target a few days earlier and that some of the memories recorded and the details to be given later about the briefing for Schweinfurt were really spread over two separate mornings. On the 17th, the 303rd Bomb Group at Molesworth decided not to give its enlisted men a second briefing and the bewildered members of the only crew which had missed the first briefing asked for some details. Technical Sergeant Dale Rice, the crew's engineer, remembers, 'They gave the six of us our own briefing. It didn't take long. The officer just opened the curtain and said, 'This is it. This is the big one,' and gave a few more details. By the time it was finished and we realized how far we were going, I think we were all in a state of shock.'

A few groups briefed all their flying crews together, but most had separate briefings for officers and enlisted men. The briefing officers settled down to their dual task of informing the crews about what lay ahead and providing them with as much encouragement as possible. One group commander says, 'We were expected to put something special across that day. If we did that the crews would probably do a better job.' There was little difficulty in selling the importance of the factory at Regensburg as a target to men who had seen so many Messerschmitt 109s in the air on previous raids. The Regensburg bombardiers were not warned of the proximity of the civilian hospital on the edge of the factory; it was not the policy to tell them anything which might cause any distraction when bombing. There was obvious interest in the details given about the flight to North Africa and the airfields there. No firm details were given about the return flight to England; the job in hand that day was big enough for everybody's attention for the time being. (By good fortune, the briefing notes for both officers and enlisted men at Great Ashfield, home of the 385th Bomb Group, have survived and are included as an appendix.)

For the Schweinfurt groups, however, there was much mystification over why factories making ball-bearings warranted the risk of flying such a dangerous mission. The comments of Lieutenant Donald Perkins, a bombardier in the 305th Bomb Group, are probably typical.

> At first we thought, 'What's so important about a ball-bearing factory in that little town so deep in Germany?' If they'd told us something like an aircraft factory, or the Ruhr Valley, or an oil refinery like Ploesti, we could have understood it. They had to explain why ball-bearings were so important. Then they stressed that we even had to hit individual buildings in Schweinfurt – right down the pipe. We had to hit that building or nothing. The crews really took a lot of convincing that it was such an important target.

The only thing one gunner recalled about the briefing was that 'it was brought home to me how important a little ball-bearing was in our mechanized world', while a pilot says that Schweinfurt and its ball-bearings were 'the guts of the day; Regensburg was important but Schweinfurt was the crucial target'. Many men also remember that they were told that the R.A.F. would follow up their raid with a general attack on the town area of Schweinfurt that night. This was a good morale-boosting point but one which had probably been left over from the earlier Schweinfurt briefing in the non-moon period of the month. The R.A.F. would not be going to Schweinfurt.

There could be no hiding the fact that both raids were dangerous operations. The bomber crews listened intently to details of the German fighter strength likely to be encountered and of Flak zones, although the planners had been able to pick routes avoiding the worst of the Flak areas and both targets were believed to be only lightly defended. Fighters were obviously going to be the danger of the day. The men of both B-17 forces knew they had to fly right through the most heavily defended part of the Germans' air defences and deep into their homeland. The Schweinfurt force would have to retrace its steps through that hazardous area. The expectation that the Regensburg force would have to bear the brunt of the fight going in, while the Schweinfurt force would expect their big battle on the return flight, was carefully explained and listened to with great attention. The toughest opposition was expected to be encountered between the coast and a point roughly halfway to the targets; after that, the crews were told, they could expect to meet little more than a few twin-engined night fighters pressed into day work. The truth is that no one had any idea what the Luftwaffe had in the centre of Germany; the forecasts of what might be met between Regensburg and North Africa were even more vague.

There was a final exhortation to the crews that they were carrying out an operation which, if successful, could significantly shorten the war. The historical significance of the first American shuttle raid and the anniversary of the first Eighth Air Force raid a year earlier were both mentioned. The briefings ended.

It is probable that the contents of the briefings produced less anxiety among the men going to Regensburg and on to North Africa than to those going to Schweinfurt. The Regensburg men knew that they would only have to challenge the main strength of the Luftwaffe once. After that there was worry about getting over the Alps, possibly with battle-damaged planes, and then the long flight over the Mediterranean and the difficulty of finding airfields on a strange continent while on the limits of fuel. Fuel – that would be the main worry for the Regensburg force, not German fighters. But there was much excitement about that flight to Africa. This is what two of the Regensburg men thought of that prospect.

> The real fear was the Med and the gas. I reckon most of us felt we had only a fifty-fifty chance. But it was a strange thing that, once we had got over the original shock of seeing that map, everyone wanted to go. We saw it as a great challenge. I know that none of the pilots in our group were going to turn back for anything if we could help it. (Lieutenant Robert R. Morrill, 94th Bomb Group)

> Earlier, at breakfast, I'd seen Father Shearer sitting on his chair in the kitchen corner as usual and I had asked for his

blessing. As soon as we were dismissed from briefing, I turned and caught sight of him again and headed for him. 'Father, would you hear my confession and give me communion?' I asked. 'I thought you'd be back,' he replied. (Lieutenant Leo LaCasse, 385th Bomb Group)

The men of the new 390th Bomb Group, flying only their third raid, were dumbfounded when told they would be going so far, flying over seven countries – England, a little bit of Holland, Belgium, Germany, Austria, Italy and Algeria. Staff Sergeant Adamson says, 'We just didn't know enough about things to know how special it was. They simply woke us up in the middle of the night and told us to bring our mess kits and a blanket; then they told us we were going to Regensburg, over the Alps and on to North Africa. We were so green, we just looked at each other.'

There were several reasons why the men of the Schweinfurt groups should suffer greater anxiety. They knew that their operation had been under discussion for several weeks and had even been briefed once to crews who had since been shot down and become prisoners of war. The German intelligence services and their interrogation techniques were credited with much skill. In addition there was all the strain of the maximum effort, with tired planes and crews being pressed into service and squadrons sent to fly with strangers in composite groups. Then there was that long route, right through the German fighter belt and back again.

Our crew had been lucky so far – nine missions without any trouble, no one injured, no serious damage – but I had a distinct premonition that we were going to get it that day. I was particularly depressed because we didn't have our regular bombardier with us. He was my closest friend on the group; I'd never flown missions without him. We'd got through two raids to Hamburg and I had the definite feeling that Schweinfurt was going to be a bad one. How could it be anything but? How could you penetrate that deep and get in and out safely? (Second Lieutenant Robert E. Hyatt, 381st Bomb Group)

But there were always the optimists.

We'd had our leave cancelled to go on that Schweinfurt mission. There was a certain amount of bitching and groaning but I was pretty optimistic. Other fellows were saying we would finish up in prison camp but I was counting the missions off

– we'd done seventeen and I thought we had it made. I told them we would be home by Christmas. I felt that the might of the American Air Force was hitting Hitler's stomping ground – the so-called impregnable roof of Germany.

I felt that was the only time in my life I was doing something important – like the fellows who went ashore on D-Day or even the men who went to the moon. I felt very proud flying in that outfit – me, a peasant from the Bronx! Maybe its my youth talking a lot but we were having a good time. By day we were fighting over Germany; by night we were chasing the English girls round Bedford. We were scared sometimes but it was something you were scared not to do – it was like a dare. (Technical Sergeant Johannes H. Johnson, 379th Bomb Group)

One wonders whether many men realized how historically important the coming operation was going to be, that books would be written and films made about that day's events. It is probable that few of the ordinary B-17 men gave this a thought, but one particularly perceptive comment comes from an officer who was junior enough to fly missions regularly but was also in contact with the views of senior officers. Major Lewis P. Lyle of the 303rd Bomb Group had already finished a tour of twenty-five raids but was selected to lead one of the composite groups in the Schweinfurt force. As lead pilot many times before, Lyle had attended post-raid critiques at the headquarters of the 1st Bombardment Wing.

Although I was a mere G.I. pilot sitting at the back of these critiques and attending the preparatory discussions about that operation to Schweinfurt, it was obvious that we had problems, that we might have to give up daylight bombing. We just had to pull off a big one. It was going to be a put-up or shut-up job. We'd got to show that we were capable of doing this big mission and the enemy was not to be allowed to stop us. We just could not fail – that was the whole tenor of what was happening. The ultimate pressure was coming from Washington but the regular Air Corps officers present were also desperate to prove the daylight theory. The real struggle was over losses versus accomplishments. If we got the ratio wrong, the support from Washington would be withdrawn – probably to the Pacific where losses were a lot less.

Looking back at it now, I can see that they were dedicated to making that daylight bomber concept work and Germany was

> the place it had to be done because that was where the industrial complex was situated. Although I was not regular Air Corps – only a reserve man – I was just as fired up about it as they were to see that it was achieved. I know I was with some great people and I liked it. Nothing was going to stop me.

Major Lyle returned safely from Schweinfurt, went on to fly a total of sixty-nine missions with the Eighth Air Force and was later a major-general in Strategic Air Command, but he added this comment: 'That period was the pinnacle of my career. It was all downhill after that.'

CHAPTER 5

Revised Plans

After their briefing the crews bustled off to make their final preparations. Everyone drew flight clothing, parachutes and oxygen masks. The gunners went to the armament shops and were issued with their heavy machine-guns. All the men were then taken out by various means of transport to their aircraft. Guns were fitted and all other equipment in the planes was checked. Engines were warmed up. On this day there were more than the usual anxieties and disputes over machine-gun ammunition. One man says, 'There were almost riots over ammunition. Gunners were always trying to sneak extra ammunition aboard and, given the chance, would even steal some from the next aircraft if they could get at it before its crew came out.' On this morning some units sent extra supplies round to each aircraft by lorry and aircraft captains were asked to decide how much more their gunners could take. The problem was weight; for the groups allocated to fly in a high position, weight and fuel were already critical. Individual aircraft loadings for ammunition finished up between the standard 8,000 rounds and the 10,000 or more rounds which some crews managed to stack away in those big wooden boxes all over their planes. The combined Regensburg–Schweinfurt force would carry approximately 4,700 machine-guns into battle, and well over 3 million rounds of ·5-inch ammunition for these guns.

When all their various tasks were completed, the air crews descended from their planes to have a final few minutes of relaxation in the open. It was about 5.15 a.m. The first aircraft was due to start taxiing out onto the perimeter track at 5.35 a.m. for a take-off ten minutes later. It is not possible to say which B-17 should have moved first. Although the head of the Regensburg force was due to cross the coast fifteen minutes before that of the Schweinfurt force, the Schweinfurt groups had a more complicated forming-up process to perform and their units were also situated further inland. It does not matter. No aircraft took off at the appointed time. The English weather had intervened.

The exact nature of the weather experienced that early morning at the B-17 bases and the action subsequently taken were crucial to the outcome of the day's operations and should be described in some detail. Every single B-17 airfield was covered by cloud, the base of which was rarely above 1,000 feet as the planned commencement of the operation approached. The cloud at many airfields was so low that the conditions were the same as those produced by a dense fog. The cloud was strato-cumulus, rising only to 3,000 feet but thick and unbroken.

The Americans had been very unlucky because these conditions were present over only a small part of England. The clear, high-pressure weather, which extended over most of Europe and had caused this operation to be set in motion, was still present but the flow of moist, lower-pressure weather from the south-west, which was the normal basic feature of the English climate, still persisted. The current trough was centred some 800 miles out in the Atlantic and most of its fronts were making little impact on the European high pressure. But one warm-weather front had managed to reach the British Isles intact and charts from the British Meteorological Office show that it was now lined up over England in a familiar north-west to south-east configuration exactly covering the area in which the American bomber airfields were located. This front was moving only very slowly. A single aircraft could take off in safety in these conditions – there would be no icing or turbulence in the layered strato-cumulus which was present – but there was a serious risk of collision in the cloud when more than twenty aircraft took off from each airfield and with airfields so often situated close together. Assembly of formations above the clouds would pose no problems. Landings on return from the operation would not be in any danger; in the unlikely event of the cloud still being present in this area, there were plenty of diversion airfields available in England. There were no other weather complications. Visibility was still forecast as clear over the targets; an R.A.F. weather reconnaissance Mosquito had inspected the route in the early hours of the morning. The weather was still clear in North Africa. The only problem was the danger of collision in that local cloud in the first few minutes of the bombers' climb away from their airfields.

*

At the Headquarters of VIII Bomber Command, young Brigadier-General Fred Anderson bore his lonely burden of responsibility. He was fifty miles away from the nearest of his bomber bases and, ironically, under much clearer skies. Anderson had all the latest weather information and the commanders of the two bombardment wings were waiting for him to make his decision. Initially there was little difficulty; a short delay for every element of the operation would create no serious problem. So at approximately 5.15 a.m., twenty minutes before the first B-17s were due to start taxiing to the ends of their runways, every unit was advised that there would be a delay of one hour.

In the discussions which were taking place by telephone between Anderson and his two subordinates, it is probable that Brigadier-General Williams of the 1st Bombardment Wing played a comparatively passive role. His units could accommodate delays of many more hours before they would run out of daylight for landing. But Colonel LeMay had no such freedom. The planes of the Regensburg force had to land in Africa, further east and much further south, where the length of daylight would be shorter. The weather over the English bases was little better when the time came for the next round of discussions and Anderson asked LeMay if he could wait a further hour. LeMay was forced to reply that he could not – another half-hour, yes, but a full hour, no. So Anderson moved all the times forward again but only for that further thirty minutes. First take-offs were now to be at 7.15 a.m.; Zero Hour for the first aircraft over the Dutch coast would be 10.00 a.m. (The time being used by the Americans was British Summer Time, one hour behind that being used in Germany and by the Luftwaffe units in France, Belgium and Holland. British Summer Time will be the basis of all times quoted in this book unless otherwise stated.)

At 6.40 a.m. the three officers spoke again. There had been some improvement in the cloud conditions but not much. It was a fateful moment. The next decision was going to be critical to the outcome of the whole day's operations. The choices before Brigadier-General Anderson were threefold. These choices and the effects which would flow from them were as follows:

1. Both forces could be ordered to proceed with the operation at the end of the present holding period. Planes would commence taking off in thirty-five minutes time and all concerned would have to accept the risk of collision.

2. The whole operation could be cancelled for this day and a new attempt made on a later day. But this would risk losing the ideal weather conditions which were believed to exist all the way through Europe and on to North Africa. It was unlikely that such favourable conditions would hold for long.

3. The Regensburg force could be sent off but the Schweinfurt force held back until the weather over their bases cleared. This would more than halve the risk of collisions; only 146 planes were due to go to Regensburg compared with 231 to Schweinfurt. The obvious disadvantage of this third course was that the carefully prepared plans for the two B-17 forces to enter Germany together and for the escort and diversion operations, which had been timed to support that single entry into German-defended air space, would be completely dislocated. To split the two main forces in this way would be an extreme measure.

Everyone concerned has sympathized with the agonizing decision which Fred Anderson now had to take. There was no time for hesitation. One of those nettles had to be grasped. It is probable that Anderson now asked his two commanders whether they could take off in the present cloud conditions. Colonel LeMay replied that he believed his units could do so; conditions were not quite so severe in his area and his units had practised bad weather take-offs and assembly. Brigadier-General Williams must have informed Anderson that he was not so confident. The three factors behind Williams's judgement have all been mentioned before: his units had not practised instrument flying so intensively; he had a much more complicated assembly to achieve with his additional three composite groups made up of nine squadrons from different units; he still had plenty of daylight to spare.

Anderson made his decision. He announced that the Regensburg force was to take off at the end of the present holding period – almost immediately. The Schweinfurt force was to be held back until a new timetable could be worked out for its raid later in the day. Colonel LeMay put down his telephone and ran to the car standing outside his headquarters. We will catch up with him later.

Many important consequences flowed from that basic decision to split the two heavy bomber forces, and further subsidiary decisions needed taking. It was for this reason that the 1st Bombardment Wing was not immediately given a new Zero Hour.

The most urgent of the next round of decisions was what to do about the considerable escort and diversionary effort which had been arranged for the original joint operation. The dominating factor now was that the Schweinfurt force was likely to have to face two major air battles – going in and coming out. The two P-47 groups – six squadrons – originally allocated to escort the Regensburg force were to carry on with that force but the remainder of the direct escort force, two more P-47 groups and eight R.A.F. Spitfire squadrons, together with the whole of the main diversionary effort, were held back to support the Schweinfurt force. This delay helped those fighter and medium bomber units whose bases in East Anglia were also cloud-covered. A new timetable was soon worked out for the 1st Bombardment Wing. There was to be *a further delay of more than three and a half hours*. The first take-offs would be at approximately 11.20 a.m.; the Dutch coast would not be reached and Belgium and Germany crossed until nearly four hours after the Regensburg force had passed through. The necessary changes in orders were transmitted to the headquarters of the 1st Bombardment Wing at about 8.30 a.m.; the dispatch time for the new orders from there to the bomb groups is recorded as being 9.15 a.m.

The decision to delay the second part of the operation for such a long period was to prove the key to the high American casualties on this day. In the post-raid report which VIII Bomber Command submitted to Eighth Air Force, Brigadier-General Anderson placed his signature under the following statements:

> Due to extremely adverse weather over the bomber bases in England, it became necessary to advance the Zero Hour one hour. Since a further delay would cause the 4th Bombardment Wing forces to arrive at bases in North Africa at dusk or later, the decision was made to dispatch the 4th Bombardment Wing and to make available all the fighter escort originally assigned to both bombardment wings.
>
> A new time schedule was set up for the forces of the 1st Bombardment Wing which gave them a take-off time approximately 3½ hours after the 4th Bombardment Wing had crossed the enemy coast in order that the fighter escort would have been able to land, refuel, rearm and be available to escort the 1st Bombardment Wing forces on their penetration.

These are extraordinary statements to be contained in a report prepared at leisure after the operation. They are riddled with error. The delay in the Regensburg take-off was not an hour but one and a half hours. But this was only a small matter compared with the statements about the fighter escort. 'All the fighter escort originally assigned to both bombardment wings' was not made available to the Regensburg force; no part of the Regensburg fighter escort was ever asked to 'land, refuel and rearm' to help the outward flight of the Schweinfurt force. The interval between the flights of the two forces was too narrow to allow such a fighter turn-round. The R.A.F. Spitfires could have managed it but the longer-range P-47s would have needed at least another hour. An interval of four and a half hours instead of the three and a half ordered would have enabled the entire fighter escort force of four P-47 groups and eight Spitfire squadrons to have escorted both forces in their penetration flights, but the amendments to the field order issued by the 1st Bombardment Wing at 9.15 show that this was never intended, despite what was later written in Anderson's report.

The interval chosen was to prove the worst possible solution. Both bomber forces were denied the opportunity to have the fullest available fighter support, while the German fighter units would easily be able to fly sorties against both penetrations. The VIII Bomber Command report continues with this faulty estimate of what the Germans would do.

> It was expected that some, or all, of the enemy fighters which had been called into the area through which the 4th Bombardment Wing force passed, would have been ordered to return to their normal defensive bases by the time at which the 1st Bombardment Wing would be departing the English coast. Had this expected procedure been followed by the German fighter controllers, it is felt that the 1st Bombardment Wing units would have received very little fighter opposition en route to the target.

This expectation of the German movements could not have been more ill-founded.

It can be seen, in retrospect, that the best solution Anderson could have chosen would have been to send both forces up at the same time. At best, it might have turned out that the 1st Bombardment Wing units could have taken off through the cloud without losing planes by collision; at worst, the losses from collision would almost certainly have been far less than those subsequently suffered at the hands of the Luftwaffe. One must have much sympathy for the pressure on Fred Anderson and these comments are academic ones made with all the benefit of hindsight, but it is sad that the VIII Bomber Command report should have contained so many false statements and lame excuses. They were later accepted and repeated by the American official history* and, in turn, have appeared in other published works. It is surprising that Anderson should have passed the document and signed it; everything heard about that officer (now deceased) suggests that it was quite out of character for him to do so.

Colonel LeMay's car rushed him the fourteen miles from his headquarters to the airfield at Snetterton Heath which was the base of the 96th Bomb Group. Colonel Archie Old, the group commander, should have been aware that LeMay intended to fly with the lead plane of his group but, with LeMay's non-appearance, Old was standing at the plane ready and very anxious to take his place. The gunners had already boarded the B-17 and the officers were about to do so. Lieutenant Dunstan Abel, the navigator, describes what happened when LeMay did arrive.

> The staff car pulled up. Out got LeMay in his flying clothes and the driver carried his parachute and kit to the plane. I think that was the biggest surprise Archie Old had in his Air Force career. Archie asked LeMay what the hell he was doing there – that was his way, he cussed like a trooper – and, after a very heated discussion, LeMay made it quite clear that he intended to lead the mission himself and Archie was to stay behind.
>
> Archie threw his stuff in his car and left in a complete huff – with some indiscernible, under-the-breath comments. I have never seen Archie so mad. I heard later that he flew with the lead pilot in our high squadron.

On seven airfields – Bury St Edmunds, Horham, Snetterton Heath, Thorpe Abbots, Great Ashfield, Knettishall and Framlingham – the B-17s of the 4th Bombardment Wing started to taxi around the perimeter tracks. It was so gloomy at Snetterton Heath that the planes had to be led out from their hardstands by torchlight. At some airfields the wing-tip fuel tanks received a final topping-up with cans of gasoline before the planes turned onto the runway. The first plane to take off was piloted by Captain George Von Arb, co-pilot of the lead plane of the 390th Bomb Group, which would be flying in the high position of the lead

* W. F. Craven and J. L. Cate, *The Army Air Forces in World War II*, University of Chicago Press, 1948–58, Vol. II, p. 685.

combat wing. He took off safely from Framlingham at exactly 6.21 a.m. The early take-off of this unit will be referred to later.

The B-17s took off at forty-five second intervals and immediately disappeared into the cloud. Each group's aircraft climbed away on instruments, on a fixed heading and rate of climb. Nothing should have gone wrong in theory, but each of the heavily laden planes had slightly different flying characteristics and that climb-out was a good test of airmanship. Only one near-miss seems to have occurred, when Lieutenant Glen Van Noy's crew, 100th Bomb Group, saw another B-17 flash across their front in the murk. The other plane is believed to have been from the 95th Bomb Group. But there were no collisions and B-17s were soon 'popping out of the clouds everywhere', breaking out at about 3,000 feet into the brilliant morning sun. This safe take-off was a complete vindication of the extra instrument-flying practice ordered by Colonel LeMay, and a promising start for the Regensburg mission.

The B-17s began to form up, first into squadrons and then into group formation. A good unit could achieve this in about ten minutes and then commence the combat wing assembly. But when the first group to take off, the 390th, had formed up, it found itself completely alone in the sky, although it was supposed to join the 96th and 388th Groups to form the leading wing of the Regensburg force. The lead navigator was certain that he was in the correct place. The 390th pilots could only circle and wait for the other two groups. Two things had gone wrong. The original orders to the 390th had contained an error; the take-off time given to the group had been at least fifteen minutes too early. Then, when the take-off times for all the Regensburg units had been advanced, first by an hour and then by a further thirty minutes, the operations staff of the 390th had misinterpreted the final order and missed that last thirty-minute extension. The net result was that this group took off forty-five minutes too early and was now using up precious fuel. The waiting seemed endless and Captain Von Arb describes the anxiety of Colonel Edgar Wittan, the group commander, who was flying in his plane.

> It soon became apparent that there was something wrong. I have a clear memory of Colonel Wittan taking out his mission data folder and studying the relevant teletypes. We throttled back to the leanest mixture possible and loosened up the for-

mation so that the other planes could also conserve their fuel. Eventually, two other groups appeared and we formed the combat wing normally.

We then had a tense discussion – the two pilots, the two navigators and Colonel Wittan – about our fuel, whether we had a chance to make it all the way to Africa. It was a difficult decision. If we went back, we would reduce the defensive strength and bomb tonnage of the whole force and also have to face the anger of LeMay. If we went on, we might all finish up in the Mediterranean; we were already flying the high group position which consumed the most fuel. In the end, it was decided that we had just enough, but with no margin to spare, and we carried on.

The depletion of the 390th Bomb Group's fuel tanks was the only setback experienced in the take-off and assembly of the Regensburg task force. The other combat wings had formed up, though sometimes with difficulty because groups found themselves between two cloud layers. In addition to the normal devices employed to help assembly – the radio 'splasher beacons' located all across East Anglia, the recently introduced 'Gee' navigational aid, and flare pistols – the lead aircraft of each combat wing was displaying smoke signals. These were used for the first time on that day and were one of Colonel LeMay's inventions. A metal basket had been fastened to the fuselage of each wing leader and in these the waist gunners placed smoke grenades. One grenade at a time was not sufficient; large numbers needed to be put in at once to create the required effect. It is unlikely that this device was of much use and it was probably not employed again.

The complicated assembly procedure had taken nearly three hours from the time that the first plane had left the ground. Much of this time had been taken up in climbing. LeMay had insisted that every group should reach its bombing height – between 17,000 and 20,000 feet – before the departure from the English coast. This was so that groups could settle down to flying in really tight combat formations well before the first German fighters might appear. The three combat wings, with three minutes' flying time between each, flew over the fishing port and holiday resort town of Lowestoft, which was their departure point on the English coast. The force was five minutes late at this point but that was not a serious matter.

That stage was a tremendous relief, particularly for the pilots who had been working so hard until then, constantly changing power settings, handling controls, eyes glued to the lead ship in the element, the squadron or the group. We were all trying to fly as smoothly as possible to help others back in the formations. One sloppy pilot made an awful mess. Of the others, the gunners had the best time. They had been able to admire the whole thing; you could call them interested spectators, watching the groups form up. Everyone was amazingly surprised that, after all the difficulties, everybody got where they were supposed to be eventually. (Lieutenant Robert R. Morrill, 94th Bomb Group)

We watched that beautiful English coast pass beneath us. We hated to leave it and probably said a little prayer, hoping to see you again on the way back – although, on that mission, it would be several days before we were back. (Lieutenant Dunstan T. Abel, 96th Bomb Group)

The long, grinding climb had produced its usual crop of mechanical casualties and several planes had left to make their way back to base. These 'aborts' were a constant source of anxiety to unit commanders, weakening as they did the carefully planned structure of defensive formations. Further depletion would occur all the way across the North Sea, but after crossing the enemy coast it would usually be wiser for a plane in mechanical difficulty to fly on if possible; few aircraft survived a lone flight back across enemy territory.

In the 390th Bomb Group the loss of aircraft had actually begun before take-off. One B-17 broke through its recently constructed dispersal stand and another was found to have a last-minute fault in the ball turret. Both planes were replaced by spares. Staff Sergeant Albert Van Pelt was a gunner in one of the replacements.

We had an older model aircraft than the rest of the group and it had given us trouble back in the States. We had aborted our first mission with engine trouble and missed the second because the plane still wasn't fit. They said they would get us a new aircraft.

They dragged us out of bed that morning and told us we were needed as a spare. We were annoyed to have to get up and fly an unreliable plane but we felt that it would be just a trip around England and then we would be released. But we

> had to fill a place in the high squadron and thus found ourselves in the worst possible place – high squadron in the high group and with this unreliable plane. We were sure we would never make it to North Africa but we didn't say much. We were young and optimistic and felt it would all happen to the other guy. It would work out somehow. It was our first taste of combat.

Neither of the 390th replacement planes would complete the mission.

Eleven more B-17s dropped out either over England or the North Sea. Some would be replaced by spares and the Regensburg force would be only seven planes short when it crossed the Dutch coast. The only group to suffer severely was the 95th. The group's two airborne spares both returned to base with trouble. Two more aircraft were late taking off and one of them never caught up the formation. Four more turned back for various reasons over the North Sea. This group had a reputation for shaky morale and for unjustified aborts by some crews. One of the men who pressed on makes this comment.

> Aborting hurt a whole group; if you fly for protection and if one crew leaves a hole, the others were in more danger. To lose three or four was very disappointing. Some of them were regular aborters. There was talk of them being yellow. The faults were always followed up but they always had an excuse. They would be given a bad time later by the other crews though.

One of the last planes to turn back, just before the Dutch coast was reached, was from the leading bomb group. The plane concerned was the one in which Colonel Archie Old had taken a place when turned out of the lead plane by Colonel LeMay. An engine's propeller governor ran away. The pilot feathered the engine and decided that he was unlikely to reach North Africa with the higher fuel consumption which would result from a long flight on three engines. It is said that Colonel Old was furious but the regular pilot exercised his proper right as aircraft captain and returned to England. Lieutenant Abel, the navigator in LeMay's plane, heard about this later. 'I think that pilot was one of our more dependable ones. I'm afraid we'd have lost Archie and the aircraft had he shown less intestinal fortitude. I'm not inferring that Archie didn't realize the position and I suppose he cooled down after a bit and realized the pilot was right but I heard later that those people who stayed behind in England had one of the toughest weeks of the war with Archie until the rest of the group returned from North Africa.' Another member of this group says that the returning pilot's crew were 'from that day on always placed at or near the tail-end Charlie position on all combat missions. The entire crew became avid chapel-goers. This lasted until Old left and we got a new C.O. early in September'.

The number of crews turning back that morning was certainly less than normal. This was partly a result of the recent conserving of the B-17 force by using it for limited operations, but it is also likely that there were many men like Colonel Archie Old who wanted to press on if at all possible. Second Lieutenant Owen Roane, 'Cowboy' Roane from Texas, was the pilot of a crew in the 100th Bomb Group.

> There was much excitement and we looked forward to the flight with some anticipation. This was true for all of my crew except for two men who generally did sweat their missions out. This day they kept finding some reason for turning back. One of them was a gunner who said that his gun wasn't working properly. I wasn't particularly sympathetic to him so I told him he probably wasn't going to hit anything with it anyway. The other said that his oxygen wasn't working properly. I just told him to breathe deeply. I know they were just excuses. Actually, once we entered enemy territory, it appeared the oxygen was holding better and the guns were working and the crew behaved very well for the rest of the mission. That isn't to say that we didn't have our moments of fright during the trip.

The flight across the sea from Lowestoft to the first landfall in Holland was exactly 100 miles and took twenty-five minutes. This was the North Sea but the Americans always insisted upon calling it the English Channel, which was actually the name of a stretch of water situated further south. The weather was beautiful; the clouds beneath soon disappeared completely and the bombers made a fine sight in their tidy formations. The route led straight towards Europe without any of the zig-zags over the sea sometimes employed to deceive the Germans. There was not fuel enough to spare for this. One man says, somewhat dramatically, 'We came screaming straight in.' Everything was ready for action. All positions were manned and the guns had been test-fired. The crews were already on oxygen. The groups tightened up their formations still further. German fighter bases were well within range but no German fighters appeared before the Dutch coast was reached.

That coast was soon visible – four large islands prominently situated in the complex of wide river estuaries in this part of Holland. Each island had its own distinctive shape and the designated landfall, Schouwen Island, was easily identified. The leading aircraft of the force flew directly over it, but still five minutes behind the planned time for Zero Hour. One bombardier in the leading group knew that a German Flak battery was located here and he had to resist 'a mad impulse to drop our bomb load on it'. There was a little Flak but it was not accurate.

After making their landfall, the bomber force flew on over the wide East Scheldt River. Mainland Holland was nine minutes' flying time further on and it was at the mainland that the P-47 fighter escort was to make its rendezvous with the bombers, right over the big Luftwaffe airfield at Woensdrecht. In the bombers, it was the gunners' task to search for the friendly fighters and many eyes were peering back to England for the first sight of them. But the P-47s were not to be seen. Look-outs in the leading bombers did, however, pick up a flight of four fighters coming in from ahead. Tension turned to relief when these were identified as the big, fat, friendly P-47s. The fighter escort had reached the rendezvous a little early and was now sweeping back to meet the bombers, who were a few minutes late. The American fighter unit which had made this happy meeting was the 353rd Fighter Group, the newest of the P-47 groups in England. It had only been flying operationally for one week but had already lost its commanding officer while escorting B-17s on the Le Bourget mission the previous day. The group was now being led by Major Loren G. McCollom, on loan from the more experienced 56th Fighter Group which had been tutoring the 353rd in combat tactics. McCollom would be confirmed in command the following day.

The group was not at full strength. Thirty-seven fighters had taken off from Metfield, through the same cloudy weather that the bombers had experienced. Because of this, McCollom had ordered his three squadrons to make their way individually to the rendezvous rather than use up their slender flying time in making a group assembly. Three planes had been forced to turn back because of the unsatisfactory belly tanks which were causing so much trouble at this time. Two of the P-47s turned back while over the North Sea and their squadron commanders sent escorts back with them. It was considered bad for morale to send single-engined planes back over the sea alone. One squadron never made the bomber rendezvous at all, so that it was a weak escort of no more than twenty-four Thunderbolts which now settled down to protect 139 Fortresses spread out in a bomber column approximately twenty miles long.

The two squadrons of P-47s jettisoned their belly tanks, climbed, and took up positions 3,000 feet above either flank, weaving steadily to keep in contact with the slower bombers. If the third squadron had been present, it would have taken station above the head of the bomber force, ready to ward off frontal attacks or act as a general reserve. American bomber commanders insisted that this close type of escort was needed, with the P-47s ready to support the bombers when German fighters attacked. The fighter commanders would much rather have roamed more loosely and attempted to break up the German fighter formations before they could attack. It was the age-old conflict between bomber and fighter man. Later in the war there would be enough fighters for both roles but, with such a pathetically weak escort at this time, the fighters were probably in the best place. The Luftwaffe might decide to keep out of the way if the American fighters were visible with the bomber formation. Many of the B-17 crewmen saw little or nothing of the fighter escort, especially the men in the lower groups. If things remained quiet, they never would see the higher-flying P-47s. Colonel LeMay later grumbled that the four American fighters seen when the rendezvous was made were the only friendly fighters he saw all day; the rest of his fighter escort, he said, would have black crosses on it.

The 353rd Fighter Group was due to stay in contact for twenty minutes and would then hand over to the 56th Fighter Group. The bomber force flew on past the town of Bergen-op-Zoom, over Woensdrecht airfield and then immediately over the frontier with Belgium. The city port of Antwerp was clearly visible less than ten miles to the south. It was 390 miles to Regensburg, just ninety-three minutes' flying time. Black puffs of Flak from Woensdrecht and from Antwerp's ring of batteries were bursting around the bombers. There was no sign yet of the Luftwaffe. The Regensburg force had made a good start. The direct approach had not allowed the Luftwaffe to make an early interception over the sea or even at the coast. The German fighter-defended belt was estimated to extend 150 miles in from the Belgian border and it was hoped that the P-47s would be able to stay in contact for two thirds of that distance. There would probably be further opposition inland but it was hoped that any second-phase opposition would not be too strong.

CHAPTER 6

The Luftwaffe

The Americans were mainly correct in their assumption that the main German opposition would be met in a coastal fighter belt. It is interesting that, just as the Americans usually called the southern part of the North Sea 'the Channel', the German pilots who fought here also said they were '*am Kanal*'. Their name for the Battle of Britain which had been fought in 1940 was *der Kanalkampf*. It was exactly one year since the B-17s had started raiding Europe and challenging German-defended air-space. But units of the Luftwaffe fighter arm had been standing guard over Holland and Belgium for more than three years.

(It may be helpful here to break off the narrative of events and describe briefly the composition and naming of the German fighter units. These were split into the *Geschwader*, the *Gruppe* (plural, *Gruppen*) and the *Staffel* (plural, *Staffeln*). I prefer not to attempt translations. A *Geschwader* was usually made up of three *Gruppen* and a *Gruppe* of three *Staffeln*. The *Geschwader* can be largely ignored; it rarely went into action as a complete unit and its sub-units were usually split up among several airfields. The *Gruppe* was the all-important tactical unit. It was composed of approximately thirty fighters, all of the same type, usually based at the same airfield. It normally went into action as a complete unit under the tactical leadership of the *Gruppe* commander. In referring to these units, this book will use the standard abbreviations normally employed. The day fighter *Jagdgeschwader* is thus shortened to 'JG'. Roman numerals before the JG and ordinary numerals after it signify the *Gruppe* and *Geschwader* number respectively. So II/JG 3 was the Second *Gruppe* of *Jagdgeschwader* 3. The prefix 'N' – for *Nacht* – signifies a night-fighter unit; so II/NJG 3 was the Second *Gruppe* of *Nachtjagdgeschwader* 3. All the reader needs to remember is that any unit prefixed by a Roman numeral was a *Gruppe*, the Luftwaffe's standard tactical unit which normally went into action with a strength of between twenty and thirty fighters.)

The number of fighters which could be brought into contact with an attacking American force depended upon the number of units available locally for immediate attack, and the ability of the German control organization to forecast the future course of the American raid so that more distant units could be directed into the combat area in time to attack the bombers in the later stages of a raid, especially on the return flight. In this operation, the American bombers flying to Regensburg – and later to Schweinfurt – were routed straight through that part of the German fighter belt with the greatest density of units capable of immediate, or almost immediate, local action. The American planners had not been able to avoid this; there had been no opportunity for an indirect approach because of the great range at which the two targets lay. Six full fighter *Gruppen*, capable of putting approximately 150 fighters into the air on a first sortie, were immediately available and, if properly directed, could reach the Regensburg-bound B-17s and remain in contact for twenty to thirty minutes of combat flying time. A further five *Gruppen* were capable of reaching the American bombers but would only be able to have a few minutes combat time and would be more effective if they could transfer to a nearer airfield and refuel for later action. Finally, four more *Gruppen* could be brought in from the extreme north and south of the coastal fighter belt but could only come into action much later and after refuelling. These figures were all dependent upon the German control organization making a rapid and accurate assessment of the situation. The figures do not cover any fighter units which the Germans might have in the interior, behind the fighter belt.

The German units likely to come into action first were the *Gruppen* of JG 1 and JG 26 stationed in Holland and Northern France. No Luftwaffe day-fighter units were stationed in Belgium, but this small country was easily covered by the units on either side. There is evidence that there had been some recent movement of German units into this area from further north. III/JG 26 had been at Nordholz refitting after an exchange with a unit in Russia and fighting in the Heligoland Bight area, but only a week earlier the main part of the group had been transferred to Schiphol, the pre-war Amsterdam International Airport, only fifty-five miles north of the Regensburg route. One of the German pilots of this unit says that he believes this move was the result of the recent destruction of Hamburg and the subsequent belief by the Germans that American operations would now concentrate more on Central Germany. If this was the reason for the move, it was an astute piece of German anticipation. J G 2, further south in France, and J G 11, to the north on the coast of Germany, were the units available for later reinforcement. Of all these units, J G 1, J G 2 and J G 11 were virtually permanent units in their own sectors, but the *Gruppen* of J G 26 tended to change locations more often. Behind these units, about 120 miles inland, the Germans were reacting to deeper American raids and were thickening up their defences with parts of J G 3 brought back from other fronts. I/J G 3 had been in the West since the end of 1942 but III/J G 3 had only just arrived after serving for two years in Russia. All the German units mentioned here were equipped either with the Messerschmitt 109 or with the more modern and effective Focke-Wulf 190. Many of the Messerschmitt 109s which the Americans were soon to meet had, of course, been made at Regensburg. (The full order of battle of the German fighter units and their airfields is shown in Appendix 2.)

This is a suitable place to dispose of an old legend. The Americans had often met German fighters, Messerschmitt 109s, with yellow-painted nose sections and believed – as they still do – that these planes were from a select unit made up only of top German pilots. They were called the 'yellow-nosed Abbeville Boys' or the 'Abbeville Kids'. The legend was not a new one; the R.A.F. had been meeting these German fighters long before the Americans started flying in Europe and the R.A.F. pilots had handed the legend on to the Americans. It is now generally accepted that there was no such special unit. Several German units painted part or all of their nose sections for no other purpose than quick identification in combat. Yellow was just the most useful colour for this purpose. There was no such thing as the 'Abbeville Boys'.

On no other front was the fighting so hard and intense for a German day-fighter pilot as on the Channel and North Sea coasts. No other posting was so prestigious for an ambitious commander, so sought after by glory-hunting pilots, so feared by the timid. There were no tours of operations in the Luftwaffe, only continuous duty until removal by death or wounds. This had several results. When a pilot was shot down and survived by parachute, he was simply given another fighter and sent up again. For example, Georg-Peter Eder, a pilot who would fly later in the day against the Schweinfurt raid, was shot down seventeen times during the war and wounded twelve times. Up to three quarters of the pilots in the average *Gruppe* were experienced men and some of the pilots about to attack the American force bound for Regensburg had been in action here for years. Major Karl Borris, the commander of I/JG 26, was typical of these long-serving pilots.

> Our *Geschwader* was never out of action in the front line in the West from beginning to end. We were very proud that our efficiency did not decline with time as much as other units because we all felt responsibility for each other. We didn't have individuals who sought a lot of success without taking care of their wingmen. We always had a positive record; that is we always shot down more than we lost. I flew with the group the whole time from November 1939 to the end of the war when we finished up at Flensburg – 400 to 500 operations in all. The strength of the whole *Geschwader* at any one time was 100 pilots and we used up 1,000 during the war. At the end I felt like the last of the Mohicans.

But there was a big gap between the ability of these 'old hands' and that of the replacement pilots who made up these units. The absence of a tour system and the keeping of the experienced men in the front line meant that the Luftwaffe had no proper operational training units, and replacement pilots needed a long period to reach a reasonable combat ability, that is if they survived long enough. Feldwebel Werner Mössner, of III/JG 26, did not know that the Americans and the R.A.F. had a tour system until I told him; this was his response: *'Unsere Methode war gut für die Kameradschaft, auch gut für den Erfolge, aber auf die Dauer sehr aufreibend.'* ('Our method was good for comradeship and also for success but very grinding in the long run.')

High morale was widespread but not universal. Unteroffizier Alois Reichert belonged to an unusual unit. In 1942 JG 26 had formed a fourth *Gruppe* to fly Messerschmitt 109s in the fighter-bomber role, but this had not been a success. The Messerschmitt 109 had proved too light for such work and its commander had been killed in action at an early stage. The three *Staffeln* in this *Gruppe* had then been split up and, unusually, attached to regular *Gruppen* as an extra *Staffel* to be used mainly as a pool of replacement pilots. Reichert was in the *Staffel* attached to III/JG 26.

We had many training flights and were often in action with the parent *Gruppe* but usually on the edge of the main action. This didn't stop us suffering many casualties, more than in the main *Gruppe*. We had too many new pilots and our *Staffelkapitäns* were always changing.

The enemy forces kept coming in greater and greater strength – in ten or twenty times the strength of earlier years. We knew the Spitfire was good but the Thunderbolt was better at altitude. My *Staffel* had special planes with rubber-sealed cockpits and we had all been sent to the Austrian Alps to become used to altitude. We were supposed to fight only at the higher altitudes but we didn't have much success. The enemy were too strong and too clever in their tactics. We weren't a very lucky *Staffel* and our morale was not particularly good – the bad war news, our losses, our weakness in strength. I never saw a large formation of German aircraft but the Americans kept coming in larger formations. Our little group of pilots hadn't much lust for battle. For myself, I never managed to shoot down an enemy plane in two years of fighting.

It is only a coincidence that all the above quotations come from pilots in J G 26; a similar range of views would probably be found among men in other units.

Some of the German units in the West had recently been exchanged with other units which had been serving on the Russian Front. The reasons for this were to give pilots from Russia a change from the spartan living conditions there and to give pilots from the West a chance to share in the high scoring which was taking place against Russian aircraft. The experiment had not been a success because many of the experienced 'Easterners' had found themselves out of their depth when facing the R.A.F. and American fighters and had become early casualties. It is significant that, in the calculations of fighter-pilot success for the award of German decorations, one victory in the West was considered the equivalent of five in Russia.

The day-fighter units about to engage the Americans were generally in good condition. One or two individual units may have been affected by recent operations – a formation of fighters caught in a bad tactical position could suffer heavily in just a few minutes – but such examples were not widespread. The Luftwaffe had not yet been stretched far enough to be short of either planes or pilots. Surviving Germans also agree that the recent bombings of some of their airfields, while being a nuisance, had not had much effect upon the operational efficiency of their units. The Germans had long been masters of the arts of dispersal and camouflage. The fighters were always safely hidden away inside blast-proof earth walls or were taken away from the airfields by long taxiways to be hidden in nearby woods. The American bombing had rarely achieved more than a mass of bomb craters on the grass airfields. The units concerned quickly transferred to satellite airfields while the Luftwaffe ground staff, the Todt labour organization and pressed local labour filled in the craters. German pilots say that the most dangerous result of the bombing was the increased accident rate when their less experienced pilots were forced to operate from the small satellite airfields.

The German day-fighter control organization was split up on a regional basis under a series of *Jafüs*. (*Jafü* stood for either *Jägerführer* or *Jagdfliegerführer*, both terms meaning 'fighter controller'.) The B-17s were now flying into the southern part of the area controlled by *Jafü Holland–Ruhr*, whose area extended from the Zuider Zee to Brussels and back into Germany as far as the Ruhr. The head of the *Jafü* was Oberst (Colonel) Walter Grabmann, a veteran fighter-pilot from the days of the Condor Legion in the Spanish Civil War and from the 1939 and 1940 campaigns when he had flown Messerschmitt 110s in Poland, France and the Battle of Britain. (In the Introduction to this book it is stated that the same officer directed the main part of the German fighter defence both on 17 August 1943 and on the night in March 1944 when the R.A.F. suffered such severe losses in the raid on Nuremberg. Walter Grabmann was that officer.) The new sophisticated operations bunker, codenamed *Diogenes*, of the nearby 1st *Jagddivision* at Deelen airfield was not quite ready for use, so Grabmann was operating with a small staff from a villa in the village of Schaarsbergen near the Dutch city of Arnhem. The operations staff of the *Jagddivision* was receiving all available incoming information about Allied air movements – radio intercepts, reports from radar stations, visual sightings. A concise résumé of the incoming American raid was then relayed to the *Jafü*. Basing his judgement on this information, Oberst Grabmann then sent out orders to the various units under his control.

There had been no operations in the *Jafü Holland–Ruhr* area earlier that morning which might have indicated that a major operation was pending; in particular there had been none of the feint operations or raids on airfields which often preceded a larger operation. In fact the only Allied activity so far had been nearly 500 miles to the west where twelve R.A.F. Whirlwind fighter-bombers escorted by five Spitfire squadrons had flown from Cornwall to attack the Guipanas airfield near Brest. This force had found Brittany to be cloud-covered and had returned without attempting to bomb. But the clear weather over most of Europe would have told the Germans to expect much more than that minor sortie, and the German radio listening devices had soon started picking up tell-tale signs from the direction of East Anglia that a major raid was in its opening stages. These devices were so sophisticated that they could give an estimate of the number of individual bombers' radio sets being switched on and warmed up at the English airfields. The same devices might then have picked up the scattering of radio signals which had passed between individual B-17s and airfield control towers and later between the groups during their assembly. Although all radio messages from the American bombers had then ceased, the Germans had heard enough. The *Jafü* staff was ready. The fighter units on the airfields had been alerted. Finally, radar stations on the Dutch coast had detected the B-17 force gathering over England and started plotting its progress across the North Sea.

In view of the casualties suffered later in the day, many American airmen were convinced that there had been intelligence leaks, particularly because the Schweinfurt part of this day's operation had been under active preparation for so long and had actually been briefed to units on an earlier occasion. This is not correct. The Germans had no advance information about the American operations, although one unusual event should be recorded. At 10.20 p.m. the previous evening, a small force of Messerschmitt 110 night fighters of I/NJG 4 had taken off from Florennes airfield in Southern Belgium and flown in formation in a south-westerly direction past Paris. When near Orleans, these fighters were spotted by an R.A.F. Beaufighter Intruder of 141 Squadron. In a neat piece of work, Flight Lieutenant H. C. Kelsey and his radar operator, Sergeant E. M. Smith, had shot down the leading Messerschmitt and damaged two more. Because this took place after midnight, the Luftwaffe's casualty department recorded these casualties as having taken place on 17 August and the surviving member of the shot-down crew came into my search for Luftwaffe men engaged on that day. I found and interviewed

Unteroffizier Werner Uhlmann, the engineer/gunner in that crew.

Uhlmann stated that this force of twin-engined fighters had been ordered to make a transfer flight to an airfield further south because an Allied air operation was expected to take place *involving a flight from England to North Africa.* But too much emphasis should not be given to this statement. No other Luftwaffe men, from Oberst Grabmann down to the numerous German pilots who engaged the American bombers later that day, mention any such warnings and all the evidence of the German daylight operations on 17 August indicates that the flight from Regensburg to North Africa took the Germans by surprise. It is also significant that the unit being moved was a night-fighter unit. It is probable that it was being transferred to intercept R.A.F. bombers which were raiding a target in Italy that night and would have to return over France in the early hours of the 17th. The Messerschmitt 110s were certainly flying *away* from the area through which the Regensburg force would later pass. But the incident is mentioned here in case the German intelligence service had somehow picked up the information that a major flight of Allied aircraft was about to take place from England to North Africa. If this is so, the Germans obviously had no idea that the force would attack a target in Germany first; they gained nothing from the information and they suffered these casualties to their night fighters which had been caught by the R.A.F. Beaufighter.

There is no single comprehensive record of the orders given to the German fighter units and their subsequent activities, but enough information is available from various sources to provide a reliable picture of the German reaction on that morning. These sources are: information from Oberst (later General) Grabmann, from several German unit commanders, from the times in the logbooks of other German pilots, from the records of a few German units which survived the war and from the Allied intercepts of German radio traffic. From this information it is clear that the Germans had no difficulty in identifying the incoming B-17 force as being a major raid, but it is probable that the German reaction to the approach of that force was a fraction slower than normal. This may have been because there had been no preliminary diversionary raids and because the B-17s came straight in over the North Sea without any deviation from their course. It is also clear that the initial response to the approach of the

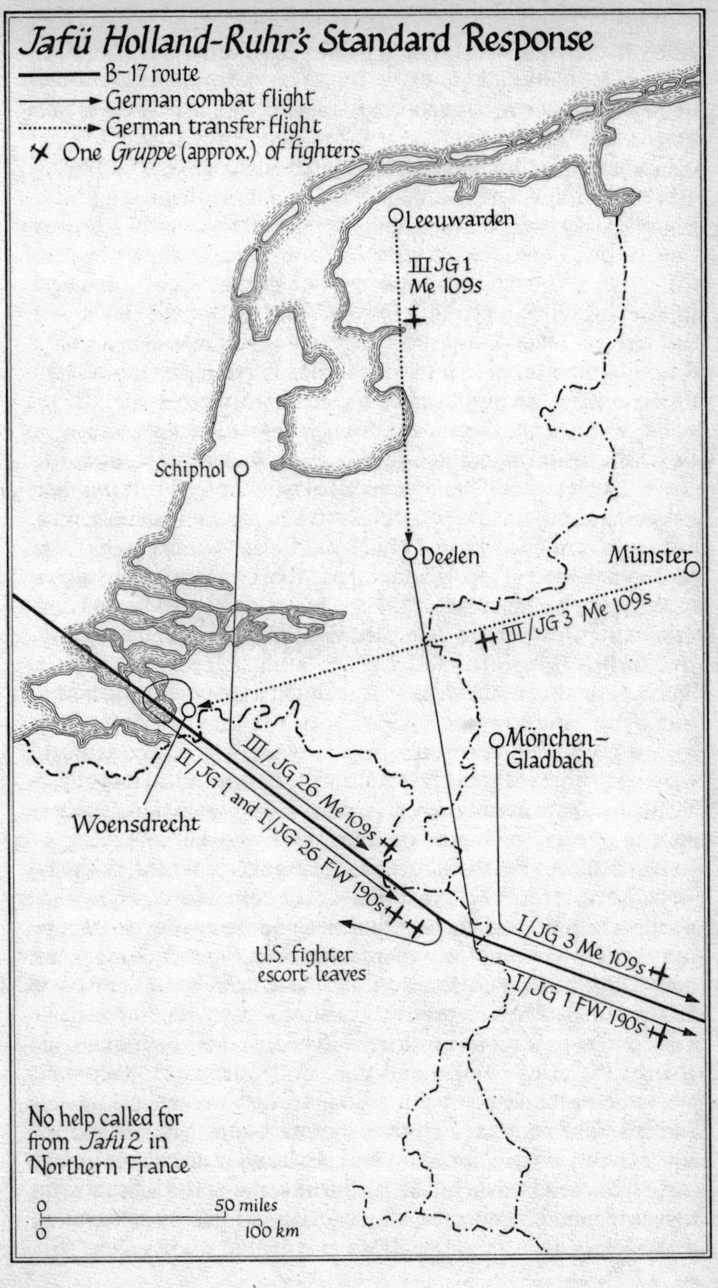
Jafü Holland-Ruhr's Standard Response
B-17 route
German combat flight
German transfer flight
One Gruppe (approx.) of fighters
Leeuwarden
III JG 1
Me 109s
Schiphol
Deelen
Münster
III/JG 3 Me 109s
Mönchen-
Gladbach
III/JG 26 Me 109s
II/JG 1 and I/JG 26 FW 190s
Woensdrecht
U.S. fighter
escort leaves
I/JG 3 Me 109s
I/JG 1 FW 190s
No help called for
from Jafü 2 in
Northern France
0
50 miles
0
100 km

American force was to engage it only with the immediately available fighter units and not to ask for any help from the neighbouring *Jafüs* to the south and north. There would be no German maximum effort at this stage of the day's operations.

Grabmann had day fighters available at six airfields – Woensdrecht, Schiphol, Leeuwarden and Deelen in Holland, and Münster and Mönchen-Gladbach just back over the German border. Each airfield contained at least one *Gruppe* of about twenty-five to thirty planes, although the full strength rarely managed to take off on an operation. At 9.45 a.m., when the B-17s were still well out over the North Sea, the units at Woensdrecht and Schiphol were ordered into the air. These fighters were to climb for height and attempt to catch the incoming force on or near the coast. The units at Deelen and Mönchen-Gladbach were ordered to take off and attempt to catch the bombers well inside the coast. The four units so far committed would pursue the bombers as far as their fuel would allow and might well land a great distance from their bases. This would leave a huge gap in the German defences. To fill this gap, the Leeuwarden unit was ordered to fly down and land at Deelen and the Münster unit would fly even further and land at Woensdrecht. These units would then be available to engage the first force of American bombers on any return flight through this area or any fresh force coming in from England later.

Oberst Grabmann sent out his instructions through a group of *Jägerleitoffiziers* who were sitting with him in that Dutch villa. These men were usually officers from the Luftwaffe signals service and, in theory, each was in touch with the 1A officer at the headquarters of the various *Geschwader* involved. Ideally, the 1A would then consult with the *Geschwader* commander who would decide which of his *Gruppen* would attempt to engage any fighter escort and which would go for the bombers. In practice, however, only JG 1 had its *Geschwader* Headquarters in this area and Grabmann's assistants probably dealt directly with each airfield. The control by *Jafü* was restricted to ordering take-off times and giving the German units initial courses and heights to help them reach the probable combat area. Thereafter, the role of the *Jafü* and his *Jägerleitoffiziers* was to broadcast further information and possibly give exhortation and advice, but not direct orders. Once a unit had taken off, its airborne commander – usually the *Gruppe* commander – took all tactical decisions.

*

The German pilots had been waiting for some time at the ready-rooms near their planes – seemingly disordered, informal places, with a few beds, easy chairs and deck-chairs, a wireless, much chatter, cigarette smoke. Fighter pilots the world over would recognize the atmosphere immediately. Then the loud-speakers blared, barking out the order to take off and providing the latest position and course of the bombers. 'We had all been anxious, on edge, unable to settle to anything while the information had been coming in earlier that the enemy formations were assembling. No one could sit still for any time. But when you sat in the plane and held the stick in your hand, then you felt different, more confident.'

The actual order to take off was given by the firing of a red flare. Speed was all-important now. The fighters were usually spread in groups of four around the airfield perimeter and each four in turn took off straight across the airfield regardless of the wind. Schiphol had its pre-war concrete runways but these were ignored; Woensdrecht was an entirely grassed field. A good *Gruppe* could assemble and be climbing on its way two minutes after the first fighter had moved. The units then flew in loose formation, spread out by *Staffeln* which in turn were flying in the small *Schwarms* of four aircraft in the standard 'finger-four' formation which the Germans had been using for years. The object was to finish up with a good height advantage and in an up-sun position when contact was made with the American bombers. Those two old fighter factors – height and sun – were all that the *Gruppe* commander had in his mind. Information continued to be broadcast from the ground, always giving the present position and the course of the enemy formation. The phrase '*dicke Autos*' – 'fat vehicles' or 'heavy jobs' – would signify that heavy bombers had been detected; if the enemy fighter escort had been seen, these would be referred to as '*Indianern*' – 'Indians'.

The Germans often had difficulty in intercepting a fast-moving enemy fighter sweep but today's fine weather and the slow-moving B-17 formation posed no problem. The first sighting could not have been easier. It was a very local affair. The Focke-Wulf 190s from Woensdrecht – I/JG 26 and part of II/JG 1 – had only to circle and gain height over their own airfield and wait in the sun for the B-17s to arrive. The Americans soon appeared, 6,000 feet below, flying calmly through the Flak bursts from the batteries stationed around Woensdrecht. Most of the Messer-schmitts of III/JG 26, coming down from Schiphol, were also present although slightly north of the American position. A German-speaking R.A.F. listener in England heard the leader of III/JG 26 asking if any 'little brothers' – Allied fighters – were present with the bombers. One *Staffel* from Schiphol is believed to have lost contact with its parent formation and not to have reached the combat area, but the main part of the *Gruppe* soon worked its way round into the sun. Approximately fifty German fighters had been led successfully into early visual contact with the 4th Bombardment Wing.

The officer leading each German unit now had to make a difficult decision. No one could advise him whether this was another short penetration raid, with the fighter escort present throughout, or whether the bombers would continue flying on towards a target in Germany and thus outrun their escort cover. The German fighters had sufficient fuel for their commanders to consider this problem for a few minutes. Their formations were safely up in the sun. The Americans had probably not even seen them yet. The Germans decided not to attack immediately.

One important matter should be disposed of before this narrative proceeds further. It was stated in an earlier chapter that the B-17 'was currently suffering severely from having to face a form of attack which its designers had never envisaged'. It was also stated that the American fighter escort force was inadequate because the U.S.A.A.F. 'had earlier convinced itself that the self-defending long-range bomber concept was valid'. These statements should now be explained in more detail.

Before the Americans had planned their new breed of bomber in the late 1930s, the standard method of attack by a fighter aircraft upon a bomber had always been from the rear. The best results had been obtained from the classic 'curve of pursuit' form of attack, which had started with a diving approach by the fighter from a height advantage to level out behind the bomber target and shoot it down with an accurate, no-deflection burst of fire. (Deflection is the angle that has to be added to the aim to allow for the forward movement of the target aircraft in the interval between the firing of a shot and that shot's reaching the path of the target aircraft.) Good deflection shooting is a difficult skill to attain. The only true no-deflection shots at a moving target are those aimed from directly astern or directly ahead. The advantage was always with the fighter; the bomber presented a larger and slower target and the armament of the fighter was greater than that which could be mounted in the bomber to protect its rear. This approach and attack from the rear had been standard since the first days of aerial combat. American fighter units had until recently been called 'Pursuit Squadrons' and the 'P' prefix in the classification of American fighter aircraft stood for 'pursuit'; the 'F' prefix would not come into use until the Korean War.

When the planners of American bombing strategy had found themselves faced with the problem of providing protection for their new family of long-range bombers, they had opted for the principle of the self-defending bomber rather than the technically more difficult provision of a long-range fighter escort. The B-17 'Fortress' had been the main result. Each B-17 could mount nine heavy machine-guns to overlap and form a huge cone of fire covering any angle of approach from the rear. The standard combat box of eighteen B-17s provided by one bomb group could provide a mass of interlocking fire from 162 guns to its rear. Two-thirds of these guns were in the top, belly and tail turrets, which had hydraulic controls and sophisticated aiming devices. The remaining, hand-held guns were never considered to be as effective as the turret guns.

In 1942 the Eighth Air Force went to war in Europe with these supposedly self-defending bomber formations. For a time they were very effective. The German fighter pilots hated tackling the American formations with the relatively slow closing approach from the rear. They called a B-17 combat box a '*Pulk*', a difficult word to translate – possibly 'herd' is the best English equivalent. In particular the Germans hated that two-gun tail turret which they had to face if they ever tried the no-deflection killer shot from directly astern. Then the Germans hit upon a simple solution. An attack from directly ahead, though at a frighteningly fast closing speed, could escape the fire of nearly all the B-17 gun positions and allow a brief no-deflection burst of fire before the attacker was forced to break off and pull away. From that moment the B-17 was obsolete as a self-defending bomber. The American bomber designers had not thought through their concept thoroughly enough.

The American bomber crews had then been in deep trouble. Neither the top nor the ball turret could quite cover that forward approach. The two hand-held guns which fired out of either side of the nose compartment – the so-called 'cheek' guns – were only a little more effective. One or sometimes two machine-guns were hurriedly fitted in the front of the noses of some B-17s, but those planes which needed to retain their bomb-sights could not be protected in this way. Back in the United States the designers started planning a new 'chin turret' to fire directly forward, but this modification had not yet arrived in England.

There was yet a further disadvantage in this new situation of frontal attack. The six gun positions covering the rear of the B-17 were all manned by enlisted men (for British readers, men who were not officers) who had graduated from a full course of aerial gunnery. They cherished and understood their guns and were dedicated to their craft. The guns in the nose compartment upon which the B-17 now depended for its defence were manned by two officers – the bombardier and the navigator – whose gunnery role had always been secondary to their other duties and whose gunnery training had been sketchy. The planned emphasis of the B-17 crew had been turned upside down. The fully trained gunners in the rear of the aircraft had little faith in the ability of the two officers at the front. The comments of this regular gunner are a little extreme but they do represent the general feeling.

> Officer gunners? An absolute minus! We were still in the States when the Germans had started their frontal attacks and the danger had been realized. These navigators and bombardiers were sent to gunnery schools but the instructors were non-coms and that didn't sit too well with these ninety-day wonders who had been told they were officers and gentlemen. They had sat at the back of the class and showed very little interest in what was going on. It was not their primary task and I think they felt that it was all a little beneath them, not realizing that when we reached Europe it could save their lives – and ours.

It was under these wickedly disadvantageous conditions that the B-17s of Colonel LeMay's force now had to face the enemy fighters. It was nothing new for the Americans; the German units they were about to meet had been using the head-on attack method for months. The B-17 crewmen would simply have to sit and take what was coming. The pilots and co-pilots would be staring straight at the incoming German fighters. The navigators and bombardiers with their jerky, ineffective hand-held guns would be frantically doing their best. Most of the six trained gunners in each crew would be able to do little more in their frustration than take hurried snap-shots as the German fighters

Head-on view of B-17 Group Formation

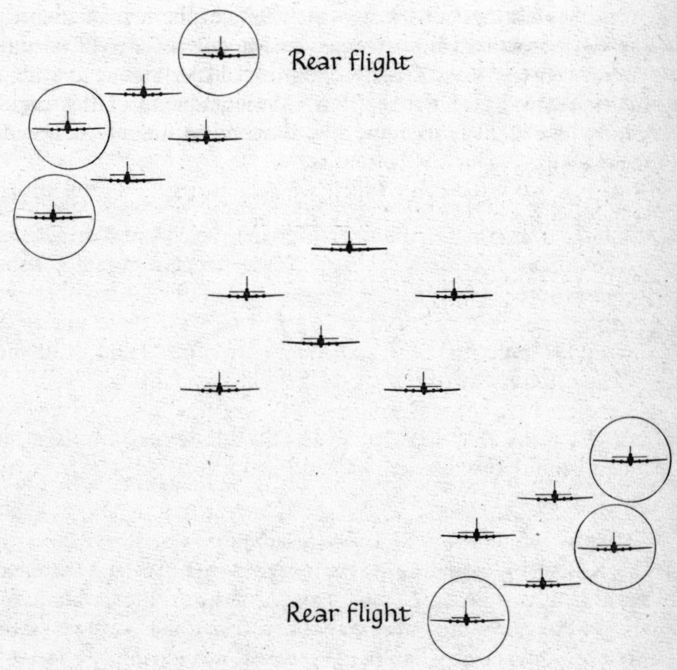

(For a good side view of a formation, see plate 16 and, for a view from above, see diagram 5.)

flashed past their ill-placed positions. Staff Sergeant Albert Van Pelt, of the 390th Bomb Group, sums up the situation well.

> The waist gunner doesn't have much chance with a head-on attack. You just saw them coming past and out of sight. Possibly you got a short burst in. I'd done a lot of hunting in my life and was aware of how difficult it was to hit something that was moving fast. We'd done a lot of air-to-air target practice but nothing moving through at that speed. I just didn't feel I was going to be hitting anything that day. I felt very inadequate.

The Americans often talk of the vulnerability of the 'Tail-End Charlie' or 'Purple Heart Corner' positions in a formation. These were vulnerable, not because they were at the rear of the formation but because they appeared on the edge of a B-17 formation when viewed by the German pilots attacking from the front and thus usually attracted the first German attacks. There was one more factor. The Germans always searched for the group which was flying the loosest formation.

These were the rules which would govern the battle about to commence.

CHAPTER 7

Going In

The American bomber force, now 139 B-17s strong, flew steadily on – indicated air speed 165 m.p.h., true air speed almost 260 m.p.h., course still south-east. Antwerp, Diest, Hasselt, Liège, Maastricht – the navigators' charts showed these to be the landmarks passing to one side or the other. This earthbound narrative will be forced to use these towns and cities to mark the milestones of the battle, but these places were three and a half miles below and only of interest to the one in a hundred men whose task it was to keep the bomber formation on its correct track. The remainder of the American airmen lived only in that vast, blue waste of the sky in which the only feature was the glaring sun. Two formations of German fighters were hiding up in that sun and a third was further north, attempting to manoeuvre into a favourable attacking position. One group of P-47 Thunderbolts was protecting the front of the bomber force; a second group had already caught sight of the tail of the force and would soon be taking over the escort duty.

The first action occurred when the 353rd Fighter Group spotted a formation of Focke-Wulf 190s to the north of the bomber formation and obviously preparing to attack the B-17s. The Germans were at 30,000 feet and the P-47s started climbing fast to put themselves between the German fighters and the bombers. Major McCollom writes:

> We spotted six or seven of them and had time only to make a hurried head-on attack. They were FW 190s and coming downhill; our closing speed must have been at least 700 miles per hour. We succeeded in two things: spraying a great deal of lead around the sky and – a bonus effect – forcing the FW 190s to make a beam attack on the bombers. I'm sure the German pilots considered that a non-habit-forming tactic.

These German planes were undoubtedly from II/JG 1 based at

nearby Woensdrecht. No B-17s and no fighters from either side were lost in this first encounter.

The P-47s had performed this useful spoiling action but the American escort was too weak to keep a watch on every avenue of approach. The commanders of the two German *Gruppen* which were hiding safely up in the sun to the south were studying the layout of the American bomber formation and had noted the wide gaps between the three combat wings of B-17s. (These gaps were necessary so that each combat wing could maintain a tight formation without flying into the turbulence of the preceding wing, and also so that there would not be congestion later when the combat wings broke out into a line of groups for the bombing run at the target.) The two German commanders watched the P-47s being drawn off to the north and independently decided that they would make a diving attack from ahead, across the top of the second combat wing and on into the last wing.

American airmen often talk of their anxiety and fear when seeing an incoming German fighter attack; to the bomber men, the Germans appeared invincible. But many of the Americans would have been surprised if they had known how the Germans felt at that moment. These two German pilots were in the units about to attack.

> I could see the fighter escort and I saw the front of the bomber formation. When I first spotted those bombers I thought, '*Oh je!*' I had never seen so many Americans before – we had just moved down to Holland from the German Bight – and I thought how weak we seemed in number by comparison. I was very depressed. (Feldwebel Werner Mössner, III/JG 26)

> The impression was a tremendous one. There were about 150 four-engined bombers and one was overwhelmed by the sheer mass of their formations but, at the same time, the hunting instinct awoke and the realization that these aircraft were full of bombs, perhaps to be dropped on Germany, was a stimulation. I didn't see any fighters with the Boeings; they were expected but I suppose something had gone wrong. If I had been more experienced, I would have been pleased to see no fighters but I knew so little and there was so much going on that I didn't think too much about it. (Leutnant Jörg Kiefner, I/JG 26)

It was probably the Focke-Wulf 190s of I/JG 26 which came

in first. In theory the *Gruppe* should have come in *Staffel* by *Staffel*, seven or eight fighters abreast, but the *Gruppe* was not at full strength and this attack was a hurried one. The Germans wanted to hit the American bombers once and then get away before the P-47s returned. They came in fast and hard from ahead, at angles of 10 or 20 degrees up from the horizontal. To the Americans – who used the all-round clockface system – it was the famous and feared 'twelve o'clock high' attack. Leutnant Kiefner again:

> We came round in a left-hand turn and attacked from ahead. When you first saw them from the front, the formation appeared quite small and our leader took us down right at the middle of the formation. They were packed in tight, like a bunch of grapes. We had to turn from side to side slightly because we still had to keep our eyes open for enemy fighters. You could always recognize an experienced pilot because he flew like a drunk – he was called an *alter Hase*, an old hare.
>
> The old hands could pick out a bomber, place the nose of that bomber in the cross-threads of their gun-sights and not open fire until the bomber completely filled the sight – just one small burst, no more than two seconds. We tried to hit the wing and engines close to the fuselage. If you hit it, then you saw the small explosions of the cannon shells striking, or even one big explosion if the tank blew up. We young chaps tried to do the same but naturally with less success.
>
> After that one burst there was no more firing, just getting through the formation. Even now it is completely unbelievable that there were no collisions as we flew through it. It seemed to take only a fraction of a second.

I/JG 26 had made its attack sweeping across the top of the 94th Bomb Group and carrying on to make a frontal attack on the 95th, the more daring Germans actually flying between the 95th's squadrons. These two groups were flying in the high positions of the second and third combat wings respectively. The Germans always say they sought out the weakest groups, and it was the 95th which had earlier lost five aborted planes. The forward-firing gun positions of the B-17s were all in action, the tracer clearly visible. To the Germans it was like 'flying through a garden sprinkler'. It was the *Gruppe* commander, the 'old hare' Major Borris, who obtained the first success when he put a devastating burst of fire into the nose of the tail-end plane in the

94th Bomb Group's high squadron. More of Borris's pilots damaged at least two B-17s in the 95th Bomb Group and left them with smoking engines. Many Americans watched Borris's own victim jerk away from its formation and go down quickly to explode and scatter into pieces around a Belgian village ten kilometres east of Diest. Technical Sergeant Arthur McDonnell was the radio operator in the shot-down B-17.

> On the intercom I heard Jake Dalinsky, who was looking out of the waist-gun window, shouting out, 'Holy Jesus, there's a mess of them out there.' Then the co-pilot, Jack Smith, called, 'Coming out of the sun,' so that meant there was another lot coming down from ahead of us. I only had that little window in the radio room; I couldn't see them. The very next thing that happened was that Jack Smith called out, 'Bale out! Bale out!' and the ship started vibrating heavily all over. That was the first intimation I had that we'd been hit. I realized they must have been hit hard up at the front – in the engines or the cockpit. None of them got out. I'm certain that it was Smith's southern accent I had heard. He was from Alabama – a wonderful guy, the girls loved him.
>
> I came out of the radio room and made for the waist and was right behind Jake. He'd already got rid of the waist door but was standing there, holding on by both hands to the inside of the ship, looking down. I tapped him on the shoulder to tell him to go and, at that moment, there was an explosion and I was thrown back inside. I was knocked down on to my hands and knees by a piece of 20-millimetre in the side of the head. It was just like being paralysed. I was only just holding on to consciousness. The 50-caliber gun in the waist was going round wildly and banging me on the head. I couldn't move. That waist gun swinging finished the job and I slumped to the floor. I was completely unconscious.
>
> When I came to, I thought I was in the hereafter. I remember thinking this was the end but there was nothing like the entire life flashing past my eyes that you hear about. There was just a sadness. The only thing I didn't understand about it was that I was going down and not up! Then I realized I was coming down by parachute. My eyes were full of blood and I couldn't breathe because my oxygen mask was still on and the tube was twisted. I ripped it off. I've thought about how I got out of that aircraft over a great many years. I still think it's a miracle.

The pilot, Lieutenant Bernard Nayovitz, together with his three fellow officers as well as the top turret and ball turret gunners were all dead, most of them probably killed by the first burst of cannon fire. McDonnell and the three survivors had escaped when the tail broke off. McDonnell, unable to see with the blood in his eyes, made a very bad landing and thumped into a tree to be crippled for life with back and pelvis injuries. (Appendix 1 contains basic details of all American aircraft losses and Appendix 2 of all the known German losses.)

Only a few seconds after the Focke-Wulf 190s of I/JG 26 had flashed through the bomber formation, part of their sister *Gruppe*, III/JG 26 from Schiphol, also came round from the sun and attacked. Their aircraft were Messerschmitt 109s and they made for the low groups of the second and third combat wings, the 385th and 100th Bomb Groups. Oberfeldwebel Heinz Kemethmüller was the leader of a *Schwarm* of four fighters.

> We couldn't see any enemy fighters around so my *Staffelkapitän* selected a *Pulk* and led us round the front of it. He decided which bomber he was going for and the rest of us spread out and selected ours. I just had time for one burst on mine and I saw pieces flying off one engine. I broke off high and to the right and circled. By this time the American formation had moved on so I was in a good position for an immediate attack again but from the rear. I looked at the bomber I had attacked on the first pass and saw black smoke pouring from the engine I had hit. It had started to lose height and was turning away from the formation. It was quite clear to me that it would never get home. Pilots who only had a few successes would have made sure of that first one but I already had seventy-two successes since May 1941 – although not all confirmed – so I didn't have to worry too much about it. I thought it better to try to get another one which still had its bombs.

Once again only one veteran pilot in a German unit gained a clear success and again the victim was the top rear plane in a high squadron, this time the B-17 of Second Lieutenant Paul Sommers of the 385th Group. Technical Sergeant Bruno Gallerini was its top turret gunner, not a regular member of this crew but a last-minute replacement that morning.

> We hadn't been under attack long. It was mostly forward stuff and I didn't see the burst of fire which hit us. I was trying to shoot at fighters as they were coming past but I do think it was a 109. Something hit the plane's left side. I knew something serious had happened because the power in my guns went out although I could still move the turret and I carried on swinging it to try to scare them but that was useless.
>
> Then I looked down and saw this gaping hole in the right-hand side of the plane. It was just behind the co-pilot's position and almost big enough to walk through. I also saw that one of the engines on the same side was smoking and there were no other planes around. We had broken formation and were losing altitude.

We shall meet both Oberfeldwebel Kemethmüller and the crew of Second Lieutenant Sommers again.

This encounter between III/JG 26 and the 385th and 100th Bomb Groups had not been one-sided. In return for one B-17 forced out of formation and others damaged, two Messerschmitt 109s were shot down by the defensive fire of the B-17 formations. One of the shot-down German pilots was badly wounded and the other, Unteroffizier Fritz Fritzlehner, was killed – the first Luftwaffe death of the day.

A German unit could never repeat the careful set-piece of a first attack. The fighters broke away in all directions and would never reform as a complete unit. Sometimes a *Staffel* of eight planes or so might manage to remain in contact with each other but it was usually a matter of fours or twos for the rest of that sortie. If a *Gruppe* commander wanted attacks to continue, the manner in which subsequent attacks were carried out and the degree to which they were pressed home would be more and more in the hands of junior pilots; there was little to stop individual pilots carrying on or quitting as they wished. As long as there was any chance of Allied fighters turning up, the basic *Rotte* of two – leader and wingman – had to stay together. The leader did the fighting; the wingman kept a look-out and protected his leader from a tail attack. There was nothing unusual in this; it was the standard procedure in all air forces. (The Germans always referred to their wingman as their 'Kaczmarek'; no one knows how this Polish surname came to be used for this purpose.)

Major Borris, the careful, experienced commander of I/JG 26, had been operating in this area long enough to know that the American fighters might reappear at any moment. His *Gruppe* had shot down one B-17 and damaged others; none of his own planes had been lost. He broadcast the order to his pilots not to attack again. They could look for stragglers on the way back to Woensdrecht but he wanted to get his units down safely and intact at their home base where they could refuel, rearm and be ready for a second sortie if the B-17s returned through this area. The Focke-Wulf 190s of this unit departed from the scene of action.

It is not known whether III/JG 26's regular commander, Major Klaus Mietusch, was leading the *Gruppe* that morning. This unit had only recently returned to the West after a six-month rotation with a unit on the Russian Front where it had operated very successfully on the Leningrad sector. The *Gruppe* had then refitted in Germany and had only moved to Schiphol four days earlier. It had not yet been in action against American bombers escorted by P-47s. Whoever was leading the *Gruppe* did not order his pilots to break off and small groups of fighters continued to wander around the rear of the B-17 force looking for opportunities to attack again. It was at this time that the P-47s of the 353rd Fighter Group, which had been operating mainly at the front of the bomber force, handed over to the newly arriving 56th Fighter Group and were passing down the northern side of the bomber force on their way back to England. Major McCollom describes how he came upon some unwary Germans.

> Shortly after we started our withdrawal I saw a 'gaggle' of Me 109s to the west and a bit south of the bombers. I made a sharp left turn which placed me to the left and a bit behind the last Me 109. I closed to about 350 yards and at this point fired about a 20-degree deflection shot with no visible result. I was still closing, and at about 250 yards and 10 degrees of deflection I gave it another long burst, three to four seconds, which registered hits on its left central section with rather awesome results and the battle was over. I then looked carefully for the rest of the gaggle but they had disappeared. We no longer had the fuel to pursue anyway so we completed our withdrawal.

Oberfeldwebel Kemethmüller was the pilot of that last Messerschmitt 109 which Major McCollom attacked.

I was thinking about making a third attack. I hadn't heard any warning about the escort and I was a little careless. Just as I turned, with my left hand on the throttle and the right hand on the control column, both the sticks were suddenly shot right through and I was left with both handles free in my hands. There were many other hits on the left hand side of my plane. My hands were slightly hurt but the armour plating behind me saved the rest of me; I felt two or three thumps there. I looked back quickly and saw the Thunderbolt just fifty metres behind me.

I had to bale out. I knew what to do; it was my fourth time – twice on the Channel, once in Russia. I knew that I should not jump at once; I would have left at the same forward speed as the fighter and the parachute opening at that speed would have been too fierce. Also, I wanted to lose height and get to where there was more oxygen. It wasn't that I was worried about being shot on my parachute by the Thunderbolt. When I did jump, I waited for my body to finish tumbling over and steadied myself with my body facing the ground before I opened the parachute.

As I was coming down the blood running out of my wounded fingers was blowing back up my arm in big waves and eventually covered the whole of the inside of my flying jacket. In the hospital I was taken to, the German doctors thought I must be severely hurt but they found that my wounds were not serious. I was the only German in the hospital; the others were all Americans.

Loren McCollom was very surprised, when told of the identity of his victim, that such an experienced German pilot should be caught so easily in this way and also that he survived the concentrated burst of bullets. Kemethmüller soon recovered and returned to fly on till the end of the war.

Major McCollom's pilots now had to return to England. It was not their fault that they could only protect part of the bomber force or that their aircraft did not have the range to go further. McCollom adds,

I don't think there was a fighter pilot in England in the business of escorting bombers who wouldn't be overjoyed to have had the capability to escort the bombers to their targets and back again. The trite expression, 'discretion is the better part of valor', pertains. We learned not to like it but to live with it. There was always the horrible vision in the back of my

> mind of staying with the bombers too long and then gracefully ditching forty-eight Thunderbolts in the North Sea.

The P-47s of this unit returned safely to England without loss. 56th Fighter Group, which had arrived in slightly greater strength than the 353rd, now had the escort duty. Parts of two German units were still in visual contact but they kept their distance, deterred by this new wave of American escorts.

The action which has been described so far in this chapter had lasted for no longer than five minutes.

There was another danger to the bombers besides the German fighters. Every sizeable town in this area had its complement of anti-aircraft batteries – Flak. The route chosen by the planners saved the B-17s having to fly directly over these Flak areas but the standard German 88-mm gun had a formidable 'slant range' and the bomber formations had been peppered by Flak ever since crossing the coast. Just after the fighter attacks faded away, a group of batteries found the correct range and caught the rearmost groups in the bomber column. Three planes – two from the 95th Bomb Group and one from the 100th – were damaged and forced out of their formations. It is believed that Flak batteries near the Belgian town of Hasselt and at the Dutch city of Maastricht can be credited with these successes.

The effect of the Flak hit on the plane of Lieutenant Claytor, in the 100th Bomb Group, was the most dramatic. Second Lieutenant Jim Nutting, the co-pilot, describes what happened.

> Everyone had been interested in the fighters; none of us had paid a whole lot of attention to the Flak that was banging away at us. All of a sudden, the mighty *Alice from Dallas* rose with a sickening lurch, then fell off to the left and started down. Frank and I fought at the controls, trying to bring her under control, and this we did somewhat. Over the interphone he kept yelling 'Bale out! Bale out!' He saw that I wasn't leaving the big bird and he asked me what was wrong with my side of the ship. A few quick glances showed me that the engines were okay but there were a few big holes in the wing. The instruments were in good shape, four engines were running and we hadn't lost any power. He still yelled for me to bale out. His wing was on fire, starting with the trailing edge and working forward. The left aileron was smashed – it was on fire and useless – and the plane kept wanting to climb and go to the

left. He was holding the stick forward and I was helping, full right aileron and full right rudder.

I finally realized that this was it. But no, it couldn't happen to us; we were going to finish our twenty-five missions so we could go home just as every boy in every crew believed or hoped. I now saw that there was a terrific blaze coming from underneath the wing on my side. I said to myself, 'Frank old boy; hope you can hold the ship for a few seconds.'

This plane had been an element leader and its erratic behaviour caused great alarm to the crews of its two wing planes. Staff Sergeant Gordon Williams was in the plane on the left wing.

The engines and wings were all on fire and it peeled off to the right. I saw some parachutes come out but then it made a full 360-degree turn and came back onto the left of the formation but it didn't quite catch up. I remember watching it just below me and to my right – flying erratically, rising and falling. It was only about 200 yards away at one stage and I could see everything very clearly. Things look closer in the air, specially when it's clear up there. I was worried a little that it might come into the formation. We were flying a tight formation and there wouldn't have been much we could have done about it. I couldn't see anyone in the pilot's compartment. It was on fire from stem to stern and I was worried that the incendiaries were still on board. It was spectacular, like nothing I'd ever seen before. I wished it would blow up or leave us but eventually it did peel off and I lost interest in it. I was looking after newer problems.

Two men died in Lieutenant Claytor's crew. One was probably killed by the Flak burst but the other was seen hesitating at the waist door. Claytor later wrote of this man: 'He was a strange boy, often airsick. I think he was actually afraid of the air. I mentioned having him removed from the crew several times but he always persuaded me to keep him. He was always brave and fearless but he had this inherent fear of the air.'

The two planes of the 95th Bomb Group hit by Flak were those of Lieutenants Walter Baker and Robert Mason. Baker's plane lost two engines and he was forced to turn back towards England. Staff Sergeant Raymond Elias describes what happened to Lieutenant Mason's plane.

The Flak hit us near the Tokyo tank in the right wing and I think a hydraulic line there was hit. There was a small fire which I could see from my position. The aluminium was actually melting; up in the sky it looked like water leaking off the wing. Mason said we'd dive and try to put the fire out and he went down steeply, about 5,000 feet, and the fire did go out.

He asked us whether we wanted to turn back or go on; he actually gave us a vote. Why did I vote to go on? I could say that I wanted to go down to Africa but the truth is that I didn't want to be one of the ones who were always turning back. I didn't want to be considered yellow. It took us about half an hour to get back in formation. It seemed like an eternity when you were down there on your own. I still can't figure out why no one came after us. By the time we got back, the others had moved up and filled our place and we tacked on to the end of the squadron.

Three damaged B-17s had turned back as a result of the recent fighter and Flak action and were attempting to reach England independently. Lieutenant Baker's crew only managed to cover half the distance to the coast before their plane's end came. Second Lieutenant 'Hank' Sarnow was its bombardier.

I heard the pilot and co-pilot trying to get it into automatic. The co-pilot was a very profane person and he kept saying, 'Horseshit, horseshit.' The damage was all on his side and he could see how bad it was. The pilot gave me the O.K. to dump the bombs and that helped us gain a little altitude. The radio operator reported that both waist gunners were hit in the legs and were lying on the floor.

The fighters had found us by now and they were after us hot and heavy. The co-pilot shot up green flares to call for friendly fighter assistance but there was no one about. While I was firing at the fighters in front of us, I heard the co-pilot asking the waist gunners if they could hold out till we reached the coast. One of them replied that their wounds were frozen over but that they had both run out of ammunition. We proceeded on, wallowing all over the place, with the fighters hammering the hell out of us. The tail assembly was fluttering and affecting the flying attitude of the plane.

A frontal attack got us in the end. A cannon shell hit the oxygen supply situated between the nose compartment and the pilots' cockpit and it burst into a white flash of flame. I was badly burned on the exposed parts of my wrists and face and my nylon scarf and rubber face mask were burned to my skin. As I pushed aside some burning fabric, I saw the co-pilot caught halfway in the pilots' compartment and the nose compartment. He had his parachute on but his flying suit was caught. He was in such a position that I had to pull him free in order to get out of the aircraft myself. I grabbed his leather jacket and pulled and pulled. He kept squirming as well and, between both of our efforts, he broke loose and we both went out the hatch as one squirming mass.

Amazingly, no one in this crew was killed although the co-pilot, Second Lieutenant Martin Minnich, was badly burned in the face and neck.

It is not known which German fighters finished off this B-17 but the other two were definitely dispatched by pilots of I/JG 26 who had broken off their attack on the main bomber force and were returning to Woensdrecht. Lieutenant Sundberg's plane was caught near Turnhout by several fighters. The bomber was soon on fire and clearly had no chance. Sundberg lowered the undercarriage as a sign to the Germans that he had ended resistance and the entire crew baled out, though the radio man died of burns several hours later. The third returning B-17 had no better luck. This was the 385th Bomb Group plane of Second Lieutenant Paul Sommers which had been badly damaged in its nose section in the earlier fighter attack. Technical Sergeant Bruno Gallerini, the top turret gunner, continues his description. As a replacement man in this crew, he had considerably more experience of operations than the other members of it.

The intercom was out so I leaned down and asked the pilot if he wanted people to bale out and he said he did. I dropped down into the nose to see the navigator and bombardier; we all needed the same escape hatch. The first thing I saw was the navigator, hit with a 20-millimetre; there was a big hole in his chest and I could tell that he was dead. I didn't wait to see any more of his wounds. I told the bombardier to bale out but he couldn't open the hatch. I remember reaching over, grabbing the seat of his pants, pulling him away and I kicked it open. I pushed him out and then two more men; I don't know who they were. I don't think they had had any practice; they didn't seem to want to go.

After the third one, I went myself. My parachute opened

O.K. I watched two fighters come past me – one on either side – just waggling their wings as they went past and carrying on after the plane.

There must have been a tragic confusion in this plane. It is not possible to piece together the full story. Gallerini has described the reluctance of the men in the front to leave. The sister of Staff Sergeant Larry Stokes, a waist gunner, says that her brother's parachute was badly holed and he went up to the front of the aircraft. The pilot was dead by then but Stokes and the co-pilot could not bring themselves to remove the seat parachute from the pilot's body and Stokes jumped with the damaged parachute, was badly injured on landing and died of these injuries soon after the war. The co-pilot, the radio operator and the second waist gunner all died but how is not known. Finally, an account by Michel Bosman, a Belgian Boy Scout at a nearby camp, describes how the tail gunner, who must also have been badly injured in the plane, was seen to come down by parachute into some pine-woods. Bosman and one of his scoutmasters found this man only because he had set light to the dry grass and branches around him to attract attention. The Belgians rescued him from the growing fire area and the American identified himself to them as 'Joe Schreppel of Pittsburg, Pennsylvania'. The report concludes: 'At Joe's request, a local man fetched a priest who talked with Joe and gave him the Last Sacraments. Then Joe passed away, very calmly.'

The two German fighter pilots who had flown past Bruno Gallerini's parachute were probably Hauptmann Rolf Hermichen and his wingman, Leutnant Jörg Kiefner. Kiefner describes what they were doing.

Hermichen led us in an attack on the two planes that had dropped out. That was the old fighter pilot's trick. The successful ones built up their scores in this way. We went for the one which was in the rear, the natural thing to do. Five or six parachutes came out while we were approaching. Hermichen and I both seemed to fire at the same time; we were attacking from below and behind. We got in so close that the Boeing seemed as large as a barn gate. After our attack, the fuselage was completely on fire. Hermichen said on the radio, 'Don't fire any more.' I can still hear him saying this. He wanted me to save ammunition. But, being only a young one, I kept on firing – it was instinct – the human being becomes an animal at moments like this. The Boeing disintegrated in the air.

That combat took us right back over our own airfield at Woensdrecht. We flew slowly across the field, as low as possible, waggling our wings to tell them we had shot down a bomber. If a pilot had shot two bombers down, he came round a second time.

When we landed, Hermichen went to H.Q. to claim the bomber but his mechanic found that the covers were still on his cannons. I had been so close to Hermichen, just a little underneath, that he had seen my tracer and thought that it was his own. I think it possible that, in all the noise and chaos and with everything happening at top speed, he had not realized that his own cannons weren't firing. Because of that, I was immediately given the credit. I hadn't even bothered to go to H.Q. – I had assumed that it was Hermichen's fire that had done all the damage.

The main bomber force had been making better progress while these actions had been taking place to its rear. Hasselt, Maastricht and Liège were safely passed without any further serious fighter attack. Much of the early German effort had slackened and the P-47s of the 56th Fighter Group were providing excellent protection. A number of Germans were still in contact but the American fighter pilots were very alert and every German approach was frustrated. A number of skirmishes took place and one Messerschmitt 109 was claimed as damaged. Feldwebel Mössner, one of the German pilots, can describe these dying actions.

We had stayed out in the sun, perhaps two kilometres off to one side, watching the bombers with the Thunderbolts flying above them. We saw one lot of Thunderbolts turn back and thought they had all gone. We started to come round to the front of the bombers to make an attack but were only halfway round when I heard someone call out, '*Achtung! Indianer.*' Then they were on us. A second lot had arrived. I was completely surprised to see them so deep in Belgium.

Then we had a real mix-up with the Americans – a real circus, all going round in circles trying to get on each other's tails. Those American fighters certainly saved their friends in the bombers from the attack of most of our unit and the first attack that we made was always the best one.

I lost my Number One at once. You must remember we were preparing an attack on bombers and were certainly not ready

> for a fighter battle. I got one of the Americans in my sights and let off two or three short bursts but I'm certain I scored no hits. I wasn't in a good enough position. The end came for me when suddenly the American fighters seemed to have disappeared. I look around for my comrades but couldn't see any of them either. The sky was completely empty except for those American bombers which I could just see in the distance. They were well on their way.
>
> I was completely disoriented; I had no idea where I was. I flew for some time over a large area of forest and then saw a lake – small but completely round. From my geography lessons at school, I realized that I was somewhere over the Eifel. I pulled the map out of the top of my flying boot, looked at the Eifel area and found that lake – it was the Marialaach. I was pleased that I had listened carefully at school – my fuel lamp was on red. At that very moment I met a Messerschmitt 110. I hadn't got the right wavelength to talk to him so I fell in beside him – only ten or fifteen metres away – opened my mouth and pointed my finger down my throat. That was our normal sign for 'I'm thirsty' – short of fuel. The pilot nodded, banked away at once and a few moments later I was safely down at Bonn/Hangelar.

The P-47s also had to give up and return to England. The B-17s would be on their own for the rest of their flight. One of the departing P-47 pilots says, 'Jesus Christ, it just made you sick, absolutely sick, to have to leave them but we just had to go.'

The bomber force was now over Eupen. This was only a small Belgian town, less than ten miles from the German border, but it is one of the significant and well-remembered names of the day because everyone knew that Eupen was where the fighter escorts left. The bomber force had now come 125 miles from the first landfall but had 300 lonely miles to fly before Regensburg was reached. This would require seventy minutes of flying time. The Americans had been a little unlucky to lose five planes so early and in their own fighter escort area, particularly the three Flak victims in an area not notorious for the intensity of its Flak defences. The combined efforts of the three German fighter units which had been so far sent into action had resulted in only two B-17s being knocked out of their formations, although they had done some useful mopping up of crippled B-17s. The American escorts had done as well as their numbers had allowed. The Germans had lost three fighters and at least five more had been damaged and would not be able to take part in operations later in the day.

The action which has taken place between the coast and Eupen has been described in great detail because the various encounters represent a very good cross-section both of the personal experiences of the men of both sides and of the tactical conditions under which air battles were fought at that time – at least in the fighter-escorted area. It must be stressed that the events described in this chapter form only a small fraction of the action which took place on 17 August 1943.

CHAPTER 8

On Their Own

The quiet conditions which had lasted from Maastricht to Eupen continued to hold after the American fighters left. A few minutes after flying over Eupen the German frontier was crossed. The next stage of the route was over the Eifel region with its extensive woods, numerous lakes and small towns and villages. There would be little to fear from Flak in this area. The weather continued to be clear and fine; the official report of the mission says that visibility to the ground was now twenty miles and increasing. There was no unexpected change in the wind and the lead navigators could easily assess their ground speed and drift and obtain a constant succession of reliable checkpoints on the ground.

The bomber crews were able to settle down after the initial burst of activity. Fresh ammunition supplies were brought to gun positions which had been in recent action. The keenest watch was being kept for further German fighters. The pilots were working hard to keep in the tightest possible formation. This called for unceasing concentration and was extremely tiring. A pilot had to use both hands – the right one on the throttles and the left on the control column – and both feet on the rudder pedals for many hours. Every formation was made up of a number of 'elements' – flights of three aircraft flying in a shallow V. The two wingmen flew slightly above or below their element leader, depending on how their part of the formation was 'stacked', trying to keep their wing-tip level with the leader's waist-gun position and as close in as possible. Element leaders had to keep station on squadron leaders, squadron leaders on group leaders, group leaders on combat wing leaders. The two thirds of the pilots who were flying in wing positions were completely dependent upon the skill of the various leaders from element up to combat wing level. Clumsy flying by leaders in the constant see-sawing of position which took place led at best to undue fatigue for the wing pilots and at worst to the danger of collision or of shaking out part of a formation into loose 'Luftwaffe bait'. The actual technique of formation flying was always one of sliding the heavy bombers around, not of banking or 'winging up', which was too dangerous because of the proximity of neighbouring planes. This sliding around required frequent throttle changes which led, in turn, to another danger, especially for the higher-flying groups – excessive fuel consumption.

This chore of formation-keeping was not unique to this flight to Regensburg but, with the fighter escort departed and several hours of flying over German defended airspace to come, there is no doubt that the pilots were working with particular concentration as that wooded frontier country of Germany was being crossed. It is not surprising that when one pilot was asked what he saw at a certain stage of the action his reply was, 'Nothing. There was no way that I could fly formation and stargaze at the same time – very unhealthy.'

The lack of German fighter attention at this stage was a further indication that the Luftwaffe had not been prepared for a deep penetration by the American force and that the undeviating route of the B-17s was still outstripping the German reaction. A few Messerschmitt 109s of III/JG 26, which had flown down from Schiphol in the north and had been in contact since the coast was crossed, were still hanging on, but not as a cohesive unit, and they were making no serious attacks. Also from the north had come the Focke-Wulf 190s of I/JG 1, the senior unit in the Luftwaffe's fighter arm, but they had either been sent up from Deelen too late or had been misdirected during their flight and they had been forced into a long stern chase and would not be able to get into a good attacking position before having to leave with fuel shortage. This unit was then forced to land at numerous airfields and three of its planes were damaged in landing accidents, mostly brought on by fuel shortage – a common cause of attrition to the Luftwaffe units. The last remaining single-engined fighter unit from the coastal belt which had any chance of catching the B-17s was I/JG 3, from Mönchen-Gladbach only forty miles to the north of the American route. These Messerschmitt 109s were just arriving on the scene with plenty of fuel in their tanks.

A few twin-engined Messerschmitt 110 night fighters were also in the vicinity. These were from II/NJG 1, whose base was at St Trond in Belgium. All German night-fighter crews received a basic day-fighter training but only in the old rear-attack method.

The Germans did not risk their most experienced night-fighter crews in these day operations; at St Trond only those with less than fifteen night successes were sent into action. Their orders were not to get involved with any Allied fighter escort or to attack the main B-17 formations, but only to search for and finish off damaged B-17s which were straggling or were attempting to get back to England alone. Ten Messerschmitt 110s had taken off from St Trond and were now searching for crippled bombers. Most of the night-fighter crews did not like this type of work; the day skies often produced unpleasant surprises. One of the Messerschmitt 110 pilots says, 'Looking back on it, one can only call the orders crazy because an Me 110, when fully equipped as a night fighter, was absolutely unfit for use in daytime action. It was far too heavy, too slow and too sluggish. I was an absolute novice at this kind of work.' This pilot, Feldwebel Otto Fries, caught up with the B-17 force and, without any orders to do so, appointed himself as *Fühlungshalter* – contact keeper. He levelled out abreast of the leading group, out of range of the American machine guns, and settled down to report the height and course of the B-17 force.

Fifty miles in from the German frontier, the head of the bomber force reached and crossed the winding River Moselle. No B-17s had been shot down or even seriously attacked during the flight from Eupen. One German fighter had been shot down. This was a Messerschmitt 109 of III/J G 26 whose pilot had rashly ventured a stern attack on the leading combat wing; gunners of the 96th Bomb Group claimed its destruction. This was probably the fighter seen by Major Preston Piper, leading the 385th Bomb Group.

> The entire plane was chequered black and white and I watched it cartwheeling from above and falling right in front of us. It was the first time I'd seen a plane cartwheeling like that. We felt it might fall into our formation but it wasn't as close as I thought and it missed us easily.

The German pilot here was probably Oberleutnant Dippel, a *Staffelkapitän* known to his friends as 'Jack-Johnnie' Dippel because he was the life and soul of many sociable evenings. Dippel parachuted safely.

Oberleutnant Dippel's attack was the last effort by his unit, III/J G 26, which had now lost four planes. The remainder of the *Gruppe* landed at several airfields. The Americans were now nearly halfway to Regensburg from the coast, had not lost a bomber since passing Maastricht nearly ninety miles back and were through or nearly through the coastal 'fighter belt' their commanders talked so much about. There was a definite air of optimism among the American airmen that perhaps the worst was over and that they might yet reach their target without serious loss.

But this belief was not well founded. The progress of this unprecedented American flight into Southern Germany was now being watched by many other Luftwaffe headquarters beyond the local one in Holland which had directed the early reaction. In theory, the American bombers were about to enter the area in which the *Jafü Süddeutschland*, believed to be located in the Munich area, would direct the German defence. In practice, however, there was probably no comprehensive plan; any Luftwaffe unit with any sort of combat capability had been alerted to send up what planes it could to engage this relentlessly oncoming force of American bombers. The Americans had passed the point at which they were likely to turn and strike at a target in the Ruhr and the sirens were now sounding in such cities as Frankfurt, Mannheim and Stuttgart. Surely that would be as far as the Americans would dare go without fighter escort?

The Luftwaffe's strength in this area had been a mystery to the American commanders. When planning this operation, they had always hoped that the Germans would be able to put up no more than a token defence here. After all, it made no sense that the Luftwaffe, hard pressed from Russia, round the Mediterranean and all along the coast in the West, should retain any properly formed combat units so deep in Germany when no serious Allied day-bomber action had ever ventured this far. If the Americans had come this way *just two weeks earlier*, a token defence is all they would have found. The only regular combat unit they would have met would have been one night-fighter *Gruppe*, I/NJG 6, equipped with Messerschmitt 110s and based at Finthen, near Mainz, just to the north of the American route. There were also a number of training units for both single-engined and twin-engined fighters which had been peacefully operating from airfields in this quiet part of Germany for many months. The instructors of these units were supposed to be able to take part in combat action if required. There were other units in this area such as those back from various fighting fronts which were now refitting with new aircraft and the 'skeletons' of almost disbanded units waiting for the production of new types of aircraft. Two weeks earlier the Germans would have been hard pressed to scrape up two dozen planes from these sources to contest the 250 miles from the River Moselle to Regensburg. Though some of the pilots of these planes were skilled and experienced men, they were not formed into the well-drilled operational units required to penetrate the concentrated firepower of the B-17 formations.

Unfortunately for the Americans a new unit had recently become established in this area. This was *Jagdgruppe* 50, an independent *Gruppe* not forming part of any *Geschwader*, and was one of two such units which had just been formed on the direct order of Goering who was becoming annoyed at the Luftwaffe's inability to catch the R.A.F.'s fast, high-flying Mosquito photo-reconnaissance planes which flew regularly over Germany. Hitler had probably expressed his displeasure about the Mosquitoes to Goering. The two new units were both equipped with Messerschmitt 109s fitted with liquid oxygen tanks for special injection into the engine above 25,000 feet, and with partial cockpit pressurization. Two successful commanders – Major Herbert Ihlefeld and Major Hermann Graf – had been brought back from the Russian Front to form these units. A small nucleus of experienced pilots had also been posted to each unit, which was then made up with men who had just graduated from pilot training schools. In this way, *Jagdgruppe* 25, under Major Ihlefeld, had been formed at an airfield near Berlin to cover the whole of Northern Germany against the R.A.F. Mosquitoes, and *Jagdgruppe* 50, under Major Graf, was at Erbenheim airfield near Wiesbaden to cover Central and Southern Germany. Graf was the most-decorated Luftwaffe fighter ace still serving with an operational unit. Both units had the secondary role of home defence against B-17 attack and had carried out some practice for this. (These two units were also designated *Jagdgruppe Nord* and *Jagdgruppe Süd* but these titles were rarely used.)

Jagdgruppe 50's airfield was no more than twenty miles from the route to Regensburg. It had flown its first operation on 12 August, when the Eighth Air Force had raided targets in the Ruhr area and the unit's pilots had claimed four B-17s shot down near Bonn. Allied intelligence kept a regular watch on the movements of all known Luftwaffe units and the formation of new ones, and at the end of each month issued a very detailed Luftwaffe order of battle covering the whole of Europe from Russia to the Bay of Biscay. The estimate issued at the end of July 1943 had not picked up the presence of this new unit. *Jagdgruppe* 50 was not to have a long history. The Mosquitoes still flew too fast and too high to catch and the unit was disbanded a few weeks later, but the casualties suffered by the Americans on 17 August 1943 would have been significantly lower had it not been for its untimely presence on that day.

Whoever was directing the German defence in this area made a very simple plan. *Jagdgruppe* 50 was ordered to send off its full available strength of twenty-six Messerschmitt 109s. The pilots had to do little more than circle to gain height above Wiesbaden and catch the American bombers as they came past. All other single-engined units in this area were told to send whatever experienced pilots they had to assemble at Erbenheim airfield, where they would be formed into a makeshift force and take off with *Jagdgruppe* 50. Leutnant Hans Harms, an instructor from the training unit JG 106 at Lachen-Speyerdorf airfield, was one of these pilots. He had arrived at Erbenheim with his Messerschmitt 109.

> We were all mixed up, all sort of planes. Another pilot came and grabbed me and told me I was flying as his Number Four. I told him I was only an instructor and I should get back to my own airfield but he told me to do as I was told. He was a 190 man and he had his own wingman. I was to be the wingman for another 109 man; the pilot was a *Gefreiter* – a corporal. The chap in charge told me to take off at once to catch the bombers. I didn't even know his name, only that his aircraft had a white tail-fin so he was some sort of leader. We exchanged first names; I forgot what his was.
>
> The four of us took off but we lost the two Focke-Wulfs after about ten minutes. We two remaining chaps went up to 6,000 metres and started looking for vapour trails. The radio was useless; our earphones were so cluttered with so many excited voices that you couldn't catch anything. I kept in touch with my Number One by hand signals.

The second part of the plan was that all available twin-engined fighters were to operate behind the incoming B-17s with a view to finishing off stragglers, but also to act as an offensive force when the B-17s, hopefully in a more weakened condition, returned to England from whichever target they were flying to attack. Approximately twenty more twin-engined night fighters of various kinds thus took off from Mainz, home of I/NJG 6, and from

Echterdingen, near Stuttgart, home of part of the night-fighter training unit NJG 101. Some planes in this twin-engined force were to see action against crippled B-17s, but most would wait in vain for the main force of American bombers to return to England.

Many of the American airmen had a perfect view of this fresh force of German fighters rising to meet them.

> I didn't feel that the break in the action would be permanent. I was sure we would have to fight our way all the way through. Of course, I was also convinced that our crew would never be shot down; we would make it. Then the gunners reported fighters climbing. I looked down to the right-hand side and saw quite a large group of them spiralling up. I realized that the next phase of the battle was about to begin. The next time I looked out of the window, the fighters were at three o'clock about two miles out, stacked up in what seemed like layer upon layer in echelon. The figure I remember was thirty-one; someone was counting them and reported it. I've always remembered that odd number. (Second Lieutenant Oscar E. Hille, 390th Bomb Group)

Leutnant Alfred Grislawski was one of the *Jagdgruppe* 50 pilots coming up from Wiesbaden.

> We climbed and made perfect contact with the Boeings. It was my first view of an American formation. There were so many of them that we were all shaken to the marrow, both our small group of old chaps from Russia and the young new pilots – the young ones a bit more than us I think. We started making frontal attacks on the right-hand-side formation; we went in in fours. I noticed that some of our new pilots broke off too soon and we never saw them again. They hadn't the heart for the tracer we had to fly through.

One German pilot says that a B-17 formation, when viewed from above, 'always looked hot – smoking with all those guns firing' and Feldwebel Fries, the Messerschmitt 110 pilot who was still watching from the side as contact keeper, says, 'You couldn't possibly imagine what sort of fireworks a tight enemy formation produced; it was almost impossible to get at it. They really were massive lumps and it took a lot to set one of them alight.'

The battle commenced. These are a selection of the American memories of it.

Second Lieutenant Gus Mencow, navigator, 390th Bomb Group:

> Some of the Me 109s came so close that I could see the expression on the pilot's face and the flaming blaze of his guns. I still shudder when I recall the big black crosses on the wings. The only consolation I remember having at the time was that the German pilots were just as much in awe of us as we were of them. I couldn't help thinking that they were as crazy as we, to fly into a formation that had about two hundred 50-caliber guns pointed at them!

Lieutenant John Brady, pilot, 100th Bomb Group:

> They kept coming in, a steady stream of them at 12 o'clock level. When they got to their break-off point they dipped down and under. A couple of the hot-dogs actually rolled as they passed under us. It was kind of like watching kids at the swimming pool, queuing up to use the diving board, then diving under us, getting out of the pool and running back along the side of it to use the diving board again – and the diving board was pointed straight at us all the time. It just seemed to keep going on for what seemed to be an eternity. That was one of the days I wished I'd been a gunner with something in my hand instead of just sitting there, driving, going straight ahead into those fighters.

Captain Everett Blakely, lead pilot, 100th Bomb Group:

> There was no question but that we realized the group was taking a beating. I could see the low squadron myself out of the left-hand window and the gunners kept reporting other aircraft going down. You could only hope that the fellows got out allright and hope also that the Germans would use up their gas and leave us but, otherwise, there was nothing we could do about it. You only sit there and do your job properly and hope that the other fellows, the rest of the crew etc., did theirs. Jack Kidd, the group leader in the right-hand seat, was the coolest man in the group. He was calling out the fighters coming in quite calmly but, otherwise, there was not a damn thing he could do about it either.

Second Lieutenant Richard H. Perry, co-pilot, 390th Bomb Group:

An armor-piercing bullet smaller than a 50-caliber hit our waist gunner in the head. He bled quite a bit. When the action slowed up, I went back to the waist. Baumgartner died in my arms. This was my first real test of war. I knew then that we were not on a training mission.

Lieutenant Robert Morrill, pilot, 94th Bomb Group:

Time after time, my entire ship shook as every gun fired. The air was filled as the formation fired thousands upon thousands of 50-calibers, the tracers leaving crossed patterns with the apex as a fighter. The fire would momentarily cease and then converge on another fighter. The guns seemed never to stop, except to reload. I glanced behind me and found the top turret gunner standing in a heap of shell cases that covered the entire floor six inches deep and flowed over into the companionway that leads into the nose.

In the cockpit, my hands were glued to the wheel and throttles. I don't believe I could have let go if I had tried. In spite of the cold, sweat was running from my hair under the helmet and down across my oxygen mask, falling onto my jacket and freezing there.

Staff Sergeant William Adamson, tail gunner, 390th Bomb Group:

Then I got hit. It was a head-on by 109s and I never saw what happened. They told me afterwards that they were coming through the formation, strafing the left-hand side of our aircraft. One 20-millimetre hit the turbo supercharger stack which caught fire and burned all the way to North Africa but we were lucky because it never did any harm except that we lost nearly all the power in that engine. The second shell hit the armor plate right below the left waist window and the explosion blew Ferris back but he wasn't hurt. The third shell hit the tail fin above and behind me. The splinters hit me in the head and the sighting glass in front of me was shot out – from the inside. The cover of my right ammunition box was holed. There was a lot of blood but no pain so I stayed where I was.

Staff Sergeant Jack Leahy, waist gunner, 385th Bomb Group:

Just before the attacks, the pilot had said that there was an empty slot further up in the group and that he was going to go round and fill it in. I don't know whether we were supposed to do that sort of thing but John Pettinger was an awfully good pilot, very aggressive. We loved him but I thought it was dumb to move in that way. When we got out to the widest part of the overtaking turn, we got attacked by several fighters. We were at least 500 yards out to the right, just a little bit out from the full group protection. We got hit by a burst of bullets and one hit the propeller and, somehow, we got slowed down. We'd have fallen back if we'd turned to go back in then, so we had to stay out there. We kept that position all the way to the target and we really were in the middle of all the action from then onwards although the fighters didn't concentrate on us.

Right in the middle of all this, I realized we had heard nothing from the ball gunner. I looked at the other waist gunner – we had pretty good rapport – and we both realized something was wrong. We both moved as fast as we could to the ball turret, hand-cranked it up so that the exit was inside the plane and opened it up but, as we did so, a couple of pints of blood hit the roof of the ship. We knew he was dead; we found a big hole in his head later. He had been a real nice kid.

I wanted to get into the turret – it was a critical position covering nine tenths of the bottom of the ship and it had two guns. We pulled him part way out but could see the bottom of the turret was covered with blood and we could never have used it so we left him there. We found out later that it was a 50-caliber from one of the planes in our group that had killed him.

A possible reason why the Germans did not concentrate on this isolated B-17 was that they may have suspected that it was a YB-40 'gun-ship'.

Staff Sergeant Earl R. Spann, radio operator, 390th Bomb Group:

The trip into Germany was a bloody battle all the way. It was mostly fighter planes but also heavy Flak at times. One plane of our own squadron to my left, as I looked back, caught a frontal attack from a fighter and immediately the wings were a mass of flames. They dropped out of formation and went down. We thought none of them got out but we learned later that they baled out and all were safe but were taken prisoners of war.

From our position, I could see behind us and there were

planes falling everywhere, a lot of ours and a lot of theirs. Many trails of smoke could be seen coming up from the ground from crashed planes. A lot of brave men had died; a lot more were destined for prison camps. This was a sight that will never leave me. I remember thinking to myself, 'Mother and Daddy and Myrtle – my fiancée – I guess I won't be coming home after all.'

Sergeant Jim Kahler, radio operator, 390th Bomb Group:

I could see another aircraft of our group off to my left, no more than 150 feet or so away. Its inboard engine, Number 2, and the wing inside the engine were burning fiercely, flames on the top and bottom of the wing, black smoke behind the flame. It was losing a little on us but not much. It was an awesome, majestic sight. I counted four or five out – the bodies zipping away out of sight – then the plane skidded off out of my range of vision.

Captain Richard S. Septime, pilot, 385th Bomb Group:

One thing that stuck in my mind was seeing a B-17 spin in. When it hit the ground, it looked like a handful of silver dust would if it were thrown on the ground. Apparently the plane exploded into thousands of pieces.

This series of German attacks was being pressed home with great determination; there was little comparison with the conditions under which the earlier attacks on the B-17s had been made. The balance of advantage had changed. The Germans knew that there was no chance of Allied fighters intervening. This had the effect of doubling the German offensive strength. The wingmen no longer had to guard the tails of their Number Ones but were free to attack the American bombers. On the American side, the cohesion and firepower of some of the B-17 groups were being steadily weakened, with aircraft being shot down, crew members in other aircraft becoming casualties, guns becoming useless through damage or malfunction under the intense use to which they were being put. Ammunition was being consumed at an alarming rate. There was another factor. The B-17s were now over Germany and the German pilots knew that one of their cities was shortly going to be bombed. The next set of quotations are from men who were in some of the B-17s being shot down in this furious battle. They show a good deal of steadfast devotion to duty, but there was also some understandable human frailty and a few of the survivors would live the rest of their lives bearing bitterness or embarrassment at what they saw as failings in fellow crew members or at their own lapses under that terrible pressure of danger. Those who have not looked death in the face should never condemn the occasional flash of panic in such cases.

Staff Sergeant Albert Van Pelt, waist gunner in Second Lieutenant Tyson's crew, 390th Bomb Group, starts his quotation with a constantly recurring phrase.

> They came at us from twelve o'clock high, out of the sun, and came barrel-rolling through the formation. There was an explosion near where I was and it knocked me over backwards. A 20-millimetre had come through the roof and exploded in the floor of the plane. I had several pieces of metal in me and was looking for a spare oxygen bottle. The explosion had ripped my oxygen tube and there was an oxygen fire shooting out of the broken tube that had been connected to me. Through a hole in the floor, I could see flames coming back from something burning further forward. I don't remember feeling any panic. Things happened too fast.
>
> We helped to get the ball-turret gunner up – that was one of the waist gunner's jobs – and helped him into his parachute. He told us there was nothing but a mass of flame underneath the plane. The other waist gunner was still hooked up on intercom but nothing was coming through. Then the radio man came back and said his room was full of flames. Still no word from the front but there was no doubt and no time for delay. I opened the waist door; Whaples patted me on the back and said 'Lets go.' I think I was out first – at least, out of the back.

Second Lieutenant Mike Doroski was the co-pilot in Second Lieutenant Hummel's crew, 100th Bomb Group.

> It was definitely a new unit of 109s which got us. They had gone out to the front and carried out a classic frontal attack, level, and they started at the bottom. We were tail-end Charlie in the low squadron, the lowest element in the group.
>
> I had been trained as a fighter pilot and I watched them coming in. I knew they were aiming at us. I watched them carefully and knew at what stage I would have opened fire if I had been that fighter pilot. I shouted out to Tom Hummel to pull up at that moment to spoil the German's aim – to give him

a more difficult angle. I feel very strongly that we would never have been shot down on that first pass if we had done that but Hummel didn't respond; he just froze and it was too late. The nose and wings of the German fighter aiming at us were lit up like Christmas trees twinkling with light. At that split second we were hit. The Number 2 prop dome was hit and the feathering mechanism damaged. The blades were no longer under control. We fell right back.

The second attack was left frontal and it hit the Tokyo tank in the left wing tip; it caught fire and the bale-out order was given. There were further attacks before we could go and one cannon shell entered the right-hand side of the cockpit just below the window. I was leaning forward, trying to feather the engine that had been hit, and I think that shell just missed me. It had passed through my back-pack parachute.

I tried to alert the top turret gunner to bale out. He was slumped forward; I thought he was leaning forward to detach his oxygen bottle and would follow me, but now I think that the shell which just missed me had hit him. Later, I found the left leg of my flight suit was covered in his blood.

The cannon shell which had passed through Doroski's parachute pack had so damaged it that he came down too fast and received crippling injuries to his hip and spine.

Staff Sergeant Gordon Williams was the ball-turret gunner in the same crew.

We were hit in the nose early and I heard the bombardier saying to the navigator, 'I can't get the guts in.' I thought he'd been shot in the stomach and I thought, 'Aw jeez; that's one less person on the guns.' But he was the first person I met when I landed by parachute later and I found out that it had been his gun that had been in trouble.

I thought we were doing real well after that but they had been hitting us a lot more than I realized. I looked around and saw one of the elevators was full of holes and they told me the waist area was pretty badly shot up too. I was nearly out of ammunition by then. I could see that one of my guns only had twenty rounds or so and the other gun only had a few more. I was figuring on going back and fetching some more but then we were hit hard again.

Things happened fast after that. The engine which had been hit was the big thing; a good big sheet of flame started coming back past me. I was so close that I felt it was heating up my turret but that might have been imagination. Then the pilot peeled out of formation in case we blew up and took the others with us. Then the oxygen started burning and we got the bale-out order.

Three of us in the waist – myself, the left waist gunner and the radio man – were preparing to bale out when the oxygen exploded and blew us out but the other waist gunner was still at his gun – he was that kind of guy. We used to go out drinking a little and, when he'd had a few drinks and his inhibitions were lowered, he used to say that the rest of us would make it but he wasn't going to. He had been a good friend.

Lieutenant Dan McKay was the bombardier in Lieutenant Biddick's crew, 100th Bomb Group.

I never saw the one which got us; I was shooting at another German fighter. I heard a quick series of muffled explosions behind me. I didn't think it was serious at that time although I knew what it was; we had been hit by cannon fire before. Then, when the plane I had been firing at had passed over, I looked back and the navigator was gone – that was the first startling thing I noticed. The oxygen tanks which are located aft of the navigator's seat – six feet behind it – were all on fire and I thought that he was dead in the fire but I found out later he had baled out.

The fire was a spewing-out type of blowtorch effect. There must have been several holes in the bottles and I also assume there must have been some pressure left in those big bottles. I couldn't see beyond it – there was just this solid fire. It was actually coming forward right over the escape hatch and it was getting so hot that I could feel the skin on my face cracking. I was backing up into the nose as far away from it as possible but it was still too hot and painful. I just had to get away from there. The escape hatch was closed; the slipstream must have closed it up again after the navigator had gone. I think the plane climbed and stalled; it was certainly out of control. That's when I decided I had to get through that fire to the hatch; it was more out of desperation than anything else. I was going to get burned either way. I dived as low as I could and as fast as I could through this fire and grabbed the handle and I had to kick upwards to the roof of the nose compartment to produce enough force to get it open and get out.

My face was so burnt by then that my eyes were beginning to close and I was only semi-conscious but I do remember being able to pull the metal ring of the ripcord and, when I looked at my hand, the fingers had been so badly burned that the effort of pulling the ring had pulled every nail up so that they were all sticking up, just hanging on.

Second Lieutenant Oscar Hille was the co-pilot in Second Lieutenant Regan's crew, 390th Bomb Group:

Suddenly, the plane seemed to stop in mid-air. It was a real jolt. I knew we were badly hit. There was a lot of confusion for a brief period – a lot of that was because we lost our intercom and our oxygen. Number 1 and Number 4 engines were both hit. We feathered Number 1 but carried on using the other for some time, despite the smoke and oil coming out of it.

We kept dropping back from one group to another, not as part of a plan, it just happened that the groups came by us. Jim Regan decided to get rid of the bombs. We opened the bomb doors and were ready to salvo them when the bombardier told us to hold it; he'd got a target in sight. He did a proper bomb run – the dope! There were Jim and I flying for our lives and there he was giving us these precise instructions. There was a little profanity. Suddenly he said, 'Bombs away,' and the plane lightened. He had bombed a small town and seen the hits right in the middle of it.

The navigator gave us a heading for Switzerland but, almost immediately, we were attacked by Messerschmitts and then we were fighting again. The pilot and I were having some difficulty. We were flying the ship and having a lot of trouble. I had been taught that, if you were being attacked from the front, you turned into them and closed the distance. The pilot was trying to do something else; he was trying to bank away from them and keep on the heading for Switzerland. I was hit while all this was happening. It was a machine-gun bullet – only a flesh wound but it hurt. It came in my rear end and came out in my leg; it tore the nerves. There was a searing pain but only for a few minutes and then the leg was dead. I couldn't move it. I fainted – possibly because of lack of oxygen or of the loss of the blood plus the traumatic shock of all that had been happening. I don't know if you were supposed to faint but I did. I know it was very disconcerting to the pilot; now, with me wounded, he had new problems.

The bomb load from this plane fell on the small village of Breder and a report duly found its way from there to Berlin: 'Some damage to property and crops, ten people wounded'.* Sergeant Jim Kahler was the radio man in the same crew and describes the next round of attacks on this B-17.

> We were taking hits; you could feel the impact of the shells on the aircraft. They kept coming in from my left rear by this time and I kept shooting away. I do remember that I kept my stomach tensed – I know it sounds silly but I felt that I was going to get hit and was braced ready for it. Then this fighter came in, shooting like mad, and hit our horizontal stabilizer; it left a hole around two feet across. I could feel the whole aircraft slide across to my right when the explosion occurred.
>
> The tail gunner had been right next to the stabilizer and, by the time the aircraft had stopped sliding across, he was up in the radio room with me – clear back from the tail turret. I think he wanted to express his displeasure to me about the danger of his position. He was very upset – scared to hell. He sat down in a corner of the radio room but he only stayed a few seconds. I was still shooting and the hot cartridges from my gun were pouring down into that corner where he was and a couple of them hit him on the face and hands, burning him a little. Our guns were quite hot by then and the cartridges also. There was all kinds of noise going on but we could yell to each other and he shouted out, 'Christ, it's worse up here than back there.' So he went back to the tail.
>
> Somewhere about that time we lost another engine.

Kahler's description ties in nicely with the experience of a German contributor. Leutnant Hans Harms was the pilot from the training unit who had been hastily sent up in a hurriedly formed section of fighters.

> After about forty-five minutes of looking for vapour trails, I found myself flying over my own airfield. I was getting low on fuel so I signalled to the Number One that I was going down to land. Then, at about 3,000 metres, I saw a B-17 flying on three engines. It was the first one I had ever attacked.
>
> I carried out a normal diving approach from above and the rear, with the centre of the gun-sight aimed just in front of him so that he would have to fly through my fire. But I was too fast

* Bundesarchiv, Freiburg, RL 411/26.

– or rather the bomber was too slow – and I think I missed. I dived down steep behind to get out of the way of the tail gunner, pulled up again and tried once more but this time from a much shallower dive and I didn't fire until I was exactly the same altitude as the bomber. He was about 1,000 metres high by then.

I think that I hit the tail gunner because his guns suddenly tilted upwards as though his body had fallen forward. I was hit at the same time and I got oil and glycol all over my flying suit and the cockpit filled with fumes. I couldn't see outside because the front of the cockpit was covered with oil. I released the canopy and baled out.

Sufficient information is available to enable a more precise résumé of the loss of B-17s during this action to be presented. Nine B-17s were lost during this period, seven shot down directly out of or in the immediate vicinity of their formations and two more finished off while attempting to reach safety after being badly damaged. A tenth B-17 was forced to jettison its bomb load but was able to stay with its group for the time being.

These American casualties were caused entirely by German fighters. The Messerschmitt 109 unit, I/JG 3 from Mönchen-Gladbach, the last of the coastal belt units to remain in contact, probably gained two of the successes before being forced to break off with fuel shortage. The new unit, *Jagdgruppe* 50 from Wiesbaden, and the *ad hoc* elements scraped up from training units in this area had done the rest of the damage, although one of the B-17s which had left its formation was finished off by twin-engined fighters. The Germans had paid only lightly for their success. Confirmed German losses show two Messerschmitt 109s destroyed and two more damaged, and only one German pilot was injured. It should be stressed, however, that the German records are not complete and their losses might have been slightly higher.

One part of the recent German effort had concentrated on the high group of the leading American combat wing; the 390th Bomb Group, on only its third operation, had lost two bombers shot down, but these were the only losses in the first combat wing. The second wing had been even more fortunate, losing only one plane from the 385th Bomb Group where Second Lieutenant Leslie Reichardt had saved his entire crew by promptly lowering his wheels as a sign of surrender when the left wing of his plane burst into flames. German fighters had circled without firing as Reichardt and all his crew left safely. Most of the German attention had been concentrated on the third wing but, surprisingly, not on the 95th Bomb Group which was already so weakened by abortives and earlier casualties. The 95th had only lost one more plane. This was flown by the crew of Lieutenant Robert Mason, who had so painstakingly and gallantly regained his place in the formation after being forced to dive steeply to put out a fire caused by Flak damage over Belgium. The heaviest casualties were in the low group of this wing, the 100th Bomb Group, which was starting to incur its 'Bloody Hundredth' reputation. It is not known why the Germans should have concentrated so fiercely on this group; only one of its planes had been lost in the early part of the flight. The group's position at the tail of the bomber force may have been the critical factor but this position was not always vulnerable; the group which would fly the corresponding position in the Schweinfurt force later in the day would not suffer a single casualty. Perhaps the 100th's critics were correct and its pilots were flying a looser formation than other groups; German pilots insist that they always searched out the loosest formation to attack. Perhaps, however, it was just bad luck. Whatever the reason, the Germans had really hammered this group. Six more of its planes had been shot down and several others severely damaged.

Every bomber crew shot down in this raid had its own personal story to tell, and some of those from the nine B-17s lost in this recent action illustrate the contrasts in fortune and in human behaviour in those doomed bombers.

The crews in one group formation watched one of its planes – one wing and the fuselage blazing – being held steady while its entire crew baled out safely. This was reported on return to England and the pilot was awarded the Silver Star. But the actual behaviour of this pilot and the award to him of the Silver Star were later to be the cause of much bitterness among the men of the crew. The pilot's own brother was flying in the crew, not as a fellow officer but as the top turret gunner. It was most unusual to have two brothers in a crew and more so that one should be an officer and one an enlisted man. Another member of the crew describes what went wrong.

Having brothers aboard had worked fine until the moment

we were shot down but I found out later that, as soon as we were hit, the pilot had panicked, turned round to grab his brother and said, 'Let's get out!' They were the first two men to parachute from the front of the plane. None of us would speak to the top turret gunner in prison camp – he lived a real lonely life there – and I heard that the pilot got the same treatment in the officers' camp.

It was bad to have two brothers in the crew; that one thing that happened under pressure spoiled it all. The co-pilot was the one who held on at the controls and should have received the credit.

In the formation of the 100th Bomb Group, Second Lieutenant Owen Roane watched the plane of his room-mate, Second Lieutenant Henry Shotland, go down in flames. Roane wondered what would happen to the £300 which Shotland had won shooting crap the previous evening; Roane had 'contributed a little, not much'. Shotland survived. But, only a few minutes later, Roane and many other men in this formation were to see a truly horrible sight. The cockpit area of Lieutenant Curtis Biddick's plane was hit by a concentrated burst of cannon shells and a fierce fire started in the oxygen supply near the cockpit. (This was the plane in which Lieutenant McKay earlier described being trapped by the fire in the nose compartment before diving through the flames to the escape hatch.) Many men watched the co-pilot, Flight Officer Richard Snyder, his escape by any other way blocked by fire, struggle through a hole which had been blown or burnt in the side of the cockpit. Owen Roane saw Snyder on the burning right wing of the B-17. 'It was a dreadful thing to see him standing in the flames but you often did see dreadful things. You don't become hardened to it though. I was sick within. I watched him reach back inside the cockpit to his parachute and clip it on.' Other men in the formation then watched Snyder jump and open his parachute all in one motion. His body immediately struck the horizontal stabilizer and the parachute then caught on it. Leutnant Alfred Grislawski, of *Jagdgruppe* 50, was the German pilot who had attacked this B-17 and he observed its fate.

The bomber fell to the left and slowly circled round, lower and lower, out of control. I could see a parachute caught on the tail with a man swinging from it. I had to bale out seven times during the war and I knew what it was like. I felt very sorry for that man. Later, I saw the bomber hit the ground and explode. It did so with the blast-waves showing in exact circles, getting larger and larger.

It is probable that Flight Officer Snyder was killed when he hit the stabilizer. His parachute must have come free at a lower level because his body was found five months later hanging in an oak tree. The body of Lieutenant Biddick, the pilot, described by a fellow pilot as 'a big quiet man with a delicious sense of humour and a lot of strength of character', was never found after the explosion of his plane.

There are particularly interesting stories to tell about the two crews – from the 100th and from the 390th Bomb Groups – which were shot down long after they had been forced to leave their formations. But because what happened to these planes is closely linked to one of the long-standing controversies of this day, their stories will need to be told in detail. Such treatment here would unduly hold up the telling of the basic Regensburg story so this subject is dealt with at the end of the book in Appendix 4.

To the men in the bomb groups which had suffered the worst of the attacks, the recent fight had seemed endless.

> I had been observing in complete fascination until it suddenly came to me that, in a few moments, I would be dead and I began to wonder how it would feel. There had seemed to be no possibility of survival, so many of the enemy all around, all seemingly intent upon our destruction. Suddenly, one of the engines was hit, the right outboard, and I moved to feather it. A feathered engine is, of course, just a goad to fighters who need no goading anyway but somehow seem more determined to finish off a cripple. To make matters worse we fell out of the formation, for we were unable to keep up due to this loss of power. All seemed lost and my eyes were drawn to the earth far below and to the remains of our group now somewhat above. How pathetic they looked with the numerous gaps in the formation, hardly like a group at all, so unlike our former majestic appearance. Decimated or not, I longed to be back up with them for protection and, now, it was merely a question of when we would be finished off.
>
> Then, amazingly, the impossible happened. The sky became quiet and almost serene and we managed to get up behind the remains of the group. (Second Lieutenant John E. Wenzel, 390th Bomb Group)

So the air battle fizzled out. The German fighters had made repeated attacks on the American formations and had rapidly expended both ammunition and fuel. The German pilots fell away and looked for somewhere to land. This time there were no more Luftwaffe units left to replace them. The Americans had finally broken through and the way to Regensburg was open. The recent action had actually lasted only thirty minutes, during which time the American force had crossed the Rivers Moselle and Rhine and threaded its way through the important group of German cities – Mainz, Wiesbaden, Frankfurt, Darmstadt, Mannheim. No doubt the people in those cities breathed mighty sighs of relief when the Americans flew on without bombing. By the time the battle ceased, the B-17s were over open, hilly country again, roughly level with the old city of Würzburg twenty miles to the north.

The head of the American force was now 105 miles – twenty-six minutes flying time – from the Messerschmitt factory at Regensburg. A few German fighters still hung on but there were no serious attacks and no American casualties. The German contact keeper, young Feldwebel Fries, had given up this task to go dashing off after various crippled B-17s he had seen and he attacked until all his ammunition was gone. He landed at Stuttgart. But there was still a Messerschmitt 110 out on a flank, tracking and reporting the progress of the American formation. Hauptmann Hans-Werner Rupprecht, who had also flown from Belgium, had been flying more carefully. He had plenty of fuel remaining and had taken over as contact keeper. The great city of Nuremberg was passed, easily visible ten miles to the north, but there were few other incidents during that final approach flight to the target and the American crews were able to settle down and make their preparations for bombing. At 11.40 a.m. the leading bomber passed over Beilngries, a town twenty-five miles due west of the Messerschmitt factory. Beilngries was the I.P. – the Initial Point – the position from which the B-17s would make their final run to the target. This insignificant town had been chosen for this purpose because four roads and three rivers meeting there made it easily identifiable, and because a run from there, with the forecast wind directly behind, would result in minimum 'drift' and, it was hoped, accurate bombing. The navigator and the bombardier in the nose of the leading B-17 had no difficulty identifying the I.P. and guiding their pilot over the centre of the town. The visibility was still perfect.

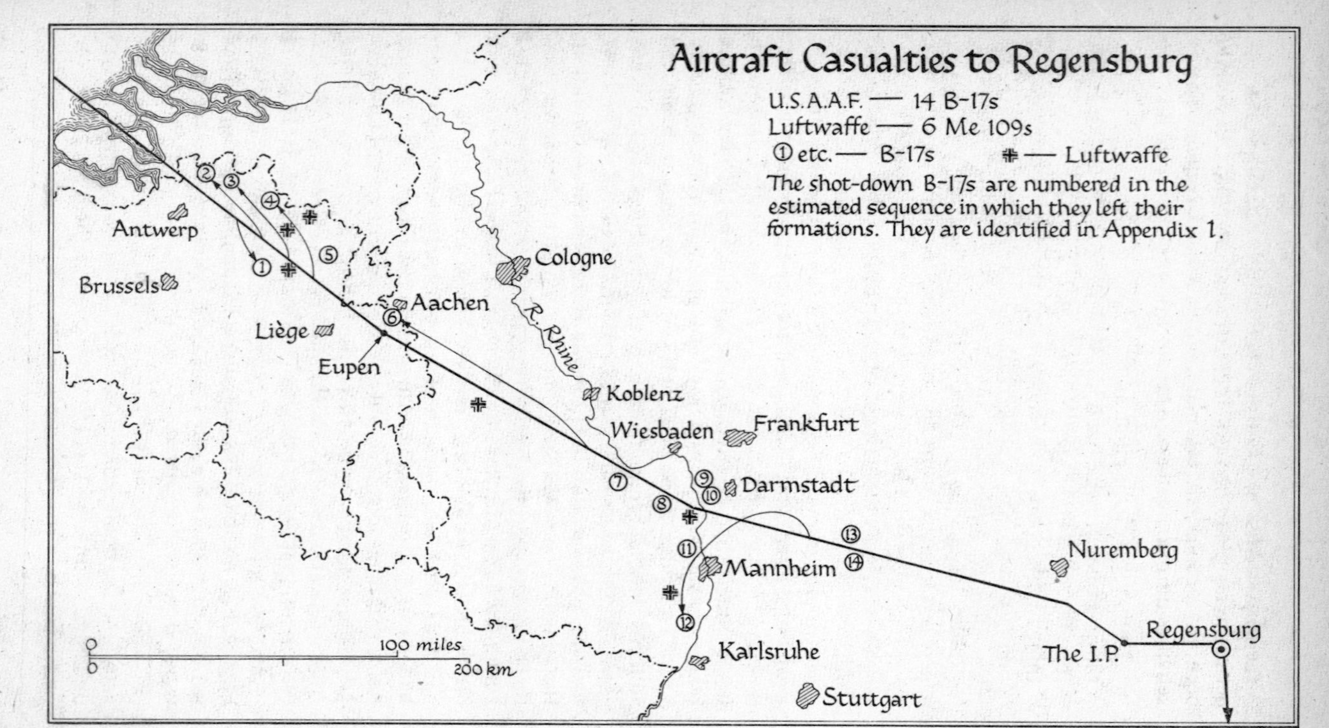
Aircraft Casualties to Regensburg
U.S.A.A.F. — 14 B-17s
Luftwaffe — 6 Me 109s
① etc. — B-17s
✠ — Luftwaffe
The shot-down B-17s are numbered in the estimated sequence in which they left their formations. They are identified in Appendix 1.
Antwerp
Brussels
Liège
Aachen
Eupen
Cologne
R. Rhine
Koblenz
Wiesbaden
Frankfurt
Darmstadt
Mannheim
Karlsruhe
Stuttgart
Nuremberg
The I.P.
Regensburg
100 miles
200 km

Lieutenant Abel, the lead navigator, had carried out his task perfectly; his plane had not been attacked and there had never been any serious navigational problems. Of Colonel LeMay's activities during the flight, Abel says:

> He stayed with the pilots most of the time. He came down into the nose once or twice but it was difficult to get down, especially for a big man like LeMay. When he did come, he enquired how things were going, but we were on the right track and the timing was correct and he made no attempt to interfere. He was a qualified navigator himself but he was completely satisfied and he even made some favourable comments on how well it was all going.

Two of the groups in the leading combat wing – the 96th and the 388th – had never been under serious attack and had so far suffered no casualties. Several men in these groups refer to the Regensburg mission as 'almost like a milk run'. But the officer observing from the tail turret of the leading plane had been sending a steady stream of reports about the action which had been taking place further back in the force and reporting those losses which he could see. LeMay was well aware that his force had suffered heavy casualties.

Of the 139 B-17s which had crossed the Dutch coast, fourteen had been shot down, two more had left their formations, released their bombs and were flying south, hoping to cut a corner and catch up later, and one of the planes still with the formation had been forced to jettison its bomb load. This left 122 planes with bomb loads available to attack the Messerschmitt factory.

The battles which had taken place during the flight of the B-17s had been intense and the American losses had been grievous, but these losses should be put into their correct perspective. The Luftwaffe had not made an all-out effort. Their response had been a conventional one and they had put up a standard defence. No one on the American side had expected that Regensburg would be reached without loss. This 10 per cent loss must be regarded as no more than the expected and acceptable cost of getting a force of bombers to this distant target when no long-range escort was available.

CHAPTER 9

Over Regensburg

Many Allied bombing raids were spoiled by last minute changes of weather in the target area, but there was to be no such problem at Regensburg. The official record says: 'Target – Clear of all cloud. Visibility 25 miles.' Nor was the bomber force scattered. Colonel LeMay had ordered the leading group to slow down to ensure that the embattled rear groups could close up. The bombardiers in the lead B-17s of each group would rarely be presented with such perfect conditions. If all went well, the seven groups of B-17s would pass over the target with only eleven minutes between the first and last planes. The shorter this bombing period, the less opportunity the Regensburg Flak defences would have to settle down to effective firing.

As they came in over the I.P., the combat wings had to shake out into 'column of groups', with the two or three groups which made up each wing forming into a 'follow-my-leader' procession. Lead groups maintained their position, low groups swung right to follow second and the only high group – the 390th – swung left to become the third group to bomb in its combat wing. All groups, however, maintained their old altitude so that they could return to their defensive formation quickly after bombing. B-17s normally bombed from 26–28,000 feet, to force the German Flak to fire at extreme range, but Regensburg was such an important target that it had been decided to give away nearly 10,000 feet of precious height advantage and to bomb from between 17,000 and 20,000 feet. The lead planes of the seven groups would actually pass over the targets at altitudes between 16,500 and 19,250 feet.

The American airmen who had struggled to reach this point were now all set for that frightening experience – the straight and level bomb run, in broad daylight, over one of Germany's important industrial targets. The lead bombardiers had already set the appropriate wind, speed and altitude calculations on the bomb-sight and were now guiding their planes directly towards the Messerschmitt factory clearly visible ahead inside a large bend in the River Danube. It should be stressed that, while one lead crew had guided the whole of the Regensburg force to the target area, the lead bombardier from each of the seven bomb groups would be entirely responsible for his group's bombing results at the target. He alone was responsible for sighting and bomb release; the remainder of his group's bombardiers would release the moment the lead plane's bombs were seen to be falling. In fact, only three other planes in each group – one wingman of the lead plane and the leaders of the high and low squadrons – carried bomb-sights, in case the leader became a casualty. There had been no such casualty on the way to Regensburg.

Captain John L. Latham, of the 96th Bomb Group, would be the first man over the target; he describes his feelings.

> As a lead bombardier I felt a great sense of responsibility because, if I missed the target, then all the planes in my formation missed. When you have flown many hours and fought hard and lost many friends from fighters and anti-aircraft fire, it is extremely difficult to condone the failure of the one person upon whom the success of the entire effort depended. This was always in the back of my mind when I was on a bomb run. At Regensburg, as elsewhere, I was always extremely tense until I knew where my bombs had hit – my adrenalin ran high – and I was always extremely tired almost immediately thereafter – but happy, although I soon resumed my general feelings of utter terror for being where I was. I did, however, enjoy dropping bombs.

The lead bombardiers took over the complete guidance of their planes approximately three minutes from the bomb release point. The pilots turned on the A.F.C.E. (automatic flight control equipment, or auto-pilot for short) which was linked to that marvellous Norden bomb-sight which the Americans had developed. For the remainder of the bomb run it would be the bombardier, making constant minute adjustments, who would bring his B-17 to that point in the sky from which his bombs would fall to strike that building in the Messerschmitt factory which had been designated as his group's aiming point. If the lead bombardiers did their work well and if their group's planes were keeping a good tight formation, the Messerschmitt factory would be destroyed section by section. It might all seem easy in theory but many things could develop to frustrate that desired result. Captain Latham commenced his final bomb run at 11.43 a.m.; the first bombs of the Regensburg raid would fall three minutes later.

An American report says, 'Anti-aircraft fire and enemy fighters, although present, did not hamper the bomb run.' This is basically true but, to the men concerned, both dangers could be very frightening. The Regensburg Flak batteries were slow in finding the range of the bombers. The lower-than-normal bombing altitude on that day actually helped the Americans; most of the German fire was too high. Staff Sergeant William Adamson, a tail gunner, was in the highest flying unit, the 390th Bomb Group.

> That bomb run seemed like it was forever and four days. We were getting some Flak – not much – but it was fairly accurate. There were black puffs, close, but not close enough for me to see the orange centre. That big tail-fin just above my head was hollow and it acted as a sounding board. Every time there was a Flak burst near by, the noise was like being inside a big drum. I heard that sound many times – that time at Regensburg was the first.

There were no direct Flak hits on B-17s but at least two planes received damage from shell fragments which would later force them to leave their formations.

The only German fighters to appear on the bomb run were a loose formation of ten to twelve Messerschmitt 109s which were seen coming in from ahead and high, but most of them did not press home their attack closely. One American pilot describes them as 'a rather inept bunch'. These German fighters came from an unusual unit. At each of their major aircraft factories, the Germans had established a small unit called an *Industrieschutzstaffel* – 'a factory protection flight' – and there was one of these at Regensburg. The commander of the unit was Oberleutnant Ladegast, who was convalescing from a wound received on the Channel coast; the remaining pilots were factory test pilots. When the American bombers had been plotted approaching this area, the necessary Messerschmitt 109s were hastily armed and fuelled, Oberleutnant Ladegast was called from his lunch, and the little unit took off. Heinz Stemmler was one of the pilots.

We took off and only just caught the bombers before they reached Regensburg. When we attacked, the leader broke away far too quickly and most of the rest followed and dived away without firing. I was left alone. I was rather curious to have a good look at the American bombers. I didn't think it was dangerous until they opened fire and then I pulled away a bit, took up position and attacked the top squadron of the leading formation. I was so close that I didn't need the gun-sight. I could see the pilots looking straight at me. I aimed at the nose and shot right along it. I think I only passed about one metre above its tail. I remember seeing the bombers on either side sheering away. Then I dived away in a steep dive because all my ammunition had gone. I didn't claim a shot down.

I think the idea of our little unit was a good one and the pilots were keen but the difference between test-flying new fighters and operational flying was just too great for us to be effective.

The bomber which Stemmler attacked was probably that of Second Lieutenant Dale Shaver, flying in the high squadron of the 390th Bomb Group. One cannon shell exploded inside the right wing of the B-17, close enough to hole the large fuel tank behind Number 3 engine but not so close as to cause the explosion which Shaver and his crew feared might occur at any moment. Fuel poured out of the tank and Herr Stemmler can claim a success because this B-17 would never reach North Africa. This was the only success for German fighters over Regensburg. Two of the German planes were damaged and, by the time they returned to the Messerschmitt factory, the landing ground was full of craters and they had to land at near-by Obertraubling instead.

At 11.46 a.m., four hours and forty-five minutes after taking off from England, Captain Latham released the first load of bombs – ten 500-pound high explosives. The seventeen other B-17s in his group released their loads within the next few seconds. The lead plane flew on a little while longer to take its bombing photographs, and then the pilot, Captain Tom Kenny, hauled the B-17 over in a steep turn to the right to commence the flight south to Africa. Lieutenant Abel, the navigator, went with Latham to a side window to observe the explosion of their bombs.

It was just as though we had the conditions made to order and we saw what we hoped to see. Our bombs fell just on the leading edge of the target. It was perfect. We saw the rest of the group's effort a split second later, moving across the target in a rapid series of bursts. Even from the height we were at you could see, just momentarily, each bomb hitting the ground, either creating a hole in the ground or sending bricks flying, and then the whitish red of the explosion followed by a cloud of dust growing bigger and bigger and spreading across the target, with the flashes of further bombs continuing to be seen in the smoke and dust.

I felt tremendous – relief and a sort of gratitude that we had done what we had come for. The whole damn trip meant nothing until we'd dropped those bombs. Colonel LeMay had been watching as well and he came down later to the nose and congratulated us.

The 96th Bomb Group's aiming point was in the left-hand side of the factory area (as viewed when flying in from due west) and the group's bombing photographs later confirmed that it had done a sound job. A dense series of bursts could be seen among the large buildings here, buildings which were among the most important of the factory. But the bombing was not quite perfect. Some bombs had fallen a little short, on the distinctly visible Thurn and Taxis racetrack and on the factory landing ground where some completed Messerschmitt 109s were parked.

The 388th Bomb Group came in next, bombing only two minutes later. Again, most of their bombing was accurate although its photographs show an unexplained group of bursts near the main entrance to the racetrack, about 1,200 yards from the group's main bombing area. At least one B-17 must have been flying this distance off to the side of the main formations. This may have been the 385th Bomb Group aircraft which had been trying to get back in formation for a long time, though its own group had yet to bomb. This group of bombs blew a few more craters in the princely racetrack and possibly hit one or two civilian houses here. Of all the bombs dropped on the Regensburg raid, these were the only ones which hit civilian housing.

The new 390th Bomb Group, on only its third operation, made a slower and more careful approach and bombed a full five minutes later. This diligence was rewarded by the best group of bombing results of the raid. A later count showed that 58 per cent of the group's bombs fell within 1,000 feet of the designated aiming point and 94 per cent within 2,000 feet. The bombing here was in the right-hand (south) part of the factory area and was particularly valuable because few other bombs fell in this area. The 390th's accuracy was also blessedly beneficial to the two large hospital buildings which were located on the edge of the factory site. Had the 390th's bombs overshot by 400 yards – about four seconds flying time – the hospital would have been blanketed by high explosive bombs. The credit for this good work should be shared between Lieutenant Douglas Gordon-Forbes, flying his first mission as lead bombardier, and the pilots of this group who were flying such a compact formation. Gordon-Forbes remembers the moment well.

> With the help of a damn good bomb-sight and by the grace of the good Lord, we did have excellent bombing results.
>
> My only goof was telling the ball-turret gunner, Duke Davidoff, to yell that the bombs hit right on the target, no matter where they did hit. I didn't want Colonel Wittan chewing on me all the way to Africa. The only trouble was that Duke yelled before the bombs were halfway to the target. Colonel Wittan kindly suggested we wait next time until the bombs reached the ground before we sounded off.

The early groups had the easiest task. The groups still to bomb were now presented with a rapidly growing cloud of dust and smoke over the target area, although the bends of the Danube and the racetrack continued to be valuable reference points just outside the target. The next group in was the 94th whose leader that day was Colonel John G. Moore. Moore's bombardier reported that the target area was too smoke-covered for him to see his aiming point properly and Colonel Moore rapidly acquiesced in a decision not to bomb on this run. A further critical decision now had to be taken quickly. The 94th could either continue flying on, holding its position in the existing Regensburg force, and drop its bombs later on a target of opportunity, or it could circle back and make a second bomb run on the Messerschmitt factory. There were problems with both alternatives. The circling-back option would require ten minutes of hard flying at a high fuel consumption rate and this might produce a serious fuel shortage later in the flight. A second run over this defended target would also double the risk of Flak casualties and of fighter attacks in what might prove to be a prolonged period away from supporting groups. To continue on to a target of opportunity would maintain the defensive integrity of the bomber force but the Regensburg factory would be spared 200 high explosive bombs. A further factor mentioned by men in the group was the anger of Colonel LeMay if the group did not bomb its primary target after the cost incurred in reaching that target. Colonel Moore decided to go round again and his plane swung left to start the long circle back to the beginning of the bomb run. Several men mention the degree of profanity among the group's crews at this move.

Flying in the same combat wing immediately behind was the 385th Bomb Group. Its lead bombardier, Lieutenant Louis Dentoni, found his aiming point satisfactorily and the group bombed, but the group leader, Major Preston Piper, was also faced with a difficult decision now: continue on as a solitary group or circle back also and keep in touch with the 94th. Piper decided that he should stay with the 94th and he turned back also. Thirty-nine B-17s, of whom half had already bombed, were thus forced to fly this long, wide circle in the target area. They met an assorted group of twin-engined German fighters which had been hovering around behind the Regensburg force looking for stragglers, but the statement that 'most of the two-engined fighters were shot down' in the papers of the 4th Bombardment Wing is not supported by any German document and is probably a mistake. One pilot of the 385th says that the first bomb run was a 'milk run' but the second was 'awesome'.

While all this was happening, the two groups in the last combat wing – the 95th and 100th – came in and bombed. These groups were severely depleted in numbers and were both carrying loads of 250-pound incendiaries. Few details of their bombing are available but there is no evidence that they did not do their work well. The 94th and 385th eventually came round for their second run; the 94th found conditions no better than before and, in the words of the group diarist, 'the bombs were hurled into the center of the smoke'. Happily, no planes of the 94th or 385th were shot down during this second bomb run although several were damaged and some crewmen were severely injured during this period.

The last bombs were dropped on Regensburg at 12.08 p.m. The bombing had lasted just twenty-two minutes. A large number of satisfied American airmen could see a huge tower of smoke over the Messerschmitt factory and there was good cause for their belief that they had carried out an exceptionally successful bombing operation. Not one American plane nor one American life had been lost in the target area, although three planes had been so damaged that they would not reach North Africa.

Colonel LeMay's first action after leaving the target was to order his wireless operator to tap out the 'strike message' which would inform his superiors in England that the 4th Bombardment Wing had bombed its primary target. The purpose of this was to allow a photographic reconnaissance flight to be made over Regensburg before nightfall. This was another task which the R.A.F. were still doing for their American friends and 540 Squadron, based at Benson in Oxfordshire, had one of its most experienced crews standing by. The flight did not take place at once, however, but was held back to allow the Schweinfurt force to reach its target also. Le May now had to decide whether to wait for the two bomb groups which had made a second run to close up the considerable gap which now existed or to press on south and sort out his formation later. He assessed, correctly, that the Luftwaffe in Southern Germany would not be a serious threat and that it was better for his scattered force to push steadily on than to delay and waste precious fuel at this stage. The Alps – only seventy miles away – were now visible ahead and LeMay ordered a course to be set for these peaks. There still remained nearly five hours of flying time and more than 900 miles of hostile land and doubtful sea to cover before the friendly airfields in North Africa were reached.

The airmen in the American formations settled down after the anxieties of the target area. Some men, for the first time, had the chance to look round and count the gaps. One of the original pilots of the 100th Bomb Group writes, 'After turning south, there was peace and quiet – but where are the rest of the group?' There was the chance to relax a little, although it was far too early to say that all danger was past. Over the Alps lay Italy, an unfamiliar enemy, and then the long Mediterranean crossing where the Luftwaffe were still strong; the latest intelligence reports suggested there might be 200 German fighters in Corsica and Sardinia, although the African-based B-17 raid to Southern France was expected to help divert this opposition.

One happy story should be told before we take leave of Colonel LeMay and the units of the 4th Bombardment Wing. During or immediately after the bombing runs, many of the American crew members saw that the ball gunner of a 385th Bomb Group plane was in serious trouble. Staff Sergeant Fred Verdun, a gunner in another group, was one of the witnesses.

> The strangest thing I saw that day was a B-17 near us and the ball turret hatch being shot off by Flak and the turret gunner falling out. I looked away before he was all the way out because, as you know, he did not have his chute in the turret with him, so the fact that he was falling out meant he was done for.
>
> Well, I reported this at briefing after we landed in Africa and, while telling the story, a guy near me called out, 'Hey! I didn't fall.' This was the man I thought had fallen. He had caught his feet on the gun sight, he said, and pulled himself back into the turret. Today, as I think of this, it could only have been done by the type of superhuman effort one reads about from time to time.

The fortunate gunner was Staff Sergeant Aubrey Bartholomew. His oxygen lines and intercom cable snapped when he fell but he managed to catch his toes under the range pedals of his turret mechanism. Bartholomew was thus left hanging upside down in the slipstream at 17,000 feet without oxygen and with no means of calling for help. After managing to haul himself back into his plane, he passed out through lack of oxygen but was spotted by a friend and revived. 'It was a memorable day,' he says.

Perhaps this was a happy omen for the remainder of the flight of the 4th Bombardment Wing. We will leave Curtis LeMay and his men at this point.

CHAPTER 10
Under the Bombs

It had been a normal workday at the Messerschmitt factory before the American bombers arrived – a Tuesday, a fine summer day, very warm. In the workshops the routine of the day shift had been proceeding smoothly. All windows and ventilators were open because of the heat; it was very noisy. A small group of Spanish Air Force officers had toured the factory during the morning and returned to the main office block for pre-lunch drinks. Also in the offices were some government auditors making their annual examination of the factory's accounts. One man who was not present was General Lucht, the factory director. It was his birthday but General Lucht was treating this as a normal working day. He had not been at Regensburg long enough to make close friends and his colleagues had not arranged a party. Lucht had taken the factory's Fieseler Storch light aircraft to make a long business trip, possibly to Berlin. He would be absent for the bombing which one colleague says 'would not be a very nice birthday present the Americans brought him'.

The German home-defence warning system gave Regensburg plenty of advance notice of the American air activity. A preliminary warning to both the town and the factory air-raid organizations was received by telephone at 11.15 a.m. – when the B-17s were still over Belgium – and three further warnings were issued in the next three quarters of an hour. (German time, one hour in advance of the time used by the Americans, will be used in this chapter.) Each warning was accompanied by details of the course and progress of the American bombers. The wailing sirens of the public alarm – the *Fliegeralarm* – sounded in Regensburg and were repeated throughout the factory area at 12.09 p.m., when the Americans were still 125 miles away and thirty-seven minutes before the first bombs were dropped.

The alarm did not cause any undue excitement among the workers. No bomb had fallen by daylight within 200 miles of

Regensburg since the small and almost suicidal R.A.F. raid at Augsburg sixteen months earlier. Only those few with access to a radio – on which regular reports about the American progress were being broadcast – or those who were in touch with someone in authority realized that there was a serious risk of the factory being bombed. The alarm sounded during the workers' mid-day break. Their cooked lunches had been prepared in a central kitchen and then taken out to the canteens which were situated alongside the main workshop halls and at the apprentice school. There were so many workers that most of these canteens served three sittings of twenty minutes each. So, when the alarm sounded, approximately one third of the workers were eating lunch while the remainder were relaxing in various other places near by.

Many people took shelter during the ample interval which followed the alarm. Most of the German workers went to the changing rooms under their canteens, although a few preferred the earth shelters outside, even though these were intended mainly for the foreign workers. But some people failed to take shelter. Nothing seemed to be happening; perhaps this was another practice alert similar to the one which had been held at the same time the previous day. It seemed a pity to spend one's precious lunch break in a crowded underground shelter. (The standard German 'underground' shelter was actually only three quarters below ground level. Fitted in the upper wall, just above the ground, were hinged steel plates to keep out bomb blast and splinters but capable of being pushed open and used as an emergency means of escape if the normal exits were blocked.)

The following accounts describe the opening of the raid. Engelbert Dimper was a foreman in the *Metalbau Halle* where the wings were fitted to the Messerschmitt 109 fuselages. He was also a member of his workshop's auxiliary fire-fighting team.

> We took up our position in front of the assembly hall; we had our own little shelter inside but we wanted to get a good look at what was going on. The first thing we saw was some of the new Messerschmitt 109s taking off with the test pilots. Suddenly, I saw three formations of bombers, side by side; it was a wonderfully sunny day with only a little high haze and there was no difficulty in seeing them. We didn't think we were going to see an air battle but I said to my pal that there appeared to be a flash of something up there – like a little flash of lightning. I think it may have been the sun reflecting on the

bombs being released. The next thing we heard was the whistling as those bombs came down.

Emil Stang worked in the welding shop of *Halle VI*.

I had really been expecting a raid. For weeks, I had taken a pair of binoculars; I kept them in my cabinet in the changing room. There was an old earth wall, three metres high or so, nearby. I ran to get my binoculars and climbed up onto it. I was desperately interested to see how bombs were released from an aircraft; I hoped that I would be able to spot that with my binoculars. I could see the bombers coming along – twenty or thirty or so in the first formation – and not only could I see the bombs being released but I could follow them down. I actually watched them coming right towards me and then jumped for safety at the last moment. I wasn't frightened – I never was the type to get frightened. I dived into a big hole near by which was full of foreign women, Russians I think.

André Robert was a Belgian.

The Germans were very nervous, calling out '*Raus! Raus! Alarm.*' Their attitude showed how afraid they were of what was about to happen. I reached my shelter in an open trench without difficulty. There was no panic. We believed that it was a simple exercise or practice like the day before. Some men even took their plates so as not to miss their meals.

Suddenly there was a deep rumbling and we saw in the distance something like a black line high up in the air, driving straight towards us. The noise grew stronger and then we caught sight of the individual bombers. There were three formations. It was very impressive and, although we were still convinced that they would pass over without anything happening, I must admit that we were worried. All of a sudden, there was a dull sound like a latch click about a hundred metres from me followed at once by terrible explosions getting louder and louder. The raid had started. Strings of bombs started to fall on the factory and, inevitably, all about us.

All the clocks in the factory stopped at 12.48 p.m.

It is only possible to give a rough outline of the progress of the bombing throughout the different areas of the factory. In the photographs which the American crews brought back the pattern of bomb bursts of each formation sometimes overlapped and, towards the end of the raid, it became difficult to distinguish individual bomb bursts at all in the cloud of smoke and dust. Neither are the accounts of German and foreign workers reliable in this respect – most of them say their areas were hit 'by the first bombs' – although such accounts do provide a vivid picture of the general experience. The description which follows may not, therefore, be in perfect time sequence.

It is clear that the first bombs – those of the 96th Bomb Group – fell in a very tight pattern, starting on the racetrack and running across a corner of the factory containing a hangar under construction, the gun-testing range and the important assembly building where fighters had their tail units fitted. This last building was right in the middle of the first bombing area and photographs showed that it was struck by no less than twenty-three bombs; it is not surprising that it collapsed in a heap of ruins. The canteen alongside was also destroyed and the roof of the crowded shelter below collapsed. There was severe loss of life here and it would be several days before all the debris was cleared and the bodies recovered. It is not known how many survivors there were from this shelter. One eye-witness says, 'There were 200 people inside; not many came out alive'. There were no survivors from this place among the people who answered my appeals. So concentrated was this group of bomb bursts that one of the most important buildings in the factory, the *Endmontage* – the final assembly line – which was situated only a hundred metres away, was not hit by a single bomb.

The bombing of the 390th Bomb Group extended the attack into the southern area of the factory which contained the main office block, the central canteen, the stores and various workshops. The canteen was badly hit but most of the office personnel who had been lunching there earlier had returned to their own building and were now sheltering in its basement. Four bombs struck the office block and one is reported to have penetrated to the basement, but this particular section of the basement may have been empty and there was no great loss of life. Kurt Obermeier, a buyer for the factory, was in another part of the basement where the visiting Spanish Air Force officers were sitting with their hosts.

> Some of them were sitting with their backs to the outside wall and the steel plates which covered the openings at the top were

blown in by the blast and threw them to the floor. No one was injured but we were all shaken up; it was the first air raid of our lives. We couldn't breathe for some time; we thought they were gas bombs. I ran into the photographic room which was near by and dipped my handkerchief into a tray of water until I realized that there was no gas.

There were two pregnant women in the shelter – they had to work up to four weeks before the expected births – and they were very badly shaken. They were sent to hospital for observation but there were no ill-effects.

On the roof of the office building was a small tower on which was mounted a four-barrelled 20-mm Flak position which was manned by office employees who had been given a short period of training. When they saw the high-flying American bombers these men soon realized that the B-17s were far too high to engage and rushed to abandon their exposed position. One man is reputed to have jumped or been blown off the building and suffered multiple fractures. The remainder were halfway down the stairs when a bomb scored a direct hit on the Flak position and sent it crashing down the stairwell. Some of the gun crew escaped but two or three men were trapped and crushed by the collapsing stairway. Herr Obermeier, who was here soon after the bombing, found 'an arm sticking out and I can remember to this day that it was that of a married man because there was a ring on his finger'.

The bombing became more confused when the later American formations arrived and it is not known which unit dropped the bombs which caused the second major tragedy of the day. In the north-eastern corner of the factory area – on the extreme left-hand side as the Americans approached – was the apprentice school. The factory had a large apprentice department with approximately 500 boys carrying out a three-and-a-half-year training period. The boys of the first two classes remained in the training school all day. The third year boys spent part of their time at the training school and part of it out in the various factory workshops, while the fourth year boys were all out in the factory. All the boys were supposed to return to the school canteen for their lunch, but many of the older boys considered themselves to be grown up and did not do so. This would save some of their lives. The apprentices who were present in the school had taken shelter in the usual changing rooms under their canteen.

One room was full of Russian women who were also being trained in the school for some delicate machine-handling work. Jakob Eisenschenk, fifteen years old, was a second-year apprentice.

> I was in Room 2A, the one allocated to the thirty boys in my class. There were five classes to a year. We were running around, joking, sparring and messing around generally when we suddenly heard the noise and felt the vibration of bombs exploding in the main works. We still didn't worry too much. Our teachers told us the factory was under serious attack and we should behave ourselves. I put my fingers in my ears when the bombs got nearer. A few moments later bombs fell right on top of us and all around us with a tremendous impact. The blast caused the steel traps to fly open, the room doors flew open as well and the walls separating the rooms collapsed. The ceiling fell in but I couldn't see daylight.
>
> When the air cleared a bit, I found there was only one other boy and myself left. I have no idea how the others got out but, when I got into what was left of the passage outside where there used to be a row of metal frames for parking bikes, I saw one boy with a piece of this metal blown right through him; one end was sticking out of his stomach. I ran through the rubble to a dark corner where I could see seven or eight other boys scrambling through a hole in the wall. I got out in the open and the canteen was no more than a mountain of rubble before me.
>
> Most of the boys in the next room to me were killed; they got a direct hit. There was a roll call afterwards and I think that seventy-eight of the boys in my year were killed. We suffered the most casualties. After the raid, I saw a pregnant Russian woman who had been killed. The blast had ripped open her stomach and I could see the baby inside. That was a sight which a young lad like me would never forget.

Among the dead was the headmaster of the apprentice school. The total death roll is not known. It may have been as high as that resulting from the worst incident in the main factory but the deaths of the apprentices made this the most emotional event of the raid, and one which is still well remembered in Regensburg.

Bombs fell throughout the factory area and there was a scattering of casualties in many places. Most of the workers sat out the raid in shelters which withstood the bombing, although every shelter had its near misses and individual experiences. These are a selection of accounts from people who were in those shelters. Michael Bleicher worked in *Halle III*, the metal shop.

There was a lady called Marie who had been married for only fourteen days and I had taken her across to the conical concrete shelter which we called the *Zuckerhut*. I did this out of consideration for this recently married lady; normally it was only for big shots like the air-raid wardens and the works police. I had left my meal coupons in a drawer at my workplace. If I had had these, I would have gone down into the canteen shelter. I fetched my coupons and, at that very moment, a bomb exploded in the hall – one of a string which fell right across this area. They were the first bombs of the attack. I dived right through the nearest window – they were always left open because it was so hot – straight out into that zig-zag trench which ran the whole length of the hall outside. I found myself among a bunch of Belgians.

It became very dark with the dust of the bomb explosions and smoke from all the fires which were starting. It was just like night-time. I got covered with all sorts of earth and suchlike rubbish but none of us was hurt. The Belgians were very calm throughout all this.

It was all over in a good quarter of an hour. When I saw what had happened to the canteen, I realized how lucky I had been to go back for my meal coupons. That was the worst day in my life.

Fräulein Franziska Setzer (now Frau Manhart) was a twenty-year-old shorthand secretary to the manager of *Halle III*.

I ran into an earth-covered shelter which was nearby; I was with some other Germans and many foreigners. I had always felt that, if a raid came, the canteen basement would not be the best place. I was worried about that roof falling in. Nothing happened for a bit so I climbed the steps to see what was going on outside. Four or five of us were there doing the same thing. We saw these bombers coming in from the west and discussed whether they could be German, British or American. I couldn't see whether they had four engines or not. Anyway, I wasn't clever enough to know that that would have meant they were enemy planes.

When the bombs fell, we all shot back into this trench. What happened next was terrible. We felt bombs falling some distance away and then one burst very close. The concussion was terrible.

In a small interval between bombs, one of our men dashed back into the hall to retrieve all the bicycles which were there – including mine. He threw them out onto the grass outside. I was most impressed by his courage. I think that we all thought that we were going to die. We were all scared stiff – Germans and foreigners, men and women, all the same. Now, looking back, I thank God that I survived. Next day, I had to carry out my secretarial work at a table in the open and I watched them taking the coffins into the remains of the canteen and bringing out the bodies. I realized that, if I had obeyed instructions, I would have been in one of those coffins.

Jules Pollet was a Belgian forced worker.

There was no panic among the Germans I saw. It was their first time; they had no idea what was coming. It was different in later raids; they were very worried then about their precious machinery. I ran from my workplace as though trying to break a record and reached the nearby earth shelter. There were eighty or more people there, all sitting along the small benches.

We all got under the benches when the bombs started dropping; we were all panic-stricken. Some men were praying, some shouting. Your life passed in front of your eyes in those thirty seconds and you thought it was the end. I can only give you a vague idea for you to put down on paper; you can't really describe the real thing. The walls shook, earth and dust came down from the roof and you could hardly see anything. A German at one entrance was hit by blast and fragments of bomb; he had a broken jaw. The German at the other entrance was blown against a wall by blast and killed. The rest of us were all right; we just swallowed the dust.

Frau Rose Poschenrieder worked in the main stores.

Our boss came and told us all to get out fast. 'Leave your bags and get into the shelter,' he said. That was unusual because he was normally the calmest of men. I went to the splinter trench entrance and we were looking out of it at those little planes which we could see against the steel-blue sky – a lovely sight. I had started to count them – I had no idea they were enemy aircraft – when this inferno erupted.

There we were, a bunch of human beings – there were at

least five nationalities in there – and we were all huddled up together, partly thrown together by the blast which forced all the breath out of us and partly by the instinct which humans have when they face danger. That was a terrible moment for me. I never wanted to work at the Messerschmitt factory. Before they directed me to go there, I had been working in a music shop in Regensburg – selling Beethoven, Mozart, Schubert – that beautiful classical music – also, of course, the latest hits – Lala Andersen was the big star at that time. And then I had been sent to this factory. Reputable girls like me had never worked in factories till then. And now I was landed up in this terrifying position. I was not hurt in the body but this whole thing revolted me, shocked me. That feeling lasted for a very long time. It went away in the end but it does reappear when I have to discuss it again.

A few people delayed so long in taking shelter that they never did find proper cover. Engelbert Dimper was the auxiliary fireman who had stayed outside to study the enemy bomber formations.

One of the first bombs fell only fifty metres away so I ran back into the hall where I was supposed to be at my fire-fighting duty. The windows blew out, bits were coming down from the roof where chunks of concrete and soil were falling onto the roof. I felt I would be safer outside so I climbed through one of the windows which had been blown open, then over a three-metre wooden fence – when you are scared you can climb beautifully – and ran down a slope onto the concrete terraces of the firm's football field and joined a little group of people huddled in a corner of a concrete wall. The dust from the bombing was about fifty metres thick by this time.

Then, we heard another bomb whistling. We all thought that was the one that was going to get us. It landed so close that the edge of the crater was only four metres away. There was a tremendous crash which I can remember to this day but none of us was killed. We were saved by that little angle of concrete wall but the shock wave was enormous and I lost consciousness. My friend woke me up. I was bleeding in the head and couldn't move my arm. My kidneys were damaged as well. I found later that my steel helmet had two big dents in it. Two of the other men had no helmets. They held their hands over their heads and got the top of their hands burnt.

Jean Jacquet was a Frenchman who had decided not to go into a shelter but to crouch with a group of Germans behind a bank of earth where the new hangar was being built.

> The first wave dropped high explosives which smashed all the iron framework and the roofs of the workshops. Machines often weighing several tons were thrown into the air and pieces of metal, wood and also, unfortunately, bits of human bodies were fluttering in all directions. It was terrible. As for us behind our earth mound, we were open-mouthed, scared, shaking with fear at this apocalyptic vision, petrified, paralysed – but unhurt, at least for the time being.
>
> The second wave arrived and I was buried under a heap of earth. Providence must have been with me that day because I was lucky enough to have one arm sticking out of the heap and one of the Germans had the presence of mind to pull me out of my grave. Both of us then ran across the landing ground towards the Danube. We were caught up on the way by a motor cycle with a sidecar. It was driven by a German pilot who gave us a lift – my saviour behind the rider and me in the sidecar. The third wave of bombers attacked while this was happening. I couldn't get out when we reached the river because my legs had become paralysed. Two Germans – a civilian and a soldier – helped me, but the soldier told me they only did so because the cushions were covered with blood from my left arm which nobody had noticed was hurt.

The patients and staff of the civilian hospital, situated at the south-eastern corner of the factory and only 200 yards from the nearest factory building, had been terrified. A large red cross was painted on the roof of the biggest building in the hospital and, although this was clearly visible on the bombing photographs taken by the Americans, their bombardiers had not been warned of the hospital's presence. When the air-raid sirens sounded the patients were taken down to the basement storerooms – there were no air-raid shelters – and they spent the raid in crowded and stiflingly hot conditions. The patients from the maternity ward cared for their own babies; some of these had been born that morning. One of the new mothers, Frau Eva Imlohn, says, 'We were very frightened that the Messerschmitt factory would be bombed and the hospital hit but we kept our fears to ourselves; those were the days of the Third Reich. It was the most terrible experience of my life. I couldn't sleep for several weeks for the memory of it.' When the bombs started to drop the religious sisters and brothers led the patients in prayer but could not stop the screams of terror from their more nervous charges.

The hospital was blessedly – some would say miraculously – fortunate. Two bombs fell on the hospital's back fence, near the little burial plot for the religious community which staffed the hospital, and a third burst in its orchard. Many windows were smashed by the blast. A few people may have been cut by flying glass but there were no deaths and no serious injuries. The people of Regensburg were full of admiration and respect for the accuracy of the American bomber crews. One lady made me promise to record her comment: 'Everyone in the town was surprised that the Barmherzigebrüder Hospital was untouched when almost every building in the factory was hit. We all said that it was a perfect example of precision bombing.'

Another good-luck story can be told about a camp for foreign workers, very close to the hospital but actually inside the factory site. Here were nine wooden barracks, built very close together, in which the night-shift of foreigners had been resting. Approximately forty bombs dropped within 250 yards of this camp but not one of them fell among these flimsy buildings.

Turning to the performance of Regensburg's defences, it has already been stated that the light Flak positions in the factory area were ineffective against the high-flying B-17s. As far as is known there were only three batteries of heavy Flak guns in the Regensburg area to engage the American formation. Each battery had either four or six guns, many of them old captured 85-mm guns which had been rebored to take the standard German 88-mm shell. There was no radar-controlled gun-laying equipment and the gun crews were the usual home-front mixture of elderly or war-wounded German soldiers, Russian 'volunteers' and the sixteen-year-old local schoolboy *Flakhilfers* carrying out their one year's compulsory service of combined schooling and Flak duty. Unfortunately there is no official report available about the activities of these batteries but there is a good personal contribution from Hans Jordan who was one of the schoolboy gunners at a battery sited on a hill in a park only one kilometre south of the factory.

We were probably not in class because it would be the summer holidays. We received the warning and stood ready at the guns for more than an hour before the first bombers appeared. We were lying out in the sun by our gun when one of the *Unteroffiziers* who used to give us lectures on aircraft recognition called out, 'Ah, what a lovely formation of Heinkel 111s.' The normal routine was that we could not open fire before receiving the order to do so and this had not come from the local Flak Headquarters.

The next thing we saw was bombs falling, but still no order came and the major would not allow us to open fire. That order about opening fire was an extremely strict one. The first formation of bombers flew right away without our battery firing a single shot at them. I don't think the other batteries were firing either. I think the whole Flak organization was caught completely by surprise.

We watched the first bombs exploding in the Messerschmitt factory and then came the order to open fire just as the second wave was bombing. I think our first shells went up just as their bombs came down.

We tried our best but I don't think we did much good. The reason for this was that we had been taken too much by surprise – also we were a bit nervous; it was our very first action. But at least we hoped to cause a bit of confusion even if we couldn't shoot any of them down. We didn't know whether they were Americans or English and the *Unteroffizier* who was the identification expert kept quiet after that first big mistake he made.

The last bombers passed over and we could see great clouds of smoke coming from the whole Messerschmitt factory area. A few minutes later some pieces of paper started fluttering down from the sky. We thought they were leaflets dropped by the bombers but found that they were documents from the Messerschmitt factory.

As the American bombers flew away, many other people in Regensburg were watching in horror the huge clouds of smoke billowing up from the factory. There was one part of the town where the people had a particularly good view of the scene and a particularly good reason for fear. When the Messerschmitt factory had been established, an associated workers' housing estate had been built on a piece of high ground in the south of the town.

This was named the Hermann Goering Estate and the roads in it were named after 1914–18 German fighter aces. Many anxious women on that high ground watched the smoke billowing upwards and wondered whether their husbands had survived.

CHAPTER 11

The Diversions

Meanwhile, the next stage of this day's long round of operations was being played out nearly 500 miles to the west, where the main Allied diversionary and harassing effort on the Channel coast had been launched. Five squadrons of medium bombers, fourteen squadrons of fighters and five of fighter-bombers were attacking five different targets. This effort was originally intended to help both the Regensburg and the Schweinfurt B-17 forces, but when these two operations were split, the diversionary effort was all held back to help the Schweinfurt force. The Allied aircraft involved – mostly provided by the R.A.F. – would produce a continuous presence over German-defended territory for nearly two hours, their effort ending just before the second B-17 force assembling over England started to appear on the German radar screens.

Three of the raids were on German airfields – at Bryas, Lille and Poix – and two were on railway yards at Dunkirk and Calais. Because of the limited range of the R.A.F. fighter force, all five diversions were concentrated into the Pas de Calais area, some eighty miles south of the B-17 route to Schweinfurt (see map on page 45). Although one obvious purpose of the raids on the airfields was to cause damage to the ground facilities and, it was hoped, to German planes and airmen on the ground, the primary aim of most of the diversionary effort was to draw the powerful Luftwaffe units in Northern France into action and prevent them from intervening in the outward flight of the Schweinfurt operation. These German units had not been involved in the earlier engagements with the B-17s flying to Regensburg and were thus quite fresh. But the operations being carried out were mostly of a type which had been flown over that limited aerial battlefield of the Pas de Calais by the R.A.F. since 1941. It was unlikely that the Germans would have any difficulty in recognizing what was happening, and they would engage the Allied forces or not as they chose.

The first raid was to the German airfield at Bryas, thirty-five miles inland from the coast. The American 386th Bomb Group, thirty-six B-26s strong, rendezvoused with six squadrons of Spitfires over the Channel. The Spitfires quickly sorted themselves out into close cover, escort cover and high cover and the force then made the forty-mile crossing to its landfall at Le Touquet. A further two squadrons of Spitfires now joined as 'forward target support'. There were now no less than ninety Spitfires escorting thirty-six bombers. No German fighters were seen before the target was reached. The B-26s found the grass airfield without difficulty and bombed it from 12,000 feet, although seven planes were not able to release their loads for various technical reasons. A total of 232 bombs – 300-pound high-explosives – were dropped. Photographs taken later showed that about 60 per cent of these burst on the airfield and none hit the nearby French village. Bryas was not a major Luftwaffe airfield, although it may have been in use as a place to which units were dispersed when their regular airfields were bombed. It is believed that one *Staffel* of II/JG 26 from Lille may have been in residence at the time of this raid but their planes had probably taken off by the time the B-26s arrived.

German commanders faced a dilemma when they had to decide how to respond to these minor raids. The Luftwaffe had little chance of winning a prolonged battle of attrition with the growing Allied fighter forces, but it was bad for the morale of the German pilots and a source of encouragement to the French civilian population if every such raid was ignored. If the Germans did choose to engage, however, they knew they were falling in with Allied wishes and fighting partly on their enemy's terms. On this occasion the Germans did choose to oppose the raid and at least three *Staffeln* – two of Messerschmitt 109s and one of Focke-Wulf 190s – were ordered up. The German-speaking R.A.F. radio listeners in England heard the German controller urging these to gain height and warning them of the presence of the Spitfire escort. Most of the Germans who were now about to engage the Allied force were from II/JG 26; the several Messerschmitt 109s reported by Spitfire pilots to be carrying Italian as well as German markings may have belonged to a part of JG 27 which had recently returned from the Mediterranean, although there are no German documents to show that this unit was in action.

The German fighters attacked a few minutes after the bombers had left the target. The Focke-Wulf 190s tried to dive through to the bomber formation but Lieutenant M. Bouguen, an alert Spitfire pilot in 341 (Free French) Squadron, saw them, called out and dived straight into the attack. He caught the last German fighter from dead astern and had the satisfaction of seeing it dive away on its back 'emitting great volumes of black smoke'. The other Germans in this unit realized they had lost the advantages of surprise and height and, apparently having no wish to tangle with the superior R.A.F. strength, dived away fast. The French pilot did not follow them because, in the hectic manner in which fighter operations often developed, his squadron was itself set upon by the Messerschmitt 109s. One of the less experienced French pilots, Sergeant L. Poirier, was seen to dive away with white smoke streaming from his engine, probably from a hit in his glycol system. Sergeant Poirier parachuted to become a prisoner of war. The Focke-Wulf 190 which Lieutenant Bouguen had hit a few moments earlier may have been the plane of Unteroffizier Karl Hadraba, of the 4th *Staffel* of JG 26, who was killed somewhere in this area.

The second Spitfire squadron in the high cover quickly became involved with another formation of Messerschmitt 109s. (The entire action being described here took place in a fraction of the time the description of it takes to read.) This squadron was 485 (New Zealand) Squadron, which, with the French squadron, formed the famous Biggin Hill Wing and was being led in action on this day by a veteran R.A.F. ace, Wing Commander Al Deere. Detailed combat reports are available but it would not be profitable to go into too much detail. None of the New Zealanders was shot down and one of their pilots, Flying Officer Jack Rae, claimed two Messerschmitts destroyed, although he was only given credit for the one which was seen to crash after a long chase down to ground level. There are several reasons why the New Zealand squadron came off best in this encounter. The German unit involved was the 11th *Staffel* of JG 26, one of the extra *Staffeln* nominally attached to a regular three-*Staffel Gruppe* but used as a pool for replacement pilots and usually sent up on minor operations like this. Unteroffizier Alois Reichert was one of this unit's pilots.

> We were being led that day by Oberfeldwebel Hoffmann, an old hand from 1940 but who had then gone back to Germany as an instructor until a few weeks earlier. I think he had been

out of the battle area too long and was out of touch. He made a mistake. We were getting into position to attack the bombers when their high escort came down on us. We hadn't seen them until then. That's when Hoffmann made his mistake; he tried to climb and meet the Spitfires – and that was the last we saw of him. The young officer who was with us took over then. There was a short combat but we saw a lot more Spitfires about and dived steeply away inland.

After we landed a message came that Hoffmann's aircraft had been found and that he was dead. We young pilots were shocked. If an old hand like him could be killed, what chance had we got? He had been a good comrade, we missed his jokes. He left a wife and some children; he was one of the few in the *Staffel* who were married.

Flying Officer Rae, in a letter, agrees that the man he shot down was an experienced pilot, but thinks that the German did not realize that 485 Squadron was flying one of the comparatively new types of Spitfire – the IXB – which could at last hold its own with the Messerschmitt 109 G at altitude. When Hoffmann dived for safety, Rae managed to hang on long enough to shoot him down.

There was no further action and the Spitfires and B-26s returned to England. This first diversion had achieved all of its objectives: many German fighters drawn into action, two German fighters destroyed, two German pilots killed, one airfield bombed – all at a cost of one Spitfire lost and one pilot taken prisoner. (Of the successful Allied pilots, Flying Officer Rae, the New Zealander, was taken prisoner just one week later when his engine failed and he had to force-land a few miles south of the scene of this recent action, and the Frenchman, Lieutenant Bouguen, would be killed the following winter test-flying a Spitfire for the dive-bomber role.)

The next two supporting operations were more harassing raids than diversionary ones. Two forces of R.A.F. Fighter Command Typhoons were to carry out dive-bombing attacks on German airfields and attempt to hurt the Luftwaffe on the ground. The Hawker Typhoon was one of the R.A.F.'s more modern fighters, a wartime development intended to replace the famous Hawker Hurricane which had borne the brunt of the Battle of Britain, although the more glamorous Spitfire had received more publicity. The Typhoon was a heavy, thick-winged, sturdy 'work horse' of a plane which, when the Second Front opened, would become the R.A.F.'s main ground-attack fighter. The dive-bombing of German airfields was just one of several roles which had been devised for the Typhoon to carry the war to the Germans during the long wait before the invasion. In official reports and in the press, the Typhoon was often called a 'Bomphoon' when operating in the dive-bomber role, but this was not a term which the pilots used. The Typhoon was also capable of operating as a combat fighter and its squadrons were out over France, Belgium and Holland on most days, either carrying out sweeps or acting as escorts for medium bombers, but only as the plodding close escort, not in the high-cover role which was likely to see more action. One pilot says, 'The Typhoons were a bit like a shire horse compared with a racehorse' – the 'racehorse' being the Spitfire. Another says, 'In our heart of hearts, many of us would have rather been on Spits but at least we knew we were doing something positive with the Typhoon. We heard stories of Spit pilots doing sweeps for months on end without shooting anything down.'

The first Typhoon operation would be an attack by eight planes of 181 Squadron escorted by twelve more Typhoons of 182 and 247 Squadrons against the airfield of Vendeville (now called Lesquin), near Lille. The second raid was to be by another eight planes of 183 Squadron, escorted by eleven Typhoons of 486 (New Zealand) Squadron, on Poix airfield. The bombing force was usually restricted to eight planes in this type of operation; it had been found that when more were used, the last few to go down in the bombing dive were too vulnerable to Flak. The bombing and escort duties were regularly rotated between squadrons. The pilots involved were told nothing of the part these operations were playing in the grand design for the day. The two airfields being attacked were both important ones and were the home bases of major German fighter units, although both airfields had been heavily bombed in the past two days by B-17s and parts of the German units there had been dispersed to smaller fields.

The three squadrons of the Lille force took off from their airfields in the Romney Marsh area and flew out over the Channel, as fast and low as possible to avoid being detected by the German coastal radar. The aim of this type of operation was to achieve surprise. Twelve miles from France the Typhoons climbed hard to cross the German coastal defences at about 5,000 feet and to arrive over their target at 10,000 feet. It is unlikely that the German controllers had time to send any new fighters up to engage the Typhoons, but one of the German units that had been hunting for the Allied force which had bombed Bryas airfield a short time earlier was either vectored onto the Typhoon force or encountered it accidentally. Two Focke-Wulf 190s managed to get into a position from which they made just one short, long-range firing pass at one of the Typhoons in the escort. It was either extremely good shooting or a piece of luck. The Typhoon went down in a spin and, although it was seen to recover and turn back towards England, it never arrived; nor did the Germans ever find the wreckage, and it must be presumed that it crashed into the Channel and joined the host of wartime aircraft which litter the bed of that stretch of sea. Flight Lieutenant W. H. Bewg, a Londoner, was the first R.A.F. death of the day. It is ironic that, like Oberfeldwebel Hoffmann, who had been killed a few minutes earlier, Bewg was a veteran pilot from the early war years who had just returned to front-line work after serving as an instructor.

The remainder of the Typhoon force reached Lille. Each of the eight bombing aircraft carried two 500-pound bombs. Flying Officer A. E. S. Vincent, one of the pilots, describes the bombing method used.

> We formed an echelon of eight on the C.O., usually lined up to his starboard. At the commencement of the attack, the C.O. half rolled and then went down vertically. The others followed, gun-sights on, the red dot in the middle of the target. We then pulled the nose slightly up 'through' the target; that had been found by practice to be the best aiming method. The last ones got their dives in as quickly as possible; the Flak was coming up thick and fast by then. The last one was sometimes so anxious that he went down parallel with number seven, although he might get told off for cutting corners.
>
> We released and pulled out at 4,000 feet but the aircraft might 'mush' another 500 to 1,000 feet lower. The C.O. climbed back to 8,000 feet and throttled back, on course but waiting to let the others catch up and watching for fighters, taking a quick look back at the bombing results. He was keen to get the formation together again now. The lone aircraft was always

vulnerable. When everything was okay we set course for home, hoping to meet German fighters; we could then perform two roles in one day, not one.

The official report says that 'bomb bursts were seen across the airfield and close to the north dispersals and hangars'. It was always the hope that such an attack would catch German fighters in the open, refuelling after an operation, and this attack nearly succeeded in that object. The Messerschmitt 109s of the 11th *Staffel* of JG 26 had just landed after their fight with the top cover of the Bryas diversion, but Lille was a front-line airfield which had been bombed in one way or another many times and the ground organization had quickly got all their planes inside the dispersal pens so that none was hit. But the attack had come as a surprise and few of the Germans had time to do more than hug the ground. One hangar was hit, a man working inside it was wounded, and someone would have to fill in yet another batch of bomb craters.

This attack may have had a sequel that was particularly useful for the Allied cause on that day. The main part of the German *Gruppe* whose home base this was, II/JG 26, had not yet been in serious action. Its planes had been dispersed to smaller airfields because of the recent B-17 bombing. The Germans were intending to concentrate the *Gruppe* at Lille during the day so that it could operate as a complete unit. It is possible that the Typhoon attack delayed this assembly and saved the Schweinfurt force from the attention of one of the Luftwaffe's best units because II/JG 26 did not collect at Lille in time to take off again and operate against the American bombers when they flew in over Belgium towards Schweinfurt two hours later.

The three squadrons of Typhoons returned safely to England without further encounter with the Germans.

The story of the second Typhoon raid, on Poix airfield, can be told more quickly. 183 and 486 Squadrons, from Tangmere, made their attack without being engaged by German fighters, concentrating on cratering the runways. Three Typhoons were damaged by Flak but all returned safely to their bases. Parts of the local German unit, II/JG 2, are believed to have concentrated elsewhere, however, and this raid did nothing to prevent their coming into action against the Schweinfurt-bound B-17s.

There remained two straightforward, old-fashioned diversionary raids before this phase of the day's action ended. These were both all-R.A.F. affairs. Seven Mitchell bombers of 226 Squadron and six more from 320 (Free Dutch) Squadron, each with three squadrons of Spitfire escorts, were to bomb railway yards at Dunkirk and Calais respectively. Neither force would make any deep penetration of France; it was the approach flight from England which was intended to draw up the Luftwaffe. The small forces of bombers were no more than bait; the Germans could soon repair a few bombed lines in the railway yards. The Calais raid took place without incident, but the Dunkirk force turned back before reaching the French coast. There had been many changes of orders for all the morning's diversionary raids – due to the major changes in timing forced on the American B-17 operations – and this final diversion never got properly organized. One squadron of the escort did not make the rendezvous and the seven Mitchells did not reach the correct bombing height approaching France. The leader of the force called the operation off and returned to England. The German fighter controllers appear to have ignored both of these diversions completely.

The diversionary effort to support the flight of the American B-17 units to Schweinfurt had now run its course. No one ever expected massive results from these operations but there had been some modest success. Three airfields had been bombed. The timetable of at least one important Luftwaffe unit had been frustrated and other smaller units had been drawn into the air. In return for two Spitfires lost, the R.A.F. claims of two German fighters shot down are confirmed by German documents, and these also show that two more German fighters were destroyed in landing accidents at airfields just to the south of the area in which the diversionary raids were taking place. Neither of the German pilots concerned was hurt but the destruction of these two further German planes can probably be credited to the diversionary effort.

CHAPTER 12
Up at Last

On the nine airfields in England at which were based the units of the 1st Bombardment Wing, more than 2,000 B-17 crew members had been enduring the mental anguish of the delay forced upon them by the changes of plan earlier in the day. The first aircraft was not due to take off until 11.18 a.m. Many men had been woken up eleven hours before this time and most were forced to wait out at their planes for more than five hours, restricted to the sometimes nervous and irritating company of their fellow crew members. There had never been a delay as long as this one and many men have spoken or written of the growing anxiety with which each hour passed. One man writes, 'Perhaps the thing that still remains most vivid in the memory of that long and arduous day was the awful wait as take-off was postponed again and again. If there be a limit to human endurance of that sort of thing, we must have approached it that day.' This had always been a potentially dangerous mission and most of the men knew enough about the air war to realize that the long delay could only help the Germans prepare a more vigorous defence. The news that the Regensburg force had already left had not been released to most of the 1st Bombardment Wing men. That really would have knocked morale to zero.

The delay allowed the 91st Bomb Group to make a change in one of its crews. The group was short of navigators and when a new crew arrived at Bassingbourn that morning its navigator was ordered to leave his suitcases unpacked, collect flying clothes and fly with a crew which was short of a qualified navigator. As his B-17 would be shot down soon after crossing the Dutch coast, Second Lieutenant Edgar Yelle would thus become a prisoner of war after what a fellow crew member describes as 'an operational career of twenty minutes'.

The warm front which had brought the excessively low cloud

conditions over the airfields moved away to the north only very slowly. Ridgewell and Bassingbourn, in the south of the 1st Bombardment Wing's airfield area, were clear of trouble early but the other airfields continued to be affected by the low cloud for most of the waiting period. It is not known whether a further delay or even a cancellation was considered but the cloud eventually started to break up sufficiently for the operation to commence at the revised time.

That long delay had, however, led to an important change being made in the plan. The original plan called for the whole of the 1st Bombardment Wing to fly past Schweinfurt to the south, then turn and make an east–west bomb run on the three ball-bearing factories. This 'going-round-the-back' method had been chosen primarily because of the position of the sun at the original target time – 10.30 a.m. English time, 11.30 a.m. German time. (The original route can be seen on Map 4, page 45.) There would have been several advantages for the bombardiers in having the sun behind them on their bombing run. The biggest disadvantage of the originally planned run was the extra flying time required to get round to the Initial Point east of Schweinfurt, but this flight would have been partly protected by the presence of the Regensburg force just ahead. With the five-hour delay, however, two important factors had changed. The Regensburg force would not be present to give support and the sun would now be more in the west than in the east. A decision was therefore taken that the bombing run over the target would be reversed. It would now take place from west to east with the sun behind and with the more direct approach saving seventeen valuable minutes of dangerous flying time. There were, however, two disadvantages to the new plan. The final approach to the three factories would be over open, almost featureless countryside and the bomb run would be downwind with less time for making final adjustments. The necessary orders were issued but it remained to be seen whether this very late alteration to the plan would cause any confusion over Schweinfurt. The studies of the Schweinfurt area and the different approaches to the town which the lead bombardiers had made in recent weeks would be put to a severe test.

The waiting at the airfields finally ended.

Jeeps kept coming out to us with someone telling us of a delay. We were just milling around, smoking, nervous. Then

> another jeep – another hour's delay! Then an officer would come out and confer with the pilot – yet another delay! It was really unnerving; the sweat was on. We were hoping not to go but word finally came round that we would be going soon. Everyone just stomped out their cigarettes, put on the rest of their flying gear, got in the aircraft and were ready to go. Well, at least we were on the way now! (Staff Sergeant John P. Thompson, 384th Bomb Group)

The first planes of the Schweinfurt force were moving out ready to take off soon after 11.00 a.m., at about the time that the men of the Regensburg force were fighting the fiercest part of their battle on the way to their target. The first aircraft to take off was probably from the 511th Bomb Squadron, part of the 351st Bomb Group at Polebrook, which had to fly nearly fifty miles to join squadrons from other groups to form a composite group in the first of the Schweinfurt combat wings. The 511th Squadron's commander was the extrovert Major Clinton Ball, who insisted that all the planes in his squadron incorporate the name 'Ball' in their nose titles. He was up in *Linda Ball*, the plane of Lieutenant Harry Morse, at 11.18 a.m. The take-off and assembly of the nine regular groups and of the three composite groups proceeded smoothly. There is no need for a long description of this part of the operation. The only salient features are the prolonged period required to get this unwieldy force properly formed up, and the large areas of England criss-crossed during the process. Peterborough to the north, Oxford to the west and Herne Bay in Kent, south of the River Thames, all appear on the American flight charts. The average flying time was one and a half hours before the final departure points on the English coast were reached. Only two of the planes designated to take part in the operation succumbed to mechanical trouble and failed to take off, and one of these was replaced by a spare aircraft. Inevitably there were other aircraft which had to give up and return to their bases with mechanical defects but the number of planes affected was surprisingly small considering that the groups were flying their third operation in three days, that this was a maximum effort for the 1st Bombardment Wing and that many of the crews were tired and fed up. Only ten planes turned back during the assembly over England and the flight across the North Sea. This was 4·3 per cent of the planes involved and compares favourably with the 7·5 per cent of abortives experienced by the 4th Bombardment Wing earlier in the morning. Unfortunately, because of the maximum effort, there were no 'air spares' flying with the groups and only two of the abortives were replaced by crews landing, switching quickly to spare aircraft on the ground and catching up their parent groups later.

There is a number of examples of crews carrying on when the condition of their planes would have given them reasonable cause for dropping out and returning to their bases. This example, described by Second Lieutenant Clive Woodbury, co-pilot in a 91st Bomb Group crew, describes the determination of his pilot, Lieutenant Eugene M. Lockhart.

> Lockhart had been badly wounded in his hand in 1942 but had insisted on returning to flying duty although he could have gone back to the States. He was a man who was determined to do his tour of duty or die. The supercharger which was needed to boost power at altitude failed on one engine after we assembled. We should have turned back. The other three engines had to be set at full power and there was little chance of us getting back with the increased fuel consumption. But Lockhart made the decision to carry on because he was an element leader – quite an experienced one – and our two wingmen were both inexperienced.
>
> He felt that he could and should stay and lead those two new boys through to the target but with the full knowledge that there were nine chances out of ten that we would have to ditch. I thought he was crazy – he knew it too – but I consider he was a real hero.

It is sad to have to record that Lockhart's guardianship of his two new wingmen came to naught. One of them was himself forced to turn back later and the second was shot down, with nine crewmen being killed, long before Schweinfurt was reached. Lockhart's plane was badly damaged and jettisoned its bomb load and, as its crew expected, they had to ditch in the North Sea on the return flight. Lieutenant Lockhart was then awarded a Distinguished Flying Cross and offered a release from his prolonged and difficult tour after twenty-one operations, but he insisted on finishing the normal twenty-five. Happily, he did so safely.

The successful take-off and assembly of the units of the 1st Bombardment Wing, with the absence of any collision and loss in the difficult cloud conditions which still existed in some places and the low number of abortives, gave the Schweinfurt force the best possible start. But the commanders who had been involved in the decision to hold back these units for three and a half hours after the Regensburg force departed must later have spent much time reconsidering that decision. Perhaps they had underestimated the ability of the 1st Bombardment Wing crews and should have risked the earlier take-off. Though an earlier departure would have been in poorer weather conditions and would have required considerable blind-flying ability, it would almost certainly have incurred a much smaller loss than that inflicted by the Luftwaffe because of the separation of the two American forces. But that was all hindsight, a luxury not enjoyed by wartime commanders.

The leading aircraft of the Schweinfurt force left the English coast at Orfordness, a little promontory on the Suffolk coast, at 1.13 p.m. The second half of the force left from the seaside town of Clacton-on-Sea eight minutes later. Both formations were on time and had achieved their assigned altitude of 14,000 feet; they would climb to 21,000 feet as they crossed the North Sea. The two parts of the force merged during the half-hour sea-crossing and the bomber stream, fifty to sixty miles long and 222 B-17s strong, made landfall on the Dutch coast at the island of North Beveland. An escort force of R.A.F. Spitfires appeared at the same time. Two of the most famous as well as the most beautiful and graceful planes to fly in the Second World War were now flying in company with each other.

The German fighter controllers had never before experienced anything like the events of this day. For years they had been experiencing the efforts of the R.A.F., and more recently of the Americans, to outwit them. Now the Germans were facing a mainly American operation which seemed to present the Luftwaffe with an unbelievable chance of success. Again there is no comprehensive record of the latest German appreciation and reaction but the scattered sources which helped with the reconstruction of the Regensburg air battle also helped to clarify the extensive German moves made in the interval between the flight of the 4th Bombardment Wing through to Regensburg and the arrival of the 1st Bombardment Wing at the Dutch coast.

After the Regensburg force had passed through the coastal fighter belt and flown so far into Germany on a course which was almost a straight line on the map, the German commanders had made all their moves on the simple assumption that, because of the known fuel capacity of the B-17, the Regensburg force could only return to England by the same route. There had not been the slightest suspicion that the Americans might fly on to North Africa. There was also an awareness that the Americans had so far used only approximately half of the B-17 strength known to be available in England and that a second operation might develop, but it cannot be stressed too strongly that most of the next German moves were designed to catch the 4th Bombardment Wing returning to England from Regensburg. Another aspect of the moves is also clear. For the first time, the Germans believed, the Americans had fatally overstepped themselves in flying so deep into Germany and had allowed the German commanders sufficient time to bring into action, by means of transit flights, a considerable further strength of fighters from the north and the south. The necessary orders rapidly went out and the whole of the Luftwaffe organization in the West from the Danish frontier down to Britanny was set in motion to move as many fighters as possible to airfields astride the expected return route from Regensburg, and to get those fighters refuelled and ready for action. It would not be an exaggeration to say that the Germans had put in hand an extreme 'maximum effort'. The direction of this effort was no longer in the hands of Oberst Grabmann at the *Jafü Holland–Ruhr* control room. The decisions were made and the orders issued through the joint efforts of the staffs at XII *Flieger Korps*, located at Zeist in Holland, and the *Luftwaffe Befehlshaber Mitte* (Central Command) in Berlin. Oberst Grabmann and his staff would, however, take tactical control of many of the incoming units when they had landed at the airfields in his area and refuelled.

So the great migration took place. The whole of the *Geschwader* which normally defended Northern Germany, in the area known as *Jafü Deutsches Bucht* (German Bight) were dispatched to the south. II/JG 11 flew from Jever down to Rheine and then down to Gilze Rijn. III/JG 11 flew direct from Oldenburg to Woensdrecht. There is some doubt about the move of I/JG 11, whose base at Husum, well north of Hamburg, was more than 300 miles north of the likely battle area. German records show that this *Gruppe* later suffered casualties in the Wiesbaden area; it may have arrived there by means of an intermediate landing at Vechta. The movement of these units left the whole of Northern Holland and Northern Germany without any fighter cover at all. These

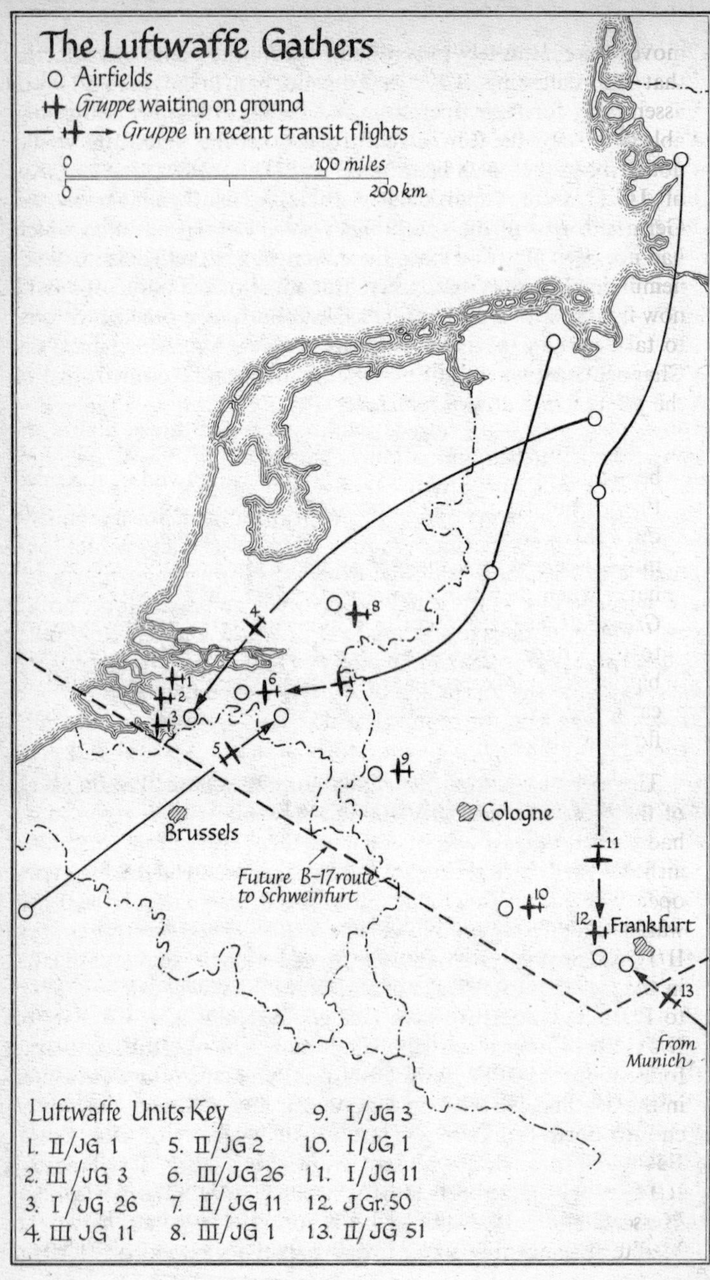
The Luftwaffe Gathers
Airfields
Gruppe waiting on ground
Gruppe in recent transit flights
0
100 miles
0
200 km
Brussels
Cologne
Frankfurt
Future B-17 route to Schweinfurt
from Munich
Luftwaffe Units Key
1. II/JG 1
2. III/JG 3
3. I/JG 26
4. III JG 11
5. II/JG 2
6. III/JG 26
7. II/JG 11
8. III/JG 1
9. I/JG 3
10. I/JG 1
11. I/JG 11
12. J Gr. 50
13. II/JG 51

moves were definitely put in hand before the Germans detected that the remaining B-17s in England had taken off and were assembling for their operation and they represented a considerable gamble by the German controllers that the Americans would not strike in the north later in the day. The three strong *Gruppen* of JG 11 were a particularly valuable reinforcement to the German forces in the south. They were well-rested units which had not been in action since the Americans raided Kiel and Warnemünde eighteen days earlier. But some of the pilots of JG 11 now flying south were apprehensive about leaving their own area to take part in the rough-and-tumble air battles for which the Channel coast was notorious. Leutnant Heinz Rose was one of the pilots flying down from Jever.

> I am sure we thought, 'What is all this nonsense!' My unit had been built up on the coast of the German Bight and we regarded that as our own operational area. We were used to carrying out convoy protection duties, to escorting Junkers 52s on their mine-sweeping flights and to attacking American bombers, but never when they had fighter escort. We always operated as a *Gruppe* in set-piece operations. Now we were on our way down to the Channel which we regarded as a completely different battlefield, a place where individual pilots were expected to carry out what we called '*freie Jagd*' operations. I had never flown in this way.

There was less support available from the south. The bombing of the German airfields in Northern France during recent days had caused at least two major units there to disperse to smaller airfields, and it has been seen how the round of diversionary operations being flown that morning drew some of the Luftwaffe strength in this area up into action. The powerful *Gruppe* II/JG 26, normally based at Lille, would not be available until later in the day. South of Lille, in a spread of airfields running down to Paris and Brittany, were located the units of JG 2. Part of II/JG 2 had moved north to Eindhoven and would be available for action, but I/JG 2, in the Paris area, would not move until later in the day and III/JG 2, in distant Brittany, was only moved far enough north to fill the gap left by the departure of other units. But a reinforcement was sent from the interior of Germany. II/JG 51 was at an airfield near Munich re-equipping with new Messerschmitt 109s after a long period of operations in the Mediterranean; only sixteen days earlier its pilots had been in action against the famous American raid on the Ploesti oil refinery. This unit flew north to an airfield near Frankfurt for the expected return flight of B-17s from Regensburg to England. And there was still plenty of fight left in the six *Gruppen* which had already been in action against the Regensburg force. Most of the planes in four of these units had, by the careful action of their commanders, been able to return to their home airfields; the pilots of the remaining two *Gruppen* had been forced to land at scattered airfields along the route to Regensburg. Although these units would not be able to operate quite so efficiently on a second sortie, most were capable of putting up a reasonable second effort and – a poor prospect for the return flight of the B-17s from Schweinfurt – even make a third flight.

Two important developments had surprised the Germans while the extensive moves of their units were taking place. At approximately 12.30 p.m. (1.30 p.m. German time), the German inland reporting organization finally realized that the American force which had bombed Regensburg half an hour earlier would not be returning to England. At about the same time the coastal radar and radio detection service confirmed that a second, larger group of enemy bombers was leaving England and crossing the southern part of the North Sea. The Germans can be excused for their surprise and for not being able to detect any logic in the American plan. The large-scale transfer of their own units was concluded in a most impressive manner and these would all be ready for action when called upon to take off and engage the new American operation. The VIII Bomber Command report, 'Enemy Tactics, 17 August 1943', which later condensed and analysed the mass of radio interceptions heard that day, pays this tribute to the Germans.

German Fighter Action

The extended interception area now necessitated by the scale of the Allied daylight offensive, and for which the German defenses in the West have been forced to arrange, seems at the moment to be causing German controls less anxiety than one might have expected. The development of the air situation had been evidently foreseen and prepared for. Fighter pilots themselves evince little consternation in being dispatched so far out of their normal areas. Evidently, before they set out, they have instruction as to their possible area of combat and all details of landing grounds in the strange territory. The organization is complete with pilots receiving appropriate cards for the coded place-names in the affected area. Controllers in France and Holland appear also to be in possession of a bird's eye view of the situation and know of the raiders' progress deep into Germany. They can, in this way, calculate well in advance, how best to fit their particular fighters into the interception scheme.

The Germans had managed to assemble a force of thirteen *Gruppen* of single-engined fighters, twelve of them located within seventy-five miles of the route the B-17s would be taking to Schweinfurt. More than half of the German units were fresh. It is difficult to say exactly how many fighters were available in total. American reports suggest 300. It might be prudent to say that the average strength of each *Gruppe* was no more than twenty fighters. This would give an available strength of 260 aircraft. To this can be added the twin-engined effort from night-fighter and training units and a small further number of single-engined fighters from various scattered sources. The combined strength now ready for action was slightly more than double that which had earlier intercepted the Regensburg force.

The German pilots had been resting out at their planes, sitting in the hot sun, meeting old comrades, relaxing before the test they knew was soon to come. Orders to take off started to come in when the B-17s were plotted halfway across the North Sea. The first Germans up were the four *Gruppen* at Woensdrecht airfield, which was again right on the American route. Leutnant Jörg Kiefner had been at Woensdrecht, waiting to make his second operational flight of the day.

> The loudspeaker which had been reporting the progress of the first American formation over Germany now informed us that a new formation was coming in from England. We had been waiting to operate against that earlier unit on its return flight; we were looking forward to that. We were surprised at this new force coming in and disappointed that we must face a fresh new enemy rather than the battered formation coming back. We had been psychologically ready to go for that returning formation which we had already ripped apart.
>
> There was growing excitement. By now there were three or four extra units at Woensdrecht and the whole airfield was ringed with fighters. There were many reunions with comrades from former days and a great feeling of strength. I had never seen an airfield so packed with our own aircraft; it was a change from our usual inferiority of this period. We were

normally the hunted ones but we felt strong that day. The Messerschmitts were away first, taking off straight across the field from their waiting positions. There was a great feeling of enthusiasm at this mass take-off – terrific noise, dust, a great new experience to see all these planes taking off from one airfield. We followed in our Focke-Wulf 190s.

Every one of those thirteen German *Gruppen* assembled for action would succeed in making contact with the new American force.

The force of B-17s now flying in over the Dutch coast would have the protection of more than twice as many friendly fighters in its escort as had earlier helped the Regensburg force, although the critical range limitations remained. Eight squadrons of R.A.F. Spitfires met the B-17s at the coast and would remain in company until Antwerp was reached, just fifteen minutes or so of B-17 flying time. Two American fighter groups would then take over and carry on to Eupen, another twenty-five minutes distant. The eight R.A.F. squadrons which were now with the B-17s were provided by the North Weald, Hornchurch, Northolt and Kenley Wings and were all equipped with the Mark IX Spitfire, the most advanced at that time. These eight squadrons illustrate the truly 'Allied' nature of the R.A.F. at that time. There were two nominally British squadrons, although one of these, 222 Squadron, had two Frenchmen, two Czechs, a Rhodesian, a Canadian, a New Zealander and an American among the twelve pilots flying that day. The remaining squadrons were two Polish, two Canadian and two Norwegian. The four wing leaders came from Britain, New Zealand, Poland and Denmark. The Spitfire squadrons had flown from two forward airfields – Bradwell Bay in Essex and Manston in Kent – and had no difficulty in finding the B-17s, although they were very careful not to get too close to the American formations. Major Kaj Birksted, the Danish pilot leading the Norwegian wing, says, 'You could pick the B-17s up twenty miles away on a good day like that one. They looked like a swarm of mosquitoes at first and then got larger as you closed up. But we were very wary of those American gunners. I always warned my pilots to keep out of machine-gun range.' Flight Lieutenant Philip Tripe, a Canadian pilot, also remembers the meeting and pays this tribute.

To me, the high degree of disciplined formation flying by the

1 and 2. Messerschmitt 109 production at the new Regensburg factory.

3 and 4. B-17 crews prepare for the mission. Despite the importance of the 17 August 1943 operation, there was almost no photographic coverage of the preparations and representative photographs from other raids will have to be used to cover many stages. These scenes show a general briefing and gunners dressing in their electrically heated flying suits and outer clothing.

right 5. Out to the aircraft.

8★ 381BG ★.532 SQ
2SQ

6 and 7. The German fighter pilots wait for action. The top photograph shows pilots of the newly formed *Jagdgruppe* 50 at Wiesbaden who are not yet dressed for immediate action. The bottom group are pilots of the 9th *Staffel* of JG 26 at an airfield near the coast.

8. The sirens sound at Schweinfurt and a Hitler Youth boy directs people to an air-raid shelter. This cannot be August 1943 because nearby buildings are already damaged, but the scene is a typical one.

9. The first bombs of the Regensburg attack fall across the race-track and in the buildings of the aircraft factory. The B-17s are flying from right to left of this picture. The factory landing ground is bottom right. The town hospital buildings are inside a dark-edged perimeter just left of centre.

above 10. Regensburg – the later stages of the attack. The wide loop of the River Danube enabled the American bombardiers to find the factory easily. The B-17 seen is flying north, so this picture must have been taken from one of the two groups which circled to make a second bomb run.

11–13. Bomb damage in the Messerschmitt factory.
Bottom left is the main office block. The picture at top right shows how bombs have penetrated a workshop floor and collapsed it into the changing rooms below which were used as an air-raid shelter. There was heavy loss of life here.

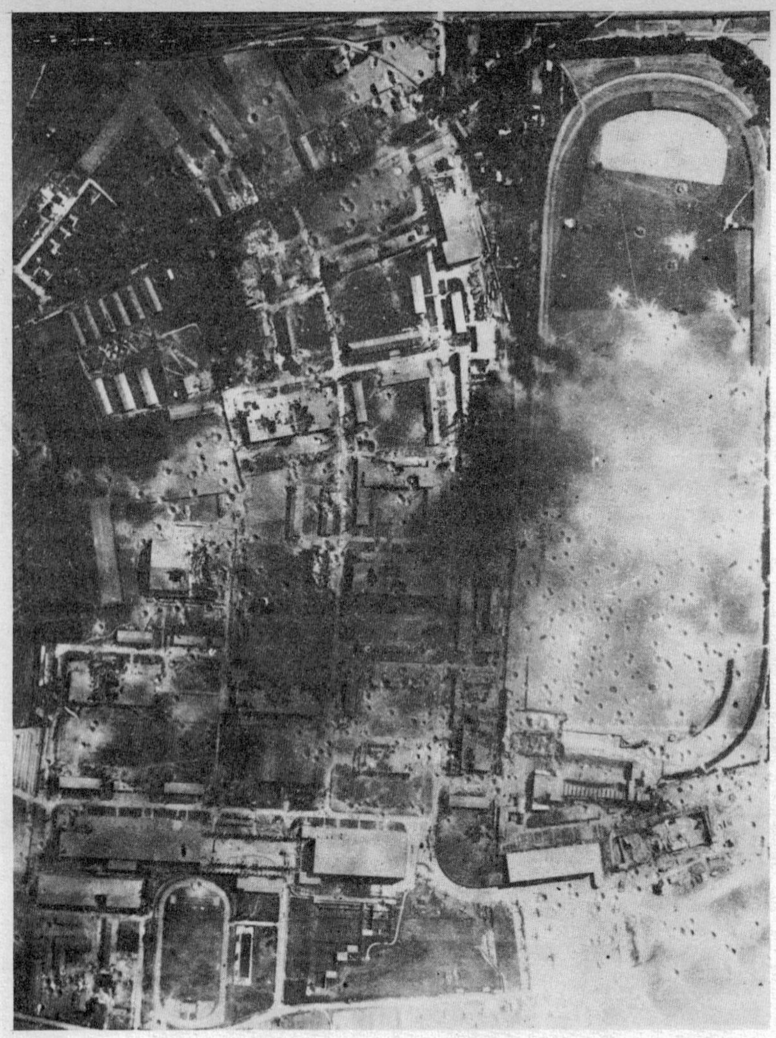

14. Photograph of the Regensburg factory taken by an R.A.F. Mosquito later in the day. Parked fighters can be seen on the landing ground, bottom right. The apprentices' school buildings are extreme bottom left. Centre left is the orchard of the hospital with one of the hospital blocks at the edge of the picture.

15. The waist gunner in action. He wears Flak jacket, sunglasses and oxygen mask but he has removed his intercom headphones.

overleaf 16. This fine photograph shows the three groups of a standard combat wing in use at the time of the Schweinfurt and Regensburg raids. If this was taken in a combat area, the gap between the lead group and the two other groups is too great for safety and the lead group is not tightly enough formed. The high group is in near-perfect formation. A straggler from the lead group is sheltering between the two rear groups.

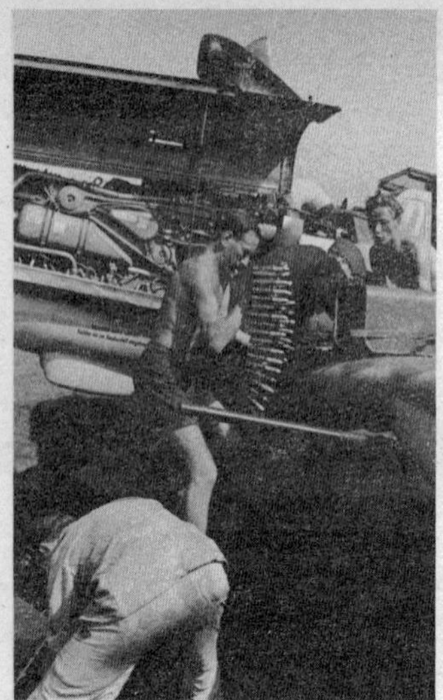

top left 17. Ground staff of *Jagdgruppe* 50 re-arm an Me 109.
top right 18. An FW 190 which has crash-landed. The blackened patch on the side of the fuselage suggests there has been an engine fire.

19. Crashed B-17 in Germany, a scene typical of many on the routes to Regensburg and Schweinfurt, although this photograph was not taken on that day.

20. Wounded. A waist gunner is treated in the plane – another typical scene after heavy action.

overleaf 21. Schweinfurt. Widespread bombing and smoke as one of the last bomb groups leaves the target.

22. The tall figure of Lt Hiram Skogmo, in the centre, and his crew after their landing at the 390th Bomb Group's base in England on the return from North Africa. Maj. Robert Good, right, the squadron commander, had flown as co-pilot and deputy group leader. Skogmo and some of the men in this picture were killed on 11 December 1943 on a raid to Emden.

23. Killed in action. The Margraten American Military Cemetery in Holland, in which many of the men killed flying to Schweinfurt and Regensburg are now buried. The cemetery lies directly under the route both forces took to their targets.

B-17 units was simply incredible. The marshalling of such large formations and the precise timing, so necessary for such operations to ensure rendezvous with fighter aircraft at specific points en route, required a degree of skill in planning and execution which earned the respect of all fighter units which were associated with this type of operation. The Spitfires were short-range fighters compared to the American fighters and, as a result, did not have the same opportunity to observe the B-17 boys under heavy attack. On the few occasions I did witness German fighters attacking and in fact shooting down one or two B-17s, the disciplined flying of the remaining units in the bomber formation was outstanding.

The Spitfire squadrons positioned themselves above the B-17 formations but their general attitude was not to maintain such a rigid close escort as the American fighters practised and which the B-17 crews liked. The R.A.F. believed that it was more important to break up German formations well away from the bombers.

Some of the Spitfires were in action within five minutes of joining the B-17s. A pilot of 222 Squadron spotted a German formation over the water and sandbanks of the Scheldt estuary, an estimated 23,000 feet below him. The reader may think that a sighting at such a distance was an incredible achievement, but Pilot Officer H. E. Turney, one of the R.A.F. pilots involved, pointed out to me that such feats were the whole purpose of a fighter pilot's life. Turney goes on to describe the pilot who first saw the Germans, Flying Officer R. B. Hesselyn, D.F.M. and Bar, a New Zealander and a veteran of the Malta air fighting.

Ray was the world's worst flyer; I reckon I was his Number Two because I was the only one who would stick to him. I think he concentrated so much on watching for the enemy that he didn't bother about keeping station with the rest of the squadron. But he had this uncanny knack of being able to spot an enemy aircraft, often before anyone else, but then he would go straight down and get it; he never hesitated. Normally, if you saw enemy aircraft, you would report their position and wait for orders. Hesselyn would just steam straight down and only report what he had seen when he was halfway there. He was an absolute genius, quite devil-may-care.

Turney went down to protect Hesselyn's tail and the two were soon followed by the section leader, Flight Lieutenant Tripe; Tripe's Number Two had turned back with engine trouble. Unfortunately the remaining eight planes in the squadron could see nothing, probably did not understand what was happening, and stayed up above the B-17s, otherwise an even more substantial success would probably have been gained. A formation of Messerschmitt 109s were caught quite unawares. Flying Officer Hesselyn shot two of them down; Flight Lieutenant Tripe shot down a third and damaged a fourth which later landed in Holland. German documents confirm all four of their casualties. It was a perfect interception. The German formation broke up in confusion and it is unlikely that the R.A.F. pilots even had a shot fired at them. The diary of 222 Squadron describes this as 'RED LETTER DAY FOR THE SQUADRON. The best day since September 11th 1940.'* (The squadron had claimed four German bombers destroyed and four damaged on that day in the Battle of Britain.)

The German unit involved now was III/JG 3, which had earlier transferred from its home base at Münster to Woensdrecht. The *Gruppe* had only been back in Germany for a few days following two years' service in Russia. Its planes were old and worn and there had not even been time since the return from Russia for any of the pilots to have leave. This was their first action in the West since their return. The War Diary† of this unit blames the *Jafü* controller for leading them under the Spitfire formation, but the unit's lack of experience in this theatre of war was probably more to blame. Hauptmann Walther Dahl was the *Gruppe* commander.

> We took off and were being directed out over the sea, climbing gently and carefully because hardly any of the pilots had flown over water. But, when we had reached about 2,000 metres, we were jumped. I was expecting something but nothing as fierce as what developed.
>
> There was the usual mix-up. When it finished we were all over the place and I ordered the pilots to reassemble at the coast near Woensdrecht. From what I had heard in my earphones I knew we had suffered some losses but not how many. I was disappointed that our first operation in the West had

* Operations Record Book, 222 Squadron, Public Record Office AIR 27/1372. The Record Book and the Combat Reports (AIR 50/85) both state that Flight Lieutenant Tripe spotted the German fighters first but personal accounts from Tripe and Turney both say that Flying Officer Hesselyn made the sighting.

† *Kriegstagebuch* III/JG 3, Bundesarchiv Freiburg RL 10-639.

> turned out like this but the direction from Deelen had been useless. They should have warned us. It was a completely new type of air war for us. Personally, I preferred Russia, despite the winters.

None of the three shot-down German pilots was killed although one, Leutnant Hans Schleef, a Russian Front ace and *Ritterkreuz* holder, was wounded.

222 Squadron's sister squadron, 129, was soon in action as well. The whole squadron had dived down onto a German formation also seen over the Scheldt but only one pilot managed to get into a firing position. This was Flight Lieutenant Tony Gaze, an Australian, who outstripped both his wing leader and the rest of his squadron in the dive and, before his cannons jammed, put just enough cannon shells into the German fighter he was attacking to cause an explosion in its right wing and force the German pilot to bale out. There are no documents to identify the German unit involved or confirm the destruction of this fighter but its crash was observed by other pilots in the squadron and a strip of gun-camera film clearly identifies the German plane as a Focke-Wulf 190.

It was unusual for the Spitfires to see so much action. There was more to come. Just in from the coast, 303 (Polish) Squadron spotted a section of three Focke-Wulf 190s trying to approach one of the B-17 formations. This story can best be told from the German side. Leutnant Jörg Kiefner of I/JG 26 had earlier been in action against the Regensburg B-17s; now he was the most junior pilot in this small section of German planes.

> We were high cover this time, climbing so hard that we were almost hanging on our propellers. It all happened quickly. We had reached 6,000 metres – the others were below us – when we caught sight of all these American bombers at 8,000 metres, possibly higher. There were a lot of fighters – Spitfires – a whole lot, buzzing all around. We expected trouble.
>
> We came in from the left on the same course as the bombers but Ahrens slid us under the formation to the right side. He told me afterwards that he wanted to make his attack without being caught by those fighters. Suddenly, however, we realized that the fighters had manoeuvred into a new position and were coming down on us. I saw them and warned Ahrens. He must have seen them at the same time because he flicked over and

dived away. The other chap did the same but I – the young hero, the new boy – I made a much slower and wider turn and the Spitfires got me.

I felt a slight bump against my left knee; later I found I had a bullet in it. The wings of my aircraft were full of holes; we called them cauliflowers because of the burst-open metal skin. The controls had gone and the machine was starting to spin, fluttering down like a maple leaf. I realized I had to get out. I hit the lever which got rid of the canopy and unfastened my seatbelt but I couldn't get out because I was pinned by the centrifugal force. I watched the altimeter whizzing round at great speed. That heavy plane fell like a stone.

I realized that I had to get out if I was to save my young life. When the altimeter read 1,500 metres, I mobilized all my strength and forced myself out the left side. It suddenly became very easy. I hit my head on the tail-fin and my parachute opened. I called this my second birthday.

I landed in a field and was attacked by some cows.

The Polish pilots later submitted claims for three German fighters destroyed and one probable, but this was a clear case of overclaiming and Kiefner was their only victim.

The Spitfire squadrons now handed over to the first of the American P-47s which were arriving. The recent action represented a minor success. Although the B-17s had only covered just over fifty miles while under the protection of the R.A.F., not one of the many German fighters then in the air had been able to attack the American formations, five German fighters had been shot down, and the whole of one *Gruppe* had been temporarily scattered. The Spitfires returned to England without having suffered any loss.

The American take-over of the escort duty was only partially successful. The plan called for two groups of P-47s to meet the bombers near Antwerp and stay with them until Eupen was reached. The 4th Fighter Group was to cover the leading two combat wings and the 78th Fighter Group the two rear wings. The 78th picked up its formation satisfactorily near Antwerp but the 4th Fighter Group was not able to find the leading wings at the position expected. The pilots of this unit then commenced a long and frustrating search for their part of the bomber force which ended only twenty minutes later, by which time they were almost at the limit of their escort time. The search had taken the P-47s well north of the bomber track and the B-17 formation they were seeking could be seen to the south, surrounded by German fighters, but the American unit could do nothing to help and was forced to return to England.

The 4th Fighter Group, led on this day by Lieutenant Colonel Don Blakeslee, later a very successful leader, was criticized for its failure to link up with the B-17s. This group had been formed from the three Eagle Squadrons in which American pilots had served with the R.A.F. before their own country's entry into the war. There was some jealousy among other American pilots of the publicity the Eagle Squadron pilots attracted, and this carried on to create a rivalry between what became the 4th Fighter Group and those American fighter units which arrived in England later. The reason for the failure to meet the B-17s and carry out this escort might have been bad timing or faulty navigation at the rendezvous by the 4th Fighter Group, but the main cause was probably the fact that at the rendezvous position the leading bomber wings were at a lower altitude than planned – of which more later.

There were bitter recriminations because of what had happened, and at the joint conference of bomber and fighter commanders held on the following day it was suggested that fifteen B-17s were shot down because of this failure. The fighter commanders were heavily outnumbered at the conference and could do little to refute this charge, which was made in the immediate aftermath of a bitterly disappointing and costly operation. It is true that the German fighter attacks on the leading combat wings did commence during the period in which the 4th Fighter Group should have been present, but only one B-17 was definitely shot down before Eupen was reached, although several others were damaged during that time and would succumb to later attacks. The wanderings of the 4th Fighter Group may even have had one beneficial result. A radio listening station in England reported hearing during this period 'a certain amount of agitated questioning caused by the controllers being unable to give exact information about the presence of Allied fighters'.

The second P-47 unit, the 78th Fighter Group, led by its commander, Lieutenant Colonel James J. Stone, made a sound job of its escort duty and remained with the B-17s until Eupen was reached. These P-47s even managed to provide a partial cover for the first half of the bomber force. The Germans kept their distance from the American fighters and only one section of four P-47s experienced any combat. On their last sweep before leaving the bombers, the flight of Major Eugene Roberts spotted a mixed formation of twin- and single-engined German fighters which were climbing to engage the B-17s. Roberts led his pilots down and, after a brisk little combat, Major Roberts claimed a Messerschmitt 110 destroyed and Flight Officer Peter Pompetti a Messerschmitt 210 destroyed. Two German pilots were later seen descending by parachute. German records show only one aircraft, a Messerschmitt 110, lost here, with its two crew members both seriously wounded. Peter Pompetti's claim was almost certainly the same plane as that claimed by his flight leader and the credit for it should be shared between the two American pilots. It is most unlikely that a Messerschmitt 210 was present. The plane shot down was from the *Ergänzungsstaffel* of NJG 2, the replacement flight of a night-fighter unit. It may have been helping a small single-engined formation of German fighters with their navigation in a strange area.

The head of the Schweinfurt force passed Eupen at approximately 2.10 p.m. The long column of combat wings had closed up considerably in anticipation of German fighter attack. Colonel Gross, commander of the first half of the force, had already made a major change from the operation's plan. His aircraft had crossed the Dutch coast at the ordered height of 21,000 feet, but soon afterwards he had seen ahead what he later reported as 'a peculiar cloud formation that, from a distance, looked to be about 19,000 to 25,000 feet high cirrus'. Colonel Gross decided that his groups could not fly in formation through such cloud and he gave the order to lose altitude and fly under the cloud bank. The first half of the bomber force thus descended 4,000 feet, although the orders stated that lead aircraft should be at 21,000 feet at all fighter rendezvous points. This may have been an ill-judged decision and it certainly contributed to the failure of the 4th Fighter Group to find the bombers at the rendezvous. A post-mission report says that the second half of the bomber force experienced no difficulty in flying this part of the route at the prescribed altitude.

This action by Colonel Gross raises the interesting and sometimes contentious point of the relationship between 'air commanders' like Colonel Gross who were not regular combat pilots and the more experienced lead pilots with whom they flew. It was generally conceded that the lead pilot's task was to fly the mission 'as briefed' and to take all the airmanship and tactical decisions required to achieve that, while the air commander's role was to make the decisions and take the responsibility for any major departure from the plan, such as the complete abandonment of a mission, the switch to an alternative target or the making of a second bomb run. Borderline decisions between these two areas of responsibility sometimes caused problems and some lead pilots resented relatively inexperienced air commanders issuing orders of a tactical nature. The presence of Brigadier-General Williams, commanding general of the 1st Bombardment Wing, in a B-17 flying just behind Colonel Gross had a different purpose. He could be consulted by radio if a really dramatic change of plan was being considered but his presence was more a morale-boosting one. This is the comment of Major Bill Rader who was leading a group further back in the Schweinfurt force.

> I think you will find in our American history that the minions always liked to think that our commanders were prepared to lead us into action. Most of our generals were smart enough to know that you don't fight wars with older people and they had enough sense to leave the combat part of it to the younger people who had the recent experience. The fact that an aircraft captain, possibly in the low group back in the formation, knew that the general was up there in front had a good effect. The 'old man' was in the same boat as the rest of us. Most of them had never met the general but they knew he was up there somewhere.

So the four combat wings of the Schweinfurt force flew the length of Belgium and crossed the German border just beyond Eupen. One more B-17 turned back with mechanical trouble; it bombed an airfield and returned to England safely. There was little difficulty in evading the worst of the German Flak concentrations. One B-17 had been shot down but at least six German fighters had been destroyed by the Allied escorts. It would require only forty-eight more minutes' flying time to reach Schweinfurt. But all the earlier efforts of the diversionary forces and the more recent support of the fighter escorts had now been played out. The men in the B-17s of the 1st Bombardment Wing were about to be exposed to the full consequences of the decision to send them to Germany three and a half hours after the Regensburg force. According to the plan, it would be two hours and seven minutes before friendly fighters were seen again. The bomber crew members watched the P-47s depart.

They wiggled their wings and went back to their barracks and beer. It brought a lump to your throat because you knew what was coming next. The pilot was on the intercom, telling us to watch with special care. We all knew we were going to be meeting the Germans soon. It was an awful empty feeling watching our fighters go. (Second Lieutenant Robert E. Hyatt, 381st Bomb Group)

We were very down: now we were on our own; now we knew the Luftwaffe would be coming after us. I had seen them before; they were very fine fighters but I think they were specially good that day. (Staff Sergeant Harold H. Schultz, 91st Bomb Group)

I watched a large number, an overwhelming number, of fighters steadily climbing straight on course, possibly a couple of miles away, just specks in the distance. My position was on the port side looking north and the sun picked those fighters out absolutely clearly in my vision. It was the greatest concept of massing of enemy fighters that I ever saw in my tour and I knew we were in for it. There was no question of it. (Lieutenant Edwin D. Frost, 381st Bomb Group)

We could see the Germans forming up in front of us – turning to start their head-on attack. The thing I remember most vividly is that the Germans turned and started making their initial attack almost exactly at the same time as the P-47s above us made their 180-degree turn to return to their base. I felt that German intelligence knew the exact range of our fighters.

Looking back at it now, I think that very moment, when the P-47s left and we went on to suffer all those casualties, was the major turning point when the Air Force had it proved to them that their idea of sending B-17s unescorted on a deep penetration just wasn't valid. It broke the back of the theories of the advocates higher up who were convinced that the Flying Fortress could protect itself if you had good formation discipline and that excellent fifty-calibre gun we were supposed to have. (Lieutenant William H. Wheeler, 91st Bomb Group)

CHAPTER 13

The Dream Fades

It is unlikely that anyone would dispute that 17 August 1943 was a turning point in the air war. Lieutenant Bill Wheeler, soon to find himself on the end of a parachute, was correct when he further narrowed down that turning point to the moment when the American fighter escort departed and the German fighter units came swarming up to give battle. The events in the period from 2.10 p.m. in the afternoon were the true heart of that historic day's operations. The Americans knew no precedent for the intensity and ferocity of the coming battle. A number of their units, although powerful, well-formed, well-disciplined and well-led, were about to be cut to ribbons by German fighter attack.

The practical difficulties of describing such an encounter are many. So far in this book it has been possible to break down action into individual events and to identify the units and even the individuals who were involved on both sides. The experiences of the Schweinfurt-bound bomber force from Eupen onwards were so hectic, however, that such identifications will rarely be possible. Furthermore, no written description can adequately convey the nature of the experiences of the men in those planes. This shortcoming may be partly remedied by the use of direct quotations from many of the men involved, but these men were the survivors, talking or writing more than thirty years later, far removed from those moments when they were, quite literally, staring death in the face. Readers who have experienced these or similar events will know exactly what it was like. Those, like myself, who have never faced such situations, will never know. The final shortcoming of a written account is that the terror and agony of the men who died can never be reported.

The German attacks had actually started before the bombers

reached Eupen, when the P-47s of the 4th Fighter Group failed to make contact with the leading units of the bomber force. But the Germans could do little to exploit this escort failure because there was only one German unit in sure contact with the B-17s at that stage. This was I/JG 26 from Woensdrecht. Its Focke-Wulf 190s started attacking the front of the American force and were rewarded by the destruction of one bomber. This was the aircraft of Second Lieutenant Don Von Der Heyde which was flying the dangerous outside corner position of the 91st Bomb Group's low squadron. The B-17 went into a vicious spin and then broke up. Only two men survived. This was the only bomber lost before Eupen was reached.

The controlling of the German fighter units was being handled with exceptional skill at this time. Oberst Grabmann at the *Jafü Holland–Ruhr* control centre near Deelen was again in charge. His team must have been at full stretch. Only two *Gruppen* – III/JG 3 and I/JG 26 – were committed at the coast but, as has been described earlier, elements of both these units fell foul of the R.A.F. Spitfire escort. The rest of the considerable German fighter force available seems to have been deliberately held back on the assumption that this new American force would penetrate well inland and outrun its escort. So, with perfect timing, these further German units were brought into contact with the B-17s just as the last planes of the American escort left. The control from the ground was so detailed that one German pilot remembers being advised that part of the American force had, surprisingly to him, lost altitude while flying over Belgium; he could not understand why the Americans were descending to an altitude at which his Messerschmitt 109 would find its best performance.

So the real battle began near that little Belgian town of Eupen, with a plane of the 381st Bomb Group being immediately forced out of formation. The next phase, between Eupen and the turning point on the River Rhine between Mainz and Darmstadt, would see the fiercest part of the battle. No less than thirteen German *Gruppen* – between 180 and 240 fighters – were in action during that time. For the historical record, these thirteen units were:

I and II/JG 1	Focke-Wulf 190s
III/JG 1	Messerschmitt 109s
II/JG 2	Messerschmitt 109s
I and III/JG 3	Messerschmitt 109s
I/JG 11	Focke-Wulf 190s

II and III/JG 11	Messerschmitt 109s
I/JG 26	Focke-Wulf 190s
III/JG 26	Messerschmitt 109s
II/JG 51	Messerschmitt 109s
Jagdgruppe 50	Messerschmitt 109s

It is estimated that at the height of this action nine of these units were in action with the American bombers at the same time. The Regensburg force had never faced more than three *Gruppen* at once during their flight earlier in the day.

There are many references in published works to the participation in this battle of twin-engined German fighter units and it is sometimes suggested that these made direct attacks on the B-17 formations. It is true that elements of various night-fighter units were up, as normal, looking for crippled B-17s, and at least one Messerschmitt 110 acted as contact keeper alongside the head of the leading American combat wing. But there is no firm documentary evidence that any twin-engined German unit was ordered into action against the main American formations, at least during this outward flight of the Schweinfurt force. In particular, reports that Messerschmitt 110s of ZG 26 and NJG 5 were employed in firing rockets at the American formations are believed to be erroneous. Such reports, doubtless based on personal accounts given in good faith, probably refer to the second American mission to Schweinfurt, on 14 October 1943, when the Germans used twin-engined rocket-firing fighters in large numbers. It is possible that one or two bold Messerschmitt 110 crews did experiment with rockets against the B-17s on 17 August and there is even a report of a Junkers 88 dropping bombs on one B-17 formation but any such twin-engined effort was confined to a handful of planes and achieved little or no result.

To read some American reports, it would seem that the Luftwaffe tried every type of attack against the Schweinfurt force, but the German success was based overwhelmingly on the head-on attack method of the standard single-engined fighter. Many of the American crews had faced this form of attack before, but never on the scale experienced during that flight to Schweinfurt. Normally the Germans split their initial attacks up into flights of four fighters, but once the B-17s had passed Eupen the Germans correctly assumed that the Allied escorts had all gone and that the American bombers were going to attempt another long flight into Germany. With the massive strength of fighters available and with plenty of fuel in their tanks, the experienced German officers who were leading each unit in the air were able to mount their attacks in the most deliberate and confident manner. They led their units well out in front of the American formation chosen for attack and deployed them by *Staffeln*, ten to fifteen fighters in line abreast. Because there were so many German units in the air at once, these attacks followed each other in relentless fashion for a longer period than any of the Americans involved had ever experienced. There was one more factor. The personal accounts of the American crew members testify to the ferocity and determination with which the German attacks were now pressed. The German pilots seemed to be 'hungry' for success and fighting with noticeably more commitment than normal.

The Americans could do little to avoid the effects of these tactics; the B-17s could only press steadily on like men bowing their heads against a rain-storm. The American pilots could carry out some evasive action against each individual attack but, with so many German planes attacking over a long period and with other B-17s all around them, the opportunity to throw off the German aim was strictly limited. The main gunnery defence was in the hands of the two officers in the nose compartment of each B-17 – the navigator and bombardier – with their rather ineffective hand-held guns; the ball turrets and top turrets were also able to contribute to the defence, although never against the same fighter. The four other gun positions were almost redundant.

Two tactical factors dictated that the onslaught would fall against those American units at the head of the bomber force. When the American 4th Fighter Group failed to make contact with the leading combat wing of bombers over Belgium, the German units which were then appearing started to gather around that unescorted wing. Then, when the Germans started to make their attacks, they found it very useful to use the unlimited air space in front of the leading bomber wing to carry out their preliminary manoeuvres. In this way, all three bomb groups in the leading wing became the object of the early German attacks. Although some of the German effort later spread to other parts of the bomber force, those leading groups quickly started suffering casualties and after that the Germans followed their golden rule – 'Go for the weakened groups.' The conditions which existed at Eupen thus dictated the main pattern of the battle all the way to Schweinfurt. Again for the historical record, the following were the American units which had to face that German onslaught on the front of the bomber force:

101st COMBAT WING

High Group	101st Composite Group made up of: 401st Squadron, 91st Bomb Group 511th Squadron, 351st Bomb Group 533rd Squadron, 381st Bomb Group
Lead Group	91st Bomb Group
Low Group	381st Bomb Group

The following accounts describe those massed German attacks made during the period after the American force crossed the German border near Eupen. All the quotations are from men who were in the leading combat wing or in the second wing to which the German attacks later spread. Lieutenant Edwin Frost was a navigator in the 381st Bomb Group.

It was just pandemonium. It seemed that every gun in the ship was firing at once and the noise was terrific. I don't know how long it went on for; it just seemed endless. I, as navigator, was supposed to log everything that happened but I just dropped everything; I don't think I put pencil to paper until I reached the Dutch coast coming out. I had one of the nose guns but not one that fired directly forward and the only time I could get in a burst was when the fighter came in and broke away on my side, but I think most of them were coming straight through – tear-assing right through us. I didn't exactly see the whites of their eyes but I remember one which seemed to be coming straight at us. Our bombardier accused me of throwing myself down behind him for cover. It was just an instinctive reaction; I had never seen them that close.

Intercom was impossible – everyone was calling out fighters and Cormany, the pilot, told us to get the hell off it, all of us. There was no question of us using intercom during all that action. The pilot was bucking and yawing all the time – trying to get out of the estimated line of fire of the fighters he could see coming in. After we landed he told me that he had never had such a work-out in his life; his arms were nearly falling off.

Never before or after did I ever see such incessant action. That was certainly the apex of my operational career and it was the most horrible experience of my life.

Staff Sergeant John Thompson was a waist gunner in the 384th Bomb Group.

I witnessed something that mankind will never see again. It was rare to see hundreds and hundreds of aircraft in the sky at once. On one occasion our formation made a small turn and I was able to look back. It looked like a parachute invasion of Germany. There were planes in flat spins, planes in big wide spins. Planes were going down so often that it became useless to report them. My God, I had never seen anything like that before; it had always been just one plane going down at a time. Even Hollywood could never match that. It is still a very vivid scene to me.

Staff Sergeant Jack Goetz was another gunner in the 384th Bomb Group.

Some of our pilots were good but I really saw some fine flying by the Germans that day. Sometimes they came in real close, actually firing as they rolled, even firing while upside down. You could see the cannons firing just like four little red blinker systems going. As we got deeper into Germany, they seemed to be even more desperate, boring in even closer on us. I did the full tour of twenty-five missions and I never saw more determined fighter attacks. That was the only day I ever swore, cursed and prayed at the same time.

This account, by Sergeant Delmar Kaech of the 91st Bomb Group, shows how ineffective was the radio operator's gun position against a forward attack.

I reversed my stand in the radio room, strapped myself to the bar on which the gun was mounted and was thus able to fire forward, although I couldn't depress my gun below about 60 degrees from the horizontal. I was in this position for about ten minutes but I got no shots in and had to give up, mainly because, though my head was not out of the open hatch, it was so far back that the huge force of incoming wind made my eyes stream with water and I couldn't see.

I had one nasty moment before we were hit. I saw this dark shape coming down just as though a high-level fighter was coming in. Your reaction has to be so quick if you are going to get a fighter that you had to take snap shots when you could. I let off just a few rounds before I saw that it was a B-17. It must have been from the group which was above us and just out of my sight, echeloned to the side. It was coming down fast and steeply – almost at a 50 degrees angle – not on fire or spinning.

It was gone in no more than three seconds – it was just a snap deal. I hope I never hit them.

Lieutenant Colonel Robert H. Burns was the deputy leader of the 351st Bomb Group.

All guns aboard were firing so the din and smell of ammo being expended exceeded anything I had experienced to this time. In fact, I never flew another mission which was even close in intensity and duration of fighter attacks as this one. At one point, I saw a Me 109 turning into a quartering head-on attack on my airplane. As he neared, 20-millimetre bursts began to 'walk' right into the cockpit. I remember counting about four bursts and knowing that the next one would be right in the windshield. But the 109 pilot just didn't squeeze off that fifth round. That's why I made it, I guess. I never flew another mission that compared to Schweinfurt.

Lieutenant Donald Rutan was a co-pilot in the hard-hit 381st Bomb Group.

There wasn't much sense in calling out fighters that day; everything was twelve o'clock level for what seemed an eternity. Each time they came in you thought that one of those times it would be our turn to get it. So many of our planes had gone. That was the fiercest we had ever had it. The fellows in my crew who were shot down on a later mission without me always said that Schweinfurt was their most vivid memory. They never forgot August 17th.

Second Lieutenant Joe Baggs was the lead bombardier of the 384th Bomb Group.

I could see the groups ahead of me, particularly the 381st which was directly in front of me. I saw B-17s doing things that day that were unbelievable. I thought I had seen the lot up to that time but I saw more that day. There were aircraft stalling, slow-rolling, wings disintegrating, chutes on fire. I counted eleven going down from just in front of us before we reached the target. They took quite a beating.

I remember praying that at least we would get to the target. I didn't think we'd ever get back – that seemed a foregone conclusion – but I did want to get to the target and do what I was supposed to do if only for the sake of those eleven crews I watched go down on the way there. In retrospect, it was a

> terrible responsibility for a young man being the lead bombardier, particularly after those losses going in. It made an old man out of me in a hell of a hurry – it also made a major out of me in a hell of a hurry.

Major Clinton Ball of the 351st Bomb Group was flying with his squadron in the composite group in the leading wing. The 'Nick' he refers to was the regular co-pilot of the plane in which Ball was flying; this man had been placed in the tail turret as 'formation observer'.

> Having several missions under my belt as observer, co-pilot, pilot and air commander, I decided that my chances of taking a shot at the Germans with a fifty-caliber gun were hopeless unless the crew had a spare pilot on board. Schweinfurt was the right and probably the only chance I'd get during a full tour. I called Nick up to the cockpit, sent a gunner back to the tail and then slipped out of the right-hand seat, turned the airplane over to Harry Morse and dropped down into the nose compartment.
>
> There I took over the right gun and stayed there until we crossed the coast on the way back. I never had a more interesting flight. I shot off all my ammunition, more than I had ever fired in my life. I am quite sure that I shot down no Me 109s, no FW 190s, no Me 110s, and no Ju 88s but that was my one chance of shooting back at the enemy pilots who had the opportunity of shooting at me every mission we flew. It really was satisfying.

Lieutenant Carl Stackhouse was a navigator in Major Ball's squadron.

> It was such a beautifully clear day that you could see everything. I remember the tremendous number of reports from our tail gunner of planes going down and counting the chutes out – we always kept hoping he'd get to ten. Then I saw a parachute on fire – that was my most vivid memory; I'll never forget it. He jumped out and there was just a plume of fire behind him. I don't know which plane or outfit he was from. When was our turn coming?
>
> I vividly remember the 'tucking up' our pilot, Carl Wilson, made to the plane over us. He put our left wing almost in between the element leader's wing and tail. It was quite a flying accomplishment for the pilots to do that for such a long period.

I guess they were somewhat inspired by seeing all the others going down. As for the Germans, their persistence and their numbers – they kept coming and coming and coming and coming and we had still got miles to go before the target. I remember thinking that there wouldn't be many of us left when we got there.

Don't get the idea that any of us ever thought that we would ever turn back – either as an individual plane or as a formation. There was never any doubt in my mind or in the mind of anyone I spoke to – even after fellows had a few drinks and got a little braver and spoke their true minds – that we would ever have turned back because of the opposition. But I still remember thinking that there wouldn't be sufficient of us left to put enough bombs down on the target to destroy it.

Although the German fighters were hammering away at all three groups in the leading combat wing, it is possible to subdivide this action somewhat. The location of crashed B-17s and the testimony of surviving crew members show that the low group, the 381st, suffered the worst of the early attacks. Four of the first five bombers to be shot down past Eupen came from this group. The first of these was the plane of Lieutenant Weldon L. Simpson, which was flying as an extra 'spare' alongside the lead squadron. Simpson decided to drop down and fill a gap left in the low squadron when a plane there had aborted earlier. This should have been a simple manoeuvre, but unfortunately the first German head-on attack caught Simpson before he could complete the move and gain the protection of the low squadron. In a spectacular display, the B-17 pulled up vertically, half rolled to the right, and was then seen to go down in an upside-down spin. Simpson later managed to regain control and flew back towards the coast but was attacked again and shot down. The next round of German attacks shot down three planes from the 381st's high squadron. By coincidence this was the 534th Squadron with which Lieutenant Simpson normally flew. The squadron had been particularly fortunate in the two months since this unit commenced operations, suffering at most one lost crew. The eight crews flying to Schweinfurt were all originals who had been together since their training days in the United States. The squadron commander and other members who were not flying this mission were deeply dismayed when four of the eight crews failed to return.

The German attacks quickly spread to the 91st Bomb Group, which was flying just above and ahead of the 381st, but the initial attacks failed to knock any of the group's planes down. Lieutenant Bill Wheeler was observing these attacks from an even higher position. His squadron, the 401st, had been detached from the 91st Bomb Group to form part of a composite group in the leading wing's high position.

> I remember the concentrated efforts of the Germans on the lead group just below me and to my left. There must have been thirty to fifty German aircraft involved and most of them were concentrating on that lead group. They were much more determined and aggressive than I had ever seen. I felt a tremendous admiration and feeling of respect for this lead organization which didn't deviate a bit from its course and didn't disperse its formation. I probably didn't think at the time about it being my own group, just that one of our American units was taking the brunt of it and behaving so well, with such dedication in trying to do the impossible.

The main part of the 91st Bomb Group managed to hold itself together without loss for the first quarter of an hour of this main battle but then their planes started to go down fast; almost half the group would be gone before Schweinfurt was reached. Lieutenant Colonel Clemens K. Wurzbach, the group commander, was piloting the leading aircraft. He was one of the many American airmen with German ancestors; he would soon be passing within a few miles of the birthplaces – Mannheim and Stuttgart – of two of his grandparents.

> I always thought it was sort of ironic that, had the Germans succeeded in shooting down my aircraft and that of my deputy leader, they would have made a lot of promotion vacancies. In my aircraft was Colonel Gross – the air task force commander, myself – the group commander, the group navigator, the group bombardier and a squadron navigator. In the aircraft of my deputy leader was Brigadier-General Williams – the bombardment wing commander, my senior squadron commander, his operations officer, his squadron navigator and squadron bombardier. The German fighters shot down aircraft all around us but did not succeed in getting either of us.
>
> My group was so seriously crippled after that Schweinfurt mission that it took several months to build it up into a first-class fighting organization again.

Both Colonel Gross and Brigadier-General Williams saw their left wingmen shot down but received reinforcements when the only two planes to survive in the low squadron came up to join them.

The high group of the leading wing, officially the 101st Composite Group, was also heavily attacked. There is no dramatic story to tell here; the Germans simply removed nearly a third of this makeshift formation's strength before the target was reached.

Although the three groups of the leading combat wing were the objects of most of the attacks during that fiercest part of the battle, a little of the German pressure spilled over onto the second combat wing, sometimes with German pilots coming straight through after an attack on one of the leading groups. Three B-17s were lost in the second wing before the Rhine was crossed near Darmstadt. But, further back still, the second half of the bomber force was almost untouched. The third and fourth combat wings each lost only one plane before the Rhine and many of the men in the units flying here were largely ignorant of the disaster being experienced at the front of the force. The scattered German successes at the rear of the force were probably achieved by fighter units which were not used to operating in this area and had little stomach for the full-blooded head-on attack method. One German unit involved in attacks on the rear half of the Schweinfurt force was the 5th *Staffel* of II/JG 11 which had flown down from Northern Germany. This *Staffel* was experimenting with unusual kinds of attack methods on American formations. In recent weeks it had bombed the Americans from above, but not with sufficient success for that role to become permanent; now its Messerschmitt 109s were fitted with a 15-cm rocket under each wing. Oberleutnant Heinz Knoke was the *Staffelkapitän*.

> I led the *Staffel* into position, three flights of four aircraft each. It took several minutes to get us all sorted out and into the most favourable position but I knew that I had plenty of time because the American fighters had left. I was very keen to get my *Staffel* really favourably placed. I chose the lowest American formation and we went into a slight dive, levelled out at the same altitude and speed as the bombers and took careful aim with the gun-sight. The main object was to burst the rockets on a timed run inside the American formation and

create confusion. My aircraft was hit in the left wing by American machine-gun fire before I could launch my own rockets, and the rocket hanging there was shot off and dropped away. It was difficult to hold the stick with the remaining rocket, the aircraft was dragging to the right and this made it difficult to aim. I fired and watched it explode in the formation but with no effect.

The rest of the *Staffel* all fired; I think Feldwebels Fest and Fuhrmann – our two experts – hit bombers which blew up. We had taken twenty-four rockets into action and had been hoping for at least five or six successes. We were optimistic in those days; we had to be in everything we did. We were very disappointed with the result. We had tried bombs and that was a failure and now it seemed that these rockets were only a limited success.

I decided to break off and land because I didn't know how badly my wing was damaged, but the rest of the *Staffel* stayed and carried out cannon attacks but I don't think they or the rest of the *Gruppe* had any more successes and Oberleutnant Koenig, the commander of the 4th *Staffel*, had to force-land when his plane was damaged. We called him 'Kegelkoenig' because he was such a bowling fan.

The records of the 92nd Bomb Group, flying the low position in the third combat wing, contained a detailed description of this German rocket attack, although the group estimated that the rockets were fired at a range of 750 yards. Knoke's hope that two B-17s had been destroyed by his *Staffel*'s rockets was not justified. The 92nd Group's report says that two B-17s which were damaged by rocket fragments were crippled and thus easily shot down by later fighter attack, but survivors from both planes say that they hardly realized they had been hit by rockets and that the subsequent shooting down of their aircraft was almost entirely due to conventional fighter attack.

Compared with the material which contributed to the earlier description of the fighter attacks on the Regensburg bomber force, there are not many good accounts available from German pilots involved in these attacks on the Schweinfurt force. Most of the German contributions give only general descriptions of a succession of frenzied, frightening attacks from the front against the American formations. The battle was so intense that it is rarely possible to 'pair' American and German accounts. One part of the battle, however, can be isolated and described from both sides. This was only a small action compared to the mass destruction of B-17s taking place at the front of the bomber force but it displays several interesting tactical aspects.

The high group in the fourth and last wing of the bomber column was another makeshift unit, designated the 103rd Composite Group. The lead and low squadrons were made up of planes from the 303rd Bomb Group and the high position was filled by the 525th Squadron of the 379th Bomb Group. Five of the six pilots flying in this squadron were original members of it; in fact their crews represented virtually the last original part of the squadron still existing. One plane had aborted over the sea and returned to England, but the remaining crews were quite happy to be flying on in this position; 'high-high' – high squadron in a high group – rarely suffered any serious trouble and while the head of the bomber force was under violent attack this formation had been flying quietly on in peaceful conditions. Suddenly, at a point near the Rhine south of Koblenz, a series of unusual fighter attacks commenced when a string of single Messerschmitt 109s came down steeply from above and levelled out before making their head-on attacks. It was the sudden appearance and steepness of the approach which surprised those who were watching.

The German fighters making these attacks were from II/JG 51, the *Gruppe* which had recently returned from the Mediterranean to re-equip with new aircraft at an airfield near Munich. Part of the *Gruppe* had flown up to Frankfurt and refuelled there before this action. It had then split into smaller sections and it was the 5th *Staffel* which was attacking the high squadron of the composite group. Hauptmann Hans Langer was the *Staffelkapitän*.

> When I first heard just how many planes they said were coming in, I went absolutely potty; I was scared – but not later when I got into the air. I took my eight planes and flew east. It was fascinating to see so many bombers after the few we had seen in the Mediterranean. They looked like clusters of grapes hanging in the sky.
>
> We had practised the frontal attack. We had to study everything very carefully because we were so small in numbers and because of the disadvantage of our equipment; the 109 was so inferior by then although I loved it. We even had a captured B-17 – I had flown it at Rechlin – and knew exactly how fast the

top turret could turn. We weren't bothered about the ball turret; it wasn't very effective. Four or five days earlier we made practice attacks on four Junkers 88s flying at 23,000 feet at the B-17's cruising speed and found that attacks from 10 degrees above and dead ahead were the best. When we tried this flying wing to wing, we found that two or more planes sometimes zeroed in on the same bomber and got in each other's way, so we tried it singly, in line, with each pilot taking his own target.

Just as I was about to start the frontal attack my fuel warning lights came on; my wingman said his were on too. I said, 'Let's run two attacks and we'll see how we get on.' We lost altitude too fast and dipped below the bombers before levelling up again with them. I saw them waving about, all trying to get in tight; I thought that was very good. Then things happened fast; we all shot at will. I passed just underneath the bomber formation. I could feel a shaking as we went past, either from their propeller wash or from the air compression with being so close.

I told the others on the radio that we would make a climbing left turn and attack from the back. I looked around and saw that two of the bombers were trailing smoke. I collected my fellows again and came right on top of the bombers. We throttled back about 300 feet above them. Then I decided to sideslip into the formation – the first time I had ever done that. This had two advantages – one that the bomber gunners would find it almost impossible to fire at me and the other that I was already very close.

I side-slipped and levelled off just behind a bomber on which I had my sights, close enough for me to see the tail gunner inside. I pressed both buttons at once and all my guns fired. I saw a stream of fire going into the B-17 and that's all – except for one more thing. The Number 3 engine – the right-inner – actually came off the wing and whipped right back over me and the wing came off immediately afterwards. The bomber flipped onto its back.

The bomber which Langer saw destroyed in such dramatic fashion was that of Lieutenant Erwalt Wagner, known to his friends as 'Bring-'em-back-alive Wagner'. Technical Sergeant Johannes Johnson, radio operator in the B-17 immediately ahead, had a grandstand view.

> I heard everyone hollering when the fighters first came through. The others were all firing but I couldn't; they came through too fast. I watched them going round again. They seemed to be concentrating on our squadron. I suddenly saw the inboard engine on the right wing of the plane behind me come off. The whole engine came out and over the top of the wing, hit the right stabilizer and tore that off. The engine dropped out of sight. The plane flopped over completely and headed straight down. I saw no more; it went out of my sight but my assumption was that it went straight down like a bomb and buried itself ninety feet into the ground. You were supposed to count chutes but there was nothing to see on that one.
>
> It was all over in a flash. The whole thing was over in less than two seconds. It happened far faster than I can tell it. That's one of the few times I got really scared – I make no bones about it. I hadn't any feelings about the men in that ship. I was just worried that it was our turn next. I don't mean to be callous but that's how it was.

There were no survivors in Lieutenant Wagner's crew.

A fighter pilot has only the most limited view of what happens in an air battle. Interview notes with another German pilot, Oberleutnant Peter Eder of II/JG 2, show how he and his wingman flew past one high group and swung in to attack a second from ahead. He describes his attack on a B-17.

> I took the centre aircraft in the high squadron. I aimed at the cockpit but hit its left wing, as seen from the front, between the two engines. I saw the left wing break off before I passed through. It was one of those pictures you never forget. I got official credit for it.

Both Langer's and Eder's accounts match perfectly the destruction of Lieutenant Wagner's B-17 and illustrate the difficulty of allocating success to individual German pilots. An interesting point is that these two had started out that morning from airfields 420 miles apart to meet here and share in the destruction of that American unit. The other four planes in that high squadron were all hit and suffered engine failures because of the German attacks. One by one the four fell back and lost height. Three of them later crashed at widely separated points, the last turned back and became one more of a growing number of lone, crippled B-17s hoping to reach safety, and whose fortunes will be described later.

There were no further losses from that composite group, but the group leader, flying in a lower squadron, was Major Lewis Lyle, whose own plane also suffered a damaged engine. Lyle allowed the propeller of the dead engine to spin so that he would not attract further German fighter attack and managed to fly on three engines to the target and all the way back to England without breaking formation. Lyle's post-raid report stated that most of the planes in the high squadron should also have been able to maintain formation on three engines as he did, but he took a less harsh view on being interviewed for this book.

> I think they were going to be shot down anyway. It was unmerciful the way they kept coming in and attacking that top squadron. In fact they were attacking so hard that when the top squadron had gone we would have been next, but fortunately the attacks seemed to fade away just after the top squadron had gone.

Thus did the 525th Bomb Squadron disappear from the Schweinfurt force. The main body of its parent group, the 379th, was flying immediately below the composite group and many of its members witnessed the loss of the squadron. The main group did not suffer a single casualty.

We return to the general description of the battle. These are a selection of the many personal accounts available from men who were in the B-17s shot down. The difficulties and frustrations of the regular gunners caused by the German head-on attacks are a recurring theme, as are the sometimes frantic efforts of navigators and bombardiers in the nose compartment to defend their planes. One of the accounts is from the only B-17 shot down before Eupen was reached; all others are from planes shot down between Eupen and Schweinfurt. Three of the accounts will be presented anonymously so as not to cause undue embarrassment to surviving crew members or distress to the relatives of dead ones. There was little that was unique about the experience of the men inside the B-17s shot down on the way to Schweinfurt; similar incidents occurred whenever the Eighth Air Force met the Luftwaffe. What was unique was that there was no precedent for the intensity of the action.

Second Lieutenant Walter Brown was the bombardier in the 91st Bomb Group plane shot down before Eupen.

We were tail-end Charlie – low plane, low squadron. The first four fighters missed us but the lead plane of the next pass had us right in the middle of his sights. I don't know how many hits we took but there was one serious one in the leading edge of the left wing between the two engines. The whole wing just flopped off outside Number 2 engine and that was it.

No one really had much chance to get a parachute on. I had seen two planes collide over England and a good buddy of mine was the only one to get out. He'd been wearing a back-pack so I always wore one after that – the only one in the crew to do so. The navigator was at his table and was able to reach out and grab his chest-pack quickly. He only got one of the clips fastened when the centrifugal force pinned us both to the floor. He was being throttled by his oxygen tube but I was able to reach up and unplug it from the wall for him. I never heard a word from or had a chance to see the others from beginning to end.

I didn't realize we were spinning – you lose the horizon and you have no idea what position you are in – but my pal in another aircraft told me that we made three or three and a half turns and then the plane disintegrated. I don't know whether there was an explosion or not; centrifugal force can be enough to tear a plane apart. All I know is that I went flying out the plexiglass window. The glass wasn't there but the nose gun was and I hit it with my back. I'm sure that would have killed me if I hadn't had the back parachute pack on. I reckon that back-pack saved my life twice.

The next thing I knew was that the parachute was open and there were bits of aeroplane falling around me. I don't remember pulling the ripcord; it may have caught in something. It was awful damned quiet, a terrific contrast.

The only other survivor in this crew was Second Lieutenant Edgar Yelle, who had only been assigned to this crew as navigator just before take-off, having arrived at the base that morning.

Staff Sergeant Paul Shipe was the top-turret gunner in Lieutenant Hamden Forkner's crew, 381st Bomb Group.

They came in from eleven o'clock high – two F Ws with yellow cowlings. I didn't see them until very late. I called out to 'Ham' to stick the nose down but, at the same time, the ball-turret gunner was saying, 'Stick the nose up', so that he could fire as well. But it was too late; it only takes a fraction of a second.

Coming in dead on the nose like that was a dirty trick; you hadn't a chance.

Number 1 engine was on fire and Number 2 was hit and spurting out oil all over my turret. We turned back and the pilot tugged at my leg and motioned to me to shoot a flare to tell the fighters we wanted assistance but there was no one there to help us. Then he waved at me to go back and check out the crew. I went back through the bomb-bay and saw all the doors open. Everyone in the back had gone. The pilot had always told us that if we went down we'd all got to get the hell out fast or he would beat us out – but he didn't do that. After he had set up the automatic pilot he gave me a push in the back and we both went out together.

This B-17 flew on for at least another twenty-five miles after Forkner and Shipe left it.

Staff Sergeant Lloyd Thomas was the ball-turret gunner in Lieutenant Bill Wheeler's crew, 91st Bomb Group.

The dead level approach of the fighters shut off the firepower from the ball turret and top turret at long range, as these guns were designed not to fire through the plane's props. My own attempts to fire at them were limited to those fleeting seconds as they passed underneath. The top turret had few opportunities to fire and the bombardier had no guns because we were flying in the lead position and were carrying a bombsight.

We were hit in the Number 2 engine position and there was soon a large tongue of flame like a giant blowtorch coming from the engine and extending practically to the tail of the aircraft. All around us there were other aircraft falling, both enemy and friend; chutes were everywhere. My first thoughts were that we could blow the fire out in a dive but, no, it continued. The bomb-bay doors opened. I saw the bombs fall and then I saw other objects falling out and realized those objects were crew members baling out.

I feel we should not have been shot down that day. We were a veteran crew in good physical condition. We knew we could expect the mission to be rough but the onslaught of fighters was like a storm. Nothing could have withstood them.

The following account comes from a navigator.

You get a really clear view of everything in front of you

when you are in that nose of a B-17 and I was definitely frightened – a gnawing feeling of desperation. They're coming in and I can't do anything about it. As an individual I was quite defenseless because my gun wouldn't bear directly to the front. The bombardier had the twin fifties right in the centre of the nose. He was not our regular bombardier. He opened fire on them far too early, when they were way out in the distance – they were just dots – but, instead of firing in bursts, he just froze on the triggers and both guns jammed. I think they burned out. I remember looking out and the barrel of one had definitely bent with the heat. He was like a crazy man when those guns stopped.

They 'can-opened' the right wing; they just gouged great holes right into the metalwork all along the front of it and both engines. An engine on the other side also had to be feathered but I don't know why. The pilot gave the order, 'Prepare to bale out', a preliminary command to which we all had to respond. The response was meant to go in a certain order commencing with the bombardier, but he never replied. If I've ever seen a personification of fear, that man had it. He just ripped his oxygen mask off and came at me and tore my oxygen mask off too. Both of us were thus without our throat mikes so we weren't able to respond. I think he thought he was trying to save my life, pushing me back to the escape hatch. I was trying to open it when the bombardier gave me a real kick in the pants, onto the door and I went straight out with the hatch clutched to my chest. I was the first one out – great honour!

Later, in the prison camp, the co-pilot accused me of cowardice and the pilot was certainly very tight-lipped about it. They said I had endangered their lives by making the co-pilot come down into the nose to see where we were. The co-pilot was so incensed when he saw me in the prison camp that he was talking of court-martial but that never evolved. The bombardier wasn't with us in the camp and I had great difficulty convincing them that it wasn't my fault. I'm not sure they ever accepted it.

Staff Sergeant John Wasche was the ball gunner in Lieutenant J. D. Stewart's crew, 92nd Bomb Group.

There was a tremendous rocking of the ship and fire was coming out of the gasoline tanks under the wings and the engine nacelles on the left wing. There was raw gasoline spraying over my turret but it didn't ignite; I don't know why. Later, when I was on the way down by parachute, I was sick because I gulped a mouthful of it when getting out of the turret.

Then, almost at once, I heard Jimmy Stewart in his slow Texan drawl use an expression he was fond of using when he was surprised at something that had happened, 'Shithouse mouse, we're going down. Abandon ship.' And those were the last words I ever heard Jimmy say. I never saw him again. I got out of the turret at once and, by the time I got into the waist, the plane was so hot that there was ammunition exploding somewhere. You could hear it. Before I put my parachute on, I made sure there was no blood. I didn't mind dying but I didn't want to be a cripple. If I had been badly wounded I would have gone down with the ship but I was all right. Steve Solga, one of the waist gunners, was badly wounded. Part of his face was shot away and the rest was covered in blood; the eyeball was partly protruding. We checked that his parachute and face were alright. His parachute was okay but we couldn't do anything about his face. Two of us kicked the door which opened at once and out went Steve Solga.

Despite John Wasche's fears, Lieutenant Stewart survived safely and Steve Solga's wounded eye was saved by a German doctor. Technical Sergeant John Collins was the radio operator in the same crew.

I was stood on a box in my radio room trying to do something useful with my gun but with little success. I remember looking down into the waist and the two men at the guns there were just going crazy with action. The plane was really very badly shot up. One of the men in the waist was wounded and he wanted to know whether we were leaving. We all knew something was drastically wrong but we had not heard the alarm bell, although I think the red warning light in my room, telling me to destroy the radio, had come on.

I wanted to go forward to ask what was happening but to do this I had to go along the catwalk through the bomb-bay. I opened the door and closed it real quick – a whole lot of flames came roaring out. I didn't get badly burned – just singed. There was no possible way of getting forward. I destroyed my radio; you just pushed a button and it detonated inside, just a dull thud. Normally a radio man doesn't like to lose his radio but I certainly wasn't worried about it that time.

We got John out of the ball turret; he was very ill with the petrol he had swallowed. I think we had a little confab in the waist to see whether we should bale out. No one took the decision; it was just a mutual agreement.

Lieutenant Tony Arcaro was a pilot in the 91st Bomb Group. He was 'a real Brooklyn boy' of humble origins and with a widowed mother, and was intensely proud of having become an Air Force officer and captain of a four-engined bomber.

There was a lot of excitement and confusion. Enemy fighters were coming in from different directions – everyone on the plane was calling out and the other planes on the squadron kept disappearing. My one thought was to keep in formation and stay with the force. Every time we lost a plane I kept moving up to fill the empty space until there was only us and one other plane left. I tucked myself very, very close in with that last aircraft, so close that my port wing overlapped with him. I had to watch that wing very closely so that I could follow every evasive action he took. I don't think I have ever concentrated so hard on flying in my life.

I remember one Messerschmitt 109 going across our nose on its back and its slipstream shook our whole aeroplane. I could see the pilot hanging upside down as he went past in front of me. The nose guns in front of me never moved, never fired a shot, that German was going so fast.

We were still in perfect condition, taking no hits; we were doing great. But then four of them came in high, from about eleven o'clock. They all seemed to be firing at my plane. I didn't see the exact extent of the hits but we were on fire. The oxygen bottles right underneath the co-pilot were hit. It was just like a blowtorch just below me. It was really serious.

I decided that I had to order the crew to abandon the ship – it was all that fuel I was worried about. The intercom was out and we didn't have a bale-out bell so I sent someone to tell them to abandon ship. I don't know how long I waited after that, probably a couple of minutes. The fire was getting bigger; it was really raging. I didn't think I was going to get out and I thought, 'Will my mother ever know I died this way?' I put it on automatic and managed to get my chest-pack on. Then I dove right from the flight deck out through the front hatch – right through the fire. I cleared it just like a champion diver; I never even bumped the side. I was real glad to be out of that thing. I think I'm a pretty lucky guy.

Two of Arcaro's gunners were killed in the German attacks and the navigator so badly injured that he died later. Sergeant Delmar Kaech, the crew's radio operator, had a particularly lucky escape.

I could see through the back of the radio room that the ball-turret gunner was hit. He was half way out and 'frozen' to the controls of his turret which was going round and round in steady circles. I wanted to help him and take over his position – that's a very important position on a B-17 – but he was definitely dead. His body was in such a position that I could not reach the dead man's switch which would have stopped it revolving.

One of the officers came back then to tell us to get out. I tried to get out through the bomb-bay but it was full of flames and I eventually went out in a very unusual way. I climbed over the frame of my own gun mounting in the radio room and got into a position where I was sitting on the top of the fuselage, holding onto the barrel of my gun. My back was towards that big vertical stabilizer but I never gave that a thought. I just let go. People say that you can't survive a bale-out from that position; you are bound to hit either the vertical or one of the horizontal stabilizers but I missed them all.

Lieutenant John Dytman was the navigator in Lieutenant Helmuth Hansen's crew, 351st Bomb Group.

Then we fell back a third time and this time Hansen couldn't get the propeller back into govern and we fell further back. Immediately those fighters queued up and started coming into us from the port side – about ten o'clock high. I think that at one time there were eleven of them out there. Every gun on the ship was firing; we were being hit all the time. I got a few fragments in both legs but was not incapacitated. I think it was about the seventh or eighth pass that they really hit us hard. It was a 20-millimetre incendiary shell into the oxygen supply system and one bottle had a small hole with a fire shooting out of it. It was just behind my position.

I got down there with my navigator's briefcase; I thought I could smother the fire with it. I put the briefcase sideways onto it but, all of a sudden, the whole area became one big fire-flame, a bright orange-red blowtorch in which I was engulfed. My wrists where the gloves met the flying suit and my face where it was not protected by my helmet were burnt. I guess they were second-degree burns but they didn't hurt at the time. Later, however, when I was coming down by parachute, the pain was unbelievable – fresh burns going through cold air!

This account is from a bombardier.

I looked up and saw seven Focke-Wulfs spread in a line across the front of our element. I felt they were concentrating on our ship; the centre of their line was directly ahead of us. I had seen that sort of thing before and survived it but never that many, that close and that determined – it was a little different this time. When you saw those seven aeroplanes with the winking lights in their wings, that terrified you. I was on my knees, firing my single machine gun, and I picked the centre one of the line – I felt he was the one who was being very personal – but I don't think my fire was very effective. You had that heavy machine gun with its ring-and-post sight suspended on bunjee cord and the movement of the aircraft made it like trying to hit something with a garden hose.

All of a sudden there was this explosion and I found myself back behind the navigator, almost back in the crawlway under the pilots' cockpit. The whole nose was full of smoke. I got up and looked out of the left side window. The left wing was on fire – the area round Number 2 engine was blazing pretty well. Then I poked my head up into the cockpit. The top turret gunner was all right; he was getting out of his turret. I could only see the back of the two pilots' seats and all I could see was that they were both immobile. The instruments were all shot away, hit from the front and blown inwards. The cockpit was full of smoke. They'd pretty well chewed us up horizontally. I heard later that the rest of the aircraft was almost untouched; there was just that one concentrated burst in the front.

The top turret gunner said, 'Let's get out of here.' I crawled back to the nose and got my chest parachute and told the navigator we had got to go. For some reason I had always had a fear of parachuting and often said that I would never do it but, when the time came, I never gave it a second thought.

Five men were lost in this crew. The pilot and co-pilot were both decapitated by the concentrated burst of cannon fire. No orders went back to the rear of the plane and two waist gunners are believed to have been trapped by the spin which developed. The navigator baled out but no one is sure how he died.

This final account, from a navigator, should also be an anonymous one.

> I turned away from my gun, picked up my parachute from the bench and put it on. Then I turned round and there was the bombardier. He had already popped his chute and I think he must have been trying to push the parachute outside because it was streaming away through the hatch in the floor. I couldn't get by him because he was sprawled right across the hole in a very awkward position. He had no chance remaining in the plane but he couldn't bring himself to go. I can't tell what was in his mind; he was in a very bad way, bleeding from the mouth. The front cockpit area hadn't been badly hit; it is possible that the parachute opening suddenly may have injured him internally. He was conscious and he told me that he didn't want me to push him out. I tried to persuade him but he just didn't want to move.
>
> That left my escape hatch blocked and it meant that I had to crawl back underneath the pilot's position and on through the bomb-bay. The bombs were still there, either side of me. I reached the waist door which was open and I looked down. Things were hot underneath me – all sorts of hell fire. The fighters were all about us and I could see tracer passing just underneath me. Some of the shots were hitting the aircraft but I only got a few slivers in the butt – nothing serious, just enough to break the skin after passing through all the clothing.
>
> Then I was going down. I delayed pulling a little but when I did I could hear the whole sky rumbling and vibrating with engine noise – just like an armada of aircraft going over.

The German attacks slackened during the final part of the flight to Schweinfurt. Many German pilots were running low on fuel and only two German units, *Jagdgruppe* 50 from Wiesbaden and II/JG 51, were able to remain in contact. The Germans had shot down twenty-four B-17s between the crossing of the Dutch coast and the Initial Point a few miles west of Schweinfurt. This represents 11 per cent of the force which had crossed the coast. The Regensburg force had lost fourteen B-17s during the equivalent period. The flight to Schweinfurt seemed to have lasted for an eternity, particularly to the men in the groups under the most determined and prolonged of the German attacks. Some of the survivors would be amazed when, years later, we calculated together that the flight time from the coast to the I.P. was only seventy-four minutes. The most intense part of the action, from Eupen to the crossing of the Rhine near Darmstadt, lasted only twenty-seven minutes – a period which saw the loss of twenty-one B-17s. Seventeen of the twenty-four shot-down planes came from the leading combat wing which had lost almost a third of its strength. Four planes were lost from the second combat wing, one from the third and two from the fourth although two more from the fourth wing were badly damaged, only loosely in contact, and would be finished off by German fighters after Schweinfurt had been bombed. Many other B-17s in all parts of the bomber force had been damaged and their crews must have been facing the prospect of the flight over the target and all the way back to England with much apprehension. The American casualties were caused almost entirely by German single-engined fighter action. The bomber force had been cleverly led around nearly all the German Flak areas by the lead navigator, Captain David M. Williams, and tributes to his good work carried out in the nose of his B-17 with German fighters attacking bombers all around him appear both in official documents and personal accounts. The vicinity of Aachen appears to be the only place where German Flak was effective. Two of the B-17s shot down by German fighters had first been damaged by Flak here.

It is more difficult to be precise about the German casualties in this battle. Firm evidence exists for only twelve fighters likely to have been shot down or forced down to crash-landings by the fire of B-17 gunners during this period. Casualties to German pilots inflicted by B-17 gunners on the way to Schweinfurt are believed to be one killed and six wounded plus another pilot killed when his Focke-Wulf 190 landed short of fuel at Koblenz and somersaulted. There is no way that the German casualties can be credited to individual American units apart from the obvious statement that the bomb groups which suffered the heaviest German attacks probably shot most of these Germans down.

Eight German units appear to have shared the credit for the shooting down of the B-17s. Most of the successes were achieved by the regular German front-line units from the Holland-Ruhr area; their pilots were well used to the rough and tumble conditions of 'Channel coast' operations. The three *Gruppen* of JG 11

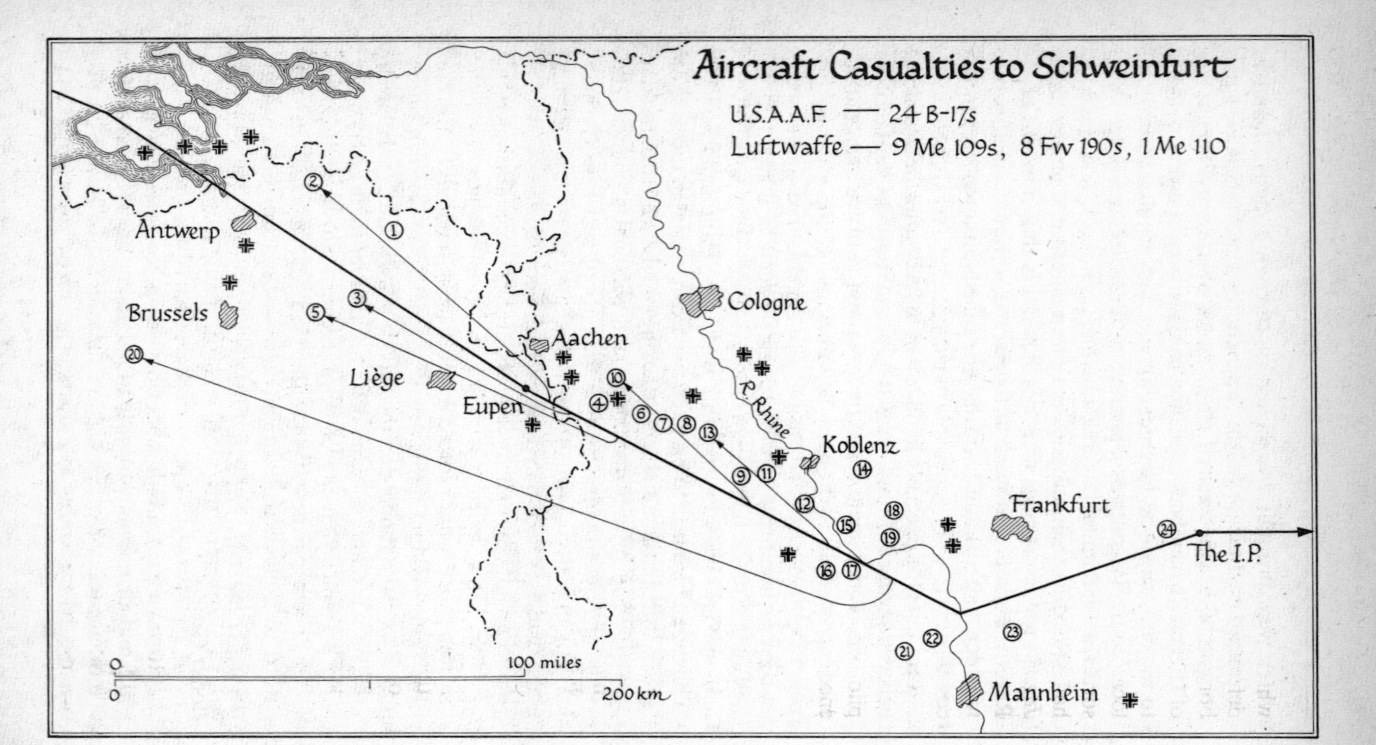
Aircraft Casualties to Schweinfurt
U.S.A.A.F. — 24 B-17s
Luftwaffe — 9 Me 109s, 8 Fw 190s, 1 Me 110
Antwerp
Brussels
Liège
Eupen
Aachen
Cologne
R. Rhine
Koblenz
Frankfurt
Mannheim
The I.P.
1
2
3
4
5
6
7
8
9
10
11
12
13
14
15
16
17
18
19
20
21
22
23
24
0
100 miles
0
200 km

which were brought down from Northern Germany cannot be definitely credited with the outright destruction of a single bomber, although seven of JG 11's own planes were lost. As one of this unit's members explained earlier, its pilots were not used to the individualistic *freie Jagd* type of fighting practised by the local units. By contrast, *Jagdgruppe* 50, flying its second major sortie of the day, had again come into action at a late stage and had scored further successes against weakened American units. *Jagdgruppe* 50 later claimed fourteen B-17s shot down from the Regensburg and Schweinfurt forces and, although this figure is too high, this new unit was experiencing an outstandingly successful day.

This chapter can end with two personal contributions each containing notes of relief. Leutnant Heinz Rose was the II/JG 11 pilot who earlier mentioned the unsuitability of his unit's experience for the hectic fighting in this area.

> It was really a new theatre of operations for us and we had approached the prospect with much apprehension. Specht, our *Gruppe* commander, liked to conduct his operations in a careful manner but I think he found this all a bit confusing. I never even fired my guns.
>
> I had to land at Hangelar near Bonn with the red lights on – not much fuel left. I was making my approach when I saw an FW 190 making a normal landing just in front of me. Because of my low fuel, I picked up speed and flew over the top and landed in front of him, forcing him to overshoot and come round again. This was forbidden but I just had to do it. I landed and taxied off to the left. A car came tearing up with the local flying control officer ready to tell me off. The propeller of my plane stopped at that moment; the last of the petrol was gone. I was doubly pleased, once to be down safely from that horrible flight and secondly to be able to prove to flying control that I had been forced to land that way. I probably met the FW 190 pilot later and apologized.

Lieutenant Edwin Frost was a navigator in the embattled 381st Bomb Group.

> It was a tremendous relief when the fighter attacks slackened off and there was a chance to catch our breath. I remember looking out to our left and seeing the sun shining on two big rivers – the Rhine and the Main – and we had an excellent view

of a big city. It was Frankfurt. That was the first time I started doing my job as a navigator since Eupen. These were the two mile-posts that I remember of that trip – Eupen when all the action started and Frankfurt when the worst was over.

I do remember, also, a typical build-up of tension as we approached the target area.

CHAPTER 14

Over Schweinfurt

The navigator of the leading B-17 guided his pilot over the Initial Point at 2.53 p.m. (3.53 p.m. German time). This was two minutes later than the time laid down by the flight plan, a seemingly small delay but one which would turn out to be important. The I.P. was the small town of Gemünden, which was situated on a wide loop of the River Main and at the junction of four roads; it was six minutes' flying time west of Schweinfurt. Of the 230 B-17s which had taken off in England, 198 arrived at the I.P., although two had already jettisoned their bombs and several more would be unable to release their loads on Schweinfurt because of combat damage. The lead planes of all twelve bomb groups had survived and none of them had suffered any personnel casualties or mechanical damage which might impair their bomb-aiming ability. That is not to say that many of the men in those twelve planes were not somewhat shaken by their recent ordeal. But Lieutenant-Colonel Wurzbach, pilot of the leading plane of the force, probably captured the general mood when he says, 'I was convinced by then that I would not survive the mission, so my only goal was to make as accurate a bombing run on the target as possible.'

The procedure by which high and low groups fell into line behind each other for the run through the target areas and the activities of the lead bombardiers were the same as have been described in the earlier chapter on the Regensburg bombing. There were only three significant differences in the Schweinfurt plan. The average bombing height was 3,000 feet higher than at Regensburg, presumably because of the stronger Flak defences expected at Schweinfurt. There were three separate targets at Schweinfurt instead of the one at Regensburg. The third difference was that the I.P. and direction of approach to the target had been changed just before the take-off of the Schweinfurt force, a bomb run from the west being substituted for the earlier planned approach from the east. This change had been made to keep the sun in a more favourable position and should have made little difference because the lead bombardiers had been studying every approach to Schweinfurt for some weeks past. But the alteration had not reached some units until very late and this change of plan was to be one of several adverse factors affecting the prospects for a successful attack.

The remnants of the 91st Bomb Group settled down on the run across the rather featureless countryside between the I.P. and Schweinfurt. Unfortunately the River Main, which ran through both places, swung well to the south here and could not be used for reference purposes. It was not ideal country for the final approach flight, but the town of Schweinfurt soon came into sight. The weather was clear and there was not yet any Flak. But all was not well behind this leading group; the units following were not settling down into the well-spaced column which was essential to give their bombardiers the chance to make a good attack.

The seeds of the trouble had been sown more than an hour earlier over Belgium when Colonel Gross, commander of the first two combat wings, decided to reduce height to fly under a sheet of cloud. That reduction in height and the subsequent climb to regain altitude when the cloud was passed had put this first half of the Schweinfurt force a little behind the briefed flight plan – two minutes at the I.P. But the second half of the bomber force had not made any height adjustments and thus gained ground on the leaders. This 'squeezing up' of the whole force had been further accentuated by the natural closing up of groups seeking mutual protection under the prolonged German fighter attacks. When the worst of the German attacks had slackened, near Frankfurt, the various elements of the force had attempted to shake themselves out and 'gain interval' for bombing, but this process was only partially successful. The second combat wing flew a large zig-zag to create its interval and this in turn affected the next combat wing, the navigator of whose lead aircraft later reported:

> Approximately halfway along this leg we observed groups of B-17s converging towards the estimated position of the target from both our left and right. We found it necessary to continue to 50·08 deg. North, 09·51 deg. East for our I.P. in order to fall in behind the left group of planes which were barely ahead of us.*

* 306th Bomb Group, Navigation Narrative.

This group thus had to start its approach run into Schweinfurt from a point ten miles north-east of the designated I.P., and presumably the other two groups of the wing had to comply. The result of all these manoeuvres was that, although the three early groups were able to make clear bomb runs, most of the nine groups following were getting in each other's way and were approaching the target from different directions.

The three ball-bearing factories, none of them large or prominent and all three located in residential areas of the town, had always been considered difficult targets. It was realized that the factory areas might be obscured by smoke towards the end of the raid and the four groups at the rear of the bomber force which were carrying incendiary bomb loads were told that, if conditions became too difficult, they were to bomb the centre of Schweinfurt and cause general damage there. One lead bombardier in an early group remembers being told: 'If you can't hit your aiming point, hit the housing, try to get some of the skilled workers and don't feel too bad about it.' It should be stressed, however, that such measures were only to be used as a last resort. Every effort was to be made to carry out precision bombing of the three ball-bearing factories.

But the bombing of Schweinfurt was not to be successful. The reports which the bomb groups filed for submission to higher command on returning from the raid put as good a gloss on the efforts of their bombardiers as possible, but the bombing photographs brought back by the B-17s and the excellent photographs obtained by an R.A.F. photographic reconnaissance plane two days later revealed the true position. The failure which unfolded was not the result of inadequate preparations and study; it was not due to poor weather conditions; it was not due to the interference of the German defences at Schweinfurt. This was a case of an unduly large bombing force becoming confused and congested on its approach run to the target. A combination of several seemingly minor factors had combined to withhold from the American airmen the reward of accurate bombing of those three small ball-bearing factories. The men of the 1st Bombardment Wing had been struggling against bad luck all day. Even the best-planned endeavours in wartime sometimes go that way.

The leading groups of a bomber force normally had the best chances of carrying out an accurate attack – there being as yet no smoke and dust to obscure their aim – but the three groups flying in the leading combat wing over Schweinfurt – the 91st, the 381st and the 101st Composite – made little use of this advantage. Photographs brought back by the surviving crews showed an extraordinary situation in which the planes of these units appear to have released their loads in no less than five concentrations spread over an area *nearly four miles long*. Two of the concentrations fell across the corners of the V.K.F. No. 1 and Kugelfischer factories, but even here most of the bombs fell among civilian housing near the V.K.F. factory and in the area of the railway station near the Kugelfischer factory. Two further concentrations fell in open fields well short of any target and the fifth concentration of bombs fell on the south side of the River Main nearly *two miles beyond* the furthest factory. The records of the units concerned do not contain any detailed explanation for such disappointing bombing results.

The three groups of the second combat wing – the 351st, 384th and 306th Composite – arrived three minutes later. Most of their planes had survived the fight through to the target and theirs was really the last chance to put right the catastrophic course of events in the Schweinfurt bombing. Unfortunately for the American cause, this did not happen. The 351st Bomb Group obviously led this combat wing into the target from too far to the south and was then completely confused by the widely scattered dust and smoke left by the first wave of the attack. Once again the bombing started too early, with many bombs falling in and around a village nearly a mile south-west of the nearest ball-bearing factory and the remainder of this wave of the bombing spreading across the river to fall harmlessly in open fields.

The next combat wing, containing the 92nd, 305th and 306th Bomb Groups, also arrived with its original strength almost intact, but this was the wing which had been forced north by the congestion at the Initial Point. They were still too far north when they arrived over Schweinfurt and the lead bombardiers could see nothing of the three ball-bearing factories, only an extensive cloud of smoke more than two miles long. The photographs brought back by these groups show that all three lead bombardiers gave up any idea of trying to hit the factories and decided to bomb the town centre. The first bombs, from the 306th Bomb Group, did fall right in the centre of Schweinfurt, but the loads of the succeeding groups were released too soon and

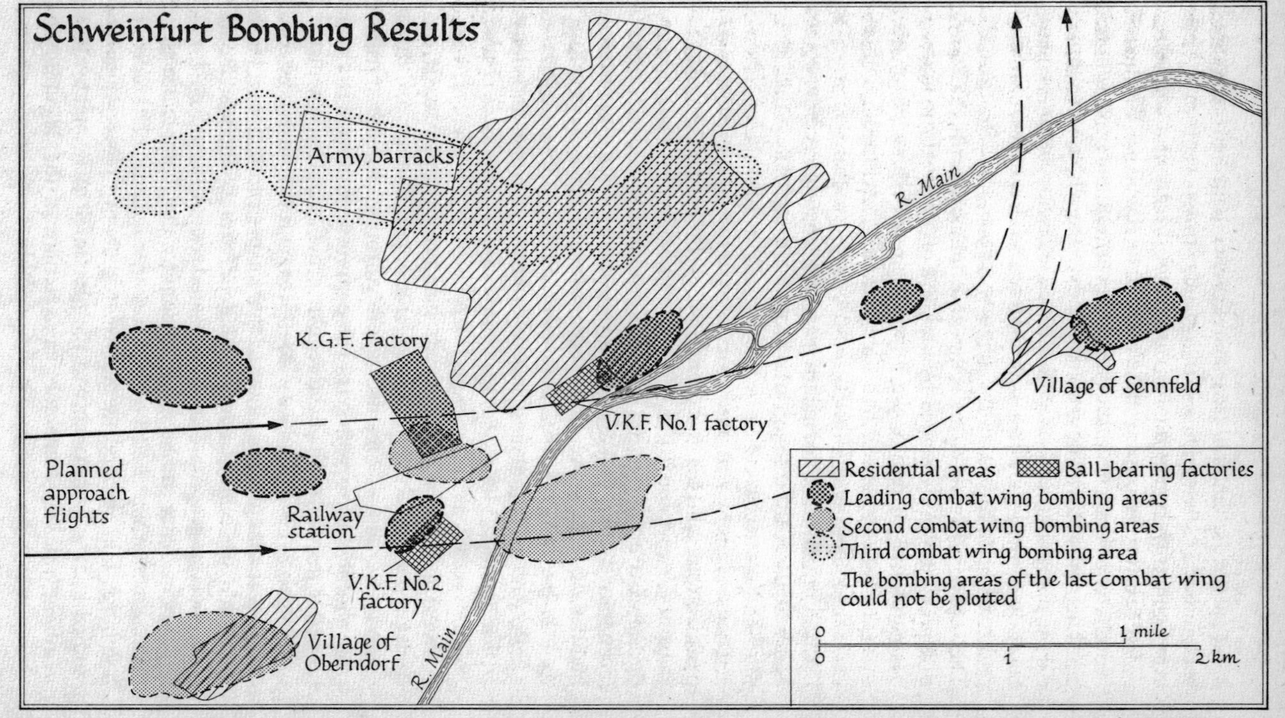

Schweinfurt Bombing Results
Army barracks
R. Main
K.G.F. factory
V.K.F. No.1 factory
Village of Sennfeld
Planned approach flights
Railway station
V.K.F. No.2 factory
Village of Oberndorf
R. Main
Residential areas
Ball-bearing factories
Leading combat wing bombing areas
Second combat wing bombing areas
Third combat wing bombing area
The bombing areas of the last combat wing could not be plotted
0
1 mile
0
1
2 km

burst in a now familiar pattern two miles long and extending back into the countryside. No industrial premises were under this heavy concentration of bombs, but the local army barracks were.

The last three groups over Schweinfurt – the 303rd, 379th and 103rd Composite – had little chance of carrying out any accurate bombing. Smoke was now billowing over the whole target area. All the planes in this wave of the attack were carrying incendiary bomb loads and they had been ordered to drop these into the centre of Schweinfurt if the factory targets were not visible. There were other problems – the lead bombardier of the 303rd Bomb Group was wounded by Flak fire on the final run and his navigator had to release the bombs manually, and the bomb-sight mechanism in the 379th's lead aircraft developed a fault at the last moment and affected the proper release of this group's loads. For all these reasons it is impossible to say where the bomb loads of these final three groups fell; it is likely that they were well scattered.

The last bombs went down on Schweinfurt at 3.11 p.m. (4.11 p.m. German time). The raid had lasted twelve minutes. As far as can be ascertained, 184 B-17s dropped 380 tons of bombs in the Schweinfurt area – 265 tons of high explosive and 115 tons of incendiaries. Some planes of the 305th Bomb Group also released bundles of leaflets over the target; a report from Schweinfurt records the titles: *Angriff* and *Adolf Hitler erklärte Krieg am 11. Dezember 1941 an die Vereinigten Staaten* (*Attack* and *Adolf Hitler Declared War on the United States on 11 December 1941*).

The American bombing results had been very poor. Of the twelve groups involved – nine regular group formations and three composite groups – three had possibly dropped some bombs on their allocated factory targets. The composite groups performed no better nor worse than the regular groups. Only a few of the men in the B-17s flying away from Schweinfurt realized the true extent of the failure, although the more experienced among them knew that something serious had gone wrong. The lead bombardier of one group which claimed good results, though no documentary evidence can be found to confirm this, complained that many other groups had bombed early; he called it 'hit-and-run bombing'. He regarded the Schweinfurt 'bomb plots' which he studied later as comparable to the plots of R.A.F. night 'area-bombing' raids he sometimes saw. A pilot in the 381st Bomb Group, which had suffered severe casualties on the way to the target and which seems to have scattered its bombs all over Schweinfurt, says, 'If the lead bombardier was shaking as much as I was, he had a reason to miss. We didn't hear till later that we had done so badly. There was no emotion about it; the main thought was – I've survived! But there was soon talk that we would have to go back again.'

Schweinfurt's defences were considerably stronger than those at Regensburg. Hitler's personal attention had been drawn to the importance of the ball-bearing industry town and there were eleven batteries of 88-mm Flak in and around Schweinfurt; at least some of these batteries had radar-controlled gun-laying equipment. A German historian, Friedhelm Golücke, who has written about Schweinfurt's air war says that 'in relation to its size, Schweinfurt was the best-defended town in Western Europe but the industry here was so important that every single battery was needed.'* But the Schweinfurt Flak defences had never been in action before and there were some shortcomings in their performance on this day. Although many of the batteries were situated on the B-17s' approach run to the target, none opened fire until just after the first wave had released their bombs. Herr Golücke's book describes how, even then, the German batteries were in some confusion. The smoke which soon covered Schweinfurt affected the firing of some batteries, and faults or unfamiliarity with the radar gun-laying equipment produced other problems. Golücke reports that some of the German guns were firing at such a low angle that shells were exploding just above the roof-tops of Schweinfurt. The German ex-Flak soldier who contributed this story to Golücke's book blames the gun-laying equipment problems on the metalized strips which, he says, the B-17s were dropping to jam the German radar. This was the device called Window by the R.A.F., who had just started using it, and *Düppel* by the Germans. This part of the story is incorrect; no Window was dropped over Schweinfurt, only harmless leaflets. Many of the Schweinfurt batteries soon settled down to effective firing. Schweinfurt also had extensive smokescreen protection but it was slow in coming into action on this day and it was not German-produced smoke which obscured the ball-bearing factories from the American bombardiers.

* Friedhelm Golücke, *Schweinfurt und der strategische Luftkrieg 1943*, Schöningh, Paderborn, 1980, p. 173.

The leading plane of the whole Schweinfurt force was hit by one of the first shells. Lieutenant-Colonel Wurzbach was the pilot.

> Almost immediately after 'bombs away', the blast from the first four-gun battery exploded around me and lifted my aircraft about a hundred feet. One 'eighty-eight' shell went through one of my fuel tanks in the wing but luckily didn't explode on contact. To this day, I would like to meet the Frenchman or other forced worker who put the defective fuze in that shell so that I could thank him and shake his hand.

The shell left a huge hole in the wing of Wurzbach's plane.

The German gunners steadily increased their effectiveness and succeeding waves of the attack suffered casualties; the lower groups received the most attention. The 303rd Bomb Group, flying the low position in the last wing, had ten of its planes damaged by Flak. Three B-17s in various groups were damaged so badly that they crashed within a few miles of Schweinfurt. An eye-witness account is available from each of these planes. Second Lieutenant William Lockhart was the bombardier in Lieutenant Jarvis's crew, 381st Bomb Group.

> We had just dropped the bombs and I was going back to my machine-gun when we were hit. I think it caught the two engines on the right-hand side of the ship. I was hit too. It was like being hit in the face by a brick, like someone hitting you with a baseball bat; the physical impact of being hit and stopping it with your body was considerable. A piece of shell had hit me in the chin, passed through the cheek and lodged behind the left eye. I remember being spun round and I lost my headset so that I was not aware of the trouble we were in. Actually I was in a state of shock and not really aware of anything much. I was a sorry sight. I don't remember pain then but it was extreme later on. Also, I wasn't able to get my oxygen and breathe properly.
>
> I think the pilot talked of trying for Switzerland but there was no hope of getting there. In fact the rest of the crew were all out so fast that the pilot and I were the only ones left. I managed to crawl to the escape hatch and baled out. I still don't know how I did it. The pilot followed me.

The plane of Lieutenant Donald Merchant, 379th Bomb Group, had earlier lost one engine to fighter attack and now lost a second to Schweinfurt's Flak. Technical Sergeant Johannes Johnson was the radio man.

> The pilot said he was going to try to get back. We'd had Boeing engineers come out to the group and tell us how good their planes were and that the B-17 could fly on two engines. But they were liars – we lost altitude. I heard someone say, 'Let's go to Switzerland; it's ninety miles due south.' The next thing I heard was the panic alarm button go no more than five minutes later. I thought the pilot had made a mistake so I called him up, 'Hey, Merchant' – we never bothered with ranks – 'Do you want us to bale out?' He said, 'That's right.'
>
> I went down to the waist with the other gunners. They were all ready. One of them had always said he was going to be first if it ever came the time to be out of this bird. So I pulled the pins, kicked the door out and motioned him to go. But he shook his head; he didn't want to go now. I was wearing my flying jacket and I tapped my tech. sergeant's stripes to show I was the senior non-com and out he went first.

The parachute of Technical Sergeant Gene Hecht, the engineer-gunner in this crew, did not open in time and he was killed. Hecht became the first American to be buried at a new prisoner-of-war camp at near-by Hammelburg. Lieutenant Merchant was too low to bale out and he had to crash-land; he did so safely. Five German batteries claimed the destruction of this B-17; the local Flak commander decided to allocate the credit for it equally between them all.*

The third B-17 whose loss can be mainly attributed to Schweinfurt's Flak defences is referred to in contributions from both the American and German sides. The B-17 concerned was that of Second Lieutenant Oliver Sweningsen, 384th Bomb Group. Sweningsen was in a flight of planes whose regular leader had been shot down earlier and which became detached from the main group at the Initial Point. Sweningsen describes the Flak hit. 'Carlos' was Second Lieutenant Stewart, his co-pilot.

> The windshield in front of me was blown in and the concussion knocked me against the armor plate, stunning me momentarily.

* Report of Flakgruppe Schweinfurt (Flakregiment 179) filed with Missing Air Crew Report No. 1765, U.S. National Archives. The five batteries were 2nd Battery, 482nd Flak Battalion; 1st and 3rd Batteries, 639th Battalion; and 1st and 3rd Batteries, 906th Battalion.

The plane fell out of formation in a left diving turn. Carlos noted my condition and took over the controls, but without much success. After a few moments I gathered my wits and took off the tin helmet which had become jammed down over my flying helmet and was covering my eyes. Together Carlos and I managed to get the plane back to level flight some distance from the formation and below it. At first I thought the plane was still airworthy although damaged. The controls were partly severed, the windshield was gone in front of me and there was a big hole in the nose. The tail gunner reported a leg wound and the navigator was wounded in the left shoulder. Carlos and I were struggling to get *Snuffy* back into the formation.

About that time, perhaps thirty seconds after the explosion, the left waist gunner reported over the intercom that we were on fire. I looked out and saw fire streaming out the wing below the outboard engine and eating away the wing between the engines. By this time *Snuffy* was beginning to fall off again. We could no longer hold the wing up so I gave the order to bale out. When I met the crews again two years later they told me the words I used were, 'Man the lifeboats.' I stayed at the controls until I believed all had gone. The engineer, who was still manning his turret, shooting back at a twin-engined fighter, left just ahead of me.

This twin-engined German plane was a Messerschmitt 110 piloted by Leutnant Josef Springer, a trainee night-fighter pilot from II/NJG 101 based at Kitzingen. Here is Springer's story.

Only the instructors were supposed to fly against the Americans but there was a spare aircraft – the radio had gone wrong – so I asked to fly it. I wanted to get in the two hours of operational flying which entitled me to better rations. I had never flown on operations before. My radar man came with me and we took off.

A Leutnant Busse volunteered to guide us to the main group of our planes which had taken off a little earlier but, in the general confusion, Busse never showed up. Then I saw some Flak to the north and said to myself that where there is Flak there must be the enemy. So I decided to go along and have a look. I saw two formations in the distance and then three four-engined aircraft 500 metres below me – American Fortresses! I was astonished to find them so close and I was frightened; I had been making a nice steady approach on those formations in the distance and, suddenly, there I was alone, just above these three Fortresses which we regarded as so well armed that they were virtually indestructible.

I banked over onto the starboard wing in order to get into position for an attack on the one on the left-hand side and I pressed the button to get in a test burst. We had been trained to attack from the rear – in order to knock out the tail gunner first – but I was really in a perfect position, 500 metres above and behind, and I made the attack from a diagonal direction.

I gave it one long burst and saw hits all over the left wing in the engine area. An engine immediately started to burn. I didn't know whether their gunners were firing; when I landed there were no bullet holes in my plane. I shot past it and underneath, then climbed again up to the level at which the American was flying and prepared to make a text-book attack from the rear. The other two had carried on, leaving this one behind. I must add that I was in a highly tense state by now. I closed to 300 metres, firing, and suddenly saw a white ball, growing in size, coming towards me. Then it blossomed into a parachute and I assumed that the tail gunner had baled out. I felt much happier then and was able to concentrate on the left wing again. I was astonished to see the bomber banking to the right; that showed me how powerful the engines were, that the pilot was able to control the aircraft with the two left engines out. I continued firing and the left wing eventually fell off.

I went back to my airfield and flew low over it, waggling my wings on the approach to show my success. But I had to come round again because they had forgotten to change the wind-direction marker on the ground. I waggled my wings on the second circuit and they thought that I had shot down two planes. That, for a student pilot, would have been fantastic.

I thought I should have had the Iron Cross Second Class for my success. I believe the reason I didn't get it was that the bomber had been hit by Flak over Schweinfurt and the complete success could not be credited to me. If you find the crew of that American plane, invite them to visit me in Erlangen.

Leutnant Springer's attacks on this B-17 probably continued after all the survivors had left – two men in the bomber died – and this type of attack by twin-engined German planes hunting for stragglers in the area is not unusual. The two other B-17s abandoned by their crews after receiving serious Flak damage over Schweinfurt were both 'attacked' and 'shot down' by German pilots anxious to claim a success. Two other B-17s left their group formations at this point. Both had been badly damaged by fighter attack before reaching Schweinfurt but had managed to hang on long enough to bomb. One of these two planes – that of Lieutenant Harry Smith of the 381st Bomb Group – soon went down under further fighter attack, although all of its crew parachuted safely. The second – a 384th plane – dived hard to try its luck at hedge-hopping back to England and its story will be told in a later chapter.

The bomber force which was leaving the target area had now lost twenty-nine of its number and still faced the return flight to England. The only other aerial event at Schweinfurt was the flight over the town two hours later of the R.A.F. Mosquito which flew out to take photographs of both Schweinfurt and Regensburg. The pictures taken at Schweinfurt showed little but smoke, however, and another Mosquito had to repeat the run two days later.

CHAPTER 15

In Schweinfurt

The air-raid siren had sounded in Schweinfurt at 3.44 p.m. German time, only fifteen minutes before the first bombs fell. It was a time of day when a large number of people were away from their homes and it was exactly the time when the early and late shifts in the workshops at the ball-bearing factories changed over. Both workforces were present, many of the outgoing shift staying on a few minutes to have a coffee and a chat with friends before going home. The office staff worked more normal hours and it was still over an hour before their working day would end. The town's main railway station, situated between the Kugelfischer factory and the V.K.F. No. 2 factory, was crowded with trains bringing in or taking home the workers who lived in surrounding villages, or visitors to the town's market which was being held on that day. One person says that a troop-train had also halted at the station but that cannot be confirmed. It was a hot and sunny afternoon and as at Regensburg the people had not the slightest conception of the implication of the wailing sirens – 'another reconnaissance plane' was the common thought.

The first bombs fell across the southern end of the Kugelfischer factory – the most important in Schweinfurt – and into the nearby railway station. The two personal contributions which are available from Kugelfischer's illustrate extremes in how people in shelters reacted to the subsequent bombing. Alfons Kuhn was a sixteen-year-old German.

> The factory had its own siren but many people never heard it because of the noise of the machinery. Those who did hear called out and each operator stopped his own machine and went to the shelter. The slow ones were hurried on by the foreman and then someone switched off the main electricity because of the fire risk.
>
> I wasn't really concerned; I thought it was just another false

alarm. I sat next to an older man in the shelter who had just arrived for the second shift. This old chap – he was about forty – reassured me that nothing would happen. I thought he knew what he was talking about and because it was very warm in the shelter and crowded with people I promptly went to sleep. I stayed asleep right through the raid and they had to wake me up to carry out my air-raid duty in the factory that had been hit by the bombing.

When I did wake up, the old chap told me that I had been lucky to have been asleep; it hadn't been much fun.

Adela Nieroda (now Mrs Kamianowska of Warsaw) was an eighteen-year-old Polish forced worker who was a machinist.

We should have gone to the basement shelter but I and three other girls ran to the main concrete shelter although it had 'Only for Germans' written on it. The one-legged factory policeman who was on duty to make sure only Germans went in spotted us; he saw the 'P' on our clothes. He could speak Polish and was often rough with us. He shouted, 'You Poles go to your own place,' and he actually got hold of two girls by an ear each and dragged them back to their own shelter.

There were possibly a thousand people inside, mostly foreigners. There were explosions and the electricity went out. It was pitch dark. Some of us started to panic and cry and some men tried to keep everyone calm. I was scared that if the factory was hit I might survive but be trapped under the ruins of the four or five factory floors above. I was so frightened; I don't want to remember it even now. I found another Polish girl, a friend of mine called Julia. We put our arms around each other and we talked. We thought that the war was coming to an end soon and that we would be killed just before the end. The whole shelter was swaying but the building above us was not hit. We found out afterwards that the bombs hadn't been very far away. When we eventually came outside, the Germans were very excited and the works security men in particular were very angry with the foreigners, pushing us around.

This chapter is intended only to describe the general effects of the raid in Schweinfurt; details of the material damage caused and the effect upon production will be given later. But, on the basis of a detailed report from the Kugelfischer factory, it can be said here that, of the several thousand people present in the factory at the time of the raid, thirty Germans and seven foreigners were killed. There are fewer details available from the two V.K.F. ball-bearing factories but it is believed that the damage and casualties there were much less. The only contribution available from either of these factories is from Ernst Zillmann, an engineer. He remembers little of the bombing – there were so many raids on Schweinfurt during the war – only this incident immediately after the raid.

> There was an unexploded bomb which had come through four stories of the factory and was lying on the floor. I was amazed at its size; it looked like a big dead pig. A fireman picked me up by my trousers and sat me astride it. I had my air-raid service steel helmet on and I could really feel my hair standing on end with fright under the helmet.

Many of the B-17s in the second wave of the attack dropped their bombs in a dense concentration south-west of the main factory area. Here was located the small village of Oberndorf on the main road from Schweinfurt to Würzburg. The village had been officially incorporated into Schweinfurt after the stretch of open countryside which had formerly separated the village from Schweinfurt was filled by the expansion of the factories and the building of the new railway station. Approximately two thirds of Oberndorf's inhabitants now worked in the town, but the remainder still engaged in farming and 'all of us still regarded ourselves as true Oberndorfers and were proud of our village'. The lady who made that remark, Ellen Hess (now Frau Nauhauser), worked on her father's farm and she goes on to describe the bombing.

> We never gave a thought to there being any danger in living next to those important factories. If we did go into the cellars when the alarms sounded, it was not for any fear of danger but only because the air-raid wardens would have been round harassing us if we didn't. The whole concept of an air raid was just beyond our imagination.
>
> It was the end of the afternoon break and we were all in the yard getting ready for more work when the sirens sounded this time. It was harvest time. We heard Flak some distance away but never saw the bombers. The next thing we knew was the whistling of the bombs. My sister, mother, grandmother and the other people who worked on the farm all ran into the

house. Father was out in the fields. I was a bit curious and hung on a little to see what was happening. I only just got inside the house when the door itself was blown off its hinges and fell on my back. It didn't hurt me and I really raced down into the cellar. There were two bombs, one in the courtyard and one on the corner of the house. I found out later that the blast was so strong that a pear tree in the yard was uprooted and thrown right over the roof from one side of the house to the other, and 300 young chickens were all killed by the blast. Father gave them away to neighbours afterwards. My uncle's house, 200 metres nearer the town, was hit by another bomb and my aunt and her sister-in-law were killed when the granary in which they were standing was hit and collapsed and the roof timbers fell on them. They had been on their way to the cellar under the granary but were too slow.

We were so absolutely dazed that even after the bombing had finished we stayed in the cellar until father came back from the fields. He knocked on the door and shouted, 'Who's in there? How many of you?' On the way from the fields they had told him that his wife and daughter had been killed, but they had confused us with my aunt and her sister-in-law.

Father had the first tractor in the village and that night he took us all out to a barn deep in the country. We were quite panic-stricken; the fear was worst at night. Many of the other people in the village went into the country as well that night. I think we went out there every night for a week.

Because the village officially formed part of Schweinfurt there are no separate figures for deaths here; Frau Nauhauser believes that no more than ten people died there. The village was lucky; if the main concentration of bombing in this wave had been a little *nearer* to the factories, the village would have been virtually flattened.

The third wave of the bombing fell on the army barracks and across the residential area between the barracks and the town centre. Hauptfeldwebel Erhard Kreisl, a wounded veteran from the siege of Stalingrad, was at the depot of the 36th Panzer Regiment.

The men who were in the barrack areas had normal air-raid shelters to go to but the procedure for those of us who were out in the large tank sheds was to take shelter in the tanks themselves. We had up to eighty of these – Marks II, III and

IV – and ten men or so could get into each, close the top down and be fairly safe.

Then the bombs came down, some of them all around us. We tried to count them; there were at least sixty in our immediate area. For those few moments it was far worse than being in Russia. As a soldier in Russia you could take some action to look after yourself but here we could do nothing except wait and hope for the best. We always felt that we were technologically superior to the Russians, but with the American bombers attacking us we felt it was the other way round. Also this was happening in our own country to our own people, not far away in a foreign country.

One bomb fell into the shed next to our tank and we thought it was all up with us but no one panicked, not even the new recruits. In fact, we were quite safe; a wall next to us took most of the blast and, although the tank shook, it didn't collapse when the girders and the roof all fell on top of us. We had to wait in that tank until 8.00 p.m. when bulldozers cleared away the debris. We could do nothing but twiddle our thumbs until then.

We added up later that exactly thirty soldiers were killed in our barracks. First to go were the fire-fighting pickets and the crews of the light Flak on the roofs of the barrack blocks, then there were always the dumb ones who wouldn't follow orders. Some of them were killed. Most of the men in the shelters and the tanks were safe.

Another German report says that sixty Wehrmacht men were killed in this barracks and in the one adjacent to it.

At least a third of the American bombs fell in residential areas of Schweinfurt, mainly in the long swathe of the third-wave bombing which extended from the army barracks right into the centre of the town. A detailed map of wartime Schweinfurt shows no industrial premises of any kind in this area, but many of the private houses would have been the homes of workers in the ball-bearing factories. A total of 144 private houses were destroyed and just over 1,000 were damaged. Several public buildings in the old town centre were hit. A hotel – the *Kroner* – which had been converted to a wartime hospital was destroyed; the *Welt Bio* cinema was almost destroyed and four schools and three churches were damaged. It can be estimated that approximately twenty men, sixty women and forty-eight children – nearly two thirds of

Schweinfurt's total death roll on this day – were killed in the residential town areas and at the railway station. Nearly 400 people were wounded. Once again the civilian death roll would have been less if people had taken the warning alarms more seriously and taken shelter immediately but, having been a war-time schoolboy in an English market town only a little smaller than Schweinfurt, I can understand the 'it won't happen today' attitude; most alarms led to nothing, but if anything was going to develop we wanted to watch until the last moment.

The Germans could be the most diligent compilers of statistics. A report* on this raid prepared by the police authorities at Nuremberg for submission to the Bavarian state governor at Munich carefully lists the damage and casualties in the villages around Schweinfurt. Sixteen farmhouses and thirty farm buildings were destroyed and exactly 68·96 tonnes of hay and straw burnt. Apart from the dead people previously mentioned in Oberndorf, six men were killed in Sennfeld, a village two miles east of Schweinfurt which unfortunately found itself under a strong concentration of American bombs. The report even lists the farm animals killed in the villages – two horses, nineteen cows, one pig, two goats, 300 rabbits, 300 chickens, ten geese and 500 pigeons.

There are two good personal accounts available which describe the scene in Schweinfurt immediately after the bombing and the effect on the morale of some of the ordinary people there. Alfons Kuhn was the sixteen-year-old boy who had earlier slept through the raid in a shelter at the Kugelfischer factory. He was now in that corner of the factory which had been bombed.

> My duty after the raid was to report to one of the office blocks for rescue work. On the way to it I passed one of the machinery shops which had been hit. The oils which needed to be constantly fed to the grinding machine tools, together with the reserve oil tanks nearby, had all caught light and were now a roaring inferno, and the fire had spread to the offices which were all in flames as well. Everyone was running around in circles. No one seemed to know what to do.

* *Bayerische Hauptstaatsarchiv*, Munich, reference *Reichsstaatthalter* 704. The routine *Polizeipräsident*'s report which should have been produced by the Schweinfurt police was never compiled. It is said that complacency had prevented the necessary system of collecting reports in Schweinfurt being established. It appears that the Nuremberg police had to come in and complete this task.

I went across to some low buildings which faced the railway station and climbed onto the roof. I wanted to see what was happening over the road there. A lot of people were trying to sneak off from the factory and I wanted to see if there was any chance of getting on one of the trains. But I could see that all the trains in the station were on fire and there was no chance of getting away that way. There was nothing I could do at the offices so my group leader told me to go across to the carpentry shop. When I got there I found that this was burning like mad. What was really happening was that all our carefully prepared air-raid plans had gone to pieces. The people in charge were just improvising as best they could.

No one was watching, so I decided to clear off. I ran across the fields to the next station on the railway line and found trains held up there because of the raid. I managed to get on one of them to my home out in the country. The important thing for me was that I had survived and reached home.

Johannes-Curt Rust was a fifteen-year-old apprentice who also worked for Kugelfischer, but on that day he had been sent to a small box-making workshop out in the village of Oberndorf.

We youngsters knew nothing about bombs. We didn't know what a bomb sounded like and we certainly didn't know what it all meant. I was frightened but not as much as in later raids when I knew more about it. After the bombing finished I ran home. I wanted to know what had happened to my mother. It was on the way back there that I began to realize what bombing meant.

I ran flat out all the way. At the station the trains were all burning and the people from the trains were all standing around with their luggage not knowing what to do next. The bomb craters were already filling with ground water. Trees were blasted all over and splintered. Opposite the station there was a large wooden Red Cross hut where the passengers could rest and eat. It had received a direct hit and I saw my first dead people. I looked away; I daren't look at them. There were arms and legs blown off – it was all terrible.

Then I ran along the main street into the town. I saw smoke and flames pouring out of the Kugelfischer factory, fire engines, great numbers of people running out of the factory and the surrounding houses. Then I saw the first ordinary houses destroyed; some of them were razed to the ground and people were pulling bodies out. Then there were other houses not touched by the bombing but the people were crying, shouting and screaming.

I arrived in my own street and saw that my own home was intact although the doors and windows were blown out by blast. I ran up the stairs to our flat and found mother. There she was, already starting to clear up the mess. She said, 'You and I are alive. What more do you want?' There was only she and I left in the family. She was a widow and my two elder brothers had been killed in Russia.

CHAPTER 16

The Cripples

When a B-17 was so badly damaged that it could no longer keep up and remain within the protection of its formation, its pilot had a difficult decision to make. There were plenty of German pilots delighted to increase their score by finishing off such crippled solitary bombers; indeed the twin-engined German fighters were usually sent up for just this purpose. The natural instinct of the pilot of a crippled plane was to attempt to return to England or, if that was not possible, to fly to the nearest neutral country. But most of the American pilots had seen, on previous missions or earlier on this one, the way in which German fighters pounced on any cripple and usually shot it down. Some thought that it was better to dive hard and attempt to escape at low level, but it was a long, lonely descent to ground level from operational height; other pilots thought it better to bale their crews out in safety while all were still alive, and statistics show that this was probably the more prudent course. But nine pilots of B-17s forced to leave the main formation during the flight to Schweinfurt and in the target area decided to make a run for it alone, often after a vote among their crew. All were attempting to reach England. This short chapter describes the fortunes of some of the ninety men in those planes.

Five B-17s had been forced to turn back during the first German attacks between Eupen and Koblenz. A mere thirty to forty-five minutes of flying time would have seen all of them to the Dutch coast. The account of Staff Sergeant Peter Katsarelis, a gunner in Lieutenant Challen P. Atkinson's crew of the 381st Bomb Group, is probably typical of the experiences of the men in those planes which had to turn back from the main battle area.

> We tried to hang on, keeping among other groups which were following, but these passed us and although they were still in sight no one was near enough to support us. Then we

had trouble with another engine; a great stream of blue smoke came pouring right back past my position and eventually the bell – the bale-out signal – rang. The ball-turret gunner got out of his turret, kicked the escape hatch out of the side of the aircraft and out he went. Within a few seconds we had a burst of bullets through the floor – a long line of holes. I think the Germans saw his two guns hanging in the vertical position, which they did when the ball gunner left his turret. I actually saw the fighter that did it – an FW 190 – and he was hanging almost in a stall underneath us but I couldn't get my gun down onto him. Then I heard Tex Atkinson say, 'Cancel the bale-out order. Hold tight.' He told us he was going to put it into a dive and put the fire out. He put her down in a turn towards home, so steeply that I was pinned to the floor by the centrifugal force; I couldn't move an inch. Eventually he got straightened out and level and the fire did go out but of course that engine was finished as well. The fighters continued circling round us but they only took pot-shots; they weren't taking any risks now. They were just waiting for us to crash on our two engines. We were firing back when we could.

We were able to keep going for some time. I know that I had about 250 rounds left at the end of the dive, and by the time the end came I only had a few which I was keeping in case I got a close-up shot. The tail gunner was right out of ammunition and the pilot kept flying in a zig-zag course to give each of us waist gunners a chance to fire at the fighters behind us. When the bell went again I got onto the intercom to check that this wasn't another false alarm but then I saw three bodies coming past my position from the front and I heard someone shout 'Get out!'.

All of these first five planes were shot down, with fifteen crewmen killed, within twenty minutes of leaving their formations but, ironically, the cripples which left their formations when more deeply into Germany all had a much longer run for their money, and their stories become progressively more interesting. The crew of Lieutenant Jack Hargis, 91st Bomb Group, had only just resumed operations after a spell in a rest camp following their ditching in the North Sea while returning from a raid to Hamburg. The regular navigator had refused to fly again; his replacement, Second Lieutenant Carlyle Darling, describes this crew's fortunes after leaving formation near Mainz.

The group seemed to be going up but it was really us going down. It was a sickening feeling. Hargis told me he wanted me to work out a route home; it only took three or four minutes and then we were off, going home on our own. We weren't attacked by fighters for some time and I think we all thought we would make it. We were very confident; we were even looking for something to drop our bombs on. We saw some barges on the Rhine and thought about those but I suppose we were over them too soon without getting lined up. We were told that over Germany you could drop them anywhere – even on a farm – but over France and the Low Countries you had to pick a proper target. We eventually unloaded them somewhere to pick up air speed.

About thirty minutes later the fighters caught us – Me 109s, just two or three of them; they didn't seem to have the skill of the earlier ones. They didn't press their attacks too close and, once they had made one pass, they just fell off and we didn't see them again for another ten minutes or so. I think we were attacked like that about three times. On other raids I had looked down and seen a lone B-17 down there with five or six fighters going round like Indians round a wagon-train until they killed that B-17, but they didn't persevere like that with us. We still felt confident that we would get back.

Then came the *coup de grâce*. All hell broke loose but not one of us saw the fighter which did it. A cannon shell blew the plexiglass in the nose right apart. Another engine blew up – he even shot the cowling off it. I reckon something else was hit because she was just bouncing then, just fluttering, whereas a moment earlier she had been flying smoothly. That fighter had come right out of the sun and I don't think any of us ever saw him. We got raked over real good.

Lieutenant Hargis and one of the gunners died and the B-17 crashed near Tournai in Belgium only twenty minutes from the coast and after flying 200 miles alone.

The B-17 of Lieutenant Clayton R. Wilson of the 384th Bomb Group had been badly hit by fighters on the approach to Schweinfurt. Most of the bomb doors were blown away and the oxygen system so badly damaged that some of the crew members started passing out. Wilson managed to stay with his group long enough to bomb but then peeled off and dived hard, still under fighter attack, down to tree-top level where all could breathe more easily. Staff Sergeant Eugene Penick, one of the gunners, said that his pilot was 'an eager beaver with a very aggressive attitude', and this plane now commenced what Eugene Penick describes as 'a hell of an exciting ride, seeing Germany from tree-top level'.

Lieutenant Wilson knew that after bombing Schweinfurt the main B-17 force was going to turn and return to England by a northerly route. He felt that his lone flight back to England stood a better chance of avoiding fighters if he took the southerly route. He felt confident: 'There we were, right down on the deck in the heartland of Germany, but the aircraft was basically sound and all four were turning.' The exact route taken is not known but the B-17 certainly roared right across Sandhofen airfield on the outskirts of Mannheim, shooting up the airfield as it passed. It was then intercepted by a Dornier 217 from the night-fighter training unit, NJG 101. The B-17's tail guns both failed when the gunner fired too long a burst and burnt out his guns, and the top turret was hit and jammed. Lieutenant Wilson received a bullet wound in his arm but his worst concern was a huge hole blown in a fuel tank. Because of earlier damage, the fuel transfer mechanism to another tank could not operate. 'We just sat there, sick, watching our hopes of survival pouring away like a severed artery. Gone was our chance of reaching England.' The Dornier was eventually shaken off when Wilson banked and gave his ball-turret gunner a chance to fire. The German plane was seen limping away with smoke coming from an engine.

Wilson now asked his crew whether they preferred to make for Switzerland – 130 miles away – or get as near as they could to England – more than 300 miles away. A three-day pass was due for the crew and every man opted for England, even if they could get no further than the Channel – such was the confidence which the Americans had in the R.A.F.'s air-sea rescue service. This adventurous crew flew low level a further 180 miles and reached the area of Rheims, in Northern France, before their luck and their fuel finally ran out. The co-pilot, Second Lieutenant Dewey Brown, flew much of the way because of his pilot's injury, but Wilson now took over the controls and made a perfect belly landing in a field. After wasting valuable time trying to set their plane alight, the crew split up into pairs in attempts to find an escape organization. Four of them succeeded in reaching England.

*

Two of the nine crews forced to attempt individual flights had better luck. The B-17 of Lieutenant Elton Hoyt of the 379th Bomb Group lost two engines in a fighter attack and Hoyt brought it down to low level, jettisoned his bomb load and set off back towards England from the Mainz area. Another action-packed low-level flight across Europe ensued, on a more northerly route than that taken by Lieutenant Wilson. A prisoner-of-war or internment camp was flown over, as was a Luftwaffe airfield around which a number of Messerschmitt 109s were taxiing. Four of these took off and gave chase but the German pilots were not used to attacking well-defended bombers at tree-top level and were shaken off. Hoyt's gunners believed that two of the fighters were either shot down or flew into the ground but, as so often with such claims, this cannot be confirmed. Holland was reached safely and the B-17 flew up a wide river along the banks of which people were swimming and picnicking – 'a rather peaceful scene, inconsistent with the experience we were having,' says Hoyt. The river opened into a harbour from which several German naval vessels opened fire, sending up huge 'geysers' of water through which Hoyt had to fly. The co-pilot was injured here.

Two Spitfires met the B-17 over the sea and escorted it safely to land at Chipping Ongar airfield, home of a B-26 group which had finished flying for the day. It was the B-26 commanding officer's birthday and Lieutenant Hoyt and his crew were invited to join in an alcoholic celebration. Later that evening they were flown to their own airfield. As Lieutenant Hoyt says, 'We were a rather bedraggled but happy-to-be-surviving bunch. We learned we were the only survivors from our squadron on the raid and really recognized our extreme good fortune that our two remaining engines, stressed beyond any reasonable level, had performed so well.' Hoyt's B-17, *Battlin' Bobbie*, was repaired but was shot down over France on its next mission, to Nantes on 16 September, although Hoyt and all his crew survived.

The experiences of the only other solitary B-17 to reach England safely must be recorded more briefly because no personal contribution was available at the time of writing. The plane concerned was that of Second Lieutenant Judy of the 91st Bomb Group, believed to be flying his fourth mission. This is the official report; the reader must imagine the drama and courage behind these lines.

This aircraft reached a point 15 to 20 miles south-east of Frankfurt. Three 20-mm hits exploded in left wing and directly under the pilots' compartment, setting fire to the aircraft. Immediately the navigator and bombardier baled out. Due to smoke and fire, the pilot temporarily lost control of the aircraft but was able to bring it out of a slow spin at 6,000 feet. Bombs were released safe by the pilot pulling emergency release. The top turret gunner, who was already wounded in leg and chest, fought the fire in the pilots' compartment while the co-pilot was aft, directing the ditching of the waist gunners, radio operator and tail gunner. Co-pilot Layn saw to it that all harness adjustments were made before these men jumped. It was necessary to use force in some cases as the men would have jumped with their chutes improperly adjusted. Layn stated that all chutes opened properly.

All during this time there were persistent enemy attacks. After learning that T/Sgt Cherry, the top turret gunner, was wounded and burned and that Cherry's parachute had burned up, Lt Judy decided to try and make home. Fires broke out intermittently but were brought under control by Cherry and Layn who, in their spare time, continued to fire at the enemy fighters. Layn burned out both waist guns. Judy immediately lost altitude until he was at 100 feet then came across enemy and enemy-occupied territory on a zig-zag course.*

The B-17 crash-landed at Manston airfield but was not worth repairing and was written off. Second Lieutenant James D. Judy, Second Lieutenant Roger W. Layn and Technical Sergeant Earl M. Cherry were all recommended for the Congressional Medal of Honour – America's highest award for gallantry – but these decorations did not materialize. Judy and Layn both became prisoners of war in later raids but Judy was killed in a flying accident in 1955.

There is one more 'cripples' story that should be mentioned, although the crew concerned did not have to fly back to England alone. The plane of Lieutenant David A. Tyler, 305th Bomb Group, was badly damaged by fighter attack in the main battle area on the way to Schweinfurt. There was a violent explosion in the waist section of the plane which left one gunner dead, two injured and the oxygen supply in that area quite useless. The 'abandon aircraft' alarm bell in the tail section of the plane is believed to have sounded and, in circumstances which no one ever criticized, the four surviving men there baled out. The four officers, and the top turret gunner, who was also wounded, stayed with the plane, although one engine had failed and there were a

* Missing Air Crew Report No. 283, National Archives.

host of other technical problems. The combined efforts of these five men kept the plane in formation and it eventually crash-landed at Martlesham Heath, the first airfield found on reaching England. The story of this flight will not be described in detail here because it has been well covered before* and the balance of this book dictates that it is time to return to the main story. The five men of this crew who came back did not have to fly with the Eighth Air Force again because they had now completed their tours, but the bombardier, Lieutenant Louis Nelson, was later shot down in a B-29 mission to Tokyo.

* See Edward Jablonski, *Double Strike*, pp. 173–6.

CHAPTER 17

'Herr Gott Sakrament!'

The twelve individual group formations left Schweinfurt and reformed into their four combat wings. After a short flight to the north, the B-17s wheeled westwards to face the long return flight. Now that the bombing was completed it was no longer necessary for the entire force to fly in a long column and the two halves of it turned at different points to commence the next leg level with each other but about seventeen miles apart, but this gap would gradually close because both formations were aiming for the fighter rendezvous point at Eupen. As the bombers settled to that long flight, their crew members looked back at the target area with mixed emotions. Second Lieutenant Darrel Gust, a navigator in the 303rd Bomb Group, says, 'I thought our bombing results had only been fair and, after we left the target, the bombardier confirmed this. I recall saying to myself, "And we got our asses shot off only to come this far and missed the damned target."' But Captain David Wheeler of the 306th remembered the hard fight to reach the target: 'I knew we had to go back all the way through the German fighters. It would be an awful long time before we met our own fighters again. For me that was the most anxious time in the mission. I wished we had been able to go on to North Africa like the Regensburg boys.'

So the groups settled down on the long leg to Eupen, 190 miles or sixty-eight flying minutes away from the turning points north of Schweinfurt. The first three quarters of that long run would be over quiet country areas, past the towns of Fulda, Giessen and Wetzlar, but once the Rhine was crossed the bombers would enter the area of the German coastal fighter belt again. The American plan called for both halves of the bomber force to hold their altitude, with lead groups maintaining 21,000 feet for the whole of the run to Eupen, but, again, Colonel Gross decided to lose altitude and descended to 16,000 feet. He later claimed this was to keep well under the old cloud belt which he had met on his outward flight. Colonel Gross must have remembered the importance of altitude at the fighter rendezvous because a radio message was sent to England about the change, although this does not seem to have reached the American fighter commander concerned. Colonel Gross also exceeded the planned speed, with the result that his half of the force gradually pulled ahead of Colonel Turner's. Once again, Colonel Turner experienced no difficulty with cloud. He could have increased speed as well but he had at least three crippled aircraft in his part of the force – one a group leader – and he was prepared to sacrifice speed in order to give the crews of those three planes a chance of keeping up.

The flight from the target area as far as the Rhine was a blessedly quiet one for most of the American units. The Luftwaffe did not put in a big effort here, even though it would be the last substantial opportunity for the Germans to attack the B-17s without the danger of interference from Allied fighter escort. There were two explanations for the German failure to exploit this vulnerable stretch. The first was obviously that the fighter units which made such effective attacks when the B-17s were flying to Schweinfurt needed time to refuel and rearm. The second reason is an interesting one. The Germans had to guess which way the bombers would turn after attacking their target. There are a number of German reports which show that they gambled on the bombers turning south at Schweinfurt, either to fly on to North Africa like the earlier Regensburg force or to return to England by a southerly route. Several German fighter units were ordered to fly to Würzburg, which was twenty-five miles southwest of Schweinfurt and well placed for either of these eventualities. Not only did the B-17s' turn to the north cause this disposition to be faulty, but the German inland reporting system was slow in passing on details of the northerly return route to their fighter units. Some German fighters were still over Schweinfurt at 3.40 p.m., asking on their radios where the American bombers were, nearly half an hour after the last B-17 had left Schweinfurt. It was the first major German error of the day and a valuable opportunity was wasted by the fighters which were up at that time.

American reports say that only a few single-engined fighters appeared during the hour after the bombers left Schweinfurt. The German attacks were not pressed strongly and no B-17s were lost to them. There was, however, one little gem of action halfway along that route to the Rhine. The German night-fighter unit at

Mainz/Finthen, I/NJG 6, sent up six Messerschmitt 110s as soon as the turns north and west from Schweinfurt had been detected. For the first time in the day, the twin-engined fighter crews were ordered to attack the American main formations and not confine themselves to attacking stragglers. The Messerschmitts took off and went into action in two flights of three. Oberleutnant Hans Engels was leading one of the flights which caught up with the more southerly of the two American formations just south of Giessen.

> I made a great mistake. I told the others that we would attack from below and behind; this meant we were climbing when we attacked. As night fighters that was our normal method of attack and, really, I didn't spend much time thinking about it. It was a semi-automatic reaction. You've heard of *Jagdfieber* – combat fever – well that's what I was suffering from.
>
> Night fighters never fired from long range. We approached this formation slowly and the Americans opened fire first. I had no idea that their firepower was so strong. We attacked in echelon, myself leading on the left, and my aircraft was the first to be hit. They got me in the right engine; the propeller jerked once or twice, then stopped. That was when I realized I had made a mistake and I yelled out to the other two to break off. I banked away but my plane was hit again in the tail and we were out of control then. I told the radio operator to bale out but got no reply. I turned round to find that he had been shot through the head. His face was covered in blood and I am sure he was already dead.
>
> I found it difficult to get out because the plane was in a steep dive and the speed was too great for safety. In the end, the air rushing by actually plucked me out and I was thrown against the tail. My left shoulder was dislocated and my right knee badly twisted.
>
> I never saw anything of the others but I believe they did not break off when I told them to and I heard later they were both shot down. Some of my friends criticized me later for making that type of attack but my *Gruppe* commander, Wohlers, consoled me and he quoted this proverb: '*Wo gehobelt wird, fallen Späne.*'

A free translation of this proverb is 'He who is never wrong is likely to catch it himself one day.' The American gunners had swiftly disposed of Engels's flight. All three German planes were shot down and only Engels and a wounded radio man in one of the other planes survived. Thirty-one gunners of the 303rd Bomb Group, flying in the low position at the rear of the last combat wing, later submitted claims for the destruction of these German planes. There was one happy sequel for Oberleutnant Engels. A woman student doctor at a Giessen hospital watched this combat and saw an airman coming down by parachute. When Engels was brought to her hospital for treatment, the two fell in love and were married a few months later.

It is likely that the second flight of Messerschmitt 110s were more wary in their attacks. They all survived safely and they claimed the final destruction of the crippled B-17 captained by Flight Officer James N. Sexton of the 379th Bomb Group; it went down just west of Giessen. Sexton's plane was the only American bomber to be lost in the flight of nearly an hour's duration from the target area to the Rhine south of Bonn. Many Americans remember that relatively quiet flight, with every minute taking them a few miles nearer to at least the partial safety of the escort rendezvous at Eupen. But some of the Americans had a sadder memory. As their route approached the Rhine they came closer to the scene of the fierce battle they had fought on the outward flight and they could see a succession of columns of smoke rising high into the clear sky. Two navigators have recorded their feelings at this sight.

> I have a graphic memory of those funeral pyres, those tall columns of smoke which were the last resting places of our '17s. The poor bastards! Subconsciously you felt, 'There but for the grace of God go I.' You could only live from one moment to the next. (Lieutenant Edwin D. Frost, 381st Bomb Group)

> My most vivid memory of the first part of that flight back – which took place at relatively low altitude – was the view of that beautiful countryside with the coloured trees, just like Virginia in the fall. For quite a while it was fairly peaceful – not a bit of Flak, fighter attacks minimal, weather delightful. That part of the flight was almost enjoyable except for those fires on the ground from aeroplanes that had crashed earlier. I made the comment, either then or later, that this was almost like flying a light line in Texas. In our training period in Texas we would fly by night, using beacons strung out at intervals. There was no need for navigation on that part of the flight

back from Schweinfurt; all we needed to do was to follow those fires home.

But there was now a different attitude to the Germans than before – that of survival. We had fought them on the way in; we had done our work at the target and now we had this shot of adrenalin flowing which said we had been through the hard part and we had just got to hang on a little bit more and reach the Channel or our fighter escort. (Lieutenant Carl B. Stackhouse, 351st Bomb Group)

The leading B-17s flew over the River Rhine just before 4.00 p.m. They were nearly halfway to the coast from the target and the rendezvous with the fighter escort was only eighteen minutes away but, as has been seen before, great shifts of fortune could occur in short periods of time.

The Germans already knew that this was going to be a great day for the Luftwaffe. They may not yet have calculated the exact American losses so far – it was actually forty-four B-17s – but they knew it well exceeded any earlier success. (Their best previous day had been 13 June with twenty-six American bombers down in raids on Bremen and Kiel.) The inland fighter-control organization might have let one chance slip away but the veterans in the coastal belt were determined to make a final all-out effort to catch the battered American units and inflict further loss. Orders had gone out to all available German pilots to take off and close in on the B-17s before they slipped under the safety of the fighter escort known to be coming out from England.

The effort which could be provided by the units which had been in action earlier in the day – sometimes twice – was obviously limited: planes were scattered over several airfields, often suffering from battle damage or mechanical defects. The pilots were usually in better shape than their planes, but some were not as eager for action as earlier in the day. I asked one pilot why some of the planes in his unit took off and flew back to their home airfields in North Germany when they were so handily placed at Bonn to intercept the B-17s returning from Schweinfurt. His answer was: 'We felt that the unit was so dispersed that we could not be usefully employed again. We weren't used to this sort of fighting. We'd had enough.' But this was not a majority view and many German pilots now prepared themselves for the final battle. At least eight single-engined fighter units which had already flown one or two sorties still managed to get part of their strength up and into action at this stage. One measure of the German determination is the extent to which their twin-engined night force was also ordered into action. An estimated sixty night fighters, mostly Messerschmitt 110s, were sent up from airfields in Holland, Belgium and Northern France and their crews urged to attack the main B-17 formations. But the main German hopes were based on three relatively fresh, full-strength units of single-engined fighters which were at last being committed to the battle from France. II/JG 26 had flown from its dispersal airfields to assemble at its main base at Lille and was now up again and flying north. I/JG 2, based on a group of airfields west of Paris, had also assembled and was on the way. III/JG 2 had made a transit flight from its airfield in Brittany, landed and refuelled at Evreux, and was now also flying towards the battle area, but this unit would be at its extreme range if it did make contact with the American bombers. German radios were very active at this stage and the R.A.F. radio-listening service in England was able to plot the flights of these units with great accuracy. The names of *Gruppe* and *Staffel* commanders were clearly heard: 'Wutz', Matoni, Sternberg, Naumann, 'Rudi', Brille, Brenndiger. 'Wutz' was Major Wilhelm-Ferdinand Galland, commander of II/JG 26 from Lille and brother of the famous Adolf Galland. These three fresh units were all equipped with the powerful Focke-Wulf 190. The exact number of planes coming up from France is not known but it may have been around sixty.

The next stage of the action was to be extremely complex and sometimes confused. Several important events followed each other in rapid succession, and while one type of action was being fought in one part of the sky a completely different type of battle could be taking place only a short distance away. Of all the periods of action on 17 August 1943, this was to be the most concentrated.

The two parts of the B-17 force had been steadily pressing on over Germany, their crews anxious to reach Eupen and meet the friendly P-47s of their fighter escort. They were aware that the attention of German fighters was increasing but ignorant of the heavy German reinforcement approaching. It had been intended that the two halves of the bomber force would reach Eupen side by side, but Colonel Gross's part would actually reach Eupen several minutes ahead of and 5,000 feet lower than the remainder of the force. There were several stragglers from both formations. When the B-17s flew over the River Rhine they were being attacked by elements of eight different German units, but many of the attacks were only token efforts by German pilots who were all flying their second or third sorties of the day. Little impression was being made on the American formations and most of the claims made by both sides are without foundation. It was almost as though two tired boxers were flailing away at the end of a long bout but not landing any serious punches.

Only one specific incident can be identified in the first part of the fifty-mile flight from the Rhine to Eupen. The plane of Lieutenant Rothery McKeegan, 305th Bomb Group, had been badly damaged over Schweinfurt by Flak but its crew had refused to consider making for Switzerland. Now they were lagging underneath the rear of the bomber force and were the object of several German pilots' attentions. McKeegan's crew put up a tremendous fight, hoping to reach the cover of friendly fighters, but they just failed to do so. Two men were killed, three more wounded and several gun positions ran out of ammunition. At least one German fighter may have been shot down but, with all four engines finally hit, McKeegan had to bale out with the surviving members of his crew.

One of the Germans attacking this B-17 was Oberleutnant Heinz Knoke whose Messerschmitt 109 had been hit in the wing earlier in the day. McKeegan's gunners noticed that one of the German pilots was flying with particular care. Knoke describes how he nursed his damaged wing and expended all his ammunition. 'I was willing to keep firing all my guns until every shot had gone; I didn't bother with the short bursts we normally used. I was determined to get him if I could before my wing failed. It was stubbornness rather than bravery. Then they hit me. It was just like emptying a sack of potatoes onto an empty barrel. I had never heard the noise of being hit so clearly.' Knoke must share the credit for McKeegan's B-17 with the Schweinfurt Flak batteries and with other German pilots who were attacking at that time. Knoke's own plane went down to a forced landing and finished up as scrap.* In turn, McKeegan's gunners must share the credit for its destruction with several gunners in the 303rd Bomb Group who were watching this combat below them and firing on Knoke's plane.

* Heinz Knoke also describes this engagement in his book, *I Flew for the Führer*, published in various editions, 1953–79.

The many Americans who were watching out to the front of their formations, hoping to spot their own fighters as they neared Eupen, were excited to see a cloud of little dots appear, but their pleasure at what would have been an early arrival of help was dashed when these small planes spread out across their front in the familiar attitude of veteran German pilots preparing to make a head-on attack. The Focke-Wulf 190s of Major 'Wutz' Galland's II/JG 26 had beaten the American fighters to the scene. Galland's own headquarters flight was out in front and at least three *Staffeln* were spread out behind him. From the scattered evidence available it appears that Galland had either not seen or had ignored the leading part of the bomber force – the lower one – and was attacking the head of Colonel Turner's task force. The whole of Galland's *Gruppe* pressed home their first attack, the brunt of it probably falling on the leading low group, the 92nd. The plane of Captain Roland Sargent immediately dropped away; it would struggle on for another forty miles before succumbing to further attacks. Four of the German pilots then spotted a B-17 straggling well below the main formation and swooped down on it. This plane was from the 381st Bomb Group and its co-pilot, Second Lieutenant Allen Chapin, says, 'From the joy of thinking that we were going to get home came the certain realization that we would never make it. I have never forgotten how your emotions can go from one extreme to the other, almost in the snap of a finger.' This B-17 was swiftly dispatched by the four Focke-Wulf 190s.

Only a few days earlier Major Galland had gathered his officers together and stressed to them that their best effort must henceforth be directed against the American four-engined bombers which were posing such a threat to Germany. His own personal score already stood at eight such bombers. After completing his first attack he turned and led his own flight back around the side of the bomber force to prepare for a second frontal attack. And that is when the sky fell in on Major Galland and his unit, for American fighters were suddenly all around them.

The American planes which arrived so dramatically on the scene of action were from the 56th Fighter Group which had flown one mission earlier in the day as escort to the Regensburg force of B-17s. After a three-hour rest the group had taken off again and forty-six P-47s reached the Dutch coast, released their belly tanks, climbed to 27,000 feet and came into action *an estimated fifteen miles east of Eupen.* No Allied fighter had managed to reach this far into Europe before. The credit for this achievement belongs to the group commander, Colonel Hubert Zemke. 'Hub' Zemke was a tough little man, a former Golden Gloves champion for the state of Montana who had recently boxed in London under a corporal's name. Zemke had nursed the pilots of his group through four months of operations and the 56th was probably the most efficient American fighter unit in the Eighth Air Force at this time. Many thought Zemke the most skilful American tactical fighter leader in Europe; one of his pilots says that 'the old man had an uncanny knack of finding Germans'. Ironically, Zemke was of very recent German blood. An uncle had been killed flying for the Germans on the Western Front in 1916 and two German cousins died in the Russian Front in 1941 while Zemke was in Moscow on liaison duties with the Russians!

Zemke knew that the B-17s were returning from a particularly dangerous mission and would need all the help his unit could give. He was always trying to squeeze a little more range out of the leaky, faulty drop tanks his P-47s had to rely on at that time and he somehow managed to find that fifteen extra miles of range which had just surprised the Germans. The American pilots arrived with every possible advantage. Their initial approach was from out of the sun, 5,000 feet above the Germans, and they actually flew over the scene of action before turning and deploying themselves in the manner in which Zemke had ordered – one squadron on either side of the last combat wing and one squadron to cover the next combat wing ahead. This action was all around Colonel Turner's rear half of the bomber force; Colonel Gross's two wings were not under German attack. Because Colonel Turner was approaching the rendezvous point at the correct altitude and time, Zemke had experienced no difficulty in finding the B-17 force. The unsuspecting Germans did not see the American fighters sweep overhead and were thus doubly surprised when the P-47s turned and swooped down on them from out of the east. The B-17 men were, of course, delighted at this unexpectedly early intervention. Captain David Wheeler of the 306th Bomb Group remembers the moment.

> We could see two things happening almost at once. There were German fighters being called in by the gunners and then I can remember looking up and seeing the contrails of the '47s which swooped over the top of us, way high, and then seeing them

make their attacks on the German fighters. It was the greatest thing in the world to see that. It was like being attacked out in the street by a gang and then seeing a friend coming along to help you.

In theory the American fighters went down in a succession of flights of four, the leading flights attempting to break up the pattern of the German formation, with succeeding ones going in after individual German fighters 'for the kill'. That may have happened in some cases but the whole action quickly became a great mêlée, although each of the three American squadrons generally kept to their own side of the bomber force. The 61st and 63rd Squadrons, on the flanks of the bomber formation, saw most of the action. Many of the German pilots who escaped the first American pass dived hard to the east and took no further part in the battle, but the more aggressive Germans stayed to fight it out. The area of action quickly spread but the B-17s, moving steadily westwards, were always the centre point. Although there are sheafs of reports and interview notes from both sides, no written account can completely describe this great battle. The reader must visualize the brilliantly clear sky, the labouring bomber formation and up to a hundred fighters diving, zooming, banking and twisting – all trying to get on each other's tails, all trying to shoot down the other man and fulfil the whole purpose of the fighter pilot's existence.

The Americans claimed ten German single-engined fighters destroyed in the first phase of their action, together with two probables and one damaged. German losses which can be confirmed by documentary evidence were six single-engined fighters – two Focke-Wulf 190s of Major Galland's II/JG 26, three more Focke-Wulf 190s from I/JG 1 and a Messerschmitt 109 of *Jagdgruppe* 50, the new unit from Wiesbaden which had been causing the B-17s so much trouble all day. German documents show many more planes damaged. The casualty which rocked the Germans was the death of Major Galland himself. His plane was never seen by the pilots of his unit after the first American pass. Oberfeldwebel Adolf Glunz was one of those pilots.

He just disappeared. For some hours after we landed we hoped for the best, but the normal telephone call never came, only the growing realization that he was probably dead. It was a very heavy blow, this loss of such an experienced pilot. We often had 'young' pilots lost on their third or fourth flight but

> not often a man as experienced as this. We could not afford such losses. We said that as the war progressed the number of our experienced leaders available contracted rather than expanded, while the English and Americans were growing all the time, not only in numbers but also in quality – especially their fighter escort.

Major Galland's body, in the remains of his fighter, was not found until nearly two months later. It was buried four metres deep in soft ground near Maastricht. 'Wutz' Galland had flown 186 operational flights 'on the Channel' in the last two years and was credited with fifty-five successes. A younger brother, Leutnant Paul Galland, had disappeared over the sea in October 1941 after a combat with Spitfires while returning from a flight to Canterbury. A fellow *Gruppe* commander says that 'Wutz' was the best pilot of the three Galland brothers, although Adolf – 'a man without nerves' – was the best leader. Major Galland's body was buried on 15 October with full honours and in the presence of senior officers in the Luftwaffe's burial plot in the grounds of the château of the Baron de Pitteurs close to St Trond airfield. Which American pilot shot down this German ace? A study of the American combat reports shows the most likely candidate to be Captain Walker H. Mahurin, and if this is correct Galland was the first victim of a long, distinguished career for Mahurin, who went on to be credited with twenty-one German planes, a Japanese bomber in the Pacific in 1945 and three and a half MIGs in the Korean War before he was himself shot down in Korea and taken prisoner. But the man who should at least share the credit for this American success was Colonel Zemke who led the 56th Fighter Group so deep into German-defended air space and caught such an experienced German leader by surprise and at a tactical disadvantage.

Another force of German aircraft caught up in the battle was a formation of Messerschmitt 110s of I/NJG 1 from Venlo and Gilze-Rijen airfields. There were eight or ten of these and their crews were the usual junior ones who had not yet gained many night successes. On spotting the B-17s, the 110s had spread themselves out in line abreast 'to share out the Boeings' defensive fire; there was a lot of iron in the air', and had made a weakly pressed head-on attack. But this area was a most unsuitable place for a twin-engined fighter to be; the P-47s fell on them like a ton of bricks. Three 110s were shot down and a fourth so damaged that it never flew again. The destruction of one of these German planes occurred in most spectacular fashion. This is Colonel Zemke's description.

> Then I saw and the Germans saw and the bomber crews probably saw the most phenomenal scene I ever witnessed in this war. The 63rd Squadron had been drawn off in heavy action to the north and the 61st came screaming down from the front and caught an Me 110 right over the last box of bombers. Two P-47s shot at this guy at the same time – sixteen guns firing – and both of them hit him simultaneously. That Me 110 blew up as I've never seen anything blow up and fell, on fire, directly through the bomber formation. It was just a mass of flames and fire and it fell right through the bombers without hitting one of them.
>
> It was almost as though everything stopped while everyone watched it. There was certainly complete radio silence while all eyes turned to watch it happen. Then, maybe thirty seconds later, all the chatter resumed.

The Messerschmitt 110 concerned was that of Unteroffiziers Hans Neuner and Rudolf Mielmann who were, of course, both killed. The two American pilots were Captain Gerry Johnson and Lieutenant Frank McCauley. Colonel Zemke got his own Messerschmitt 110 a few seconds later. The remaining German crews fled for their lives. Unteroffizier Helmut Fischer was the radio operator in one of the crews which escaped.

> It was a nasty shock for us, as night fighters, to be treated in this way and to be shot down in such numbers. It was also an eye-opener for us to see, in that one moment when we first saw that American bomber formation, the overwhelming strength of the enemy air forces attacking our country. At night, of course, we only saw an occasional bomber now and again.

The Americans suffered some casualties. In the 62nd Squadron, Lieutenant Voorhis Day and his wingman, Lieutenant Robert Stultz, were seen to go down on some of the Messerschmitt 110s and, although their voices were heard happily talking about a possible success for Day, neither was seen again by their fellow pilots. It is probable that both were caught by German single-engined fighters. 'Daisy' Day's friends later tried to secure for him the credit for shooting down two Messerschmitt 110s, but confirmation of this was not granted by the American authorities.

The third American casualty occurred in that part of the 63rd Squadron which had remained aloft, the officer leading two flights of P-47s preferring to stay as high cover well above the battle – much to the annoyance of the other pilots in those fighters. These American fighters were then 'jumped' by two German planes coming down from an even greater altitude and the P-47 of Lieutenant Arthur Sugas was shot down. Lieutenant Harold Comstock promptly attacked and shot down one of the Germans but was later disgusted to be fined £5 by his flight leader for breaking formation without orders. Comstock says, 'My very first enemy aircraft destroyed had cost me twenty bucks! I was sorry to have seen my friend Sugas go down but I have to be honest and say that the elation of my first success was by far the uppermost emotion at that moment. I didn't know he was dead; I really thought he would get out.' Lieutenants Sugas, Day and Stultz, all original members of the 56th Fighter Group when it came to England, died. Their P-47s crashed between Liège and Maastricht. Five German pilots from three different Luftwaffe units claimed these American fighters.

Some of the American pilots were reluctant to leave when Colonel Zemke decided that it was time to break off the action and return to England.

> I had called, 'Break it off. Let's go home,' and tried to form up as best we could over the bomber formation. I picked up most of them but then I got a call from Mahurin, well to the north; you got to know the guys' voices on the R/T. 'We've got 'em cornered. There's plenty for everyone. Come on up this way.' I think he only had a flight of four planes! My reply was, 'This is a recall. Break it off Bud. Let's go home.'
>
> The entire action had lasted about twenty minutes but it had been hot and heavy. We knew we had been in a damn good action but I didn't know what the losses or claims were. I didn't know whether the bombers had been attacked while we'd been so busy but I felt we had given them fairly good protection. We had certainly broken up several German attacks. It was the biggest go, by far, we'd had up to then and that day taught us a lot of lessons.

The battle had lasted from Eupen almost to Antwerp, with the heaviest fighting in the Liège area. It was quite a famous little action and one of great assistance for the American bomber crews, completely altering the balance in their favour after so many setbacks suffered earlier in the day. The Germans would remember it as the battle in which they lost Major Galland. The radio conversations of the German pilots had been clearly heard by the R.A.F. listening station in England. At the beginning of the battle there had been anxious inquiries about the fate of Major Galland; towards the end one German pilot was heard to gasp, '*Herr Gott Sakrament!*'

The American pilots had shot down at least eleven German fighters for the loss of three of their own planes and pilots. The P-47s had not given complete protection to the bomber formations but to achieve that with only one unit of fighters was impossible. Only one B-17 was lost from the formations which the P-47s were attempting to cover. Second Lieutenant Douglas Mutschler's plane from the 305th Bomb Group went down near Diest with Mutschler and two of his crew dead. Considering the number of German fighters that had been present, the timely arrival of the 56th Fighter Group and their subsequent action must have prevented the loss of many more B-17s. Lieutenant Reginald Robinson, a B-17 pilot in the 306th Bomb Group, can speak for many of his comrades.

> Imagine our delight to see those friendly fighters! It was very comforting to be so grandly escorted back to the coast. We were able to turn our attention to our wounded and our aircraft damage. At that time emotional wounds appeared to be greater than physical ones after being under attack for five hours.

Throughout the recent action the two leading combat wings of bombers had been flying on across Belgium without any fighter protection. Colonel Gross had seen the P-47s flying high above him to the rear half of the bomber force and later expressed annoyance that his force received no escort. But by pushing on ahead and losing altitude he had for the second time that day missed the fighter rendezvous. This time, however, little harm was done. The few German fighter attacks on the leading groups gained no success and were easily beaten off.

The battle around Liège was the last major action of the Schweinfurt operation. The leading B-17s were just fifteen minutes from the Belgian coast when Colonel Zemke withdrew his P-47s south of Antwerp. Forty P-47s of the 353rd Fighter Group turned up on time, their duty being to escort the rear of the bomber force. A few German fighters were seen but they were

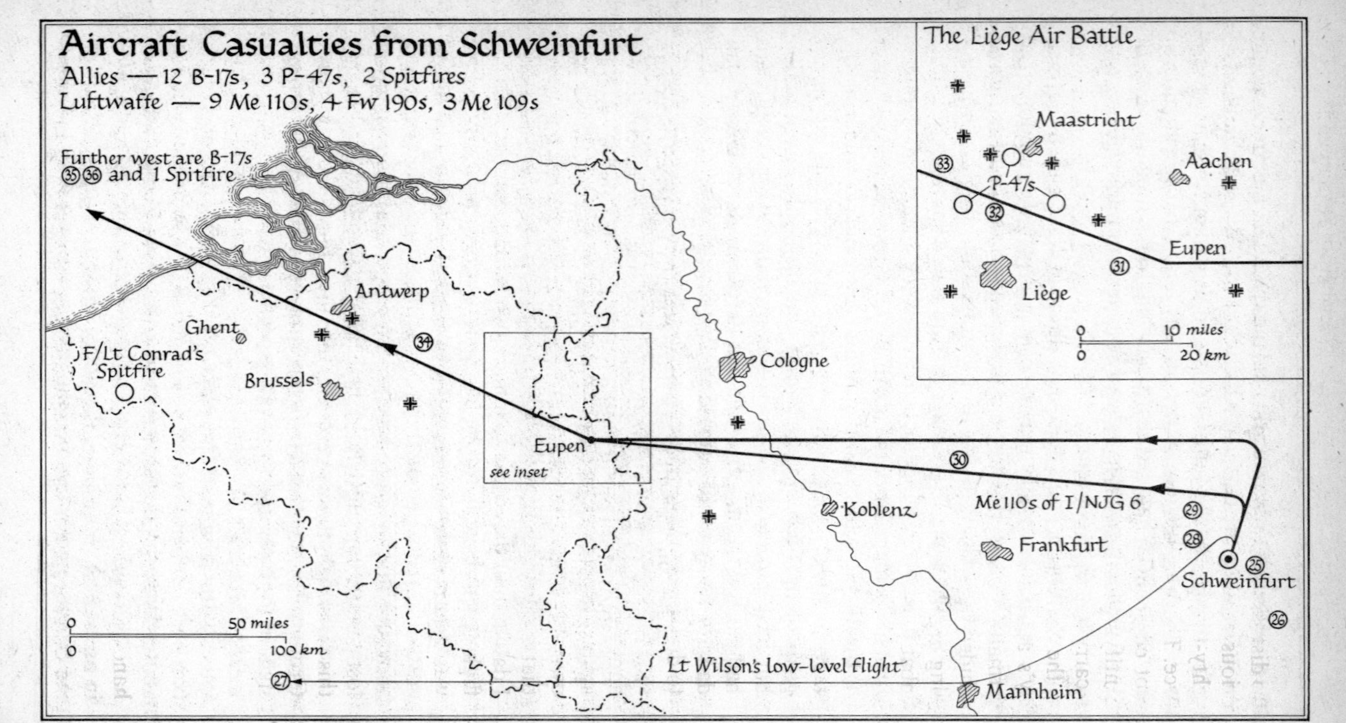
Aircraft Casualties from Schweinfurt
Allies — 12 B-17s, 3 P-47s, 2 Spitfires
Luftwaffe — 9 Me 110s, 4 Fw 190s, 3 Me 109s
Further west are B-17s
35 36 and 1 Spitfire
Antwerp
Ghent
F/Lt Conrad's
Spitfire
Brussels
34
Eupen
see inset
Cologne
Koblenz
30
Me 110s of I/NJG 6
29
28
Frankfurt
25
Schweinfurt
26
Mannheim
Lt Wilson's low-level flight
27
0
50 miles
0
100 km
The Liège Air Battle
Maastricht
33
P-47s
32
Aachen
Eupen
31
Liège
0
10 miles
0
20 km

too distant to engage and this unit completed its task without any serious combat. At the same time eight squadrons of Spitfires – eighty-two planes – appeared to cover the front of the bomber force. The Spitfires experienced a few minor incidents. One Polish pilot complained that a P-47 fired a short burst at him before identifying him as friendly and a solitary Messerschmitt 110 dared to carry out an attack on a B-17 group and was swiftly shot down by the Spitfires. The time for lengthy personal accounts of this day's actions is rapidly passing but the story of Obergefreiter Hermann Vollert, the radio operator in that German plane, is included because it contains so many interesting personal points going right back to the take-off order received while he was sunbathing at Venlo airfield.

> I was in my bathing trunks; I grabbed a few clothes and was taken out to the plane by bus. We were given a general order to go and find the American bombers, not just nice easy stragglers but to attack their main formations. It was the first time we had flown on such an operation but I wasn't worried about the danger. We knew the Luftwaffe was hard pressed and we had to do the best we could. It was our standard practice to keep a set of maps in our flight bags but I had lent my maps to another radio operator who wanted to study them; it was against regulations but he was a new fellow and hadn't got his own yet. When I looked in my flight bag on the bus I realized that I was committed to this major operation without my maps. I dared not tell the pilot because he would have abandoned the flight and I would have been court-martialled. From then on I was dreading the consequences of that map business.
>
> We took off with several other planes and were given various vectors from the ground but because I had no maps we soon lost contact with the others. [The other Messerschmitt 110s in this flight were the ones handled so severely by the 56th Fighter Group near Liège.] It was quite some time before we caught sight of the bombers. I was delighted when we made contact; it meant I wouldn't be court-martialled. We had to climb to get into an attacking position and while we did so I counted the bombers – ninety-two of them. We got a thousand metres above the formation we intended to attack and chose the left-hand corner to avoid as much of their fire as possible. We went in and let off one long burst of fire but didn't see any hits on the bombers, although three weeks later I got the Iron Cross

Second Class for my part in making that attack on our own. I can only remember that when Hauptmann Frank pinned it on my chest I took it off as soon as the parade was over and put it in my back pocket. It wasn't as important to me as getting out of that court-martial.

As soon as we got under the bomber formation we were hit very hard, a hail of bullets struck our plane and it was soon on fire. I couldn't see anything; my hair was singed. We had to get out quickly but we both managed it. The pilot landed in a street in Antwerp right next to a tramcar and I came down in the River Scheldt. Some Belgians fished me out and tried to help me to escape because they thought I was an American at first, but I was eventually handed over to a Wehrmacht Feldwebel who soon appeared. He spoke in Pomeranian dialect and I was a Württemburger. As I hadn't had time to dress properly when we took off and I hadn't got my identity tag, I had a job to persuade him I was a German and I was kept locked up and got very hungry. They only accepted that I wasn't an American after they got through to the airfield on the telephone. It was funny really because Americans with perfect Württemburg accents must have been very rare.

Having, in R.A.F. parlance, 'deloused' the B-17 formations of Germans, some of the Spitfire squadrons remained to give cover while others went hunting in surrounding areas. Wing Commander 'Johnny' Johnson, the famous English pilot who was leading a Canadian wing, took 403 Squadron on a sweep down the coast to Dunkirk. Flight Lieutenant Walter Conrad was one of the Canadian pilots.

We were ready to go home when I realized that there seemed to be five planes in the starboard section. I looked quickly at the other sections and they were complete, so it was obvious that the extra plane had to be a Hun. It was a '190'; I think he thought he could sneak up on the Number Four in that section, get in a burst and then half-roll and away. He must have been a very brave man. I yelled at Johnny that there was a 190 at three o'clock and he said, 'Go get him. I'll cover.' So Shouldice and I turned starboard just as the Focke-Wulf half-rolled.

I was determined to follow this son of a bitch all the way to Paris to get him if I had to. I had never dived a Spitfire from 29,000 feet right to the ground; she was a tricky aeroplane when she got too fast. Anyway, we caught him at about 3,000 feet and I blew his wing off. Then I said, 'Going up, Shouldie,' started to pull up, and the next thing I recall was this great big bloody four-bladed Spit prop just above my head and slightly behind me. How he got there I don't know. It was one of those things. Surely this can't be happening to me!

From then on it was just chaos. Shouldice's prop chopped off the whole of my Spitfire behind the armour-plated seat. The aircraft was way over the sky, well below a thousand feet. I was pinned against the cockpit by centrifugal force but got my toe behind the armour plate, pushed and became unstuck. I didn't count – just pulled the ripcord. I don't think I even had time to pray. The next thing I knew I hit a haystack. I don't think the parachute ever opened although it did stream.

The squadron thought I was dead because they promptly went home and looted all my razor blades and the other good things that were hard to come by.

Conrad's promotion and appointment as squadron commander had come through just before take-off that day. He came down near Armentières, was helped by civilians to evade capture and return to command another Canadian squadron later in the war. The German plane involved was probably that of Leutnant Helmut Hoppe, a II/J G 26 pilot who may have joined the Spitfire formation in error while returning to his airfield at Lille. He later claimed the destruction of Conrad's Spitfire; there is no mention of Hoppe's plane being a casualty.

The other Canadian pilot, Flight Sergeant C. M. Shouldice, was in severe trouble. After colliding with Conrad he managed to gain a little height and his comrades saw that his left aileron was missing, probably lost pulling out of the violent dive. Halfway back over the Channel, Shouldice's Spitfire suddenly dived into the sea and he was killed. Notification of his commission as an officer had arrived at his unit while he was away flying that day. Some of the other Spitfires experienced great difficulty in returning to England because in the turn-round at Manston between their first and second sorties their fuel tanks had not been properly filled. Several pilots ran short of fuel while over Belgium, but because of the great altitude at which they were operating and the flying qualities of their light and graceful Spitfires, they were able to glide fifty miles to land at Manston.

It should be stressed that, however interesting the experiences of the German radio operator Vollert and the Canadian pilot

Conrad, these were minor, isolated actions. Most of the B-17s were safely escorted without incident from Antwerp out over the North Sea. In theory, two German *Gruppen* of fresh fighters should have come into action in this area. These were I and III/JG 2, sent up from the Paris area, but their flights had been long and difficult, with several planes dropping out or losing contact with formation leaders. The few which did come within sight of the B-17s were mostly put off by the presence of the Spitfire escort. Only one part of I/JG 2, under the *Gruppe* commander Hauptmann Erich Hohagen, made a quick pass against the very front of the bomber force. The lead plane of the 91st Bomb Group, carrying the group commander Colonel Wurzbach and the task force commander Colonel Gross, received further damage but no one was hurt and the B-17 did not go down.

It took only thirty minutes for the bombers to cross the North Sea. The formations loosened out and descended steadily. The crew members were at last able to take off their oxygen masks and relax a little. Some smoked but most immediately went for their packed food and bit into sandwiches or chocolate bars frozen hard by the long flight at altitude. One man noticed that when the two waist gunners in his crew removed their oxygen masks they both wore 'what appeared to be a brass mask on their face'; the constant feeding in and ejection of the cartridges on their guns had created a brass dust which clung to the exposed part of their faces.

One crippled bomber had to ditch halfway across the North Sea. This was the plane of Lieutenant Eugene Lockhart's crew, from the 91st Bomb Group, which had been in serious trouble since crossing the Dutch coast on the outward flight nearly four hours earlier. Lockhart kept up with his group until the Belgian coast was crossed but then fell back, eventually flying on one engine until forced to ditch. Two Spitfires watched over the bomber during this process and stayed with the dinghy when all the crew managed to get out of the rapidly sinking plane. The Spitfire pilots, Norwegians Lieutenant Tor Werner and Sergeant Christen Gran, later received a letter of thanks from Lockhart's unit. The only casualty in the B-17 was the radio operator, Technical Sergeant William C. Darden, a calm, cool Texan who stayed at his set right up to the ditching and ruptured his liver because the parachute pack which should have cushioned the impact had been thrown out to save weight. Darden's perfect handling of the radio distress procedure produced an R.A.F. Walrus rescue aircraft before nightfall and this crew was safely landed at Ramsgate during the night. Darden recovered from his injury and completed his tour of operations safely. This plane was the tenth lost from the 91st Bomb Group.

A second cripple managed to get within ten miles of England before having to come down on the sea. Because it was exactly on track, two R.A.F. rescue launches which were on station waiting for the American bombers' return arrived promptly and also landed this crew at Ramsgate. This was the plane of Flight Officer George Darrow and it was the eleventh B-17 lost by the 381st Bomb Group. The happy absence of serious casualties in these two ditchings is a tribute both to the inbuilt strength of the B-17 and the skill of the American pilots and the men of the R.A.F. air–sea rescue service, about which so many Americans make favourable comment.

The first B-17 to return from the Schweinfurt operation landed at 5.47 p.m. and landings continued until 8.20 p.m. The average crew had spent nearly seven hours in the air. Various planes, damaged or short of fuel, put down at the first airfield their pilots could find – but this was all routine after a big operation. The closest shave came when the plane of Flight Officer Randolph Jacobs, on only his third mission as aircraft captain, ran out of fuel as he was circling his airfield at Grafton Underwood while waiting for planes with wounded men aboard to land first. Staff Sergeant Jack Goetz was the engineer.

> I was standing between the two pilots and they were having a discussion about a damaged wheel. Jake knew how much battle damage we had and with one wheel out as well he decided it was better to go in on the belly. They retracted the undercarriage, but only a few seconds later all four engines went dead. Jake told me to go back and get the boys ready for a crash-landing. He came in steep and fast. I'd only just got back to my normal station on the flight deck when we hit the ground. There was no time to worry; it all happened too fast.
>
> A great mass of sparks and dust came up into the bomb-bay just behind me. That was the only time in my flying career that I was really scared – when I saw that mass of sparks. No one said anything; I think everyone thought we were going to blow up. We were heading straight for one of our old B-17Es at its dispersal and it would have been good-bye if we'd hit that

because we had a pretty good speed up. But our left wing caught the earth bank protecting the dispersal, slewed us round and stopped us dead with the nose of our plane up on that bank of earth.

There were a lot of big shots at Grafton Underwood that day; it was the anniversary of the first Eighth Air Force raid which had taken off from our base in 1942. When we came down, everyone on the base – the cooks and everybody else who had been watching us return from the raid – came running out with the ambulances and the fire engines, all tearing across the field to us. We were all out of that plane before even one of them arrived. Jake had a big cigar in his mouth and he said to the first man who arrived, 'Anyone got a match? I didn't have enough gas to fill my cigarette lighter.'

This B-17 was never repaired. 'Jake' Jacobs, later promoted to captain, was killed leading his group on a raid to a flying-bomb site at Sottevaast in the Pas de Calais. Most of the other men in this crew survived the war.

There were no other accidents during the landings from the Schweinfurt mission.

CHAPTER 18

Distant Action

There had been action at other places while the B-17s were fighting their way back from Schweinfurt. Two more small raids were flown across the English Channel and the North Sea but these were not pressed home as firmly as the main round of diversions earlier in the day. The first was a further attack on the airfield at Poix in France, carried out in mid-afternoon and obviously timed to hold down any Luftwaffe fighter units still remaining in that area. This operation was only partially successful. It had been planned as a considerable effort, with the 323rd and 387th Bomb Groups each providing thirty-six B-26s and R.A.F. Fighter Command sending eleven squadrons of Spitfires as escorts, but only half of this force reached the target. The weather over the Channel was now worsening and the commander of part of the Spitfire escort decided to abandon the raid. The 387th Bomb Group thus dumped its bombs into the sea and turned back with five of the Spitfire squadrons. The remainder of the attacking force flew on and cratered the much-bombed airfield of Poix yet again. The Luftwaffe did not appear and there were no aircraft casualties on either side.

The last operation to be mounted from England took place after the Schweinfurt B-17s had withdrawn from the Continent. Five R.A.F. Typhoon squadrons provided thirty-eight aircraft for a dive-bombing force and escort in an operation against Woensdrecht airfield, hoping to catch recently landed German fighters on the ground. This entailed a long flight over the sea and, with Woensdrecht's heavy defences, one of the Typhoon pilots says that 'this sort of trip tended to make one grow old in a hurry'. But the five squadrons never managed to combine as one force. The records of those which did not reach Woensdrecht blame the failure on bad visibility caused by haze and make the charge that other squadrons were guilty of faulty navigation and timing. Only eight Typhoons bombed Woensdrecht; the remaining dive bombers found a 3,000-ton tanker off Flushing (now named Vlissingen) and attacked it, but no hits were scored. A Typhoon damaged by German fire while attacking the tanker was the only R.A.F. casualty of this operation. Luftwaffe records do not show any German casualties at Woensdrecht.

The air operations of this day – at least as far as this part of Europe was concerned – had thus turned full circle, because it was over Woensdrecht that the B-17s of the 4th Bombardment Wing had penetrated mainland Europe on their way to Regensburg more than seven hours earlier.

It is now necessary to go back to Regensburg and pick up again the story of the 4th Bombardment Wing. The time is soon after mid-day. The force of 123 B-17s has turned south after bombing Regensburg. It is not under German fighter attack but its groups are no longer in one compact force because two of the groups had been forced to make a second bomb run over the target. The airfields in North Africa are nearly a thousand miles and five hours' flying time distant. Most of the B-17s have already been airborne for five hours; some have been flying for nearly six hours. Two damaged B-17s are flying alone over Southern Germany, hoping to rejoin the main force later or to reach neutral Switzerland.

It was only a short, twenty-minute flight from Regensburg across Bavaria to the Alps. The route passed east of the city of Munich – 'a big mass of beautiful buildings, clearly visible'. The weather remained fine and clear as it would all the way to Africa. The Alps grew larger and larger. For Lieutenant John Brady, a pilot in the 100th Bomb Group, those minutes flying from the target to the mountains were the most pleasant part of the day.

> The Alps – a glorious sight that none of us had seen before. The combination of that beautiful sight and the fact that we had come through okay and the realization that there weren't any fighters around any more was pretty euphoric. We had expended nearly all our ammunition and there was an almost audible sigh of relief from everyone that we had actually survived. I walked back through the plane; I don't recall ever doing that before. I remember the guys standing among all those empty shell cases. They were a pretty relieved bunch of boys.
>
> That was before we started getting worried about whether

we had enough gas to get to Africa. At that point, that was all well in the future – a purely academic point not worth worrying about then.

The next turning point was the Chiemsee, a beautiful lake set in the foothills of the Alps. The plan allowed for this to be a 'rally point' where the force could circle and close up before the mountain crossing. But Colonel LeMay was anxious about fuel consumption. He knew his force was well strung out, but the weather over the mountains appeared clear and he decided not to delay here but to press on and attempt to close up the groups later.

There followed an interesting forty-minute flight over – or in some cases through – the Alps. The briefed route may have called for a straight flight across this area but many of the group actually threaded their way through the valley of the River Inn and the Brenner Pass, almost like tourists. It was in the Inn valley that the Americans shook off the very last German plane to have remained in contact. Hauptmann Hans-Werner Rupprecht had taken off in his Messerschmitt 110 night fighter from St Trond in Belgium and had been shadowing the bomber force and reporting its progress since the Frankfurt area. Rupprecht knew that he would soon have to leave and he closed in to try and secure a victory by making a series of attacks on the two groups flying at the rear of the American force. One of his first bursts of fire hit the lead plane of the 385th Bomb Group and caused damage to its radio equipment which was to have an unfortunate effect a week later when this plane had to ditch in the Atlantic while flying back from North Africa and experienced difficulty in radioing its ditching position to England. Rupprecht then concentrated on Lieutenant Robert Morrill's B-17 which was straggling from the 94th Bomb Group with a damaged engine. Rupprecht's fire caused a second engine on the bomber to give trouble. The German pilot then pulled away and flew back to land at Munich with his tanks almost empty. His unit put in a hopeful claim that one of the planes he had attacked might be one of the B-17s which later force-landed in Switzerland or crashed in Italy, but Lieutenant Morrill, by ordering all loose equipment to be thrown out and by some careful flying, reached North Africa safely. Hauptmann Rupprecht did not fare so well. He was killed the following month flying against an R.A.F. night raid on Hannover.

Apart from Rupprecht's attacks, the B-17 force crossed the

Alps without incident. The Americans were flying over some of the most beautiful country in Europe. The cities of Salzburg and Innsbruck were passed to left and right. The Austrian Tyrol was crossed with snow still on many of its peaks. Austria fell behind and Italy appeared with its equally beautiful Dolomites. Staff Sergeant Clarence Payne of the 390th Bomb Group remembers Lake Garda – 'a beautiful lake, it looked just like a blue mirror; we all commented on how blue it was. It nestled in a valley with mountains on either side. I was brought up in the mountains of Western Maryland and I always loved mountains and water.' Many other men talk of the beauty of the flight over the mountains, but one wounded gunner says that 'they looked more foreboding when you were hurt and scared', and another man, much concerned about fuel consumption, says, 'They were pretty enough – the storybook Alps – but we wanted to get the hell out of them. We knew where we wanted to go and it wasn't the Alps.'

Many Americans say that they flew across a corner of Switzerland but this is not correct; Switzerland was 100 miles away from the briefed route. Three crippled B-17s did reach that country, however. When the navigator of Second Lieutenant Raymond Becker's crew, of the 390th Bomb Group, advised that neutral Switzerland was below, Becker told his crew that they were free to bale out if they liked – there was little chance that he could reach North Africa – but no one accepted the offer and Becker carried on flying south. The other two B-17s were more seriously hurt and came to Switzerland deliberately to land. Both planes had shaken off German fighter attacks and then made low-level flights across the Bodensee (Lake Constance) pursued by German Flak. Lieutenant Donald Oakes of the 100th Bomb Group belly-landed at Dübendorf military airfield near Zurich and Second Lieutenant Stephen Rapport of the 390th put his plane down in a potato field near Berne.

The Swiss were very interested in these almost intact examples of the famous Flying Fortress – the first to reach Switzerland. (They had received their first B-24 Liberator – from the 93rd Bomb Group – after the Wiener Neustadt raid four days earlier.) The American crews became 'internees' who could be kept in Switzerland until the end of the war because they had deliberately flown to Switzerland and were not escapers from prisoner-of-war camps or evaders from aircraft shot down in German-occupied territory. Oakes and Rapport, however, were soon exchanged with some Luftwaffe pilots whom the Germans wanted back and the two pilots had an interesting rail journey through Germany and France to Spain. The Swiss also found means of returning most of the others, but only after many months of waiting.

The main force of bombers emerged from the Alps over Lake Garda. This was the second of the designated rally points and Colonel LeMay decided that he should pause here and allow his scattered groups to concentrate into tight combat formation again. There was every expectation that German and Italian fighters would be met over the Italian plains and near the islands of Corsica and Sardinia, where Intelligence estimated that up to 200 German fighters were stationed. LeMay led the five groups which were with him round in a series of big circles over the lake to wait for the two groups which had become separated. An enemy Flak battery fired salvoes of four shells ineffectually into the empty middle of the circle throughout the fifteen minutes it took the force to reassemble. Major Preston Piper, leading the 385th Bomb Group, was delighted that LeMay had waited for them.

> We had been feeling very lonely and isolated and I felt physically let down with anti-climax after the target. I saw this big mass of whirling aircraft ahead and thought it was another air battle. I could only think that the Italians had come up but it was LeMay doing a three-sixty to help us catch up. We were very relieved.

But the delay chafed on the nerves of many of the waiting crews, particularly those of the 390th Bomb Group who had taken off too early and had then flown the entire operation in the high position of its wing. The fuel forecasts for many of their planes were now looking critical but no move was made to release this group and send it ahead.

Further anti-aircraft fire appeared from time to time during the flight across Italy but it was never accurate and the B-17s flew serenely across the wide valley of the River Po and finally left the mainland of Europe between Genoa and La Spezia. Some Italian fighters were seen but they never attacked, being content to fly a series of spectacular aerobatics well outside machine-gun range. The Luftwaffe in Italy did not appear at all; its strength must all have been further south in the fighting around Sicily. The Americans could not believe how lucky they had been to cross this supposedly major enemy country without suffering any serious attack.

But the steady attrition of the bomb groups continued. Two

more crippled planes had fallen out over Italy. The crew of Lieutenant Ronald Hollenbeck all baled out safely before their plane flew on to crash into a mountain; this was the eighth loss suffered by the 100th Bomb Group. Lieutenant Robert Hayden's plane in the 95th Bomb Group went down next. There should have been plenty of time for its crew to parachute safely but the tail gunner opened his parachute too early and was caught on the tail. Three other gunners were presumably unnerved by this sight and refused to jump. All four were killed when the plane crashed.

Two more B-17s left their group formations as soon as they were safely out over the sea. The plane of Second Lieutenant Dale Shaver, 390th Bomb Group, had lost a lot of fuel after being damaged by a fighter of the Messerschmitt factory's 'protection flight' over Regensburg. Pilot and navigator quickly calculated that there was no chance of reaching Africa and Shaver called up his group leader to seek advice. He was told that neutral Spain, 300 miles to the west, was the best prospect and given a course to fly. Shaver duly set off into an area for which his navigator had no maps. Some time later a peninsula of land was spotted and, with fuel almost expired, a skilful crash-landing into a small airfield left the ten crew members unhurt and wondering whether they were in Spain. This hope was dashed when bursts of machine-gun fire kicked up dust all around them and Italian soldiers surrounded them. Shaver and his crew were in Southern France, not far from Toulon, and in an area occupied by Italian troops who, three weeks later, were to be on the American side! Shaver and his crew were soon handed over to the Germans.

The next B-17 to fall away was yet another 100th Bomb Group aircraft, that of Lieutenant Glen Van Noy. This was the plane named *Oh Nausea* which had such a bad mechanical record that it was reputed never to have completed a mission. It was in this plane that Colonel Kennedy, the senior officer from a gunnery school in the United States, was flying. He had certainly received plenty of first-hand combat experience, although the gun he was manning in the plane's waist had suffered an early malfunction and he had not been able to fire more than single shots. *Oh Nausea* had behaved true to form and one engine had failed very early in the flight. Several crew members felt that Van Noy should have turned back to England but the pilot had pressed on. 'He was that sort of chap; he was feisty,' says one of his crew. A second engine failed over Germany and this now became another plane which had no chance of reaching Africa. Van Noy could have landed in Switzerland but he again decided to press on and try to reach one of the airfields in Sicily which were now in Allied hands. There followed a long flight within sight of the Italian coast – the crew even saw the buildings of Rome – before Van Noy turned south near Naples for the last lap to Sicily. But this was to be another disappointed crew. When only half an hour from safety, still with enough fuel to reach Sicily, a third engine failed and Van Noy had to ditch. Technical Sergeant Bill Crabb says, 'That guy could never land an airplane properly on a concrete runway but he made an absolutely perfect landing on the sea.' The crew took to their dinghies and cranked out emergency radio signals all night, but it was a German flying boat which arrived next morning and picked them up. Friendly German officers at the seaplane base at Naples asked Colonel Kennedy why they had come down in that area; Kennedy replied, 'I thought we would go fishing.'

This is a suitable place to describe the bombing operation which was mounted from North Africa against Luftwaffe airfields in Southern France. These airfields were at Istres and Salon near Marseilles. Photographic reconnaissance indicated that large numbers of German bombers were stationed here, posing a threat to the Allied forces soon to invade Italy. Major-General Doolittle's Northwest African Strategic Air Force attempted to time this raid to coincide with the withdrawal flight of Colonel LeMay's force past the German-held islands of Corsica and Sardinia in order to split the efforts of the German fighters believed to be in that area but, because of the delays in take-off in England, the raid took place before LeMay's force appeared in the area. The 2nd, 97th, 99th and 301st Bomb Groups dispatched 180 B-17s on this operation. The two airfields were easily found and heavily bombed. The bomb loads had been composed entirely of 20-pound fragmentation bombs, so as to hit the largest number of German planes possible; 25,619 such bombs were dropped! Photographs led to a later American claim that ninety-four German planes had been destroyed on the ground and a further twenty-eight damaged. Two of a handful of Messerschmitt 109s which attacked the B-17s were shot down; two B-17s – from the 2nd and 301st Bomb Groups – were lost to Flak fire. It seemed to be a very successful raid. But German casualty records show that the mass of planes seen on the two airfields had not been bombers but were mainly the towing planes and gliders of German airborne units. The records show that at least fifty-two planes were destroyed and 135 damaged; two thirds of these were gliders.

The North African based B-17s returned over the Mediterranean about two hours ahead of LeMay's force, but they received no attention from the German fighters believed to be on Corsica and Sardinia and these B-17s landed safely back at their bases. Colonel LeMay's force then passed only thirty miles from the two islands and again not one German plane appeared. It is not known whether the Luftwaffe units believed to be in that area were a myth or whether the German reporting service failed to detect the two bomber forces. Whatever the reason, a major cause of anxiety was removed from the men of a force which would not have been in very good condition to face any determined fighter attack at that point.

The groups had started to loosen up their formations as soon as they left the Italian coast. Colonel LeMay later issued strong words of criticism over this but a looser formation made less demands on fuel and many crews were going to need every drop they could save. There followed a very long, very tedious flight at reduced power settings right across the Mediterranean. LeMay was in constant touch by radio with his group leaders; Lieutenant Abel, navigator in this plane, says that LeMay 'maintained positive control of the whole effort; he wasn't just there for the ride'. The greatest anxiety was in the lead plane of the 390th Bomb Group; Captain Von Arb, the co-pilot, says, 'Colonel Wittan obviously regretted his early decision not to return to England when he found we were up too early. There wasn't much he could do but sweat it out.' One sight remembered by many men was the stream of machine-guns, belts of ammunition and other items of equipment being thrown out of the waist windows and hatches of those aircraft with the worst fuel problems.

The force managed to reach within 130 miles of the African coast without further loss but a series of ditchings began at that point. Four planes went down, one each from the 385th and 388th Bomb Groups and two from the 390th. All four had earlier suffered combat damage but the two planes of the 390th would certainly have reached land if they had not taken off too early that morning. All the ditchings were within sight of the main formation; one man who watched all four planes go down said that they were all 'good, professional landings'. No lives were lost. A minor point of interest is that one of the planes which went down, that of Second Lieutenant Wade Sneed of the 390th

Bomb Group, was named *Blood, Guts and Rust*. 'The 'Blood and Guts' was from the sayings of General Patton, a man whom Sneed admired, and the 'Rust' was the choice of the rest of the crew who knew that one way or another the plane would finish up as scrap one day. This B-17 had flown just three missions. A major air search took place for the four ditched crews and all were picked up by friendly rescue services either that evening or the next day.

The Regensburg operation was nearly over. The coast of Africa appeared at approximately 4.50 p.m. (this was English time; local time may have been one hour ahead). It had been planned that the entire force should land at Telergma, a large airfield forty miles south of the coast that was capable of taking heavy bombers, but all crews had been given details of seven other airfields in the area and, because of their fuel situation, planes were soon landing at fields all along the coast of Algeria; an R.A.F. fighter airfield at Bône was particularly busy despite its short runway. There are numerous stories of pilots with damaged or fuel-starved planes landing blindly into sand-clouds blown up by preceding planes, and of the absolute breakdown of any form of effective flying control. But every one of the 119 B-17s still remaining from the 146 which had left England managed to land. The only serious incident was when one B-17 chopped the tail off another plane but fortunately the tail gunner had already left his turret. It was a minor miracle of that day and certainly against all reasonable odds that no lives were lost in two mass take-offs in England in poor weather conditions, in seven ditchings in the North Sea and the Mediterranean, and in these hair-raising landings on the African airfields.

The average crew in the Regensburg force had been flying for eleven hours, some on their third consecutive day of operations. Colonel LeMay's plane, with more fuel remaining than most, was one of the last to land at Telergma. He was seen 'disappearing to raise hell at the lack of facilities', but most men had little energy left. Lieutenant-Colonel Oliver B. Taylor was one of the American officers waiting at Telergma for the arrival of the B-17s from Regensburg.

> As the ships were parked, out tumbled the crews, accompanied by a general clamor as some called for help with the wounded, others indulged in bitter cursing and a few vowed vehemently

that they would never fly in combat again. I was particularly distressed by the sight of one very young sergeant climbing out, leaning his head against the side of his ship and sobbing convulsively. I guessed, or may have been told, that the blanket-wrapped, dismembered remains of an airman which were being passed out of the ship had been a buddy of his. These people had been through hell – and they showed it.

The men who had been to Regensburg also have their memories of that moment.

My crew all kissed the ground when we landed and they even went to church the next day. It would be an unusual thing for some of them to have done that. (Lieutenant Paul Vance, 390th Bomb Group)

We knew we had taken heavy losses but I don't think I detected any depression in the crews, only sadness over losing people, trying to pull ourselves together to fill in the gaps of what had happened to the lost planes. But we were very pleased with the success of the mission – we felt that we had been right on it. Alongside that was a feeling of utter exhaustion. (Lieutenant Charles Cruikshank, 100th Bomb Group)

I recall that three of us went over to the British Officers' Club that night and got very drunk on wine, which is all they had to spare. Even today, when I taste a sweet grape wine, the events of that day and night come into my mind. (Second Lieutenant Gus Mencow, 390th Bomb Group)

That night the men stretched their flying clothing on the ground under the wings of the planes and slept. I slept in the radio room and I could not have slept better on a beauty-rest mattress.

In fact, after a mission like the one we had just completed, which was more fantastic than fiction, I think we could have slept standing up. 'Sleep, sleep, fighting men; the day is dying in the West.' (Lieutenant William G. Broach, 94th Bomb Group)

CHAPTER 19
The Reckoning

In attacking Regensburg and Schweinfurt, the United States Army Air Force had given their doctrine of strategic bombing the fullest possible test. Any judgement of the joint mission will depend upon the results achieved compared with the cost incurred. It will be convenient to deal with the cost first.

The Eighth Air Force dispatched 376 B-17s to Regensburg and Schweinfurt; 361 of those crossed the coast of mainland Europe but only 301 returned to England or reached Allied bases in North Africa. Sixty B-17s were lost over Europe or ditched and sank in the sea. At least eleven of the planes which did reach safety – three from the 1st Bombardment Wing and eight from the 4th – were so badly damaged that they were written off and did not fly with their units again, although some of the B-17s left in North Africa by the 4th Bombardment Wing may have been repaired and later allocated to local units. A further 162 aircraft which did return suffered various degrees of damage. The loss of aircrews was alleviated by the saving of six full crews from the sea by Allied rescue services. Fifty-four full crews (of whom more details later) were thus missing with their aircraft and the equivalent of three more crews were lost when men parachuted prematurely or were killed or seriously wounded in damaged aircraft which returned to England. The overall loss of B-17s and crew from the raids to Regensburg and Schweinfurt was, therefore, seventy-one aircraft and forty-six crews. This was roughly equal to the total losses of the infant Eighth Air Force during its first six months of operations from August 1942 to February 1943.

The aircraft casualties can be split up between the two bombardment wings involved as follows:

Wing	*Dispatched*	*Bombed Primary (%)*	*Missing (%)*
4th Bomb. Wing Regensburg	146	122 (83·6)	24 (16·4)
1st Bomb. Wing Schweinfurt	230	184 (80·0)	36 (15·7)
Total	376	306 (81·4)	60 (16·0)

The 'missing' total does not include the ten or more aircraft written off after battle damage.

The heaviest losing groups were:

Bomb Group	*Target*	*Dispatched*	*Missing (%)*
381st	Schweinfurt	26	11 (42·3)
91st	Schweinfurt	24	10 (41·7)
100th	Regensburg	21	9 (42·9)

Only one bomb group from each force returned without losing any aircraft or crewmen killed. These were the 96th – in which Colonel LeMay was flying – and the 306th Bomb Groups. The 303rd Bomb Group suffered no aircraft losses but one gunner was killed.

In the supporting operations, American and R.A.F. fighter escorts to the B-17s flew 456 sorties and lost three P-47s and two Spitfires. The 469 sorties flown in the diversionary raids incurred the loss of only one Typhoon fighter-bomber and one Spitfire. The number of Allied aircraft missing was thus sixty-seven from 1,301 sorties flown, an overall missing rate of 5·1 per cent. (Comments in this chapter do not cover the Northwest African Air Force raids to Istres and Salon.)

But men should be of more consequence than machines. The name and eventual fate of every crew member in all the missing Allied aircraft has been identified and some interesting information is thus available. First, the following table shows what happened to the crews of the sixty lost B-17s:

	4th Bomb. Wing (Regensburg)	*1st Bomb. Wing (Schweinfurt)*	*Total*
Killed	34	68	102
Prisoners	133	248	381
Evaders	13	25	38
Interned	20	—	20
Rescued from sea	40	20	60
Total	240	361	601

('Evaders' are only those men who actually returned to England; many others were on the run for a considerable period before being taken prisoner. The ten men of the 100th Bomb Group picked up from the Mediterranean by the Germans are counted as prisoners and are not included in the 'rescued from sea' total.)

These figures can be presented in another way to separate officers and enlisted men:

	Officers	*Enlisted Men*
Killed	40	62
Prisoners	154	227
Evaders	13	25
Interned	8	12
Rescued from sea	24	36
Total	239	362

From these figures it can be seen that officers and enlisted men suffered fatal casualties in almost equal proportions, but that enlisted men were slightly more successful in evading capture.

Another aspect that was researched was the position in its bomb group formation from which every lost B-17 was shot down. (Diagrams in Appendix 1 show this information.) The German head-on attacks, which concentrated on the wingmen positions at the rear of group formations, resulted in heavy losses in these positions. With the exception of Colonel William L. Kennedy, who was taken prisoner while flying as a waist gunner in a 100th Bomb Group crew, no senior officers became casualties. The highest-ranking casualties were Captain Robert M. Knox, also of the 100th Bomb Group, who was killed, and two other captains in a 92nd Bomb Group crew who became prisoners. All other casualties, whether killed or prisoners, were first lieutenants and below. On the other hand, research also shows that every group sent its most experienced available men on the raids. Many of the lost crews were in the second half of their operational tours of twenty-five missions. Lieutenant Charles A. Bennett of the 91st Bomb Group was unlucky enough to be shot down on his twenty-fifth mission but he evaded capture. If one excludes the new 390th Bomb Group, which was only flying its third group mission, only four of the shot-down crews had flown on less than four previous missions. The crew of Second Lieutenant Henry P. Shotland of the 100th Bomb Group seems to be the only one lost on their first operational flight.

Concentrating now on the mortality rate, one is immediately impressed with the high proportion of men who survived from B-17s shot down during these daylight operations. On average less than two men in each standard crew of ten died in the B-17s lost that day; the actual figure was 1·7 men per crew. Even if the eleven aircraft which either ditched or crash-landed without any loss of life are excluded, the mortality rate only creeps up to a little over two in the crew of ten. But these overall figures could hide large variations. The 91st Bomb Group lost thirty-six men killed in its ten missing crews; the 381st had only five deaths in their eleven. This relatively high survival rate was not unusual for Eighth Air Force operations; the outcome on other B-17 missions was roughly similar. A comparison with the survival chances in shot-down R.A.F. night bombers shows almost the reverse position. The mortality rate in 213 four-engined bombers shot down in R.A.F. raids to Hamburg (four raids), Peenemünde and Nuremberg was 83 per cent! Unfortunately it would require a lengthy essay to explain the different factors involved.

The relative danger of the crew positions in a shot-down B-17 can also be presented. The following crew members were killed in B-17s on the Regensburg and Schweinfurt mission:

Crew Position	*Killed*
Pilot	15
Co-pilot	12
Navigator	6
Bombardier	6
Engineer/gunner	11
Radio/gunner	8
Ball gunner	14

Crew Position	*Killed*
Right waist gunner	11
Left waist gunner	8
Tail gunner	10

(A pilot killed in unusual conditions on the ground, which are described later, has not been included here.) There is not so much difference here from night operations. The R.A.F. bomb aimer was the safest man in his crew, and pilots – who have to remain at the controls until other crew members have parachuted – always ran the greatest risk. The higher figures above for the ball-turret gunner reflect the known danger of that cramped and isolated position from which escape was so difficult. R.A.F. bombers did not have ball turrets.

If the casualties in the returned B-17s and in the escort and diversionary operations are now added, the Allied death role for the day numbers 114 men – 112 Americans, one Englishman and one Canadian – with 393 men becoming prisoners of war and a further thirty-nine evading capture and returning to England.

The next few paragraphs will examine the performance of the Luftwaffe units on 17 August 1943. Because the true heart of this day's fighting was the attempt by American commanders to force their way right through the German defences, it will be convenient to isolate the 'Luftwaffe versus B-17' contests first. We know exactly the extent of the American effort – that 361 B-17s crossed the coast of German-defended Europe – but there are no reliable figures available for the Luftwaffe fighter effort. Adolf Galland, the general commanding day fighters, says in his memoirs that 'about 300' German fighters were in action. Oberst Grabmann, the *Jafü Holland–Ruhr*, in a private report says that '400 single-engined and twin-engined planes' were involved. Because some planes flew two or three times, however, it is preferable to talk of 'sorties flown', and I give the following estimate:

	Single-engined Sorties	*Twin-engined Sorties*
Regensburg operation	140	15
Schweinfurt outward	260	20
Schweinfurt return	70	35
Total	470	70

The next table is an estimate of the cause of loss for each of the sixty missing B-17s. It should be stated that many of the bombers were lost to a combination of causes, with twin-engined German fighters often finishing off bombers knocked out of formation by the single-engined fighters, and Flak sometimes taking a share in a bomber's destruction. Where more than one cause was involved, simple half shares have been allocated. For those B-17s which ditched in the sea or force-landed in Switzerland, I have attributed their loss to the original cause of distress even though this may have occurred several hours earlier.

Cause of Loss	*No. of B-17s*
Single-engined fighter action	47½
Twin-engined fighter action	2½
Flak	9
Mechanical defect	1
Total	60

On the basis of these estimates, it would seem that the Luftwaffe flew nearly ten single-engined sorties or twenty-eight twin-engined sorties to shoot down each B-17 on this day.

In turning to the Luftwaffe's own casualties, the greatest difficulty is experienced when one attempts to allocate successes to the B-17 gunners who submitted claims for German fighters destroyed. These young Americans had been trained for and lived for one purpose – to shoot down German fighters. Happy was the man who returned to his base, submitted his claim and received that highly desirable 'confirmed kill'. Medals and publicity followed; morale stayed high in otherwise bad times. Overclaiming, often with complete sincerity, occurred in all air forces by both fighter pilots and bomber gunners, but post-war research soon showed that the overclaiming by American bomber gunners was in a class of its own. Early in 1943, VIII Bomber Command had tightened up the confirmation procedure and issued the following instructions.

An enemy plane would be counted as destroyed when it had been seen descending completely enveloped in flames, but not if flames had been merely licking out from the engine. It would be counted as destroyed when seen to disintegrate in the air or when the complete wing or tail assembly had been shot away from the fuselage . . . Single-engine enemy planes would be counted destroyed if the pilot had been seen to bale out.*

The bomb group records for the Schweinfurt and Regensburg raids are packed with claim forms containing those essential phrases, 'in flames', 'disintegrated', 'pilot baled out'. The main problem with claims submitted by returning gunners was what to do when several men, sometimes from more than one group, were firing at one German fighter. No one had an answer to this problem and, in those urgent days, no one really worried about the hunger of posterity for accuracy. Many senior officers realized that the claims were inflated. Colonel Maurice Preston, commander of the 379th Bomb Group, says:

> I had a very low regard for B-17 gunners. I flew forty-five missions and I could never be sure that I saw a B-17 shoot down a German fighter. I saw many smoking but I knew that the fighter 'smoked' when it throttled back. There was no official policy to overdo confirmations but we were always prepared to be lenient, specially with gunners who had been through a tough mission.

These were the claims submitted by the bomb groups for 17 August 1943 and *accepted by the bombardment wings*. They do not include any casualties which the sixty missing B-17s might have inflicted on the German fighters.

	Destroyed	*Probables*	*Damaged*
Regensburg operation	140	19	36
Schweinfurt operation	148	62	67
Totals	288	81	103

The Eighth Air Force public relations unit sent out the figures almost unchanged. On 26 August *Stars and Stripes*, the American servicemen's daily paper, was headlined: 'Biggest Air Battle Cost Nazis 307 Planes, Shuttle Raid Forts Got 140, Schweinfurt Force 147, P-47s 20.' The sixty B-17s lost would not look so bad to the American public after that.

The main basis for establishing German aircraft losses are the

* W. F. Craven and J. L. Cate, *The Army Air Forces in World War II*, University of Chicago Press, 1948–58, Vol. II, p. 223.

Luftwaffe Quartermaster General's return of aircraft casualties and the Luftwaffe's central personnel casualty files.* Unfortunately, even when these two sources are combined there may be some gaps – possibly up to 10 per cent – in the compilation of Luftwaffe casualties. Some of these gaps can be filled from the personal accounts of German pilots shot down, but all comments here on Luftwaffe casualties must allow for a possible shortfall of 5 to 10 per cent. Against the B-17 gunners' claims of 288 German fighters destroyed, the actual number which can be credited to them is only twenty-one, made up as follows:

	Regensburg	*Schweinfurt*
Messerschmitt 109s	5	8
Focke-Wulf 190s	—	5
Messerschmitt 110s	—	3
Total	5	16

The 'fighter-versus-fighter' encounters resulted in exactly the same number of German fighters being destroyed – twenty-one – as were shot down by the B-17s. Thirteen victories can be allocated to the American P-47 units – eleven of them to the 56th Fighter Group in its battle near Liège – and eight to R.A.F. Spitfires in both escort and diversionary operations. The Germans lost five further fighters in take-off and landing accidents.

The Luftwaffe's total loss for the day thus numbered forty-seven fighters – twenty Messerschmitt 109s, eighteen Focke-Wulf 190s and nine Messerschmitt 110s – against Allied losses of sixty-seven planes lost in action and at least eleven further losses of aircraft written off after battle damage. But these simple figures do not tell the full story. The loss of so many of those great, powerful, four-engined B-17s with their ten-man crews outweighed all other factors. Only sixteen German aircrew were killed and nine wounded, compared to the Allied loss of 565 airmen who were killed, taken prisoner, on the run in German-occupied

* The Luftwaffe Quartermaster General's return of aircraft casualties is on microfilm at the Imperial War Museum in London and probably at various other places; the central personnel casualty files are at the Deutsche Dienststelle in the Eichborndamm, Berlin. The German system classified aircraft casualties from 100-per-cent destroyed down to 10-per-cent damaged. In this book, 60-per-cent damaged and above is taken to mean that the aircraft concerned was either destroyed or 'written off' as beyond repair.

territory or interned in Switzerland. In the air, at least, it was a clear victory for the Luftwaffe.

But the outcome of the aerial battle was only half the story. Did the results of the bombing at Regensburg and Schweinfurt justify the cost of reaching those targets? There were the usual morale-boosting and sometimes self-delusory messages and reports in the days and weeks following the operation. How valid would these prove to be in the cold light of post-war years when the German side of the story became available? In attempting to answer these questions, the immense assistance of hindsight must be acknowledged. This was still a trial-and-error period for the American commanders and any comments made here should not be regarded as personal criticism.

The bombing by the units of the 4th Bombardment Wing at Regensburg could hardly have been better; the American Official History several times quotes reports from the next few months in which various commanders express the hope that more 'Regensburgs' could be achieved.* In fact the performance of the 4th Bombardment Wing can hardly be faulted. The only minor blemish that can be found in their whole day's operations is the premature take-off time given to the 390th Bomb Group which resulted in the ditching of two damaged aircraft, though not the loss of their crews. The success at Regensburg was the more remarkable because it was achieved by seven bomb groups whose average length of operational service was only eight weeks. Whatever the judgement on the day as a whole, great credit must be accorded to the part played by Colonel LeMay and the officers and enlisted men of the 4th Bombardment Wing.

It is not surprising that the Americans believed the Messerschmitt factory to be almost totally destroyed. Photographs taken at the time of bombing showed a carpet of bursts over most of the factory area and later reconnaissance pictures confirmed that extensive damage had been caused. But the Americans had yet to learn one of the basic truths of the bombing war – that appearances could deceive. This was a modern factory with many open spaces. At least three quarters of the bombs dropped had to fall into these spaces and they caused no more than blast damage to nearby installations. Most of the buildings in this factory were not of substantial construction; they were single-storey work-

*For example, see W. F. Craven and J. L. Cate, *The Army Air Forces in World War II*, Vol. II, pp. 689 and 719.

shops with thin brick walls and asbestos roofs. Those that were hit did indeed collapse in ruins and present to aerial photographers a scene of complete destruction. But when the Germans cleared away the debris they found that most of their valuable machine tools were intact and could be relocated, switched on and quickly producing again. The stark truth was that the 250 tons of bombs dropped by the whole of the 4th Bombardment Wing on Regensburg was just not sufficient to 'destroy' this type of target, however accurately aimed. Not only was the tonnage insufficient but the actual bombs used were not heavy enough to smash the all-important machine tools. The heaviest bombs dropped on Regensburg were 500-pound high-explosives, and on Schweinfurt 1,000-pounders. British aircraft were regularly dropping bombs of up to 4,000 pounds in weight and sometimes of 8,000 pounds. The British were even developing a bomb of 12,000 pounds specifically for precision attacks on German factories! The B-17 bomb-bay was incapable of taking anything heavier than a 2,000-lb bomb at this time.

When German officials surveyed the Regensburg factory after the raid, they thus found that much of the machinery remained usable. Replacements were rapidly ordered for those items which had been damaged; a Belgian worker writes of new machine tools soon arriving from the Skoda Works at Pilsen, only seventy miles away across the Czechoslovakian border. The same Belgian tells of a large new assembly building, the tubular framework of which 'went up in one night like a large circus tent; it was unbelievable'. The Messerschmitt company had also been preparing a series of 'shadow' workshops in the towns and larger villages of Bavaria, the plan being for each unit at Regensburg to have three 'shadows' outside. This was partly to increase overall production and partly to cover the main factory against air-raid damage. This process was not complete at the time of the American raid but some of the machinery from Regensburg was immediately rushed out to the shadow sites. By such means, and because the most important building in the main factory, the *Endmontage* or 'final assembly shop', had not been hit in the raid, a limited production of fighters resumed at Regensburg in less than one month. Former Messerschmitt officials still living in Regensburg are extremely proud of the factory's swift recovery.

The German recovery plan also included a major degree of dispersal, not just to the shadow workshops but to a unique series of new production sites in Bavaria's extensive forests. Corridors of trees were cut down, the space left was covered with camouflage netting and a small part of the fighter production process was moved in. These 'forest factories' were cheap and easy to establish and the Allies never discovered them. The new workers drafted in, mainly forced labour or concentration-camp prisoners, had to put up with the primitive living conditions.

American commanders were quick to claim a dramatic cut in Messerschmitt production as a result of their raid. At the 4th Bombardment Wing's post-mission critique on 28 August, Colonel LeMay told his officers that the British Air Ministry estimated the production loss to be between 2,000 and 2,500 planes, but someone was helping morale along a little here. Although there are no official German reports available, the officials still living in Regensburg estimate the loss at between 800 to 1,000 planes, equivalent to eight to ten weeks of full production. Despite the extensive German recovery, this immediate loss due to the Regensburg raid was a major success for the Americans, and the effort which the Germans were forced to devote to recovery and dispersal must have been at the expense of other parts of their war effort. There was also one small but important effect of the raid of which the Americans knew nothing. Craftsmen at Regensburg had been preparing the jigs for the fuselage of the projected jet fighter, the Messerschmitt 262. These jigs were destroyed in the bombing and the subsequent development of the jet was delayed, but by how long is not known.

Approximately 5,000 people were in the Messerschmitt factory at the time of the raid. There are conflicting reports as to how many of these became casualties. Various unsubstantiated estimates of a death-roll of between 500 and 900 are likely to be too high. A total of 461 people were treated for injury and the Regensburg Stadtarchiv says that 402 people died, but adds that this was unlikely to be the final number. That figure of 402 dead was broken down in another report as follows:

German men	201
German women	53
German apprentices	68
German children	2
Foreign workers	78

The death-roll was undoubtedly increased by the unrealistic attitude of the ordinary people of Regensburg to the danger of air attack on their town so deep in Germany, by the reluctance of many to take shelter when the sirens sounded and by the poor protection given by the factory shelters to those who did go into them. The Germans killed were mostly skilled workers – or would have become so in the case of the apprentices – who might be regarded as legitimate targets of war. It is not known whether the two children were visiting the factory with their mother or whether they were killed by one of the very few bombs which fell on housing outside the factory area. The seventy-eight foreign dead were spread over at least five nationalities – Belgians, French, Russians, Czechs and Hungarians. The Belgians suffered the worst. A notice in a Belgian newspaper announced that a list was available at the Hôtel de Ville at Mons of twenty-five dead at Regensburg from the province of Hainault whose bodies had been returned home for burial. A sad postscript says that this was the fifty-fourth such batch of bodies to be returned from Germany, although the numbers involved were rarely as large as this. Many other Belgians were buried at Regensburg.

There was one interesting repercussion of the German casualties. Many people from Regensburg had emigrated to the United States during the inter-war years of depression and, after the raid, death notices appearing in the *Regensburger Kurier* stated that several of the casualties of the raid would be mourned in the United States. For example, twenty-year-old Fräulein Hildegard Multerer had relatives in New York and Otto Knollmüller, 'an exemplary father', had relations in Chicago. An unexpected result of this link between Regensburg and the United States was that after Curtis LeMay had been publicized in the American press for leading this raid his wife received threatening letters at her parents' home in Cleveland and had to move to friends in Alabama for a few weeks.

In judging the success of the raid we should not concentrate entirely on the material destruction and human casualties. The effect upon morale should never be forgotten. Immediately after the raid a railway official emerged from an air-raid shelter in Regensburg, saw the smoke rising from the Messerschmitt factory and told his family, 'This is the end of the road – we have as good as lost the war. If they can come all the way here in broad daylight, we have no chance.' And Martin Ettinger, a survivor of the apprentice-school disaster, says, 'We had been indoctrinated that there was nothing to match the Messerschmitt 109 we were making; nothing could ever happen to us. And then one fine day those great bombers appeared out of the sky and our whole world collapsed.'

In turning to the effects of the 1st Bombardment Wing's raid on the ball-bearing factories at Schweinfurt, we can proceed more quickly. Many of the comments made in the study of the Regensburg results about the greater tonnage and size of bombs required to knock out a target are just as valid here. The many troubles of Brigadier-General Williams's units on the day of the operation have been well covered in earlier chapters; the only thing worth repeating is that it was a tragedy for the men shot down on this mission that the bombing of Schweinfurt was so disappointing. Immediate reports circulating among the 1st Bombardment Wing units and other reports submitted by the wing to VIII Bomber Command tried to put as good a face on the results as possible. Those early assessments were wildly exaggerated and are not of much help to us. They were intended for the immediate encouragement of men fighting a tough war who had just suffered terrible losses, and for public consumption at home.

But, after the war, the Americans initiated a major investigation into the results of certain aspects of the strategic bombing offensive. This was the United States Strategic Bombing Survey – known as the U.S.S.B.S. for short – and its findings were accepted as gospel. The raids on the ball-bearing industry received special attention. The American Official History, basing its comments on U.S.S.B.S., thus reported that eighty high-explosive bombs had fallen inside the boundaries of the ball-bearing factories with 663 machines damaged or destroyed at the Kugelfischer factory and a 50-per-cent production loss for the next ten weeks in the 'ball' section there – as distinct from the cage- and roller-bearing section.* But there are aspects of the original U.S.S.B.S. report which are not reliable. It mistakenly refers to 'Tokyo Tank B-17s' making this deep-penetration raid possible, and it gives the bombing tonnage on Schweinfurt for this day as 434·8 tons when the actual figure was approximately 380 tons. The figure given of eighty high-explosive bombs hitting the three factory premises is possibly accurate – this out of the 954 such bombs aimed at the factories – but the 663 machines quoted as destroyed or damaged seems unrealistic and may be a misunderstanding by the U.S.S.B.S. officials of a term in the original German report. The

* W. F. Craven and J. L. Cate, *The Army Air Forces in World War II*, Vol. II, p. 686.

estimate of production loss in the ball section of Kugelfischer's is probably accurate but this was only one of three departments in one of Schweinfurt's three factories. Much has been made, in other books, of reports reaching England soon after the raid of panic-buying by the Germans of ball-bearings in neutral countries, and particularly of reports that men were hurrying to Germany with suitcases and knapsacks of ball-bearings, but the truth is that there were ample reserve stocks of finished bearings in Germany's war factories and still some slack remaining in the ball-bearing industry generally. A U.S.S.B.S. chart of monthly production* contains the damning evidence that more finished ball-bearings were produced in September 1943 than in August!

Quite simply, the raid of the 1st Bombardment Wing failed to inflict serious damage on Schweinfurt's ball-bearing industry, but instead led to that counter-result which many unsuccessful or partially successful British and American raids produced during the war of warning the enemy that a certain target was vulnerable. As at Regensburg, machines were hauled out of debris and relocated. There was not much immediate dispersal of production at Schweinfurt; what did happen was that low protective brick walls were built around each individual machine. If the machine tool survived, production could always be resumed. Another adverse effect was that the Germans immediately reinforced Schweinfurt's defences. It is believed that eleven batteries of heavy Flak were present for the 17 August 1943 raid; there would be twenty-three batteries ready for action when the Americans made their second visit in October.

There was damage in other parts of Schweinfurt and the results of this should not be ignored. The important firm of Fichtel & Sachs suffered hits to four of its departments and two of these stopped production for eight days. This firm was making parts for military vehicles and, by coincidence, fuel pumps for the new Messerschmitt 262. Several small industrial firms were also hit; the Rotenburger Metallwerke, just south of the railway station, was a firm making agricultural machinery and is mentioned as being damaged in all the German reports. The bombing of the military barracks has been described earlier. The main railway station suffered severe damage, an important matter because this station brought both workers and raw materials from outside Schweinfurt right into the area in which the main ball-bearing factories were located. At least one third of the American bombs

* U.S.S.B.S. Overall Report, Europe, Chart No. 14, p. 28.

fell into residential areas of Schweinfurt and the damage and casualties caused by these must have had some indirect effect upon production in the war factories. The Americans may have regarded this as a poor substitute for the precision bombing they risked flying in daylight for, but this type of 'area bombing' – attacking the whole of an industrial town or city with a view to affecting morale and stopping industrial production by indirect means – is what R.A.F. Bomber Command carried out on nearly every raid during these middle years of the war.

The death-roll was lighter than in Regensburg, but a much larger proportion of the casualties were in the town and not in the factories. The commonly accepted figure is 203 civilian dead, made up of seventy men, seventy-seven women, forty-eight children and eight foreigners. To this must be added approximately sixty soldiers killed in the bombing of the barracks.

The American airmen who flew to Schweinfurt had been told that their raid would be followed up by the full weight of R.A.F. Bomber Command attacking the town that night. Those Americans who had been shot down near Schweinfurt and were locked up in the town spent a miserable night wondering when the awesome might of the R.A.F. would fall upon them. But nothing happened on this night or on succeeding nights. The prisoners at Schweinfurt were greatly relieved at this but many Americans expressed their disappointment at what they saw as a failure by their British allies to support the American effort. There were several reasons why the R.A.F. did not follow up the American raid and, because this was an important aspect of the Schweinfurt operation, these can be covered in some detail. ('Bomber Command' in this section refers to R.A.F. Bomber Command.)

Schweinfurt was one of the most controversial subjects in the R.A.F.'s bombing war; the British Official History probably contains more references to this target than to any other in Germany. The Air Ministry had been urging Bomber Command to raid the town since late 1941 and it was mentioned in a directive waiting for Sir Arthur Harris when that determined but independently minded commander took over in February 1942. Harris had doubts about the possibility of a successful raid because of the relatively small size of the town compared with the larger city targets the R.A.F. usually attacked at night, but he wrote to the

Air Ministry on 11 April 1942: 'I am keeping an open mind on this target and, given the right conditions, I might decide to burn the town and blast the factories.'* It was a typical example of Harris's delaying tactics, but the Air Ministry never gave up their pressure on him to carry out the raid.

Nothing happened in the next year. By May 1943, the Eighth Air Force was involved in the attack on Germany and the Pointblank Directive issued to both air forces now gave Schweinfurt one of the highest priorities. The papers for the Washington Conference, which preceded the issuing of the directive, contain this statement:

> This plan does not attempt to prescribe the major effort of the R.A.F. Bomber Command. It simply recognizes the fact that when precision targets are bombed by the Eighth Air Force in daylight, the effort should be complemented and completed by R.A.F. bombing attacks against the surrounding industrial area at night.†

When the Eighth Air Force was preparing its operation to Schweinfurt, Brigadier-General Fred Anderson consulted Harris and came away believing that he had a firm commitment from the R.A.F. that they would follow up the American attack. One reason for the inclusion of incendiary bombs in the loads of the B-17s which went to Schweinfurt was to start fires which would guide the R.A.F. to the target that night.

If the American raid had gone ahead in early August as planned, it is possible that Harris might have sent his own bombers to Schweinfurt on the following night. Unfortunately, the delay until the middle of the month brought the full-moon period and the R.A.F. did not normally operate by moonlight because of the risk of heavy loss to German night fighters. In fact, however, there was another reason, a particularly valid one, why the R.A.F. did not immediately follow the Americans to Schweinfurt. Allied Intelligence had discovered that the Germans were preparing the V-2 rocket at an experimental establishment at Peenemünde on the north coast of Germany. R.A.F. Bomber Command had been given the task of raiding this target on the first moonlight night with suitable weather conditions at Peenemünde. The risk of a moonlight operation was to be accepted in return for the sure destruction of this vital target, because the outcome

* Sir Charles Webster and Noble Frankland, *The Strategic Air Offensive against Germany 1939–1945*, H.M.S.O., 1961, Vol. I, p. 348.

† op. cit. Vol. II, pp. 23–4.

of the proposed Allied invasion of Europe in the spring of 1944 might be put in jeopardy if the rocket campaign against England opened before then. The night of 17/18 August turned out to be the first suitable night for this operation. The fact that the operations to Regensburg and Schweinfurt would help by drawing the Luftwaffe's strength down to the south was a bonus for the R.A.F. aircrews. Many of the Messerschmitt 110 night fighters shot down during the day by the B-17s and P-47s would otherwise have been at Peenemünde.

The Peenemünde operation duly took place. The R.A.F. sent 560 four-engined bombers by a northerly route over Denmark and the attack was successfully carried out.* The worst attentions of the Luftwaffe were avoided by using the northerly route and by mounting a diversionary raid by a small force of Mosquitoes on Berlin, but the German night-fighter force still reached Peenemünde before the raid was over and the R.A.F. lost forty bombers, twice as many R.A.F. men being killed as the Americans lost attacking Schweinfurt and Regensburg. This special R.A.F. operation, together with the American raids to Regensburg and Schweinfurt, made this perhaps the most interesting twenty-four-hour period in the air war. It also made it possible for the Germans to claim the destruction of 100 Allied four-engined bombers in such a short period for the first time. It can only be a matter of conjecture what would have happened at Schweinfurt if, instead of having to attack Peenemünde on that night, Sir Arthur Harris had been free to send Bomber Command to Schweinfurt. The R.A.F. dropped 1,795 tons of bombs on Peenemünde compared with the 380 tons which the Americans had dropped on Schweinfurt. The moderate Flak defences of Schweinfurt and the poorly defended southern night route to Schweinfurt might have saved the R.A.F. from heavy loss, even by moonlight, but that is by no means certain.

One would have expected the R.A.F. to visit Schweinfurt during the next non-moon period but, to the dismay of both the British Air Ministry and the Americans, Harris failed to give that order. In fact the R.A.F. did not attack Schweinfurt until the night of 24/25 February 1944, the night after the *third* American raid on the town. By then much of Schweinfurt's ball-bearing production had been dispersed and what remained was immeasurably better protected than it had been in August 1943.

* For a full account of this operation, see the present author's *The Peenemünde Raid*, Allen Lane, 1982.

I will try as briefly as possible to review the reasons why Harris delayed so long in attacking Schweinfurt, despite the clear wishes of his superiors and the hopes of his American allies.

Sir Arthur Harris was deeply convinced that Germany would not be beaten by the bombing of selected industries. He did not believe that the necessary targets could be bombed with reasonable accuracy – at least by night – and he did not believe that the German war effort would be crippled by an attack on any one segment of it. In short, he did not support the 'bottleneck theory'; he thought the ball-bearing theory in particular was 'oversold'. Harris believed that the general area-bombing campaign against major German cities which he had painstakingly built up since early 1942 would cause both German morale and industrial production to collapse. Moreover, in the autumn of 1943 he believed that he was on the verge of success. The spring of that year had seen the undoubted success of the so-called Battle of the Ruhr, and the summer had brought the destruction of Hamburg. Now he was preparing for the climax, the winter-long 'Battle of Berlin' in which he hoped the Americans would join. A few weeks later he would make his now famous statement: 'We can wreck Berlin from end to end if the U.S.A.A.F. will come in on it. It will cost us between 400 and 500 aircraft. It will cost Germany the war.' And he later forecast a state of devastation in Berlin which would produce an 'inevitable surrender' by 1 April 1944.* Harris was absolutely convinced in his views about Berlin and in August 1943 and for the remainder of the year he had no intention of diverting any part of his force from that main aim. The Battle of Berlin began with a heavy raid on the capital six nights after the Americans went to Schweinfurt.

The Air Ministry did not entirely share Harris's views. In particular, Air Commodore Sydney Bufton, the Director of Bomber Operations at the Air Ministry, made every effort to persuade Harris to attack Schweinfurt. The following is Bufton's view of the matter; 'Portal' was Sir Charles Portal, Chief of the Air Staff and Harris's direct superior; 'Don Bennett' was Air Vice-Marshal D. C. T. Bennett, commander of the R.A.F. Pathfinder Force.

> Bert Harris could have gone to Schweinfurt any time but he stubbornly refused. He must have broken Portal's heart on this

* These two statements, made on 3 November and 7 December 1943, are quoted from Sir Charles Webster and Noble Frankland, *The Strategic Air Offensive against Germany*, Vol. II, pp. 9 and 56.

subject. If Bomber Command had really gone for it with determination right at the beginning, its attacks could have been highly effective. Bert Harris argued that it was difficult to find but I asked Don Bennett about this at the time and he said there was no more difficulty about finding Schweinfurt than any other target. Harris also said that his losses would be over 10 per cent but there was no reason why casualties should be any heavier on Schweinfurt than on any other target in that part of Germany.

Portal could have issued a direct order to Harris at any time he wished, but it was not the R.A.F.'s style to control commanders too closely and he did not issue that direct order until early in 1944. The ultimate responsibility for any failure by the R.A.F. to follow up the American attacks on Schweinfurt rests with Sir Charles Portal, who could have imposed his will earlier. Harris's Battle of Berlin was not a success and there was no German collapse in the spring of 1944. By then the Americans had realized that there was no such thing as a truly combined bomber offensive; in reality there were separate offensives by two air forces each with its own philosophy.

We return to the American operations to Regensburg and Schweinfurt for final comment. The Americans had now raided their four priority targets – Ploesti, Wiener Neustadt, Regensburg and Schweinfurt – and suffered severe casualties three times out of four. The American doctrine of the self-defending daylight bomber was proved to be an illusion. As so often with major events, the setback at Schweinfurt and Regensburg was really a simple story. Heavy loss would have been inevitable with any plan, but the casualties were further increased by the huge mistake of splitting the two bomber forces by just that amount of time which gave the German fighter force its best possible opportunity. The chance influence of the weather which led to this can never be ignored and should be remembered when the actions of wartime commanders are being discussed. But the major lesson was that the American bombers should not have been risked on flights deep into Germany until realistic fighter escort was forthcoming. Let me admit again that these are all observations made with the luxury of hindsight.

The other major lesson learnt on 17 August 1943 was that the bombing capacity of the American force then available was not sufficient to destroy two targets. The force should not have been split into two: the next raid on Schweinfurt, in October, would be by all the available American bombers in England. More aircraft were needed. They would come. Generally, the lesson was that the knocking out of Germany was going to be a longer, tougher job than any of the American commanders had foreseen. The necessary skills would be learned; the determination had never been lacking.

After all this talk of bomber aircraft and ball-bearings, let us not forget the most important loss of all, the loss of human life. At least 760 men and women died as a result of the air operations of 17 August 1943 – 111 Americans, one Briton, one Canadian, 565 or more Germans and eighty-six forced workers of at least six different nationalities. They were all ordinary people; not one of their names would ever become prominent in the history books but they all died helping to decide the direction of just one small step in the world's history.

CHAPTER 20

The Aftermath

When the day of the missions to Regensburg and Schweinfurt closed, survivors from the American units found themselves in no less than eight different countries – England, Belgium, Holland, France, Germany, Switzerland, Italy and Algeria – or were afloat in rubber dinghies in the North Sea and the Mediterranean. The majority of the men who were shot down were about to experience one of the basic rules of air warfare: fight over your own country and you would be given a new plane each time you were shot down and probably finish up dead or crippled; fight over your enemy's country and you could expect to be shot down only once and then see out the rest of the war in a prison camp. Nearly 400 Americans were already experiencing the first stages of that process.

It was harvest time and few of the men who came down by parachute did so without being spotted. Most were quickly met by farm workers in the fields, but country people are usually good-natured and there are numerous stories of Americans being kindly treated, especially the wounded ones. There were some interesting encounters.

> I was helped by a young French boy who was working in a field with other people. He gave me a drink of water from a wine bottle. I have always been amazed that someone so young could even look at me with my burns and all my flight suit burnt but he put my head on his knee and gave me this drink. I am certain he was French although we were well into Germany. (Second Lieutenant John W. Dytman, 351st Bomb Group)

> I fell right into a field where they were harvesting wheat. There was no chance of escape and I thought I might as well take it easy; the jig was up. I just sat on the edge of a small track, took out a cigarette and offered it to the old chap who reached me first. He sat on one side of the track and I sat on

the other, both of us smoking but not saying anything. We neither of us knew the other's language; we had tried but it had not worked. The first man to turn up from away took out his knife and told me in English that he ought to cut my throat, but he was just showing off. I think he was some high-up from the next town. (Staff Sergeant Elmer C. Smith, 351st Bomb Group)

Soon after hitting the ground, I saw an elderly couple walking along a country road and they simply pointed down the road and said, 'Luxembourg'. They never stopped talking to each other or said anything else to me, almost as though they wanted to pretend they had not seen me. I could only assume that they were tired of the war and sympathetic.

I set off in the direction they told me and met another of the crew but was then captured by a man in uniform riding his bicycle furiously down the road. It all happened in about five minutes. It quite amused me that I should be captured by a man on a bicycle; I would have expected a fast car at least.

Nine of us were soon assembled at a small farm and another elderly couple were helpful and sympathetic to us. The old lady was particularly kind; she was like a mother hen. She brought me a piece of bread and some lettuce and a drink of milk. I didn't really want the bread – I wasn't hungry – but I didn't want to hurt her feelings. I would love to know exactly where this was because I always wanted to go back there again and see that lady and let her know that I did appreciate her kindness. (Technical Sergeant John Collins, 92nd Bomb Group)

I was badly injured and was given a large helping of red wine by a Belgian farmer while lying on the ground. The Germans took me to a hospital at Leopoldsburg and when the wine made me violently sick a German medical orderly said, 'So, they give you alcohol to make you brave enough to fly!' I was too sick to reply but I felt disgusted. 'The stupid Kraut,' I thought. (Technical Sergeant Arthur P. McDonnell, 94th Bomb Group)

I was badly injured on landing and tried to crawl and hide, but within minutes I was surrounded by ten or fifteen children with a few adults. The children were particularly curious; I was the first American *Luftgangster* they had ever seen. The next big shock was when a civilian man came up, offered me his hand and said in perfect English, 'How do you do? I am from Cleveland, Ohio. How do you like it here?'

I asked him what he was doing here and he told me that, when Hitler called back Germans from the United States, he had left his grocer's shop on the east side of Cleveland and was now the Bürgermeister of his village. He stopped talking in English when some more adults came. (Second Lieutenant Wayne L. Wentworth, 384th Bomb Group)

I was searched and I showed them my identification card. Now, I've had my name pronounced in all sorts of ways all my life but that German took one look and said, 'Ah, Leutnant Egender', in the correct pronunciation and in those strange circumstances the thought flashed through my mind that I had to go through all this to get my name pronounced correctly. (Second Lieutenant Herbert F. Egender, 91st Bomb Group)

Americans with German surnames were often asked why they were fighting 'on the other side'. The Germans even gained as a prisoner Lieutenant Frank Messersmith, a navigator in the 95th Bomb Group. Another member of his crew says that Messersmith got as fed up with German taunts about his name as he had earlier been with the comments of his own crew.

There were a few cases of ill-treatment and deliberate humiliation of prisoners, the first probably at the hands of civilians who had lost relations in the bombing of cities, the humiliation usually the result of action by minor local Nazi Party officials. Prisoners captured in Germany were sometimes paraded under the gaze of local people. One party of prisoners in Belgium had all their flying clothes removed and were then marched in various states of undress through several villages and not allowed to break ranks to urinate. Local Belgians tried to show their sympathy. At the other extreme, five men from one crew captured in Belgium were taken by their escorts into an *estaminet* and treated to a round of beers which, says one of the Americans, 'after all the excitement and in that heat was the best beer I have ever tasted'. In Germany, Second Lieutenant Ronald Delaney was being threatened by women armed with long kitchen knives until someone translated a letter which had been brought out to his aircraft just before take-off. The letter was from Delaney's mother and described how well his wife was looking in her pregnancy. The German women immediately became more sympathetic.

It should be stressed that ill-treatment of Americans shot down on this day was not frequent and usually ceased when the prisoners came under any sort of military control. There is one case of a

B-17 pilot who was almost certainly shot and killed on the ground, but only after being observed by a fellow crew member running hard to escape from German soldiers. This American was definitely armed with a pistol and was known to be the type of man who would probably have preferred to shoot it out rather than surrender. In another case an American was casually shot in the stomach by a German soldier and left for dead, but he managed to survive. The bodies of four other men in this crew were not recovered after the war and much investigation took place into the possibility that these men had also been shot on the ground, but there was not enough evidence for this to be proved. Wounded men were usually given proper – sometimes excellent – treatment. The oddest 'medical' story is that of Staff Sergeant John Wasche, the ball gunner who swallowed raw gasoline before baling out. Wasche remembers nothing between being on the end of his parachute and finding himself sitting on a street kerb in a built-up area.

> There was a girl going by and I asked her why I was in the city of New York. She informed me in perfect English that I was in the city of Bonn. She gave me an apple and she also told me that we – the Americans or Allies, she meant – would soon end the war. I remember that she was a blonde.
>
> The reason I thought I was in New York was that they were driving on the right-hand side of the street like we did at home and the first car I saw was a 1941 Chrysler Town and Country. I loved cars and knew every model and year. I looked up and saw other Americans and the German guards. Then I remembered that I had baled out earlier but I never remembered anything of what happened in the interval.

The Americans were then subjected to the normal routine for aircrew prisoners of war. They were gradually gathered into groups and sent off by rail or road to the Luftwaffe interrogation centre, *Dulag Luft*, at Oberursel near Frankfurt. The first to arrive were probably Lieutenant Tony Arcaro and his six surviving crew members. Their plane had crashed not far away and they came in during the early hours of 18 August. The next few days were to see the biggest influx of Allied prisoners Oberursel had ever experienced. The Americans were taken from Frankfurt to the town of Oberursel by tramcar and then had to march to the camp. On one of the following days one American counted

144 men in his marching column. 'Everyone was very quiet, very thoughtful about our prospects for the future.'

The normal interrogation took place at Oberursel, the Americans learning how diligently the Germans had assembled information on each bomb group; even the new 390th had a bulky file. Many individual men were greeted by a smiling interrogator with, 'Welcome. We have been waiting for you,' and then shown an almost complete record of their service career, these details having been systematically culled from American home-town newspapers or supplied by German sympathizers in the United States. The subsequent questioning was rarely very thorough, although any man having previous contact with the B-29 Superfortress bomber programme was pressed hard on details of that plane and the possibility of it appearing in the campaign against Germany.

After a few days of discomfort and solitary confinement at Oberursel, the prisoners were sorted out and sent to permanent prison camps. All the officers captured at this time seem to have gone to *Stalag Luft III* at Sagan, south of Berlin, the camp from which the 'great escape' of seventy-six R.A.F. prisoners took place in March 1944 – an escape which resulted, however, in the execution of fifty of the escapers after their recapture. The American officers were not involved; the escape was not from their compound at Sagan. The enlisted men went to *Stalag VII A* at Moosburg in Southern Germany but were soon moved to *Stalag XVII B* at Krems in Austria. When liberated in 1945, few of the prisoners returned to England; they were sent to Camp Lucky Strike near Le Havre in France to await ships sailing to the United States. Only one or two determined Americans found ways of reaching England to marry their English girlfriends.

A number of shot-down Americans were never taken prisoner. The process of evading capture started during the parachute descent. The standard advice was to open the parachute early when over Germany – particularly near built-up areas – so that German soldiers could see you coming down and reach you before unfriendly civilian elements, but over the German-occupied countries it was better to delay the opening as long as possible so that the civilians who were usually so keen to help reached you first. On this day it was mostly the people of Belgium who were involved; they had never been presented with such a feast of opportunity. At some stages of the action, people on the ground thought that a parachute invasion was in progress. Those airmen fortunate enough to be met by friendly civilians on landing were usually hidden swiftly in bushes or crops; their helpers would reappear at nightfall and take them to a more secure hiding place. Other men became the objects of desperate hunts with civilians competing against the German search parties. It is obvious that a massive German operation took place along the line of the B-17 route through Belgium. Cars, motor-cycles and even soldiers on horseback were seen scouring the countryside, and at least one low-flying Fieseler Storch reconnaissance plane joined in the search. It is also obvious that the German organization was overwhelmed by the number of Americans on the run and by the enthusiasm of the Belgian civilians. It is estimated that, of the 117 men who are believed to have parachuted safely over Belgium and Holland, nearly fifty were at least set upon the preliminary stages of evasion by civilians.

But it was the second stage of the escape which was more difficult to achieve – making contact safely with the recognized escape organizations which, naturally enough, kept their identities secret. Some of the evaders were discovered by German searches or handed in by civilians too frightened of German reprisals or, sadly, by the very few who were seeking German favour or reward. A major problem for both the 'amateur' and the full-time helpers was what to do with airmen who were injured, and some of these were deliberately handed to the Germans for better treatment or to safeguard the escape organizations. There were, however, other cases where local doctors took terrible risks to treat badly injured men who eventually did reach safety. Second Lieutenant Carl Smith came down in the vicinity of a village near Ath, in Belgium, with a badly broken leg. After being hidden in bushes all day, six young Belgians – three men and three women – came at night and Smith had to listen to a long argument between the men, who wanted to turn him in to the Germans – whether because of the practical problems or for reward, Smith could not tell – and the women who were determined to help him escape. Smith was anxious to take his chance in an escape in order to return to his wife who was pregnant with their first child, rather than wait an indefinite period in a prison camp. The women won the argument and, after many adventures, Smith reached the United States just two days before his daughter was born.

There is no need to describe this aspect of the Regensburg and Schweinfurt missions in detail; this is not an escape book. The regular escape line ran 600 miles from Belgium, through France to the Pyrenees and into neutral Spain. The final stages were to Gibraltar and then by transport plane to England. The fastest escape of the Schweinfurt–Regensburg men is believed to be that of Technical Sergeant Bruno Gallerini, who was helped from Antwerp to London in just one month, but most of the evaders could be held up at any stage – getting started, at the Belgian–French frontier, in Paris, at the Pyrenees. At every stage there were further captures by the Germans in their relentless pressure to break the escape organizations and prevent the return of trained aircrew to England. For example, Staff Sergeant George Mikel was captured in Liège after being hidden there for seven months, and Second Lieutenant Carlyle Darling, who attended Christmas Midnight Mass in Rheims cathedral with an English sergeant, was captured in Southern France in April 1944. Paris hotels were dangerous places and several men were picked up there. Second Lieutenant Ken Lorch was held up for three months in Paris, travelling freely in the city and rubbing shoulders with Germans in restaurants. He enjoyed his stay in Paris, 'but there was always a little anxiety about the outcome. There was a long way to go and I wanted to get home. The waiting seemed endless.' Lorch moved on from Paris but was captured at Bordeaux and the Frenchman who was sheltering him was shot by the Germans. Lorch did not join his many fellow prisoners from the 100th Bomb Group in *Stalag Luft III* until July 1944.

Thirty-eight of the men shot down on the Regensburg and Schweinfurt missions achieved the complete escape to England. Thirty-five of these escaped from Belgium, France or Holland and they represented 30 per cent of the total number of men who came down in those countries. It was a major achievement for the brave civilians of the escape organizations. Evasion from Germany was very difficult, but Lieutenant Robert Nelson and Staff Sergeant Raymond Genz, who parachuted into the Eifel mountains, walked back into Belgium and eventually reached England. The final evader was Staff Sergeant Glen Keirsey, a member of a B-17 which came down in Italy who was successfully hidden by partisans in that country and was never captured by the Germans.

The Americans who returned to England in this way were not allowed to fly on operations in Europe again for fear of later capture, when they might jeopardize the escape lines under German interrogation. Such men were given ground duties in

England or returned to the United States as instructors or for an operational posting to the Pacific. This policy may seem curious in view of the risks the civilians in the occupied countries had taken in helping the airmen to escape; a cruel fate faced the many civilians who were caught by the Germans doing this work. One evader, Second Lieutenant Hank Sarnow, actually discussed the motives of the civilians with Madame Anne Brussellmanns, a member of the famous Comet Line in Brussels. 'She told me that they regarded their work as a debt of honour to Allied airmen, in gratitude for the risks we had taken in flying to Germany to bring back their freedom.' Many years later Sarnow was brought to London for a reunion with Madame Brussellmanns in the B.B.C. television programme *This Is Your Life*. There are still many enduring friendships. Americans who return to one village in Belgium are still treated 'like saints', and Lieutenant Charles Bennett, a pilot helped to escape by civilians at Aarschot in Belgium, speaks for many when he writes, 'Much has been written of these courageous people but I have yet to find words that describe the truly superhuman effort they displayed in getting so many to freedom.'

The men of Colonel LeMay's 4th Bombardment Wing who had bombed Regensburg and flown on to North Africa returned to England much more quickly. Their stay in that strange land of Algeria was a combination of interest and extreme discomfort. Because the plans which LeMay thought he had made for accommodation and servicing facilities had not matured, there was a delay in preparing the return flight to England during which the aircrews had to live out at their planes and carry out all their own aircraft servicing. Colonel LeMay was most annoyed by what he considered a failure to comply with reasonable requests made by him well before the operation. The trouble was that during the long delay in confirming the Regensburg mission the Twelfth Air Force Headquarters in North Africa had not passed on the detailed requirements to its Service Command. The war had meanwhile moved on and many facilities had been removed from the airfields. Lieutenant-Colonel Oliver B. Taylor describes how, when the mission was finally confirmed, he was given the unenviable task of preparing for the arrival of LeMay's units with just two days' notice.

The force expected was roughly equal in size to our own heavy bombardment establishment in the Twelfth Air Force. I discussed the various requirements with General Bartron [Brigadier-General H. A. Bartron, commander of Twelfth Air Force Service Command] and, when he reached bedding, I nodded agreement as he mentioned blankets, showed some surprise when he said cots and almost fell through the floor when he added bed-sheets! Whatever we had in the way of bed-sheets were used exclusively in our hospitals to my knowledge, and cots were still something of a rarity in the field. In any case, General Bartron concluded by telling me that I had a job to do and to 'get cracking' – a British expression that seemed to tickle his fancy.

Regarding whether LeMay's annoyance was justified, I can only guess that it was. To do more than guess, I would have to know what arrangements he had made earlier and, therefore, something about what his expectations might have been. Certainly the short notice we had in the Service Command did not permit us to do quite as much as we might have otherwise. In any case, LeMay should have been apprised of our limitations and of the fact that conditions in the field in Africa were nothing like those in England. We were only just making it with keeping our own units supplied and manned.

As to primitive conditions and inadequate facilities, that was a matter of viewpoint. What was primitive to the Eighth Air Force was the normal situation in the Twelfth. Our men had lived for prolonged periods in pup tents, slept in the mud, stood in the rain or dust storms for chow, bathed and laundered only on chance occasions out of a helmet or bucket, used open pits for latrines and garbage etc. The Eighth could be admired for their combat performance but it was difficult to sympathize with them about 'primitive' conditions to which they were exposed for only a few days.

LeMay's men eventually prepared most of their aircraft for a return flight to England. Major-General Eaker flew in from England and, in view of the recent heavy loss of the Regensburg operation and the uncomfortable living conditions, told LeMay that he could send his crews back on a relatively safe night flight without attacking a target on the way. But LeMay believed that it would be good for the morale of his men if they could make the return an operational mission and it was agreed that a Luftwaffe airfield near Bordeaux would be the target. Eighty-five of the 115 B-17s which had reached Africa were made ready for the operation and this was successfully flown on 24 August with only three planes lost.

During their stay in Africa many of the Americans had made pets of small donkeys bought from local Arabs and some of the donkeys were flown back to England equipped with makeshift oxygen masks. Men from five different bomb groups claim to have taken off with donkeys but it is believed that some of these claims are duplicates and that only two reached England. The report that one donkey in a 96th Bomb Group aircraft expired through oxygen failure and that its body was thrown out over the target at Bordeaux may be apocryphal. One of the surviving donkeys was in the plane of Second Lieutenant 'Cowboy' Roane, 100th Bomb Group. On arrival at his base in England, Roane fired a red distress flare – normally used when a wounded crew member needed urgent attention – and radioed his now famous message that he had 'a frozen ass' aboard. His plane was met by a puzzled ambulance driver.

The crews left behind in North Africa repaired some of their planes and flew them back to England individually by a wide and safe route over the sea, but a few of the B-17s had to be left behind and their crews returned by transport plane. Many of LeMay's men would later regard their whole experience since leaving England as the most interesting of their lives.

The stunned city of Regensburg recovered slowly from the raid. Three days after the bombing, 184 of the German dead were buried together in the town's Catholic cemetery. But the dominant tone of the event was not religious; the swastika was more prominent than the cross and party officials had more to say than priests. I do not have the text of the orations but the *Regensburger Kurier*, party-controlled of course, published an emotive notice about the funeral ceremony in that morning's edition under the headline THEY ALSO DIED FOR GERMANY. The final paragraph is a typical example of the high-flown Nazi prose which made use of a specially created emotive vocabulary and appealed to the mystical streak in the character of some Germans:

> Our thanks to the dead will consist of our solemn vow, confessing ourselves yet more fervently to the community of fate which is our Nation, with which we are bound together for all eternity and which unites us in the iron struggle of our age. Loyalty to our Leader, our faith

in the life of our Nation and our love for our native land – all of these acting as a shield to our soldiers in their arduous battles against the enemy's onslaught – will be even more strengthened and intensified by our sacrifices.

Reference was also made to the 'innocent victims of the recent cowardly British terror attack'; it is not known why the authorities should wish to pin the blame on the British and not the Americans. Four days later, the *Kurier* helped morale in Regensburg along by announcing that 109 four-engined enemy bombers had been shot down in Southern Germany on the day of the Regensburg raid.* A service for some of the dead foreign workers took place afterwards. Pierre Jouvin, a French worker who attended, gives this emotive description.

> A prisoner-priest gave the blessing and, after the lowering of the coffins which took place to the sound of military music and blasts of stupidity from the Nazi mugs, the general who was the factory director gave us a very collaborationist speech. This poor cretin had learnt nothing and dared to talk to us of 'making amends for the disaster'.

But several people say that the common experience of the raid improved relations between the foreigners and the ordinary Germans working in the factory.

The effect of air raids on morale was always important and the views of the Germans in Regensburg and Schweinfurt on this subject have been recorded several times. Léon Vêche, a Belgian worker at Regensburg, writes: 'My impressions of the raid were firstly of fear but, little by little, my friends and I realized that this operation was a symbol of release for us. That was the first serious blow to the enemy of which we were the witness.' By contrast, more than 500 miles away at his headquarters in East Prussia, Hitler gave Generaloberst Hans Jeschonnek, the Chief of Staff of the Luftwaffe, a severe telling off, presumably for the failure of the Luftwaffe to defend Germany. That night, after hearing news of the R.A.F. raid on the rocket research establishment at Peenemünde which followed the daytime bombing of Regensburg and Schweinfurt, Jeschonnek shot himself.

* The funeral notice was from the *Regensburger Kurier* of 20 August 1943 and the claim of aircraft shot down was published on 24 August 1943.

Regensburg had a relatively fortunate war, despite further air raids. The Americans came at least four more times, but always by daylight, and the targets were always outside the town – the Messerschmitt factory again, another factory at the Obertraubling airfield a few kilometres away, the railway yards, the local oil depot. The R.A.F. attacked only once, and not until 1945 when a small force came by daylight and also attacked the oil depot.

The war ended for Regensburg on 27 April 1945. There had been an ugly incident a few days earlier after the local S.S. commander had ordered Regensburg to be defended 'to the last stone'. About 1,000 civilians, led by the deacon of the cathedral, gathered to protest at the order and ask that Regensburg be declared an open city. The deacon and another man were seized by the S.S., tried and condemned on the spot and publicly hanged that night near the cathedral. But there was no fighting when American troops appeared and Regensburg escaped a final battle.

Earlier in this book I wrote that Regensburg had been 'a centre of culture and civilization for nearly 2,000 years'. It was the greatest good fortune for the people of Regensburg that their city was never chosen as a target for an R.A.F. area-bombing night raid. Only about 10 per cent of Regensburg's buildings were hit by bombing during the entire war and the original character of the city remained unchanged. A city guide describes present-day Regensburg as 'the only fully preserved medieval town in Germany'.

Schweinfurt, by contrast, had a terrible war; it became one of the most bombed towns in Germany. The whole of the Eighth Air Force returned on 14 October 1943 and the full weight of R.A.F. Bomber Command finally fell on the town in the night of 24/25 February 1944, with a second but smaller R.A.F. raid in the following month. The R.A.F. ignored Schweinfurt after that but the American campaign continued until October 1944 with six further major attacks. It was then decided that the ball-bearing industry at Schweinfurt was no longer a profitable target.

Schweinfurt had been a veritable battleground. Its Flak batteries were strengthened over and over again; the Luftwaffe fighter force always fought ferociously in the town's defence. The attacks of the Americans and the R.A.F. left little but ruins. Improved shelters and what became an acutely wary population kept the death roll of civilians down to 1,079 in all raids. Nearly half of the population had fled by the end of October 1944 and much of the ball-bearing industry had also been dispersed. Half of Germany's supply had come from Schweinfurt before the first American raid; this was only one fifth by October 1944.

An uneasy quiet followed until the spring of 1945 when American ground forces approached. Hitler had ordered an industrial 'scorched earth' policy in front of the Allied advance but Albert Speer, Hitler's armaments industry minister, persuaded the local Gauleiter in Würzburg to ignore this in the case of those of Schweinfurt's ball-bearing factories which were still functioning. There was a little shelling and some tactical bombing when the Americans finally appeared before Schweinfurt, and the town was captured on 11 April by the famous 42nd Rainbow Division – so-called because its units came from so many states in the union – supported by tanks of the 12th Armored Division. Bürgermeister Pösl committed suicide by jumping from a window. In a considerate gesture, the commander of the American force which captured Schweinfurt handed a large swastika flag found in the town to an Air Force journalist for later presentation to whichever Eighth Air Force unit had suffered the greatest loss in attacking the town. The flag was eventually handed over to the 305th Bomb Group, which had lost nineteen B-17s in the long campaign against Schweinfurt.

Schweinfurt rose from the ruins after the war. The machinery of the Kugelfischer ball-bearing factory was designated as part of the war reparations due to Russia, but the machinery only got as far as East Germany where the Russians allowed their new friends to use it. The V.K.F. factories (now S.K.F.) stressed their link with Sweden and escaped the reparations move. While post-war Germany had no need for Regensburg's aircraft factory, Germany's economic miracle, particularly the growth of the automobile industry, most certainly needed ball-bearings and Schweinfurt became once again the centre of this industry and a very prosperous town. The three factories which the Americans bombed are still there on their original sites. Their main concern now is competition from Japan.

It was not surprising that the B-17 units of the Eighth Air Force had to be rested in the period immediately following the missions to Schweinfurt and Regensburg, and only short-range operations by limited forces with continuous fighter escort took place in the next two and a half weeks. The whole future of the long-range daylight bomber concept was at stake; regular operations incurring the casualty rates of Schweinfurt and Regensburg could obviously not be accepted. Was the B-17 only viable as a short-range force under fighter protection? If this was the only answer, then an expensive aeroplane had been produced to achieve no more than could be achieved by the much cheaper twin-engined medium bomber. If this was the only answer, then Germany's vital war industries would remain beyond the reach of the Americans in daylight and the American version of 'the bomber dream' would be dead. Morale was at an all-time low throughout the Eighth Air Force and all the way back to Washington. It was a time for holding the bomber force together while a solution was found.

But it was also a time for limited experiment and two events early in September were of great significance. On the 6th, VIII Bomber Command marshalled its entire strength again to attack ball-bearing and aircraft factories in the Stuttgart area. It was to be the Schweinfurt–Regensburg plan all over again but with some important tactical lessons learnt from those earlier raids and with a shallower penetration of German airspace. The raid was a failure. The Eighth Air Force lost another forty-five B-17s and bad weather frustrated much of the bombing. The lesson for the Americans from this important raid was that the losses at Schweinfurt and Regensburg had not been unusual and could be expected on every deep penetration of Germany.

Two nights after the American failure at Stuttgart, the American 422nd Bomb Squadron, part of LeMay's old 305th Bomb Group, sent five B-17s to fly with an R.A.F. night raid. The raid, by 262 aircraft, was to a suspected V-1 flying-bomb site near Boulogne. The B-17s all returned safely. This American squadron flew by night with the R.A.F. on seven more raids in the next month, five of these being area-bombing raids on German cities. The American crews flew entirely under British control and used British bombing methods. The reader will remember that at the end of July 1943, soon after he had been appointed to lead VIII Bomber Command, Brigadier-General Fred Anderson had flown with an R.A.F. crew to study at first hand the methods used by his British allies in their night-bombing campaign. The R.A.F. had been urging the Americans for some time to give up the costly daylight offensive and throw their weight into the night battle which Sir Arthur Harris and others believed could knock Germany out of the war during the coming winter, especially if the raids were concentrated against Berlin. The total effort of the 422nd Bomb Squadron during this period was only thirty-five B-17 sorties – of which two did not return – but it was undoubtedly a trial period in case the Eighth Air Force decided to devote at least part of its force to the night offensive.

It was at this stage that the Americans might have made a major change similar to the one the R.A.F. had made much earlier in the war when British long-range daylight operations had proved too costly and the R.A.F. had turned to a night campaign which lasted for most of the war. In doing this the British saved their strategic bomber force from extinction, but they had sacrificed bombing accuracy and been forced to turn to the area-bombing of German cities. Now the Americans faced the same choice. The night offensive had its attractions. If the Germans were toppled in the coming winter as Sir Arthur Harris was forecasting, it would be a great victory for the bomber. But such a victory would entail a loss both of pride and principle for the Americans. They had brought their heavy bombers to Europe not to play second fiddle to the British but to show that there was a better way to strike at German industry than the laying waste of city after city. The Americans chose not to take this path. The decision to stick to their original policy was not consciously taken at a high-level conference; the American commanders just held steadily on and never reached the point where they were forced to make that drastic move to night bombing. No other part of the Eighth Air Force was ever transformed into a night-bombing force and after its last flight with the R.A.F. on the night of 4 October the 422nd Bomb Squadron became a specialist night leaflet-dropping unit until the end of the war in Europe.

But, amazingly, the period of hope that somehow the B-17s – and the B-24 Liberators which now rejoined the offensive – would win through without escort lasted for a further six weeks after the disastrous Stuttgart mission of 6 September. The idealists, the purists, were still in charge. After a further period of restraint during which only limited penetration raids were attempted, another great long-range offensive took place in the second week of October. Consecutive missions on the 8th, 9th and 10th saw 1,090 sorties dispatched to various German targets, but eighty-eight planes were lost. Then, after a three-day rest, came the climax on 14 October when every B-17 group in the Eighth Air Force was sent deep into Southern Germany to bomb that dreaded place Schweinfurt again, to attempt the destruction of the ball-bearing factories which had been so ineffectively attacked on 17 August. The bombing this time was much improved and serious damage was achieved; post-war assessments credited this raid with causing a greater setback to the ball-bearing industry in Schweinfurt than any other of the war. But the casualties were again enormous. Sixty B-17s were lost. The tactical rules which governed deep penetration raids to Germany remained exactly the same.

This event finally triggered off a radical change of attitude. There had existed for some time in the United States a modern fighter aircraft which had the potential for great range when fitted with the necessary engine and fuel tanks. This was the P-51 Mustang produced by the North American aircraft company. But so heavily – and emotionally, one suspects – were American leaders committed to the self-defending 'Fortress' bomber concept, that when the first output of the long-range version of the Mustang appeared in early August 1943, all were earmarked for the reconnaissance role in various theatres. It was not until the end of October, two weeks after the disaster of 'Second Schweinfurt', that General 'Hap' Arnold, the Air Force Chief of Staff in Washington, decreed that all long-range Mustangs be sent to England until the Eighth Air Force had a complete long-range fighter escort force. The first Mustangs flew with the B-17s from England on 5 December 1943, and within the next few months the full escort force was quickly built up. During this period the P-47 Thunderbolt modestly increased its range and the P-38 Lightning appeared, but it was the Mustang which turned the American heavy bomber into a viable proposition.

The appearance of the Mustang was not just a simple matter of the provision of an escort aircraft. It signified the end of the self-defending bomber dream, at least in the Second World War in Europe, and it coincided with changes in leadership both of the Eighth Air Force and of VIII Bomber Command. In December 1943 there was a big re-shuffle in preparation for the invasion of Normandy being planned for the spring of 1944. Major-General Ira Eaker was sent to the Mediterranean to command the joint Allied Air Force there. Eaker formally asked his superiors to allow him to remain with the Eighth Air Force, but his request was refused and this respected and well-liked personality had to leave England. In the same reorganization VIII Bomber Command disappeared as a separate element within the Eighth Air Force and Brigadier-General Fred Anderson left to become deputy commander in charge of operations in the newly created United States Strategic Air Forces, Europe. This was not a field command position but a coordinating one between the American bomber forces based in England and those in the Mediterranean. It should be stressed that the removal of Eaker and Anderson from the leading roles in the direction of the American bomber forces in England were in no way demotions – both were promoted and went to new positions needing men of high calibre. The new commander of the Eighth Air Force, brought in from the Mediterranean, was Major-General James H. Doolittle, famous as the man who had led a small force of B-25 Mitchell bombers from an aircraft carrier to attack Tokyo earlier in the war. It did not seem sensible to some people that Doolittle and Eaker should have been changed over between England and the Mediterranean in this way, but, as one experienced officer in the Eighth Air Force says, 'Doolittle came in with a wider perspective. He was a no-nonsense businessman type, a complete realist who looked at the whole problem with less of the dedicated bomber man's outlook.' Because there was now no separate VIII Bomber Command headquarters, it was Doolittle who controlled the tactical handling of the American heavy bombers which flew from England from then until the end of the war in Europe.

There is little more to be said. How the Mustang sounded the death-knell of the Luftwaffe day-fighter force and how the long-range American daylight bomber in its modified role made a major contribution to Allied victory in Europe are not subjects for this book, although I would like to express a personal opinion that the P-51 Mustang was the most important aircraft of the Second World War, opening up as it did the skies of Europe to the daylight 'heavies', both American and British. The men who survived the Schweinfurt and Regensburg missions in August 1943 were either shot down in later operations or finished their tours of combat duty and returned to their homes. Brigadier-General Robert Williams remained in command of the 1st Bombardment Wing – soon re-designated the 1st Bomb Division – until the end. Curtis LeMay fulfilled his early promise and went on to greater achievement. He was sent to the Pacific in 1944 to lead the B-29 Superfortress force in the offensive against Japan.

LeMay's brilliant career continued after the war. In 1948 he was the American commander in Germany who established the Berlin

Airlift and later the same year was brought home to take charge of Strategic Air Command. LeMay's nine years with this organization were perhaps his greatest success. He shook up an ailing command and made it the formidable deterrent force which, again in my personal opinion, did more to keep world peace in those years than any other factor. A large number of Schweinfurt and Regensburg veterans were proud to serve under LeMay in Strategic Air Command. He then became a four-star general and was rewarded with his service's top position, Chief of the Air Staff. On retirement LeMay dabbled in politics and in the 1968 presidential campaign was vice-presidential running-mate to the hard-line Independent, Governor George Wallace of Alabama. The stalemate in Vietnam was the issue of the moment and LeMay caused a furore when, in a television interview, he advocated the use of atomic bombs to end the war there. It was a typical, blunt piece of LeMayism and, needless to say, he and Wallace did not win the election, but the tough old general is unlikely to have lost much sleep over the reaction to his views. I do not apologize for devoting so much space to Curtis LeMay. He served my country well in the Second World War and he served my generation well in the years when we might have had to fight another war. These sentiments apply equally to many other men who flew in the Eighth Air Force.

The bodies of many of the Americans killed in the Schweinfurt–Regensburg mission were returned to their homeland after the war. The others were removed from Germany, it not being American policy to leave their war dead in what had once been enemy territory. The bodies which remained in Europe are now buried in the beautiful American military cemeteries at Neuville-en-Condroz in the Ardennes region of Belgium, at Margraten in Holland and at Saint Avold in France. The survivors of the missions are proud of their service with what is justly called 'The Mighty Eighth'. The flights to Schweinfurt and Regensburg on 17 August 1943 will remain in the minds of most of those men as the greatest experience of their lives. These are a selection of their present views.

> I'll never forget that day so long as I live – and every August 17th since 1943 has been a day of remembrance for me. The things I saw that day will live with me for the rest of my life. (Lieutenant Johnny A. Butler, 384th Bomb Group)

I can compare it a little with Henry V's comment on the eve of Agincourt or with Pickett's charge at Gettysburg. I can say that I was proud to have been part of it. (Lieutenant Edwin D. Frost, 381st Bomb Group)

I can conservatively state that I saw more enemy action in the four-plus hours of combat over the Continent in the Schweinfurt mission than I had seen in all of my previous eight or ten combat raids combined. Literally we were fighting for our lives. (Second Lieutenant James D. Penrod, 351st Bomb Group)

This was my twenty-fifth and last raid over Germany and, as I looked back at Schweinfurt, I couldn't help wondering if the battle was just another echo in the history of aerial warfare or was it some sort of aerial Gettysburg, but somehow I thought, 'Now I'll live for ever.' (Technical Sergeant Andy Berzanski, 303rd Bomb Group)

As you well know, our losses were heavy. By the time of the Regensburg mission I had been in combat several times in sixty days and already I was a seasoned war veteran. I had turned twenty-three and matured far beyond my age . . . The memories never go away. I have visited my old airfield a number of times since. The silence is always deafening and the tears are uncontrollable. (Lieutenant Leo LaCasse, 385th Bomb Group)

APPENDIX 1

American and Allied Operational Performance

This appendix will provide in statistical form the combined order of battle, details of operational performance and list of aircraft casualties for all American units taking part in the Regensburg and Schweinfurt operations of 17 August 1943 and in the American and Allied fighter escort and diversionary operations of that day. The opportunity is also taken of providing a 'roll of honour' for the men killed in those operations.

Each lost aircraft is identified by its factory serial number, its pilot's name and, where available, the personal names given to the plane by its crew. Each B-17 lost in the Regensburg and Schweinfurt forces is given a number 'down'. This number represents as accurately as possible the sequence in which B-17s were forced to leave their formations, most to crash nearby but a few to fly considerable distances before coming down. The numbers coincide with similar numbers plotted on Map 7 for the route to Regensburg and on Maps 10 and 12 for the routes to and from Schweinfurt. There is no map for the flight from Regensburg to North Africa but the sequence of losses on this route can easily be followed in the text of Chapter 18. The same numbers are repeated in the 'missing aircraft charts' which have been prepared for this appendix to show the positions in their own bomb group formations from which each B-17 was lost. So, the '1st down' shown for the B-17 of Lieutenant Nayovitz in the 94th Bomb Group entry below indicates that this was the first B-17 to be forced out of the Regensburg formation and, from the formation chart, that this was the left-hand plane, third element, high squadron, of its bomb group formation.

The dead members of each crew, except the pilot when killed, are listed in alphabetical order and their home cities or towns are also provided. The experience of the lost crews in terms of operational missions carried out is also given when known, although individual members of crews had often flown more or less missions than the basic crew; where the crew was a thoroughly mixed one, the best estimate of its average record in missions is given.

The following abbreviations will be used: Captain – Capt.; Lieutenant – Lt.; Second Lieutenant – 2/Lt; Flight Officer – F/O; Technical Sergeant – T/Sgt; Staff Sergeant – S/Sgt.

Part A The Regensburg B-17 Force

4TH BOMBARDMENT WING

(Commander: Colonel Curtis E. LeMay; H.Q. Elveden Hall, Thetford)

146 B-17s dispatched, 122 bombed primary target, 24 missing. Personnel casualties: 38 men killed, 133 prisoners of war, 13 evaders, 20 interned in Switzerland, 40 rescued from sea and returned to unit.

94th Bomb Group, Bury St Edmunds
21 B-17s dispatched, 20 bombed, 1 missing, 12 damaged. 6 men killed, 2 prisoners, 2 evaders.

B-17 42-30389 *Dear Mom* (Lt Bernard W. Nayovitz, Brooklyn, New York, killed) 331st Squadron. 1st down, by fighter attack, crashed at Lummen, 10 km E. of Diest. Also killed: 2/Lt Robert P. Allison, Moscow, Pennsylvania; T/Sgt Albert V. Beyke, Fort Recovery, Ohio; 2/Lt Murlyn F. Burnett, Oklahoma City; S/Sgt Jack H. Loveless, Congress Heights, Washington D.C.; 2/Lt James F. Smith, Montgomery, Alabama. Crew on 14th mission.

95th Bomb Group, Horham
24 B-17s took off but 7 returned as abortives or for other reasons, 14 bombed, 4 missing, 5 damaged. 5 men killed, 30 prisoners, 5 evaders.

B-17 42-30176 *Assassin* (Lt John L. Sundberg, evader) 335th Squadron. 3rd down, by fighter attack, crashed at Oostmalle, 25 km N.E. of Antwerp. Killed: T/Sgt Anthony L. Carlone, Providence, Rhode Island. 2 men evaders. Crew on 11th mission.

B-17 42-30274 *Bay-Be* (Lt Walter A. Baker) 334th Squadron. 5th down, by Flak and finished off by fighter attack, crashed at Mol, 18 km S.E. of Turnhout. 3 men evaders. Crew on 14th mission.

B-17 42-30283 *Mason's Morons* (Lt Robert C. Mason) 336th Squadron. 10th down, by fighter attack, crashed near Darmstadt. Crew on 19th mission.

B-17 42-3194 (Lt Robert W. Hayden) 334th Squadron. 18th down, by earlier fighter damage, crashed at Santa Margherita, 25 km N.W. of Parma, Italy. Killed: S/Sgt Charles E. Hill, Newark, New Jersey; S/Sgt Kenneth J. Mears, North Billerica, Massachusetts; S/Sgt Earl J. Moorer, Konawa, Oklahoma; S/Sgt John H. Riley, Cambridge, Massachusetts. Crew on 6/7th mission.

96th Bomb Group, Snetterton Heath
21 B-17s dispatched, 19 bombed, 6 damaged. No personnel casualties.

Regensburg Missing Aircraft Chart

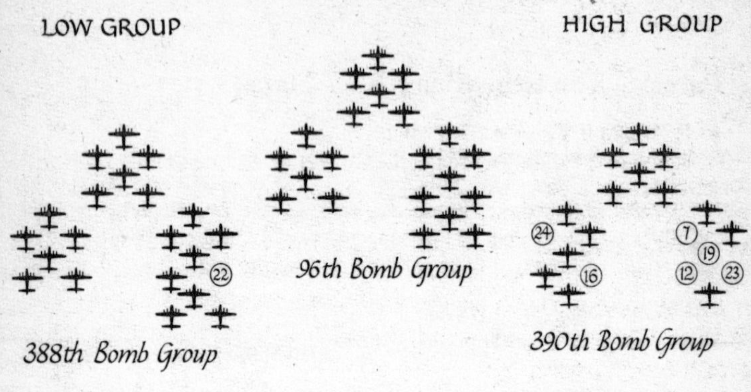

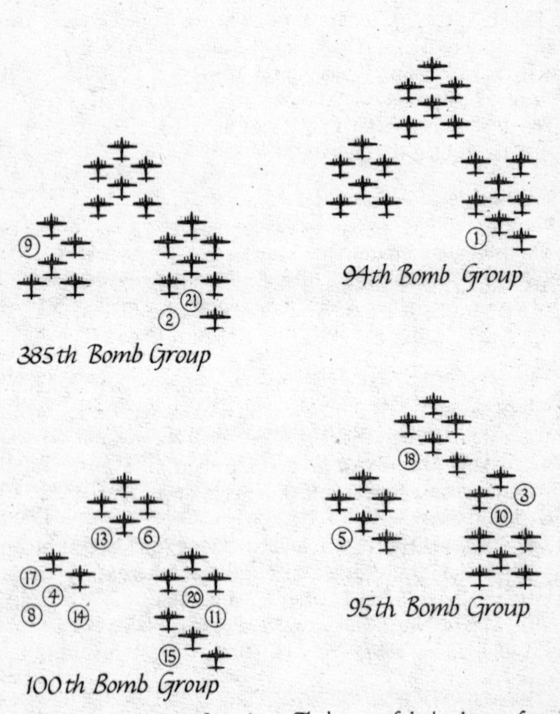

Notes 1. The formations are viewed from above. The lay-out of the bomb group formations is almost to scale; in practice their squadrons overlapped slightly more than is shown here. Distances between bomb groups are not to scale.

2. In each bomb group the high squadron is on the right, the low squadron on the left.

100th Bomb Group, Thorpe Abbots
21 B-17s dispatched, 14 bombed, 9 missing, 3 damaged. 17 men killed, 59 prisoners, 5 evaders, 10 interned in Switzerland.

B-17 42-5867 *Alice from Dallas* (Lt Roy F. Claytor, evader) 350th Squadron. 4th down by Flak, crashed at Langerloo, 8 km E. of Hasselt. Killed: Sgt William M. Hinton, New Paris, Pennsylvania; S/Sgt Edmund A. Musante, Ansonia, Connecticut. 4 men evaders. Crew on 13th mission but with some newer replacement gunners.

B-17 42-30063 *Picklepuss* (Capt. Robert M. Knox, Ardmore, Pennsylvania, killed) 418th Squadron. 6th down, by fighter attack, crashed at Schmalgraf, 7 km N. of Eupen. Also killed: S/Sgt Joseph F. LaSpada, Buffalo, New York; Sgt Alexander Markowski, Utica, New York; S/Sgt Henry A. Norton, Enterprise, Alabama; S/Sgt Frank W. Tychewicz, Chicago; 2/Lt John O. Whitaker, Wheeling, West Virginia. Crew on 8th mission.

B-17 42-30311 (2/Lt Thomas D. Hummel) 350th Squadron. 8th down, by fighter attack, crashed at Schornsheim, 15 km S. of Mainz. Killed: Sgt Richard E. Bowler, Meadeville, Pennsylvania; S/Sgt Kenneth T. O'Connor, Syracuse, New York. Crew on 5th mission.

B-17 42-30002 *The WAAC Hunter* (2/Lt Henry P. Shotland) 349th Squadron. 11th down, by fighter attack, crashed at Roxheim, 5 km S. of Worms. Killed: S/Sgt Foster Compton, Hartley, Kentucky. Crew on 1st mission.

B-17 42-5860 *Escape Kit* (Lt Curtis R. Biddick, Davis, California, killed) 418th Squadron. 13th down, by fighter attack, crashed Schweinberg, 30 km S.W. of Würzburg. Also killed: T/Sgt Robert R. DeKay, Mount Clemens, Michigan; T/Sgt Lawrence E. Godbey, Radford, Virginia; F/O Richard L. Snyder, Kansas City, Missouri. 8th mission for Biddick and his bombardier but remainder were another crew on 10/12th mission.

B-17 42-30070 *Tweedle-o-Twill* (Lt Ronald W. Braley) 350th Squadron. 14th down, by fighter attack, crashed at Pülferingen, 35 km S.W. of Würzburg. Killed: Sgt James R. Bair, Terrace, Pennsylvania. Crew on 13th mission.

B-17 42-30080 *High Life* (Lt Donald K. Oakes) 351st Squadron. 15th down, damaged by fighter attack then force-landed at Dübendorf military airfield near Zurich, Switzerland. Crew on 10/12th mission.

B-17 42-3232 *Flak Happy* (Lt Ronald W. Hollenbeck) 350th Squadron. 17th down, by earlier fighter damage, crashed at Ghedi, 20 km S. of Brescia, Italy. Crew on 10/12th mission.

B-17 42-30042 *Oh Nausea* (Lt Glen S. Van Noy) 349th Squadron. 20th down, by mechanical failure, ditched approximately 90 miles north of Sicily and crew captured by Germans. Crew on 11th mission.

385th Bomb Group, Great Ashfield
21 B-17s dispatched, 19 bombed, 3 missing, 5 damaged. 8 men killed, 13 prisoners, 1 evader, 10 rescued from sea.

B-17 42-5886 *The Jolly Roger* (2/Lt Paul A. Sommers, Maplewood, New Jersey, killed) 548th Squadron. 2nd down, by fighter attack, crashed 2 km S. of Woensdrecht airfield. Also killed: 2/Lt Herbert W. Brown, Winter Haven, Florida; S/Sgt Parker R. Crabtree, Hancock, Maine; Lt Hugh T. McClatchey, Ozone Park, New York; S/Sgt Joe Schreppel, Pittsburg; T/Sgt Olin L. Wieneke, Nokomis, Illinois. 1 man evader. Crew on 5th mission.

B-17 42-5914 *Sack Time* (2/Lt Leslie L. Reichardt) 549th Squadron. 9th down, by fighter attack, believed to have crashed S.W. of Darmstadt and N. of Worms. Crew on 7th mission.

B-17 42-5892 (Lt John T. Keeley) 551st Squadron. 21st down, damaged by fighter attack, ditched 130 miles from N. African coast. Crew on 7th mission. All or most of this crew killed in collision over England on 26 September 1943 after returning from a raid to Rheims.

S/Sgt Glenn C. Knecht, Schuyler, Nebraska, and 2/Lt David J. McMullen, Niles, Ohio, were killed in aircraft which were not shot down.

388th Bomb Group, Knettishall

21 B-17s dispatched, 21 bombed, 1 missing, 7 damaged. 10 men rescued from sea.

B-17 42-3414 *Paddlefoot* (Lt John W. Parker) 561st Squadron. 22nd down, damaged by Flak over Regensburg, ditched 80 miles from N. African coast. Crew on 2nd mission.

390th Bomb Group, Framlingham

20 B-17s dispatched, 16 bombed, 6 missing, 12 damaged. 2 men killed, 29 prisoners, 10 interned in Switzerland, 20 rescued from sea.

B-17 42-30017 *All Shot To Hell* (2/Lt Ashbrooke W. Tyson) 568th Squadron. 7th down, by fighter attack, crashed somewhere in Bingen area. Crew on 1st full mission, two earlier abortives.

B-17 42-30316 *Madie* (2/Lt James R. Regan) 568th Squadron. 12th down, by fighter attack, crashed at Bellheim, 17 km N. of Karlsruhe. Killed: S/Sgt Edward J. Jones, Ithaca, New York. Crew on 2nd mission.

B-17 42-30315 *Peg Of My Heart* (2/Lt Stephen P. Rapport) 569th Squadron. 16th down, damaged by Flak and by fighter attack, force-landed at Utzensdorf, 15 km N. of Berne, Switzerland. Crew on 3rd mission.

B-17 42-3305 *Princess Pat* (2/Lt Dale A. Shaver) 568th Squadron. 19th down, damaged by fighter attack and force-landed at Hyères, 20 km E. of Toulon. Crew on 3rd mission.

B-17 42-3310 *Blood, Guts and Rust* (2/Lt Wade H. Sneed) 568th Squadron. 23rd down, damaged by Flak and ditched 60 miles from N. African coast. Crew on 3rd mission. 2/Lt Sneed and some other members of this crew were killed on a raid to Münster on 10 October 1943.

B-17 42-3333 *Purgatory Pete* (2/Lt Raymond A. Becker) 569th Squadron. 24th down, damaged by fighter attack and ditched 50 miles from

N. African coast. Crew on 3rd mission. At least three members of this crew killed in later raids.

S/Sgt Leonard A. Baumgartner, Bensenville, Illinois, was killed in an aircraft which was not shot down.

Part B The Schweinfurt B-17 Force

1ST BOMBARDMENT WING

(Commander: Brigadier-General Robert B. Williams; H.Q. Brampton Grange, Huntingdon)

230 B-17s dispatched, 184 bombed primary target, 36 missing. Personnel casualties: 71 men killed, 259 prisoners of war, 25 evaders, 20 rescued from sea and returned to unit.

91st Bomb Group, Bassingbourn
24 B-17s dispatched, 9 bombed, 10 missing, at least 1 written off after battle damage, 9 damaged. 37 men killed (more than half of the 1st Bombardment Wing's total), 54 prisoners, 7 evaders, 10 rescued from sea.

B-17 42-5225 *Stormy Weather* (2/Lt Don Von Der Heyde, Altoona, Pennsylvania, killed) 323rd Squadron. 1st down, by fighter attack, crashed at Baelen, 9 km N.W. of Leopoldsburg. Also killed: T/Sgt Peter Comac, Frackville, Pennsylvania; S/Sgt John R. Klopolsky, Oklahoma City; S/Sgt Homer J. Mitts, Chattanooga, Tennessee; 2/Lt Donald Primeau, Lowell, Massachusetts; S/Sgt Dick Sparman, Hamilton, Montana; S/Sgt Mack D. Walton, Dickson, Tennessee; S/Sgt William F. Wannemacher, Lynbrook, New York. 1 man evader. Crew on 10th mission.

B-17 42-29559 *Stop-'n-takit* (Lt Charles A. Bennett, evader) 323rd Squadron. 5th down by fighter attack, crashed Langdorp, 13 km W. of Diest. Killed: T/Sgt William J. Barrett, Pittsburg, Pennsylvania; 2/Lt Stanley A. Dahlman, Rosholt, South Dakota; S/Sgt Thomas J. Hunt, Knoxville, Tennessee. 3 men evaders. Mixed crew but 4 members on 25th mission.

B-17 42-5437 *Frank's Nightmare* (Lt Arlynn E. Weieneth, Kensett, Iowa, killed) 401st Squadron. 10th down, by fighter attack, crashed at Hergarten, 20 km S. of Düren. Also killed: 2/Lt Clarence H. Blackmon, Yokena, Mississippi; S/Sgt Joseph D. Hall, Wilmington, Delaware; T/Sgt John J. Halloran, Stoughton, Massachusetts; S/Sgt Vernon E. Lamplot, Palos Park, Illinois; Sgt Robert McDonald, Kelso, Washington State; T/Sgt Charles E. Reidy, East Palestine, Ohio; S/Sgt Edgar A. Roe, Silt, Colorado; 2/Lt William A. Warose, New York City. Relatively new crew but number of missions not known.

B-17 41-24453 *Mizpah – The Bearded Beauty* (2/Lt Everett L. Kenner, Santa Fe, New Mexico, killed) 322nd Squadron. 11th down, by fighter attack, crashed near Mayen, 25 km W. of Koblenz. Also killed: 2/Lt George M. Bryan, Starkville, Mississippi; S/Sgt William B. Hagin,

Schweinfurt Missing Aircraft Chart

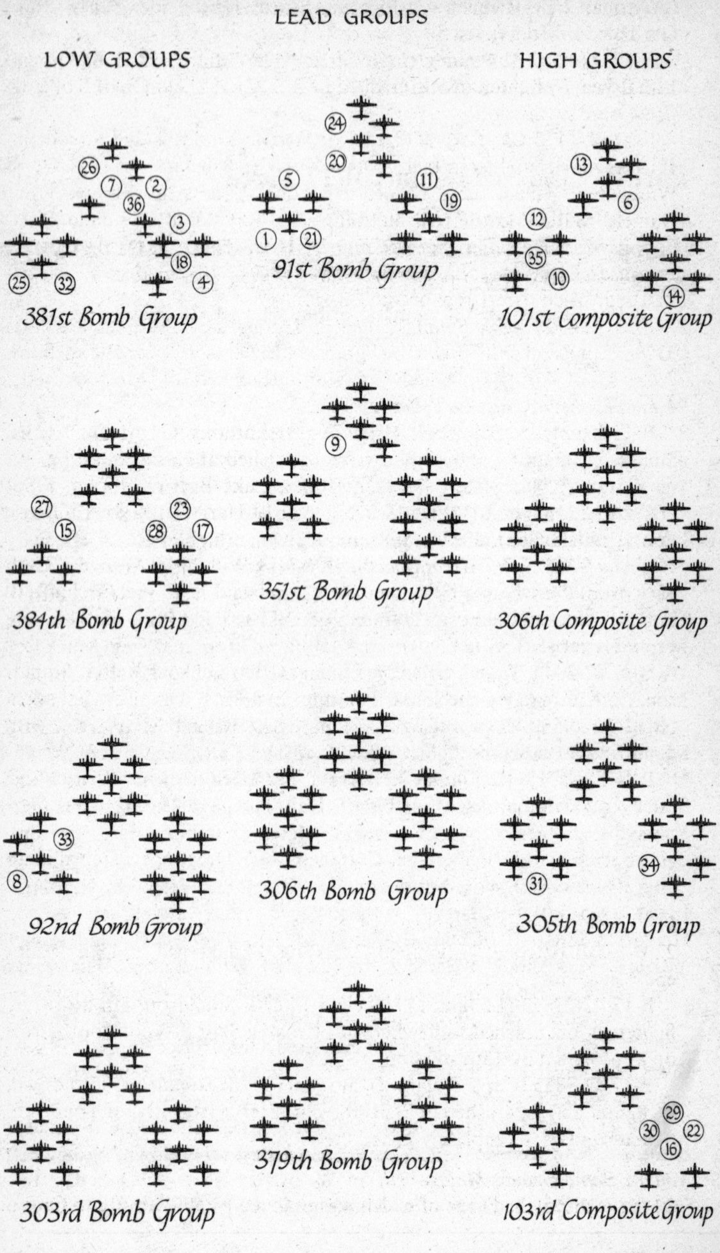

LEAD GROUPS

LOW GROUPS

HIGH GROUPS

26 7 2 36 3 18 25 32 4

381st Bomb Group

24 20 5 11 19 1 21

91st Bomb Group

13 6 12 35 10 14

101st Composite Group

27 15 23 28 17

384th Bomb Group

9

351st Bomb Group

306th Composite Group

33 8

92nd Bomb Group

306th Bomb Group

34 31

305th Bomb Group

303rd Bomb Group

379th Bomb Group

29 30 22 16

103rd Composite Group

Arizona; 2/Lt Richard G. Martin, Forest Hills, New York; S/Sgt Gardner H. Moore, Washington D.C. Crew on 7th mission.

B-17 42-5069 *Our Gang* (Lt William H. Wheeler) 401st Squadron. 12th down, by fighter attack, crashed near St Goar, 25 km S. of Koblenz. Crew on 21st mission.

B-17 42-5139 *Chief Sly II* (2/Lt Joel W. Gatewood) 322nd Squadron. 19th down, by fighter attack, crashed at Geisenheim, 20 km S.W. of Wiesbaden. Killed: S/Sgt Stanford Adams, Limestone, Maine; T/Sgt Daniel J. Butler, Seattle, Washington; T/Sgt Raymond F. Canada, Pittsboro, North Carolina; Sgt George F. Hite, Lancaster, Texas; S/Sgt Frederick F. Pearce, Niagara Falls, New York; 2/Lt George E. Riegel, Lansing, Michigan. Crew on 4th mission.

B-17 42-2990 *Dame Satan* (Lt Jack A. Hargis, Lodi, California, killed) 322nd Squadron. 20th down, by fighter attack, crashed near Wannebecq, 7 km N. of Ath. Also killed: Sgt Star Tucker, Athol, Massachusetts. 4 men evaders. Crew on 7/8th mission.

B-17 41-24524 *The Eagle's Wrath* (Lt Anthony G. Arcaro) 323rd Squadron. 21st down, by fighter attack, crashed at Harxheim, 6 km W. of Worms. Killed: T/Sgt James F. Jones, Lake Butler, Florida; S/Sgt Harold K. Michaud, Saranac, Michigan; 2/Lt Harry K. Warner, Grosse Pointe, Michigan. Crew on 5th mission.

B-17 41-24527 *The Great Speckled Bird* (Lt William S. Munger) 324th Squadron. 24th down, by fighter attack, crashed near Waldaschaff, 10 km E. of Aschaffenburg. Number of missions for crew not known, probably more than ten.

B-17 42-3043 *Hitler's Gremlin* (Lt Eugene M. Lockhart) 401st Squadron. 35th down, by mechanical failure and Flak damage, ditched in North Sea 45 miles from English coast. Crew rescued. Mixed crew with from 8 to 20 missions.

B-17 42-5712 (Lt James D. Judy) 322nd Squadron. Written off after crashlanding at Manston; 7 men had parachuted over Germany.

T/Sgt Donald F. Robertson, Cottage Grove, Oregon, was killed in an aircraft which was not shot down.

92nd Bomb Group, Alconbury

22 B-17s dispatched, 21 bombed, 2 missing, 14 damaged. 17 men prisoners, 3 evaders.

B-17 42-29853 (Lt James D. Stewart) 327th Squadron. 8th down, by fighter action, crashed somewhere in Eifel area S. or S.W. of Bonn. Crew on approximately 13th mission.

B-17 42-3435 (Capt. Roland L. Sargent) 327th Squadron. 33rd down, by fighter action, crashed at St Huibrechts-Hern, 10 km N. of Tongeren. 3 men evaders. Completely mixed crew.

303rd Bomb Group, Molesworth

29 B-17s dispatched (one of which was manned by a 384th Bomb Group

crew), 27 bombed, 17 damaged. One waist gunner in a returned aircraft was killed but group documents do not record his name.

305th Bomb Group, Chelveston
29 B-17s dispatched, 27 bombed, 2 missing, 16 damaged. 6 men killed, 19 prisoners.

B-17 42-30159 *Settun' Bull* (Lt Rothery McKeegan) 366th Squadron. 31st down, by Flak damage and finished off by fighter attack, crashed at Bilstain, 5 km N.E. of Verviers. Killed: S/Sgt Claude M. Davis, Oakfield, New York; S/Sgt Robert W. McLain, Anderson, Indiana. Crew on 10/11th mission but Lt McKeegan was not the regular pilot.

B-17 41-24564 *Patches* (2/Lt Douglas L. Mutschler, Goodrich, North Dakota, killed) 365th Squadron. 34th down, by fighter action, crashed at Averbode, 8 km N.W. of Diest. Also killed: T/Sgt Carlton J. Boberg, Lincoln, Nebraska; 2/Lt Edward L. Carter, La Habra, California. Crew on 6th mission.

Sgt Wayne Frye, Petersburg, West Virginia, killed in a returned aircraft from which four other men parachuted over Germany.

306th Bomb Group, Thurleigh
30 B-17s dispatched, 30 bombed, 17 damaged. No personnel casualties.

351st Bomb Group, Polebrook
28 B-17s dispatched, 24 bombed, 2 missing, 15 damaged. 2 men killed, 18 prisoners.

B-17 42-29839 *Cherokee Girl* (Lt Helmuth F. Hansen) 510th Squadron. 9th down, by Flak damage and finished off by fighter attack, crashed 8 km S.E. of Koblenz. Killed: S/Sgt Tuite H. A. Ambrose, Donaldsonville, Louisiana. Crew on 21st mission.

B-17 42-5812 *Cannon Ball* (Lt Max A. Pinkerton) 511th Squadron. 14th down, by fighter attack, crashed near Bad Ems, 12 km E. of Koblenz. Killed: F/O Herbert F. Berreau, Heron Lake, Minnesota. Crew missions record not known.

379th Bomb Group, Kimbolton
24 B-17s dispatched, 18 bombed, 4 missing, 10 damaged. 14 men killed, 26 prisoners.

B-17 42-29830 *Peter Wabbit* (Lt Erwalt D. Wagner, Rosewell, New Mexico, killed) 525th Squadron. 16th down, by fighter attack, crashed at Dörrebach, 10 km W. of Bingen. Also killed: S/Sgt Eldred J. Andruss, Seymour, Texas; Lt William C. Barnard, Dixon, California; S/Sgt Marvin T. Charlson, Grand Forks, North Dakota; T/Sgt Henry I. Cushman, Fall River, Massachusetts; S/Sgt Francis J. Donahue, Worcester, Massachusetts; 2/Lt Kenneth F. Gibbs, Lancaster, Pennsylvania; Lt Joseph J. Hildebrand, Wenonah, New Jersey; T/Sgt Benjamin Radensky, Sacramento, California; S/Sgt Dean J. Yates, Mona, Utah. Crew on 13th mission.

B-17 42-30158 *Mary Jane II* (Lt Howard O. Koeppen, Walworth,

Wisconsin, killed) 525th Squadron. 22nd down, by fighter attack, crashed near Abenheim, 7 km N.W. of Worms. Also killed: S/Sgt Jack Posemsky, Brooklyn, New York. Crew on 16/18th mission.

B-17 42-30191 *The Bolevich* (Lt Donald W. Merchant) 525th Squadron. 28th down, by fighter attack and Flak damage, crashed at Elfershausen, 10 km S.W. of Bad Kissingen. Killed: T/Sgt Gene R. Hecht, Plainview, Nebraska. Crew on 18th mission.

B-17 42-30309 *Raging Red* (F/O James N. Sexton) 525th Squadron. 30th down, by fighter attack, crashed at Niederwetz, 7 km S. of Wetzlar. Killed: S/Sgt Talmadge C. Naron, Kosciusko, Mississippi. Crew on 6th mission.

381st Bomb Group, Ridgewell

26 B-17s dispatched, 16 bombed, 11 missing, 14 damaged, 5 men killed, 85 prisoners, 11 evaders, 10 rescued from sea.

B-17 42-30245 *Lucky Lady* (Lt Weldon L. Simpson, Lubbock, Texas, killed) 534th Squadron. 2nd down, by fighter attack, crashed at Oostmalle, 15 km W. of Turnhout. 1 man evader. Crew on 8th mission.

B-17 42-3227 (Lt Hamden L. Forkner, evader) 534th Squadron. 3rd down, by fighter attack, crashed at Meerlaan, 10 km N. of Diest. 3 other evaders. Crew on 10th mission.

B-17 42-30028 *Sweet Le Lani* (2/Lt Neil H. Wright) 534th Squadron. 4th down, by fighter attack, crashed at unknown position south of Düren. Crew on 11th mission.

B-17 42-3092 *Strato Sam* (F/O James C. Hudson) 533rd Squadron. 6th down, by Flak damage and fighter attack, crashed at Pesch, 6 km S.W. of Münstereifel. Killed: 2/Lt Kenneth E. Robinson, Cleveland, Ohio. Crew on 8th mission.

B-17 42-30140 *King Malfunction II* (Lt Jack B. Painter, Columbus, Ohio, killed) 532nd Squadron. 7th down, by fighter attack, crashed at Esch, 8 km S.E. of Münstereifel. 2 men evaders. Crew on 13th mission.

B-17 42-29983 (Lt Challen P. Atkinson, Premont, Texas, killed) 533rd Squadron. 13th down, by Flak damage and fighter attack, crashed at Kesseling, 8 km S.W. of Ahrweiler. Also killed: S/Sgt James C. McGoldrick, Johnstown, Pennsylvania. Crew on 13th mission.

B-17 42-29978 *Hell's Angels* (Lt Reinhardt M. King) 534th Squadron. 18th down, by fighter attack, crashed at Bad Schwalbach, 10 km N.W. of Wiesbaden. Crew on 10/13th mission.

B-17 42-3220 *Damfino* (Lt Harry M. Smith) 535th Squadron. 25th down, by fighter attack, believed crashed at Marksteinach, 7 km E. of Schweinfurt. Crew on 15/16th mission.

B-17 42-29731 (Lt Leo Jarvis) 532nd Squadron. 26th down, by Schweinfurt Flak, believed crashed at Ebrach, 30 km S.E. of Schweinfurt. Crew on 14th mission.

B-17 42-3225 *Chug-a-lug Lulu* (Lt Lorin C. Disbrow, taken prisoner but killed in action in Korea) 535th Squadron. 32nd down, by fighter attack, crashed near Tongeren. 4 men evaders. Crew on approximately 15th mission.

B-17 42-29735 (F/O George R. Darrow) 532nd Squadron. 36th down, by fighter attack, ditched in North Sea, 20 miles E. of Felixstowe. Crew rescued. Crew missions record not known.

384th Bomb Group, Grafton Underwood
18 B-17s dispatched plus one crew in a 303rd Bomb Group aircraft, 12 bombed, 5 missing, 1 written off after crash landing, 10 damaged. 6 men killed, 40 prisoners, 4 evaders.

B-17 42-29956 *Vertical Shaft* (Lt Jesse D. Hausenfluck, Georgetown, Texas, killed) 544th Squadron. 15th down, by fighter attack, crashed at St Goarshausen, 30 km S.E. of Koblenz. Also killed: 2/Lt Donald B. MacKenzie, Stamford, Connecticut. Crew on 11th mission.

B-17 42-3230 *Mary Kathleen* (Lt Drewry T. Wofford) 545th Squadron. 17th down, by fighter attack, believed crashed at Weiler, 2 km W. of Bingen. Crew missions record not known.

B-17 42-3222 *Deuces Wild* (Lt Frank G. Mattes, Mount Vernon, Washington State, killed) 545th Squadron. 23rd down, by fighter attack, crashed at Reichenbach, 15 km S. of Darmstadt. Also killed: 2/Lt Adam Konefal, Pine Bush, New York. Crew on 13th mission.

B-17 42-30147 *M' Honey* (Lt Clayton R. Wilson) 544th Squadron. 27th down, by fighter action, crash-landed near Rheims. 4 men evaders. Crew on 11/13th mission.

B-17 42-30139 *Snuffy* (2/Lt Oliver Sweningsen) 545th Squadron. 29th down, by Schweinfurt Flak, finished off by fighter attack, crashed at Stangenroth, 10 km N.W. of Bad Kissingen. Killed: S/Sgt Richard S. Grover, Erin, New York; 2/Lt Victor T. Kelly, Hoboken, New Jersey. Crew on 9th mission.

B-17 42-29728 *El Rauncho* (F/O Randolph G. E. Jacobs) 544th Squadron. Written off after crash-landing at Grafton Underwood.

Part C American Fighter Escorts to B-17 Units

276 P-47 sorties dispatched, 3 missing, 13 German fighters destroyed. (Successes noted here for both U.S.A.A.F. and R.A.F. escorts are those which can be confirmed from German sources.)

4th Fighter Group, Debden
48 P-47s dispatched. No successes, no losses.

56th Fighter Group, Halesworth
101 P-47 sorties in two operations, 3 P-47s missing. Destroyed 6 FW 190s, 1 Me 109 and 4 Me 110s.

P-47 41-6398 (Lt Robert M. Stultz, Wapakoneta, Ohio, killed) 62nd Squadron. Shot down by German fighter, believed crashed at Freeren, 3 km S.E. of Tongeren.

P-47 42-7891 (Lt Voorhis H. Day, Buffalo, New York, killed) 62nd Squadron. Shot down by German fighter, crashed at Warsage, 22 km N.E. of Liège.

P-47 41-6372 (Lt Arthur Sugas, Kalamazoo, Michigan, killed) 63rd Squadron. Shot down by German fighter, crashed at Wilwe near Maastricht.

78th Fighter Group, Duxford
48 P-47s dispatched. Destroyed 1 Me 110, no losses.

353rd Fighter Group, Metfield
79 P-47 sorties in two operations. Destroyed 1 Me 109, no losses.

Part D R.A.F. Fighter Escorts to B-17 Units

180 Spitfire sorties dispatched (all squadrons flew two operations). 2 Spitfires missing, 6 German fighters destroyed.

129 Squadron, Hornchurch
23 Spitfire sorties. Destroyed 1 FW 190, no losses.

222 Squadron, Hornchurch
25 Spitfire sorties. Destroyed 3 Me 109s, no losses.

303 (Polish) Squadron, Northolt
19 Spitfire sorties. Destroyed 1 FW 190, no losses.

316 (Polish) Squadron, Northolt
17 Spitfire sorties. No successes, no losses.

331 (Norwegian) Squadron, North Weald
21 Spitfire sorties. Shared 1 Me 110 destroyed with other squadrons, no losses.

332 (Norwegian) Squadron, North Weald
24 Spitfire sorties. Shared 1 Me 110 destroyed with other squadrons, no losses.

403 (Canadian) Squadron, Lashenden
27 Spitfire sorties, 2 missing. Shared 1 Me 110 destroyed with other squadrons.

Spitfire LZ997 (F/Lt W. C. Conrad, evader). Crashed near Armentières after collision with Spitfire MA615.

Spitfire MA615 (F/Sgt C. M. Shouldice, Chesley, Ontario, killed). Crashed in English Channel after collision.

421 (Canadian) Squadron, Kenley
24 Spitfire sorties. No successes, no losses.

Part E Diversionary and Supporting Operations

Units here did not suffer casualties or shoot down German fighters unless stated. All Spitfire sorties were escorts; Typhoons were escorts unless noted as bombing.

U.S.A.A.F. Units

323rd Bomb Group, Earls Colne
36 B-26s bombed Poix.

386th Bomb Group, Boxted
36 B-26s to Bryas Sud, 29 bombed.

387th Bomb Group, Chipping Ongar
36 B-26s to bomb Poix but recalled.

R.A.F. Units

3 Squadron, Manston
8 Typhoons bombed Woensdrecht.

19 Squadron, Newchurch
24 Spitfire sorties to Calais and Poix; Poix flight recalled.

41 Squadron, Westhampnett
25 Spitfire sorties to Bryas and Poix.

56 Squadron, Manston
6 Typhoons to Woensdrecht.

65 Squadron, Kingsnorth
26 Spitfire sorties to Bryas and Poix.

91 Squadron, Westhampnett
25 Spitfire sorties to Bryas and Poix.

122 Squadron, Kingsnorth
22 Spitfire sorties to Bryas and Poix.

132 Squadron, Newchurch
24 Spitfire sorties to Calais and Poix; Poix flight recalled.

174 Squadron, Lydd
7 Typhoons to Woensdrecht but only reached Flushing.

175 Squadron, Lydd
8 Typhoons to bomb Woensdrecht but bombed ship off Flushing instead.

181 Squadron, New Romney
8 Typhoons bombed Lille/Vendeville.

182 Squadron, New Romney
6 Typhoons to Lille/Vendeville, 1 missing.

Typhoon DN553 (F/Lt W. H. Bewg, West Norwood, London, killed). Presumed crashed in English Channel after earlier damage by German fighter.

183 Squadron, Tangmere
8 Typhoons bombed Poix, 3 damaged by Flak.

226 Squadron, Swanton Morley
7 Mitchells to bomb Dunkirk but operation not completed.

245 Squadron, Lydd
9 Typhoons to Woensdrecht.

247 Squadron, New Romney
6 Typhoons to Lille/Vendeville.

320 (Dutch) Squadron, Attlebridge
6 Mitchells bombed Calais.

341 (French) Squadron, Biggin Hill
25 Spitfire sorties to Bryas and Poix; Poix flight was recalled. 1 Spitfire missing and 1 FW 190 destroyed on the Bryas flight.

Spitfire MH419 (Sgt L. Poirier, taken prisoner but killed flying after the war). Shot down by German fighter and crashed approximately 10 km N. of Hesdin.

401, 411 and 412 (Canadian) Squadrons, Staplehurst
Approximately 35 Spitfires to Dunkirk but recalled.

402 (Canadian) Squadron, Merston
18 Spitfire sorties to Bryas and Poix.

416 (Canadian) Squadron, Merston
22 Spitfire sorties to Bryas and Poix.

485 (New Zealand) Squadron, Biggin Hill
24 Spitfire sorties to Bryas and Poix; the Poix flight was recalled. 1 Me 109 destroyed on the Bryas flight.

486 (New Zealand) Squadron, Tangmere
11 Typhoons to Poix.

602 (City of Glasgow) Squadron, Newchurch
24 Spitfire sorties to Calais and Poix; Poix flight recalled.

APPENDIX 2
Luftwaffe Operational Performance

Because of the lack of some German unit records, this appendix may be slightly incomplete. In particular, German aircraft losses may have been up to 10 per cent higher than are recorded here.

It was a German custom to name some of the day-fighter *Geschwaders* after famous men. Baron von Richthofen (JG 2) and Ernst Udet (JG 3) were First World War fighter aces; Walter Oesau (JG 1) and Werner Mölders (JG 51) were aces of the Spanish Civil War and the early years of the Second World War. Albert Leo Schlageter (JG 26) fought in the First World War but did not become famous until he blew up a railway bridge near Düsseldorf in 1923 as a protest against coal being sent to France as post-war reparations. He was caught by the French occupation authorities and shot at Golzheimer Heide (now Düsseldorf airport). He is said to have met his death with great courage and the Nazi Party later adopted his memory as a symbol.

The following abbreviations for ranks are used: Major – Maj.; Hauptmann – Hptm.; Oberleutnant – Oblt; Leutnant – Lt; Oberfeldwebel – Ofw.; Feldwebel – Fw.; Unteroffizier – Uffz.; Gefreiter – Gef.

Single-engined Fighter Units

JG 1 (JAGDGESCHWADER 'OESAU')

I/JG 1, Deelen

FW 190s engaged in all three B-17 flights with unknown success. 3 of own planes lost, 4 damaged.

FW 190A-5 710014 (Ofw. Hübl) 1st *Staffel*. Believed shot down by P-47 of 56th Fighter Group, crashed at Stolberg, 10 km E. of Aachen.

FW 190A-6 550457 (Lt Johannes Feustel, died of wounds on 21 August) 2nd *Staffel*. Shot down by P-47 of 56th Fighter Group, crashed 10 km S. of Louvain.

FW 190A-5 840131 (Fw. Bodo Nette, wounded) 3rd *Staffel*. Shot down by P-47 of 56th Fighter Group, crashed E. of Maastricht.

II/JG 1, Woensdrecht and Schiphol
FW 190s engaged in Regensburg and Schweinfurt outward flights, 3 B-17s claimed on Schweinfurt outward. 4 of own planes lost, 4 damaged.

FW 190A-4 5561 (Ofw. Gerhard Ubert, wounded). Shot down by B-17, crashed near Maastricht.

FW 190A-4 5565 (Ofw. Bernhard Liper, wounded) 4th *Staffel*. Shot down by B-17, crashed at Halgers, near Maastricht.

FW 190A-5 410037. Shot down by B-17, crashed at Liers, 4 km N. of Liège.

FW 190A-6 550152 (Gef. Herrman Gottwald, killed) 6th *Staffel*. After operations set out on a further flight to unit's rear base in Germany but lost way and crashed while landing at Dortmund.

III/JG 1, Leeuwarden
Much uncertainty about this unit's activities. Me 109s probably engaged in Schweinfurt outward flight with some B-17s claimed. Unofficial reports of five or more own casualties not confirmed by official documents.

JG 2 (JAGDGESCHWADER 'RICHTHOFEN')

The *Stab* (Headquarters Flight) of JG 2 suffered two accidental losses, while taking off or landing from operations against diversions or for transfer flight to main operational area.

FW 190A-5 550145 (Oblt Fritz Edelmann). Overturned at Beaumont-sur-Oise.

A second FW 190 crashed at Beaumont-sur-Oise. Pilot unhurt but no other details.

I/JG 2, Conches and St André
FW 190s in possible action against diversions and then, after a long flight north, engaged with Schweinfurt homeward flight but little combat. No successes or losses reported.

II/JG 2, Poix and Vitry en Artois
Me 109s engaged in both Schweinfurt flights. Unofficial claims of 4 B-17s and 1 P-47. 2 of own planes damaged.

III/JG 2, Brest and Vannes
Some of its FW 190s probably in action against diversions. 1 plane lost.

FW 190A-5 2609. Engine caught fire while on operational flight, crashed at Quatremare, 25 km S. of Rouen. Pilot unhurt.

JG 3 (JAGDGESCHWADER 'UDET')

I/JG 3, Mönchen-Gladbach
Me 109s engaged in all three B-17 flights, some successes but number not known. 1 of own planes lost, 2 damaged.

Me 109G-6 18855 (Lt Harry Börner, wounded) 2nd *Staffel.* Shot down by B-17, crashed at Worms.

II and *IV/JG 3* were in Russia and Italy at this time.

III/JG 3, Münster/Handorf
Me 109s engaged in all three B-17 flights, 1 B-17 and 3 P-47s claimed. 4 of own planes lost, 2 damaged.

Me 109G-4 19583 (Uffz. Pankalla) 7th *Staffel.* Shot down by Spitfire of 222 Squadron, crashed at Yerseke, island of Beveland.

Me 109G-6 20444 (Lt Hans Schleef, wounded) 9th *Staffel.* Shot down by Spitfire of 222 Squadron, crashed at Arendskerke, Beveland.

Me 109G-6 20460. Shot down by Spitfire of 222 Squadron, crashed S.W. of Roosendaal.

Me 109G-6 20023 (Fw. Rudolf Thies, wounded) 7th *Staffel.* Hit by B-17 fire and force-landed at Schwabhausen, 15 km S.W. of Bad Mergentheim.

JAGDGESCHWADER 11

I/JG 11, Husum
FW 190s engaged in Schweinfurt outward flight but with no record of any successes. 3 of own planes lost, 1 damaged.

FW 190A-6s 530346 and 550448 crashlanded at Wiesbaden/Erbenheim airfield, possibly after being hit by B-17 fire, both pilots unhurt.

FW 190A-6 530113 had similar experience at Niedermendig airfield.

II/JG 11, Jever
Me 109s engaged in Schweinfurt outward flight, 5th *Staffel* making rocket attacks resulting in two B-17s being damaged; no other success recorded; some pilots made individual attacks on Schweinfurt homeward flight with some success. 2 of own planes lost.

Me 109 (Oblt Hans-Heinrich Koenig, wounded) 4th *Staffel.* Shot down by B-17 fire, crashed at Rheinbach, 15 km S.W. of Bonn.

Me 109 (Lt Heinz Knoke, wounded) 5th *Staffel.* Crash-landed near Bonn after being hit by B-17 fire.

III/JG 11, Oldenburg
Me 109s engaged in Schweinfurt outward flight but with no record of any successes. 3 of own planes lost, 1 damaged.

Me 109G-6 15637. Force-landed with engine trouble at Haverbeek, 10 km N.W. of Brussels.

Me 109G-6 15870 (Lt Wolf Scharff, wounded) 9th *Staffel.* Force-landed at Bonn/Hangelar airfield, probably after being hit by B-17 fire.

Me 109G-6 19856 (Oblt Franz Ströbl, wounded) 9th *Staffel.* Similar experience to last aircraft.

JG 26 (JAGDGESCHWADER 'SCHLAGETER')

I/JG 26, Woensdrecht
FW 190s engaged in Regensburg and Schweinfurt outward flights, probably shot down 4 B-17s. 1 of own planes lost, 3 damaged.

FW 190A-4 2386 (Lt Jörg Kiefner, wounded) 3rd *Staffel*. Shot down by Spitfires of 303 (Polish) Squadron, crashed St Leonard, 7 km S. of Antwerp.

II/JG 26, temporarily dispersed to *Beauvais/Tille* and other airfields. Some FW 190s engaged against diversionary raids and then main *Gruppe* in Schweinfurt homeward flight, claimed 2 B-17s, 1 P-47 and 1 Spitfire in main operation. 3 of own planes lost, 3 damaged.

FW 190A-5 41001 (Uffz. Karl Hadraba, killed) 4th *Staffel*. Shot down by Spitfire of 341 (Free French) Squadron, believed crashed near Fruges, 17 km N.E. of Hesdin.

FW 190A-6 530125 (Maj. Wilhelm-Ferdinand Galland, killed). Shot down by P-47 of 56th Fighter Group, crashed at Hees-Vlijtingen, 5 km W. of Maastricht.

FW 190A-5 1243 (Uffz. Heinz Gomann, wounded) 5th *Staffel*. Shot down by P-47 of 56th Fighter Group, crashed at Genk, 12 km. E.N.E. of Hasselt.

III/JG 26, Schiphol, with detachment at *Lille/Vendeville*
Me 109s engaged in all three B-17 flights and against diversion raids, probable successes against B-17s but no details available, probably shot down 1 Spitfire on diversion raid. 6 of own planes lost, 2 damaged.

Me 109G-4 19216 (Ofw. Heinz Kemethmüller, wounded) 9th *Staffel*. Shot down by P-47 of 353rd Fighter Group, crashed near Leopoldsburg.

Me 109G-6 19466 (Fw. Werner Kraft, wounded) 9th *Staffel*. Believed shot down by B-17s, crashed near Beverloo.

Me 109G-6 16494 (Uffz. Fritz Fritzlehner, killed) 12th *Staffel*. Shot down by B-17s, crashed near Hasselt.

Me 109G-6 18833 (Oblt Dippel) 9th *Staffel*. Shot down by B-17s, crashed at Geroldstein, 60 km W.S.W. of Koblenz.

Me 109G-3 20225 (Ofw. Hermann Hoffmann, killed) 11th *Staffel*. Shot down by Spitfire of 485 (New Zealand) Squadron, crashed 10 km W. of Fruges.

Me 109G-6 15923 (Lt Kehl). Crash-landed at Antwerp/Deurne due to fuel shortage.

One *Staffel* of JG 27 was probably in action against diversion raids in Pas de Calais area. No other details available.

II/JG 51 (Jagdgeschwader 'Mölders'), Neubiberg
Me 109s engaged in Schweinfurt outward flight, some successes. No casualties recorded.

JG 104, Fürth
Planes from this training unit took off but no details of whether in action.

JG 106, Lachen-Speyerdorf
Me 109s engaged in Regensburg flight and possibly in Schweinfurt flights, at least 1 B-17 shot down. 1 of own planes lost.

Me 109 (Lt Hans Harms) shot down by B-17, crashed near home airfield.

Jagdgruppe 50, Wiesbaden/Erbenheim
Me 109s engaged in all three B-17 flights, claimed 16 B-17s shot down but some of these were on behalf of pilots from training units who flew tactically with *Jagdgruppe* 50. Two of own planes lost.

Me 109G-5 18852 (Uffz. Dietrich Barth, killed). Shot down by B-17s, crashed at Simmern, 40 km S. of Koblenz.

Me 109G-5 15915 (Fw. Horst Bilfinger, killed). Shot down by P-47 of 56th Fighter Group, crashed at Monschau, 15 km S.E. of Eupen.

Industrieschutzstaffel Regensburg sent up its Me 109s to engage B-17s bombing Regensburg, one B-17 hit and later crashed; some of own planes slightly damaged.

Twin-engined Fighter Units

I/NJG 1, Venlo and Gilze Rijen
Me 110s engaged in Schweinfurt homeward flight, only success a possible share in one B-17. Five of own planes lost, unknown number of others damaged.

Me 110G-4 4866 (Uffz. Werner Oldenhove, killed) 2nd *Staffel*. Also killed: Uffz. Herbert Strauch. Shot down by P-47s of 56th Fighter Group, crashed at Bilsen, 20 km S.E. of Hasselt.

Me 110G-4 5551 (Lt Josef Nabrich, wounded) 3rd *Staffel*. Killed: Uffz. Fritz Heim. Shot down by P-47s of 56th Fighter Group, crashed at Flémalle, 7 km S.W. of Liège.

Me 110G-4 5542 (Uffz. Hans Neuner, killed) 3rd *Staffel*. Also killed: Uffz. Rudolf Mielmann. Shot down by P-47s of 56th Fighter Group, crashed at Aubel, 20 km N.E. of Liège.

Me 110G-4 4869, written off at Venlo airfield, possibly as a result of combat with P-47s of 56th Fighter Group.

Me 110G-4 5544 (Ofw. Hellenbrück) 1st *Staffel*. Shot down by Spitfires of 331, 332 and 403 Squadrons, crashed at Schelle, 8 km S.W. of Antwerp.

II/NJG 1, St Trond
Me 110s sent up to attack stragglers of Regensburg and Schweinfurt outward flights, possibly 5 B-17s finished off, some of own aircraft lightly damaged.

Ergänzungsstaffel/NJG 2, Gilze Rijen
At least one Me 110 engaged in Schweinfurt outward flight, no success, 1 of own planes lost.

Me 110G-4 5590 (Lt Siegfried Elsässer, wounded). Shot down by P-47s of 78th Fighter Group, crashed at Vogelsang, 26 km E. of Eupen.

Aircraft of *NJG 4*, based at airfields in Northern France, were sent to engage the Schweinfurt homeward flight but no serious contact ensued.

I/NJG 6, Mainz/Finthen
Me 110s engaged in Regensburg and Schweinfurt homeward flights, finished off 3 damaged B-17s. 3 of own planes lost.

Me 110G-4 5433 (Oblt Johannes Engels, wounded). Killed: Uffz. Horst Janisch. Shot down by B-17s, crashed near Nidda, 30 km S.E. of Giessen.

Me 110G-4 5564 (Lt Rolf Heideklang, killed). Shot down by B-17s, crashed at Bingenheim, 27 km S.E. of Giessen.

Me 110G-4 4614 (Uffz. Bernard Reindel, killed). Also killed: Uffz. Fritz Schumann. Shot down by B-17s, crashed at Echzell, 25 km S.E. of Giessen.

NJG 101
Various aircraft types from this training unit engaged stragglers of the Regensburg and Schweinfurt flights and finished off three damaged B-17s. None of own aircraft lost, possibly some damaged.

APPENDIX 3

Briefing Notes of 385th Bomb Group for the Regensburg Operation

OFFICERS' BRIEFING

(1) The Primary Target is the MESSERSCHMITT Factory at Regensburg. Bomber Command states that this is the most important target ever attacked by aircraft.
  (a) Production estimated at 200 to 300 aircraft per month.
  (b) This represents 25 to 30 per cent of the total.
  (c) The plant is the second largest of its kind in Europe.
  (d) Percentage increase in recent months has been tremendous because they have not been bombed.
  (e) The plant is almost self-sufficient. Complete assembly takes place here and everything but engines are manufactured.
(2) The Secondary Target is the FW 190 Engine Plant in Munich.
  (a) Plant manufactures 250 to 275 FW 190 engines per month. Destruction of this plant would greatly handicap construction of FW 190 planes.
(3) The Last Resort Target is the center of the city of Munich.

SCREEN GOES UP

This is the big deal Gentlemen, as you can see. You are going on through the target and land in North Africa.

The route in has been picked to keep you away from A.A. fire except at extreme range.

Along your route in you will find A.A. batteries at the following places in these concentrations:

(A) WOENSDRECHT – 1 Battery
(B) ANTWERP – Heavy guns can reach formation at extreme range.
(C) VISE – EIGHT HEAVY GUNS.
(D) AACHEN – 38 guns AT EXTREME RANGE.
(E) LIÈGE – 60 guns – also at extreme range.
(F) There are undoubtedly some other guns on course at cities and airdromes. Suggest evasive action be used in these areas as low altitude will make heavy A.A. fire inaccurate.

AT TARGET – There are 27 heavy guns mostly to the east of the target.

AT THE SECONDARY – There are 130 guns – mostly south of the aiming point. Don't forget that there are many guns in Northern Italy and any towns you pass over you should use evasive action. There are 75 heavy guns at La Spezia on the coast of Italy near Genoa, 30 at Bolzano and 110 at Genoa.

Targets (1) River pattern – right in bend of river – railroad coming into Regensburg. Island, at intersection of Danube and river; large oval. Every bombardier will carry one of these map photos. Navigator will show him his position especially at I.P. Target area = 3,500 × 20,000 ft. MPI = 350′ × 175′

(2) 2 railroads leading to Munich – woods – white patches (gravel pits), stream running around target.

Opposition: Both single-engined and twin-engined near coast but diversions and escort which S-3 will describe should nullify most of them. Inland there are 60 twin-engined fighters within 150 miles of target.

Convoys: Nil.

Photographs: Cameras by W.G. [waist gunner?] Did great job.

Security: Remember you have a long trip and a different landing field; therefore be extra careful about talking. If forced down near target, head for Switzerland and be sure to say you are *escapees* not evaders. If forced down in Italy, hide out until Italy surrenders. If forced to surrender do so to Italians so as not to be shipped to Germany.

Any officer who has not had prisoner-of-war lecture please report in my office after briefing.

In each bombardier's folder there is an interrogation form and combat form. If you do not land with the group, aircraft captain *must* interrogate.

Take off: 05.40

GUNNERS' BRIEFING

Targets: To-night you are making history, not only because of the importance of the Target, but because this is a new extension of air power.

(1) Messerschmitt assembly factory at *Regensburg* making 200–300 aircraft a month – 30 per cent of total single-engined – the most important target to be attacked by any aircraft to date.

(2) FW 190 Engine plant at *Allach*. Destruction of this plant will make construction of 190's impossible for many months.

(3) Center of Munich – remember that beer hall!

Route in and out: as free from Flak as possible.

Time: In flight – 10 hours; under oxygen – 8 hours, 28 minutes; over enemy territory – 3 hours, 33 minutes.

Enemy Opposition:

Both single-engined and twin-engined near coast; only twin-engined night fighters inland – 60 within 150 miles of target. Fighter escort and other diversions should take care of enemy aircraft near coasts.

Support:

(1) 6 Squadrons of P-47s from Woensdrecht as far as possible. Beware of shooting at your escort.
(2) Diversions by R.A.F. and medium bombers on coast.
(3) 1st Air Div. is attacking Schweinfurt. Security risk.
(4) 4th Air Div. has 7 Groups attacking this target.

Security:

Remember you have a long trip and a different landing field; therefore be extra careful about talking. If forced down near target, head for Switzerland and be sure to say you are *escapees* not evaders. If forced down in Italy, hide out until Italy surrenders. If forced to surrender, do so to Italians so as not to be shipped to Germany.

Pick up guns and go to ship. Radio operators go to drying room. Cleaning equipment will be on ships; only one armorer knows this. Don't get cocky; be alert throughout.

APPENDIX 4
The 'Wheels-Down' B-17 Crew

In Chapter 8, which describes the flight of the 4th Bombardment Wing through Germany to Regensburg, it was stated that two B-17s had been forced to leave their formations after German fighter attacks and were later shot down well away from those formations. The experiences of these two planes are linked to the most persistent legend of this day's operations. The story is best told from the beginning.

A plane of the 100th Bomb Group was forced out of formation with a damaged engine soon after it crossed the River Moselle. The pilot of the plane was Captain Robert M. Knox. After leaving his formation, Knox asked his navigator whether a route to England or one over the Alps to Switzerland offered the best prospect. The navigator advised England and the rest of the crew enthusiastically concurred. Knox turned back the way he had come; it was nearly 300 miles to England. (This is aircraft number 6 on map 6, page 142.)

The B-17 nearly managed to reach the German border. It may have been attacked by single-engined fighters during that flight but if so the gunners fought them off. Just near the border, however, at a position south of Aachen, the B-17 met a flight of three Messerschmitt 110 night fighters which had been sent up from nearby St Trond airfield to hunt for returning cripples. The German pilots were Hauptmann von Bonin, Oberleutnant Barte and Leutnant Witzke and they attacked this lone B-17 with great determination. Their planes carried a powerful armament of four 20-mm cannons each. Oberleutnant Barte describes the fierce combat.

> Von Bonin attacked first, from the rear, firing a long burst. I saw him go straight down with smoke coming from an engine. Witzke did the same thing and he also went down smoking. So I came round from the front and got off just one short burst – that was all there was time for from the front. The bomber seemed as big as a barn door when I pulled up over it. One wing fell completely off – the right one – and the bomber span down. I think I saw three parachutes.
>
> I landed soon after that and found that the others had both landed on one engine. Von Bonin's plane had been hit by over twenty bullets and I think we counted twenty-six in Witzke's. That tail gunner must have been really good.

Von Bonin, in his account of this action, says that it was the left waist gunner who caused most of the damage to his plane. The three parachutes seen belonged to the navigator and two of the gunners. A fourth survivor, the bombardier, escaped at a low altitude when he was blown out of the disintegrating wreckage and was also able to open his parachute. Captain Knox and the two gunners whose defence the German pilots had admired, Staff Sergeant Henry Norton in the waist and Staff Sergeant Joseph LaSpada in the tail, were among the men killed.

There grew up around the loss of this aircraft the legend that Captain Knox had lowered his wheels in an act of surrender, that German fighters had closed in to 'escort' it down to an airfield in the normal manner of such incidents, but that the B-17 gunners had then taken advantage of these targets and had shot down some of the escorts. The legend goes on to claim that German fighter units thereafter sought out the ◻D tail identification of the 100th Bomb Group and caused the heavy casualties suffered by this unfortunate unit on some later raids.

The first part of this supposition was based on statements made by Second Lieutenant Ernest Warsaw, the navigator and one of the B-17's survivors, who was later held prisoner at an airfield near Cologne. Because Warsaw could speak a little German he was visited by German fighter pilots for conversational purposes. Warsaw later recounted that one German officer complained bitterly that he had been shot down by a B-17 which had its wheels lowered in surrender. Warsaw was also subsequently quoted as saying, probably under questioning by authors who naturally wished to follow up this interesting story, that he 'saw that our wheels were down' during the final stages of the flight; but in a later version he said that he was only 'vaguely aware' that the wheels were down.*

There are a number of weaknesses, however, in the assumption that the events attributed to Captain Knox's crew occurred in the way suggested. Firstly, it is unlikely that an experienced pilot like Knox would deliberately increase the drag on his seriously damaged aircraft by lowering the wheels, although it is sometimes suggested that the wheels could have descended without the pilot's knowledge because of damage to the mechanism. Secondly, Second Lieutenant Edwin Tobin, the bombardier who was trapped in the aircraft for some time after Warsaw left, states that he was not aware that the wheels were down and that he thought the plane was so badly damaged that it could never have flown with the wheels down. Thirdly, the Messerschmitt 110 pilots who were contacted, von Bonin and Barte, have no memory of the bomber's wheels being down. (There can be no doubt that it was these pilots who finished off Captain Knox's plane.) Fourthly, the German officer who later spoke to Warsaw did not directly accuse him of being a member of the crew

* Edward Jablonski, *Double Strike*, Doubleday, 1974, p. 84, and Thomas M. Coffey, *Decision Over Schweinfurt*, McKay, 1977, p. 275.

which had lowered its wheels and then shot down its escort. Fifthly, German records show no evidence of any German fighters shot down by Knox's gunners. Two Messerschmitt 110s were forced down with damaged engines, as already described by one of the German pilots, but the only single-engined German fighter recorded as crashing in this area is one from III/JG 26 which must have been shot down in the main battle earlier; this fighter had taken off from Schiphol and could not still have been airborne when Captain Knox flew back through this area.

The claim by the German pilot who spoke to Second Lieutenant Warsaw, that a B-17 had lowered its wheels in surrender that morning and then shot down one of its German escorts, is in fact based on an incident which did actually happen on the morning of the Regensburg raid. However, it was a B-17 of another group which was involved. The crew concerned was that of Second Lieutenant James R. Regan of the 390th Bomb Group. Contributions from four members of the crew can be combined to provide a composite description; none of the four disagrees with any basic part of the story.

Second Lieutenant Regan's B-17 was hit by a standard head-on attack in the middle of the fiercest part of the German fighter action south of Frankfurt. Two engines were damaged; one had to be feathered but the other continued to provide some power for a time. The B-17 fell back but continued to obtain protection from other groups. When these finally passed, Regan decided not to continue eastwards on his own and turned south to follow the River Rhine in the hope of reaching Switzerland. The B-17 then suffered further fighter attacks which affected communications within the plane; the intercom link with the gunners in the rear was broken. The co-pilot was injured (see Second Lieutenant Hille's account on page 135 in Chapter 8). The second damaged engine was about to fail and there was now no hope of reaching Switzerland. The pilot, watched by the co-pilot, lowered the wheels in the traditional act of surrender. This was possible in the aircraft's damaged condition because it was descending steadily and maintaining a good speed. Unfortunately, the men in the rear of the aircraft could not be told that the wheels were down or that they should start baling out, and the officers in the front were not willing to leave until the gunners were safe. This was an inexperienced crew, on only their second mission and involved in serious action for the first time.

While all this was happening two Messerschmitt 109s appeared, flying off the left wing of the B-17. Sergeant Jim Kahler can describe what happened next.

> No one had told us to relax. I discovered that I still had two arms and two legs and my gun was O.K. I was looking round to see what was going on and all of a sudden there were two Me 109s off our left-hand wing. They were flying parallel with us – just out of range. The one

> that was closest to us then drifted into what I calculated to be shooting distance. I had my gun trained onto him and apparently the other gunners were doing the same. I opened fire first. As soon as I started, the top turret started, and then the waist gunner on that side and the ball turret. The German plane started to smoke and went down in flames. I felt pretty good – we had knocked one enemy aircraft out of the sky. As soon as this happened the other one seemed to spin round and I could see the fire coming out of his spinner from his 20-millimetre cannon and both wings were alight with the firing of his machine guns. All our guns were shooting away at him like mad, just as before. Apparently we did not hit him but he sure as hell hit us. The aircraft was jolting each time one of the 20-millimetres hit and he hit a lot of vital parts. He swooped underneath us and out of my line of fire. I could feel we were going down.

The next part of the story has little connection with the 'wheels-down' episode but is too interesting to omit. The crew were now in a highly disorganized and confused state. The plane was still flying but losing altitude fast. The wounded co-pilot was alternately fainting and recovering. The top turret gunner was sent back to tell the men in the rear to bale out. The pilot was trying to tell the two men in the nose to do the same. By the time the gunners in the back were finally alerted and ready to leave, however, the plane was so low that it was clearly dangerous to jump. Two gunners did insist on jumping and one was killed when his parachute did not open in time. The plane was approaching a field. The co-pilot came out of one of his fainting bouts to find himself alone in the cockpit.

> I presumed they thought I was dead and had all baled out until I heard voices and noises down at the escape hatch. I pushed on the left rudder pedal and the aircraft righted itself just as we hit the top of some trees – a horrible sound. Right in front of me was a large field – wasn't that convenient! – and a big haystack so I just put it down in the field, right through the haystack. We blew that apart, naturally. Somehow I kept from fainting and then we came to a halt. The wheels had come off when we hit the trees; if they had still been on and down, we would certainly have bounced all over the place and been smashed up. Talk about dumb luck!

The B-17 made as good a landing as possible in the circumstances. The plane broke into two parts and seven men emerged with no serious injury. Hille was helped out and soon taken away to a civilian hospital at Speyer. He left his leather flight jacket behind.

The unwounded Americans were eventually taken to Speyerdorf airfield and the following day were submitted to a rigorous interrogation. Sergeant Kahler describes it.

> They lined us against a wall and one highly agitated German pilot

> kept yelling at the interpreter and the interpreter kept yelling at us, 'Why were you shooting?' We were looking out of the sides of our eyes at each other, dumbfounded. He was staring me right in the eyes and his nose was an inch or so from mine; he kept yelling. I replied, 'Christ, you are the enemy.' The questions continued – why did we shoot the last fighter down? I gave the same reply again. The others were all asked the same thing. Then he said, 'But you had your wheels down – the international sign of surrender.' You could have driven a truck through our mouths at that. We gunners had no idea the wheels had been down.

Eventually the Germans did accept that the gunners had not been in communication with the pilot and had fired in good faith. As far as Second Lieutenant Regan and his crew were concerned, the incident ended there.

It is now that we come to the probable link with Second Lieutenant Warsaw of the 100th Bomb Group in his prison cell at an airfield near Cologne. German records show that a Messerschmitt 109 from I/JG 3 was shot down that morning near Worms; this was very close to the path which Regan's B-17 took in its flight south down the Rhine, although it was about twenty-five miles north of the position at which the B-17 eventually crash-landed. (The 390th Bomb Group aircraft is number 12 on map 6, page 142; the German crash is also shown.) The pilot of the shot-down Messerschmitt 109, Leutnant Harry Börner, was wounded. This was probably the escort shot down by Regan's gunners. I/JG 3's home airfield, Mönchen-Gladbach, was only twenty-five miles from Cologne and it was probably one of Leutnant Börner's friends who visited Second Lieutenant Warsaw and complained about a B-17 with its wheels lowered shooting down a German fighter.

It is my opinion that Second Lieutenant Regan's crew was the only one which was involved in any wheels-down confusion on that day. I am surprised that their story has remained undiscovered for so long. Second Lieutenant Warsaw's evidence, which led to the 100th Bomb Group being considered responsible, was given in good faith. He never claimed that the Germans had made a direct accusation against his crew and, since he knew of no other crew which might be responsible, it must have seemed reasonable to him that it was his own crew which was involved. The 390th Bomb Group never suffered any special attention from German fighters after this date . . . and neither did the 100th. Former German pilots will laugh if it is suggested that they had the time or inclination to single out a particular identification mark in a B-17 formation. The subsequent heavy losses of the 100th Bomb Group were no more than the result of unfavourable tactical conditions encountered on several subsequent raids.

APPENDIX 5
A Gunner's Letter

This letter was written by a B-17 gunner to his mother in the autumn of 1943.

'Somewhere in England'
September 1943

Dear Mother:

I've put off writing this letter for quite a while but since we began operations I've seen quite a bit. Things happen amazingly fast in combat work, so I am writing this letter tonight.

All the family pictures are before me on the table. I can close my eyes and imagine myself in our own living room at home, talking with you.

You probably felt the bad news more than you thought I could possibly know but, believe me, I do. Now it's time you should begin to feel resigned, and in a way, happy for my sake, and that may puzzle you. By now our ranks have been considerably thinned and refilled again with replacements. In combat mess almost every face is unfamiliar. We are not fighting for our country, but each of us for our own family, for our own plot of ground back home.

If you could stand with me at the briefing room door and watch the boys as they go out, you'd understand. Every face, if a bit tense, has a grin on it. A bunch of cannon-fodder if you wish, but each one knows the score, has a cause, and is not afraid to die for it.

You know mother, even now I just can't visualize not coming home. You wouldn't be reading this if that had been in the cards. Dying can't be hard, it's the uncertainty which makes one fear it. This business makes a person quite religious!

In closing, I send my love to each and every member of our family. You've got a swell gang there to keep you occupied and happy. Will be seeing you all again, sometime, somewhere.

Until then,
Lots of Love,
your son, John.

(John survived the war safely but prefers his full name not to be mentioned.)

Acknowledgements

I wish to record my sincere gratitude for the willing and friendly help given by the following men and women who all participated in the events of 17 August 1943. (All ranks are those held on that date.)

UNITED STATES ARMY AIR FORCE

91st Bomb Group: Lt Anthony G. Arcaro, Lt Charles A. Bennett, 2/Lt Walter S. Brown, T/Sgt Ford C. Cowherd, T/Sgt William C. Darden, 2/Lt Carlyle H. Darling, 2/Lt Herbert F. Egender, 2/Lt William F. Glover, Sgt Delmar E. Kaech, 2/Lt Roger W. Layn, T/Sgt Orlo Natvig, S/Sgt Harold H. Schulz, 2/Lt Carl N. Smith, S/Sgt Lloyd H. Thomas, S/Sgt Gerold Tucker, Lt William H. Wheeler, 2/Lt Clive M. Woodbury, Lt Col Clemens L. Wurzbach. *92nd Bomb Group:* T/Sgt E. John Collins, S/Sgt Kenneth F. Fahncke, 2/Lt William D. Kissinger, Capt. Roland L. Sargent, S/Sgt John E. Wasche. *94th Bomb Group:* Lt William G. Broach, S/Sgt Gerald G. McClure, T/Sgt Arthur P. McDonnell, Lt Robert R. Morrill, S/Sgt James W. Tolbert, S/Sgt Vance van Hooser, Lt William S. Winneshiek. *95th Bomb Group:* S/Sgt Raymond J. Elias, 2/Lt Henry P. Sarnow, T/Sgt Lester E. Schwab, Lt Rodney E. Snow, T/Sgt Warren D. Thomas, T/Sgt Earl J. Underwood, S/Sgt Francis L. Verdun. *96th Bomb Group:* Lt Dunstan T. Abel, Lt Carroll J. Bender, S/Sgt Arthur H. Bloche, Lt Charles A. Blumenfeld, S/Sgt Frank M. Cardamon, Lt Lewis E. Feldstein, Capt. John L. Latham, 2/Lt Raymond L. McKinnon. *100th Bomb Group:* 2/Lt Howard Bassett, Capt. Everett E. Blakely, S/Sgt William M. Blank, Lt John D. Brady, T/Sgt William W. Crabb, Lt Charles B. Cruikshank, S/Sgt Sam J. Cusmano, 2/Lt Michael C. Doroski, Lt Howard B. Hamilton, Lt John K. Justice, 2/Lt Kenneth R. Lorch, Lt Dan B. McKay, 2/Lt Raymond J. Nutting, Lt Floyd C. Peterson, F/O Owen D. Roane, 2/Lt Edwin F. Tobin, S/Sgt Gordon A. Williams, 2/Lt Robert H. Wolff. *303rd Bomb Group:* T/Sgt Andy Berzansky (died 1981), Lt C. W. Campbell, 2/Lt Darrell D. Gust, T/Sgt Howard E. Hernan, Maj. Lewis E. Lyle, T/Sgt Dale Rice, T/Sgt George W. Vogel. *305th Bomb Group:* T/Sgt Fred Boyle, 2/Lt Martin D. Fetherolf, Lt Rothery McKeegan, Lt Donald F. Perkins, S/Sgt Lee F. Quinlivan, 2/Lt Malvern R. Sweet, S/Sgt Frank E. Williams. *306th Bomb Group:* Lt William P.

Cassedy, S/Sgt John E. Corcoran, Lt Immanuel J. Klette, 2/Lt H. Kenneth McCaleb, Maj. William S. Rader, Lt Reginald L. Robinson, Capt. David W. Wheeler. *351st Bomb Group:* Maj. Clinton F. Ball (died 1981), Lt Col Robert W. Burns, 2/Lt John W. Dytman, 2/Lt Joseph S. Koffend, 2/Lt Howard G. Maser, Lt Jack H. O'Mohundro, 2/Lt James B. Penrod, S/Sgt Elmer C. Smith, Lt Carl B. Stackhouse. *379th Bomb Group:* 2/Lt Bohn Fawkes, Lt Elton P. Hoyt, T/Sgt Johannes H. Johnson, Lt Noble M. Johnson, Col Maurice A. Preston, S/Sgt Edgar van Valkenberg, 2/Lt Gordon F. Ward, S/Sgt Fred P. Weiser. *381st Bomb Group:* S/Sgt Frank M. Beech, 2/Lt Allen J. Chapin, 2/Lt Ronald T. Delaney, Lt Hamden L. Forkner, Lt Edwin D. Frost, 2/Lt Clifford M. Haverkamp, 2/Lt Robert E. Hyatt, S/Sgt Peter A. Katsarelis, 2/Lt William J. Keays, 2/Lt William D. Lockhart, S/Sgt Joseph E. Lyons, T/Sgt Robert Roeder, Lt Donald J. Rutan, Capt. George G. Shackley, S/Sgt Paul F. Shipe, Lt Frank J. Shimek, S/Sgt Kenneth Stone, Lt Alan F. Tucker, S/Sgt Joseph J. Walters. *384th Bomb Group:* 2/Lt Joseph W. Baggs, Lt John A. Butler, 2/Lt Robert C. Chapin, S/Sgt Robert Compton, S/Sgt Jack K. Goetz, S/Sgt Alfred Meyer, S/Sgt L. Corwin Miller, T/Sgt Walter A. Miller, S/Sgt Eugene Penick (died 1982), S/Sgt John F. Schimenek, 2/Lt Oliver Sweningsen, 2/Lt Arthur J. Thompson, S/Sgt John P. Thompson, 2/Lt Wayne L. Wentworth, T/Sgt Harvey R. Wiegand, Lt Clayton R. Wilson. *385th Bomb Group:* S/Sgt Aubrey R. Bartholomew, 2/Lt James L. Cooper, Lt Al Corriviau, T/Sgt Bruno Gallerini, Lt Donald E. Jones, Lt Leo LaCasse, S/Sgt Jack C. Leahy, Capt. Vincent Masters, T/Sgt Roger D. Palmer, Lt John F. Pettenger, Maj. Preston Piper, Lt Leslie L. Reichardt, Capt. Septime S. Richard, Lt Paul R. Schulz, 2/Lt Carl Tuke, Lt Frank B. Walls. *388th Bomb Group:* Lt Paul Arbon, Lt Andrew A. Chaffin, T/Sgt Elliott H. Hewes, Lt Loyd P. Humphries, T/Sgt Thomas J. Morey, S/Sgt George A. Petersen, Lt Francis E. Tierney. *390th Bomb Group:* S/Sgt William W. Adamson, Sgt Kenneth Black, 2/Lt Harold B. Boyd, 2/Lt Robert D. Brown, 2/Lt Caesar Bruschi, 2/Lt Lyman B. Burbank, S/Sgt William R. Carter, 2/Lt Oscar E. Hille, Sgt James R. Kahler, T/Sgt William J. Kubitzki, S/Sgt Marion E. Laird, S/Sgt Owen E. McWilliams, 2/Lt Nathaniel Mencow, Lt Douglas I. Gordon-Forbes, 2/Lt Burgess W. Murdock, S/Sgt Clarence E. Payne, 2/Lt Richard H. Perry, 2/Lt Stephen P. Rapport, 2/Lt Dale A. Shaver, S/Sgt Earl R. Spann, S/Sgt Albert W. van Pelt, Capt. George W. von Arb, Lt Paul W. Vance, 2/Lt John E. Wenzel.

56th Fighter Group: Lt Harold E. Comstock, Lt Paul Conger, Capt. Gerald W. Johnson, Col Hubert Zemke. *78th Fighter Group:* F/O Peter E. Pompetti, Maj. Eugene P. Roberts. *353rd Fighter Group:* Maj. Loren G. McCollom.

I would like to thank the wives of many of the above men for their most generous hospitality.

Eighth Air Force H.Q.: Maj. Gen. Ira C. Eaker, Lt Col George W.

Jones. *4th Bombardment Wing H.Q.:* Capt. Mark Brown, M/Sgt Hyko Gayikian, Lt Edward J. Kobeske, Col Curtis E. LeMay, Capt. Chankey Touart. *Twelfth Air Force Service Command, Algeria:* Lt Col Oliver B. Taylor.

ROYAL AIR FORCE

3 Squadron: F/Sgt S. B. Feldman, F/Sgt C. A. Tidy. *129 Squadron:* F/Lt F. A. O. Gaze. *181 Squadron:* F/O A. E. S. Vincent. *182 Squadron:* F/Lt W. H. Ireson. *222 Squadron:* F/Lt P. V. K. Tripe, P/O H. E. Turney. *303 (Polish) Squadron:* F/Sgt E. Martens. *331 (Norwegian) Squadron:* Maj. K. Birksted, Sgt C. K. Gran, Capt. M. Gran. *332 (Norwegian) Squadron:* Capt. W. Christie. *341 (French) Squadron:* Commandant B. Duperier, Sous Lt P. Laurent. *403 (Canadian) Squadron:* F/Lt W. G. Conrad. *485 (New Zealand) Squadron:* F/Lt M. G. Barnett, F/O J. D. Rae.

LUFTWAFFE

I/JG 1: Oblt Rudolf Engleder. *II/JG 1:* Lt Fritz Wegner. *III/JG 1:* Hptm. Robert Olejnik. *I/JG 2:* Hptm. Erich Hohagen. *II/JG 2:* Oblt Georg-Peter Eder, Oblt Friedrich Karch. *III/JG 3:* Hptm. Walther Dahl. *II/JG 11:* Oblt Heinz Knoke, Lt Heinz Rose. *III/JG 11:* Hptm. Anton Hackl. *I/JG 26:* Hptm. Karl Borris (died 1981), Lt Alfred Heckmann, Lt Jörg Kiefner. *II/JG 26:* Ofw. Adolf Glunz. *III/JG 26:* Ofw. Heinz Kemethmüller, Fw. Werner Mössner, Uffz. Alois Reichert. *II/JG 51:* Hptm. Hans Langer. *JG 106:* Lt Hans Harms. *Jagdgruppe 50:* Lt Alfred Grislawski. *I/NJG 1:* Uffz. Helmut Fischer, Obergef. Hermann Vollert. *II/NJG 1:* Oblt Walter Barte, Fw. Otto Fries, Uffz. Alfred Staffa, Hptm. Eckart von Bonin. *I/NJG 4:* Uffz. Werner Uhlmann. *I/NJG 6:* Oblt Hans Engels. *II/NJG 101:* Lt Josef Springer. *Jafü Holland–Ruhr:* Oberst Walter Grabmann.

THE PEOPLE OF REGENSBURG

Michael Bleicher, Mathilde Bork (formerly Steinkohl in 1943), Engelbert Dimper, Max Dömges, Franziska Eckert (formerly Bucher), Jakob Eisenschenk, Martin Ettinger, Hermann Heid, Martin Hirsch, Hedwig Hubel (formerly Bayerl), Eva Imlohn, Dr Hans Jordan, Josef Lambeck, Maria Macht, Franziska Manhart (formerly Setzer), Helmut Müller, Rosl Neumann, Elisabeth Nirschl, August Obermeier, Kurt Obermeier, Rose Poschenrieder, Anny Raith, Anni Ruf, Kurt Schnitke, Emil Stang, Heinz Stemmler, Martin Vielhuber, Dr Ernst Wedemeyer, Alois Weigert.

Belgian: André Dobbelaere, Georges Dutrieux, Marcel Paindaveine, Jules Pollet, André Robert, Jean Thibaut, Leon Vêche, Lucien Waroux.

French: Emile Colaprisco, Jean Jacquet, Pierre Jouvin, Emile Locchi, André Marre, Robert Melin, Albert Nicolas, J. Viti.

THE PEOPLE OF SCHWEINFURT

Willi Bach, Erhard Kreisel, Alfons Kuhn, Ellen Nauhauser (formerly Hess), Johannes-Curt Rust, Ernst Zillmann.

French: Henri Chabbert, René Defranoux, Henri Salvatella, Joseph Vivances.

Polish: Adela Kamianowska (formerly Nieroda), Stanislaw Kozlowski.

Personal Acknowledgements

I am pleased to be able to record my thanks to the numerous people in different countries who have provided valuable help in the preparation of this book.

I am particularly grateful to Paul Spitzer of Zug, Switzerland, who has translated with great diligence most of my German and some of my French correspondence and who interpreted for me on interviewing visits to Schweinfurt and Regensburg. Also worthy of special mention are: Jack Owen of Cynthiana, Kentucky, for tracking down so many of his former 8th Air Force colleagues, Chris Everitt of Eton Wick for carrying out all the Public Record Office research and Paul Andrews of Montreal for research work in the United States. Special thanks are also due to my wife Mary for her careful preparation of the maps, checking of the typescripts and help with the index, and to my regular typist Janet Mountain, who, for the seventh time, has coped with an extensive correspondence and two drafts of a manuscript with great skill and amiability.

Whom to mention next is a great problem; I am confronted with a mass of names of very kind people who have helped in many different ways. A listing by countries and in alphabetical order is the only convenient way to express my heartfelt thanks for so much valuable help.

My biggest task was the finding of men who flew in the air operations of 17 August 1943 and I thank the following hard-working officials and supporters of various unit associations in the United States for publicizing my appeals to their members or searching membership lists for individuals: Frank Betz, Jim Brown, John Ford, Art Frankel, Frank and Dottie Halm, Ed Huntzinger, Sheldon Kirsner, Leroy Nitschke, R. W. Owens, Ben Schohan, Paxton Sherwood, Russel Strong, James Vaughter and Joseph Vieira. Most of the American associations are stoutly supported by a band of enthusiasts in England and almost as much information on the location of former American aircrew members came from East Anglia as from the United States; for this I wish to thank Stan Bishop, David Crow, Colin Durrant, Stewart Evans, Mick Gibson, Richard Gibson, Chris Gotts, Peter Harris, Ian Hawkins, Ron Mackay, Keith Paull, Geoff Ward and Barry Willsher.

In my search for individual American participants I was still left with a long list of men I particularly wanted to find. These were men who had been in shot-down B-17s, whose wartime addresses were listed in the Missing Air Crew Reports but who had not joined the post-war associations. I therefore wrote to 'The Mayor' of every community named on that list, asking if any information could be obtained on the present whereabouts of the man concerned. Nearly all the mayors – or the civic leaders in smaller communities – who received these letters responded with action of some kind and many valuable contacts were thus made. I am most grateful for this help and pleased to be able to list these helpful communities by name: Alabama – Odenville; California – Piedmont, San Bernardino, Santa Cruz, Stockton, Vacaville and Vallejo; Connecticut – Bethany, Norwich and Waterbury; Georgia – Augusta, Comer and Savannah; Idaho – Caldwell and Weiser; Illinois – Berwyn, Moline and Urbana; Indiana – Bedford, Marion and Wheatland; Iowa – Le Mars; Kansas – Erie, Topeka and Wichita; Massachusetts – Assonet, Belmont, Boston, Greenfield and Longmeadow; Michigan – Bay City and Lake Odessa; Minnesota – Buffalo, Deephaven, Perham and St Paul; Montana – Great Falls; Nebraska – Grand Island; Nevada – Carlin; New Jersey – Trenton, Union City and Westfield; New York State – Cutchogue, Ellicottville, Elmira, Kenmore, Rochester and Webster; North Carolina – Asheville; Ohio – Celina, Cleveland Heights and Toledo; Oklahoma – Oklahoma City and Wynwood; Oregon – Portland; Pennsylvania – Pineville, Pittsburgh, Shamokin and Uniontown; South Dakota – Mobridge; Tennessee – Memphis, Nashville and Waverly; Texas – Austin and Brashear; Utah – Provo; Virginia – Martinsville and Pulaski; Wisconsin – Jefferson, Milwaukee and Three Lakes.

For various kinds of help in connection with my work in Europe I thank the following: in Holland, Ab Jansen of Oudorp and Adrie Roding of Enschede; in Germany, Christof Anetter, Dr Wilhelm Kick, Edith Seltsam and the town Stadtarchiv in Regensburg; Dr Hermann Renn and Herr Hanns Jarosch (S.K.F.), Dr Adolf Lauerbach and Herr Heinz Langhammer (F.A.G. Kugelfischer Georg Schäfer & Co.) and Helmut Bach in Schweinfurt; and old friends Arno Abendroth of Berlin, Norbert Krüger of Essen and Gus Lerch of Frankfurt. Thanks are due also to the following English people: V. C. D. Baker, Air Vice-Marshal S. O. Bufton, Mike Hodgson, Air Commodore W. I. C. Inness, Peter Pountney, Ted Sylvester, Annie Taverner, Alan Taylor and Cornelius van Emmerich.

For help in tracing Norwegian and French pilots flying with the R.A.F. I acknowledge the help of the Forsvarets Høgskole of Oslo and the Amicale des Forces Aériennes Françaises Libres in Paris; also Horst Amberg of the Gemeinschaft der Jagdflieger for finding some of the former Luftwaffe fighter pilots for whom I was searching. In general research matters I wish to thank helpful staff members at the National Archives at Washington and Suitland, the American Battle Monuments Commission, the 1361st Audiovisual Squadron U.S.A.F., various Ministry of Defence departments in London, the New Zealand Ministry of Defence, the Royal Geographical Society, the Cranwell College Library, the Belgian Air Force, the Swiss Air Force and the Deutsche Dienststelle in Berlin.

I acknowledge permission given by H.M. Stationery Office to quote from the British Official History.

Finally I would like to express my thanks to the following publications for publishing appeals for participants. United States: *Air Force, 8th A.F. News, Jewish Veteran, National Jewish Monthly, Retired Officer, T.W.A. Skyliner, United Airlines Newsletter*. United Kingdom: *Air Mail, Air Pictorial, R.A.F. News*. Europe: *Regensburg Mittelbayerische Zeitung, Schweinfurter Tagblatt, Luxembourger Wort, Echo* (Belgian Fédération des Travailleurs Déportés et Réfractaires), *Le Déporté du Travail* (French forced workers association).

Bibliography

Official Histories

Craven, W. F., and Cate, J. L., *The Army Air Forces in World War II*, University of Chicago Press, 1948–58

Webster, Sir Charles, and Frankland, Noble, *The Strategic Air Offensive against Germany, 1939–1945*, H.M.S.O., 1961

Other Works

Coffey, Thomas M., *Decision over Schweinfurt*, Robert Hale, 1978

Freeman, Roger A., *The Mighty Eighth*, Macdonald, 1970, and *Mighty Eighth War Diary*, Jane's, 1981

Golücke, Friedhelm, *Schweinfurt und der strategische Luftkrieg 1943*, Schöningh, Paderborn, 1980

Jablonski, Edward, *Double Strike*, Doubleday, 1974

Knoke, Heinz, *I Flew for the Führer*, Evans, 1953, and Bantam Books, 1979

LeMay, Curtis, and Kantor, MacKinlay, *Mission with LeMay*, Doubleday, 1965

Nilsson, John R., *The Story of the Century*, a history of the 100th Bomb Group published privately in 1946

Saundby, Sir Robert, *Air Bombardment*, Chatto & Windus, 1961

Wiener, Ludwig, *Schweinfurt sollte sterben,* Verlag Neues Form, Schweinfurt, n.d.

Index

'Abbeville Boys', 91
Abel, Lt D. T., 80, 83–4, 143, 147, 276
Adamson, S/Sgt W. W., 63, 71, 129, 146
Air Ministry (British), 24, 289, 294, 296
Air Ministry (German), 32
Anderson, Brig. Gen. F. L., 19, 27, 41–4, 76–80, 294, 312, 314–15
Antwerp, 87, 105, 260–61, 264, 266
Arcaro, Lt A. G., 213–14, 302
Arnold, Gen. H. H., 23, 41, 314
Atkinson, Lt C. P., 241–2
Augsburg, 33, 35

Baggs, 2/Lt J. W., 62, 199
Baker, Lt W. A., 114–15
Ball, Maj. C. F., 50, 176, 200
Barte, Oblt W., 341–2
Bartholomew, S/Sgt A., 152
Bartron, Brig. Gen. H. A., 307
Battle of Berlin, 296–7
Battle of Britain, 55, 89, 94
Baumgartner, S/Sgt L. A., 129
Bayerische Flugzeugwerke, 32–3; *see also* Messerschmitt factories
Becker, 2/Lt R. A., 272
Belgian workers, 38–9, 155, 160, 288, 291, 309
Bennett, Lt C. A., 282, 306
Bennett, Air Vice-Marshal D. C. T., 296–7
Berlin, 54; *see also* Battle of Berlin
Berzanski, T/Sgt A., 317
Bewg, F/Lt W. H., 171
Biddick, Lt C. R., 134, 139–40
Birksted, Maj. K., 184
Blakely Capt. E. E., 49, 128
Blakeslee, Lt Col D. J. M., 189
Bleicher, M., 159
'Blitz Week', 19
Bône airfield, 277
Börner, Lt H., 345
Borris, Maj. K., 92, 107–8, 111
Bosman, M., 117
Bouguen, Lt M., 168–9
Brady, Lt J. D., 128, 270
Bremen raid, 252
Broach, Lt W. G., 278
Brown, 2/Lt D. C., 244
Brown, 2/Lt W. S., 208
Brussellmanns, Madame A., 306
Bufton, A/Cdre S. O., 296
Burns, Lt Col R. H., 199
Butler, 2/Lt J. A., 50, 316

Canadian squadrons and airmen, 55, 184, 283, 298, 329, 331
Casablanca Directive, 20
Chapin, 2/Lt A. J., 255
Cherry, T/Sgt E. M., 246
Churchill, Winston, 20, 22
Claytor, Lt R. F., 113–14
Collins, T/Sgt E. J., 212, 300
Comet escape line, 306
Comstock, Lt H. E., 260
Conger, Lt P., 56

Conrad, F/Lt W. G., 264–6
Cormany, Lt, 197
Crabb, T/Sgt W. W., 275
Cruikshank, Lt C. B., 68, 278

Dahl, Hptm. W., 186
Dalinsky, S/Sgt J. J., 108
Darden, T/Sgt W. C., 266–7
Darling, 2/Lt C. H., 242, 305
Darrow, F/O G. R., 267
Davidoff, S/Sgt D., 149
Day, Lt V. H., 259–60
Deere, W/Cdr A., 168
Delaney, 2/Lt R. T., 301
Dentoni, Lt L., 150
Dimper, E., 154, 161
Dippel, Oblt, 123
Directives, *see* Casablanca Directive *and* Pointblank Directive
Doolittle, Maj. Gen. J. H., 27, 275, 315
Doroski, 2/Lt M. C., 132–3
Dulag Luft (Oberursel), 302–3
Dutch squadron and airmen, 173, 331
Dytman, 2/Lt J. W., 65, 214, 299

Eaker, Maj. Gen. I. C., 27–8, 41, 44, 54, 307, 314–15
Eder, Oblt G. P., 91, 207
Egender, 2/Lt H. F., 301
Eisenschenk, J., 158
Elias, S/Sgt R. J., 66, 114
Engels, Oblt H., 250–51
Ettinger, M., 35, 290
Eupen, 119, 121, 123, 184, 189, 193–7, 201, 208, 220, 241, 248, 251, 260

Fest, Fw., 204
Fichtel & Sachs, 31, 292
Fischer, Uffz. H., 259
Fischer, M., 30
Foreign workers, 37–40, 289, 298
Forkner, Lt H. L., 209–10
Frank, Hptm. H. D., 264
Frankfurt, 46, 124, 141, 220, 271, 302
French squadron and airmen, 55, 168, 184, 331
French workers, 38–40, 162, 290
Fries, Fw. O., 123, 127, 141
Fritzlehner, Uffz. F., 110
Frost, Lt E. D., 192, 197, 219, 251, 317
Fuhrmann, Fw., 204

Galland, Gen. A., 253, 258, 283
Galland, Lt P., 258
Galland, Maj. W. F., 253, 255, 257–8, 261
Gallerini, T/Sgt B. M., 109, 117–18, 305
Gaze, F/Lt F. A. O., 187
Genz, S/Sgt R. A., 305
German Army units, *see* Wehrmacht
Glunz, Ofw. A., 257
Goetz, S/Sgt J. K., 198, 267
Golücke, F., 227
Gordon-Forbes, Lt D. I., 149
Grabmann, Oberst W., 94, 96, 98, 177, 194, 283
Graf, Maj. H., 125
Gran, Sgt C., 266
Grislawski, Lt A., 127, 139
Gross, Col W. M., 54, 190–91, 202–3, 222, 248–9, 253, 256, 261, 266
Gust, 2/Lt D. D., 68, 248

Hadraba, Uffz. K., 168
Hamburg, 11, 18–19, 36, 41, 90, 282, 296
Hansen, Lt H. F., 214
Hargis, Lt J., 242–3
Harms, Lt H., 126, 136
Harris, Air Chief Marshal Sir A., 27, 43, 293–7, 312–13
Hayden, Lt R. W., 274
Hecht, T/Sgt G. R., 229

Hermichen, Hptm. R., 117–18
Hess, E., 235–6
Hesselyn, F/O R. B., 185–6
Hille, 2/Lt O. E., 127, 135, 343–4
Hitler, Adolf, 29, 36
Hoffmann, Ofw. H., 168–9, 171
Hohagen, Hptm. E., 266
Hollenbeck, Lt R. W., 274
Hoppe, Lt H., 265
Hoyt, Lt E. P., 245
Hummel, 2/Lt T. D., 132
Hyatt, 2/Lt R. E., 71, 192

Ihlefeld, Maj. H., 125
Imlohn, E., 162

Jacobs, F/O R. G. E., 267–8
Jacquet, J., 162
Jarvis, Lt L., 228
Jeschonnek, Gen. H., 309
Johnson, Capt. G. W., 259
Johnson, W/Cdr J. E., 264
Johnson, T/Sgt J. H., 61, 72, 206, 229
Joint Chiefs of Staff, 20–22
Jordan, H., 37, 163
Jouvin, P., 309
Judy, 2/Lt J. D., 245–6

Kaech, Sgt D. E., 198, 214
Kahler, Sgt J. R., 131, 136, 343–4
Katsarelis, S/Sgt P. A., 241
Keirsey, S/Sgt G. H., 305
Kelsey, F/Lt H. C., 95
Kemethmüller, Ofw. H., 109–12
Kennedy, Col W. L., 59, 275, 281
Kenny, Capt. T. F., 147
Kidd, Maj. J. B., 64, 128
Kiefner, Lt J., 106–7, 117, 183, 187–8
Kiel raid, 252
Knoke, Oblt H., 203–4, 254
Knollmüller, O., 290
Knox, Capt. R. M., 281, 341–3
Koenig, Oblt, 204
Kreisl, Hptfw. E., 236
Kugelfischer ball-bearing factory (K.G.F.), 30, 224, 233–4, 239–40, 291–2, 311
Kuhn, A., 34–5, 233, 238

LaCasse, Lt L., 71, 317
Ladegast, Oblt, 146
Langer, Hptm. H., 205–7
LaSpada, S/Sgt J. F., 342
Latham, Capt. J. L., 145–7
Lay, Lt Col B., 59
Layn, 2/Lt R. W., 246
Leahy, S/Sgt J. C., 129
LeMay, Col C. E.
  his character and background, 47–8, 61, 312
  preparations for the mission, 50, 53–4, 76
  on the mission, 80–82, 84, 87, 143–4, 148, 150–52, 271, 273, 275–7, 319
  comments on his performance, 287
  immediate aftermath, 289–90, 306–8
  later career, 315–16
Liège, 105, 118, 260–61, 286, 305
Lindbergh, C., 42
Lockhart, Lt E. M., 177, 266
Lockhart, 2/Lt W. D., 228
Lorch, 2/Lt K. R., 305
Lucht, Gen. R., 33, 36, 153
Luftwaffe
  Units
  Befehlshaber Mitte, 179
  XII Flieger Korps, 179
  1st Jagddivision, 94
  Jafü Deutsches Bucht, 179
  Jafü Holland-Ruhr, 94, 179, 194, 283
  Jafü Suddeutschland, 124
  JG 1, 90–91, 98, 332
  I/JG 1, 122, 194, 257, 332
  II/JG 1, 99, 105, 194, 333
  III/JG 1, 194, 333
  JG 2, 91, 181, 333

Luftwaffe – *contd.*
I/JG 2, 181, 253, 266, 333
II/JG 2, 172, 181, 194, 207, 333
III/JG 2, 181, 253, 266, 333
JG 3, 91, 333
I/JG 3, 91, 122, 137, 194, 333, 345
II/JG 3, 89, 334
III/JG 3, 91, 186, 194, 334
IV/JG 3, 334
JG 11, 91, 181, 217, 219, 334
I/JG 11, 179, 194, 334
II/JG 11, 179, 195, 203, 219, 334
III/JG 11, 179, 195, 334
4/JG 11, 204
5/JG 11, 203
JG 26, 90–93, 335
I/JG 26, 92, 99, 106–7, 109, 111, 116, 187, 194–5, 335
II/JG 26, 167, 172, 181, 253, 255, 257, 265, 335
III/JG 26, 90, 92, 99–100, 106, 109, 111, 122–3, 195, 335, 343
4/JG 26, 168
11/JG 26, 168, 172
JG 27, 167, 335
II/JG 51, 181, 195, 205, 216, 335
5/JG 51, 205
JG 104, 336
JG 106, 126, 336
JGr. 25, 125
JGr. 50, 125–7, 137, 139, 195, 216, 219, 257, 336
ZG 26, 195
Ind. Schutzst. Regensburg, 146, 274, 336
I/NJG 1, 258, 336
II/NJG 1, 122, 336
NJG 2, 190, 337
II/NJG 3, 89
I/NJG 4, 95
NJG 5, 195
I/NJG 6, 124, 126, 250, 337
NJG 101, 127, 337
II/NJG 101, 230
179th Flakregt, 229n.

Airfields
Abbeville, 43
Beaumont-sur-Oise, 333
Beauvais/Tille, 335
Bonn/Hangelar, 219
Brest, 333
Bryas, 166–7, 172
Conches, 333
Deelen, 94, 98, 122, 194, 332
Eindhoven, 181
Evreux, 253
Fürth, 334
Gilze Rijen, 179, 258, 336–7
Husum, 179, 334
Istres, 27, 280
Jever, 179, 181, 334
Kitzingen, 230
Lachen-Speyerdorf, 126, 336, 344
Le Bourget, 42–3, 86
Leeuwarden, 98, 333
Lille/Vendeville, 24, 27, 53, 166, 170–72, 181, 253, 265, 335
Mainz/Finthen, 124, 126, 250, 337
Mönchen-Gladbach, 98, 122, 137, 333, 345
Münster/Handorf, 98, 186, 334
Neubiberg, 335
Nordholz, 90
Oldenburg, 179, 334
Poix, 43, 166, 170, 172, 269, 333
Rechlin, 205
Rheine, 179
St André, 333
St Trond, 122–3, 258, 271, 336, 341
Salon, 280
Schiphol, 90, 98–9, 109, 111, 118, 122, 333, 335, 343
Stuttgart/Echterdingen, 127, 141
Vannes, 333
Vechta, 179
Venlo, 258, 263, 336
Vitry en Artois, 333

Wiesbaden/Erbenheim, 125–7, 216, 336
Woensdrecht, 86–7, 98–9, 106, 116, 179, 183, 186, 269–70, 333, 335
Lyle, Maj. L. P., 72–3, 208

Maastricht, 105, 118, 121, 124, 258, 260
McCauley, Lt F. E., 259
McCollom, Maj. L. G., 86, 105, 111–12
McDonnell, T/Sgt A. P., 108–9, 300
McKay, Lt D. B., 134, 139
McKeegan, Lt R., 254
Mahurin, Capt. W. H., 258, 260
Mannheim, 124, 141, 202
Marshall, Gen. G. C., 23
Mason, Lt R. C., 114, 138
Mencow, 2/Lt N., 128, 278
Merchant, Lt D. W., 228–9
Messerschmitt GmbH and factories, 22–6, 33–4, 53, 153–65, 287–90, 310
Messerschmitt, Prof. W., 33
Messersmith, Lt F. E., 301
Mielmann, Uffz. R., 259
Mietusch, Maj. K., 111
Mikel, S/Sgt G. L., 305
Minnich, 2/Lt M. G., 116
Moore, Col J. G., 149–50
Morrill, Lt R. R., 70, 83, 129, 271
Morse, Lt H., 176, 200
Mössner, Fw. W., 92, 106, 118
Multerer, H., 290
Munich, 29, 32, 46, 270
Mutschler, 2/Lt D. L., 261

National Archives, 24n.
Nayovitz, Lt B. W., 15, 17, 109
Nelson, Lt L., 247
Nelson, Lt R. F., 305
Neuner, Uffz. H., 259
New Zealand squadrons and airmen, 55, 168, 184–5, 331
Nieroda, A., 234
Norton, S/Sgt H. A., 342
Norwegian squadrons and airmen, 55, 184, 266, 329
Nuremberg, 11, 29, 32, 94, 141, 238, 282
Nutting, 2/Lt R. J., 113

Oakes, Lt D. K., 272
Obermeier, K., 156–7
Old, Col A. J., 80, 84–5

Payne, S/Sgt C. E., 272
Pearl Harbor, 17, 47, 55
Peenemünde raid, 43, 282, 294–5, 309
Penick, S/Sgt E., 244
Penrod, 2/Lt J. D., 317
Perkins, Lt D. F., 69
Perry, 2/Lt R. H., 128
Pettinger, Lt J. F., 130
Piper, Maj. P., 68, 123, 150, 273
Ploesti raid, 22–3, 69, 182, 297
Pointblank Directive, 21, 24
Poirier, Sgt L., 168
Polish squadrons and airmen, 55, 184, 187–8, 263, 329
Polish workers, 38–9
Pollet, J., 160
Pompetti, F/O P. E., 190
Portal, Air Chief Marshal Sir C., 296–7
Poschenrieder, R., 37, 160
Pösl, Bürg. L., 30, 311
Preston, Col M. A., 28, 61, 285

Rader, Maj. W. S., 191
Rae, F/O J. D., 168–9
Rapport, 2/Lt S. P., 272
Regan, 2/Lt J. R., 135, 343, 345
Regensburg
origins of raid on, 19–28
description of, 31–40
planning of raid, 41–54, 76–9
briefing notes for raid, 338–40
actual bombing, 144–65, 287–91

Regensburg – *contd.*
aftermath of bombing, 308–10
Reichardt, 2/Lt L. L., 137
Reichert, Uffz. A., 92, 168
Rice, T/Sgt D., 68
Roane, 2/Lt O. D., 85, 139, 308
Robert, A., 155
Roberts, Maj. E. P., 190
Robinson, Lt R. L., 261
Roosevelt, President, 20, 22
Rose, Lt H., 181, 219
Rouen raid, 44
Royal Air Force
Bomber Command, 11, 18, 20, 24, 27, 41, 43, 293–5, 297, 310
Fighter Command, 55, 169
Eagle Squadrons, 56, 189
Squadrons
3 Sdn, 330
19 Sdn, 330
41 Sdn, 330
56 Sdn, 330
65 Sdn, 330
91 Sdn, 330
122 Sdn, 330
129 Sdn, 187, 329
132 Sdn, 330
141 Sdn, 95
174 Sdn, 330
175 Sdn, 330
181 Sdn, 170, 330
182 Sdn, 170, 330
183 Sdn, 170, 172, 331
222 Sdn, 184–7, 329
226 Sdn, 173, 331
245 Sdn, 331
247 Sdn, 170, 331
303 Sdn, 329
316 Sdn, 329
320 Sdn, 173, 331
331 Sdn, 329
332 Sdn, 329
341 Sdn, 168, 331
401 Sdn, 331
402 Sdn, 331
403 Sdn, 329
411 Sdn, 331
412 Sdn, 331
416 Sdn, 331
421 Sdn, 329
485 Sdn, 168–9, 331
486 Sdn, 170, 172, 331
540 Sdn, 151
602 Sdn, 331
Airfields
Attlebridge, 331
Benson, 151
Biggin Hill, 331
Bradwell Bay, 184
Hornchurch, 184, 329
Kenley, 184, 329
Kingsnorth, 330
Lashenden, 329
Lydd, 330–31
Manston, 184, 265, 330
Merston, 331
Newchurch, 330–31
New Romney, 330–31
Northolt, 184, 329
North Weald, 184, 329
Staplehurst, 331
Swanton Morley, 331
Tangmere, 331
Westhampnett, 330
Ruhr, the, 36, 69, 124–5, 296
Rupprecht, Hptm. H. W., 141, 271
Russian workers, 38, 158, 290
Rust, J. C., 37, 239
Rutan, Lt D. J., 199

Sargent, Capt R. L., 255
Sarnow, 2/Lt H. P., 155, 306
Saundby, Air Marshal Sir R., 24
Schäfer, G., 30
Schleef, Lt H., 187
Schottenheim, Oberbürg. O., 32
Schreppel, S/Sgt J., 117
Schultz, S/Sgt H. H., 192
Schulz, Lt P. R., 67
Schweinfurt
origins of raid on, 19–28

description of, 29–31, 35–9
planning of raid, 41–54, 76–9, 175
actual bombing, 221–40, 291
aftermath of bombing, 309–14
Septime, Capt. R. S., 131
Setzer, F., 159
Sexton, F/O J. N., 251
Shaver, 2/Lt D. A., 147, 274
Shipe, S/Sgt P. F., 209–10
Shotland, 2/Lt H. P., 139, 282
Shouldice, F/Sgt C. M., 264–5
Simpson, Lt W. L., 201
Smith, 2/Lt C. N., 304
Smith, S/Sgt E. C., 300
Smith, Sgt E. M., 95
Smith, Lt H. M., 232
Smith, 2/Lt J. F., 108
Sneed, 2/Lt W. H., 276
Snyder, F/O R. L., 139–40
Solga, S/Sgt S., 212
Sommers, 2/Lt P. A., 109–10, 116
Sottevaast raid, 268
Spann, S/Sgt E. R., 130
Specht, Hptm. G., 219
Speer, Albert, 33, 311
Springer, Lt J., 230–31
Stackhouse, Lt C. B., 200, 252
Stalingrad, 32, 36
Stang, E., 155
Stemmler, H., 146–7
Stewart, 2/Lt C. P., 229–30
Stewart, Lt J. D., 211–12
Stokes, S/Sgt L. R., 117
Stone, Lt Col J. J., 189
Stulz, Lt R. M., 259–60
Stuttgart, 124, 202, 312–13
Sugas, Lt A., 260
Sundberg, Lt J. L., 116
Sweningsen, 2/Lt O., 229

Taylor, Lt Col O. B., 277, 306
Telergma airfield, 277
Thomas, S/Sgt L. H., 210
Thompson, S/Sgt J. P., 68, 176, 197
Thurn und Taxis family, 32–3, 36, 148
Tobin, 2/Lt E. F., 342
Tripe, F/Lt P. V. K., 184, 186
Turin raid, 43
Turner, Col H. M., 54, 249, 255–6
Turney, P/O H. E., 185
Tyler, Lt D. A., 246
Tyson, 2/Lt A. W., 132

U-boat bases and yards, 18, 20–22
Uhlmann, Uffz. W., 96
United States Army
12th Division, 311
42nd Division, 311
United States Army Air Force
bombing policy and early raids, 17–22, 312–14
policy on long-range fighter escort, 55–6, 192, 297, 314
Strategic Air Command (U.S.A.F.), 73, 316
8th Air Force, 17, 19–24, 27, 41, 56, 61, 70, 78, 279, 285, 294, 307, 312–15
9th Air Force, 20, 22–3
12th Air Force and Service Command, 306–7
15th Air Force, 27
N. W. African Strategic Air Force, 27, 275, 280
VIII Bomber Command, 24n., 27, 41, 43–4, 46, 48, 76, 78–79, 182, 284, 291, 312, 314–15
1st Bombardment Wing, 24n., 44, 46–53, 61–2, 76–9, 174–8, 191, 279–81, 291–2, 315, 323
4th Bombardment Wing, 24n., 41, 44, 46–54, 59, 63, 78–80, 100, 150–52, 177–9, 270, 279–81, 287–8, 306, 319
Bomb Groups
2nd B. Gp, 275
91st B. Gp, 53, 60, 174, 177, 192,

U.S. Army Air Force – *contd.*
197–8, 202, 208, 210, 213, 222, 224, 242, 245, 266–7, 280, 282, 301, 323
92nd B. Gp, 62–3, 204, 211, 224, 255, 282, 300, 325
93rd B. Gp, 272
94th B. Gp, 15, 66, 70, 83, 107–8, 129, 149–50, 271, 278, 300, 319
95th B. Gp, 63, 66, 81, 84, 107–108, 113–14, 138, 150, 274, 301, 319
96th B. Gp, 53, 80–81, 83, 123, 143, 145, 148, 156, 280, 308, 319
97th B. Gp, 275
99th B. Gp, 275
100th B. Gp, 49, 59, 63–4, 68, 81, 85, 109–10, 113, 128, 132, 134, 138–40, 150–51, 270, 272, 274, 278, 280–82, 305, 308, 321, 341–2, 345
301st B. Gp, 275
303rd B. Gp, 61–2, 68, 72, 205, 226, 228, 248, 251, 280, 317, 325
305th B. Gp, 47, 54, 61, 69, 224, 226, 246, 254, 261, 311, 312, 326
306th B. Gp, 61, 222n., 224, 248, 256, 261, 280, 326
323rd B. Gp, 269, 330
351st B. Gp, 65, 176, 197, 199–200, 214, 224, 252, 299–300, 317, 326
379th B. Gp, 28, 61, 67, 72, 205, 208, 226, 228, 245, 251, 285, 326
381st B. Gp, 61, 71, 192, 194, 197, 199, 201–2, 209, 219, 224, 226, 228, 232, 241, 251, 255, 267, 280, 282, 317, 327
384th B. Gp, 50, 61–2, 68, 176, 197–9, 224, 229, 232, 243, 301, 316, 328
385th B. Gp, 59, 67–9, 71, 109–10, 123, 129, 131, 137, 148, 150, 152, 271, 273, 276, 317, 321
386th B. Gp, 167, 330
387th B. Gp, 269, 330
388th B. Gp, 65, 67, 81, 143, 148, 276, 322
390th B. Gp, 54, 63, 65, 71, 80–84, 104, 127–32, 135, 137, 140, 146–9, 156, 272–4, 276, 278, 282, 287, 303, 322, 343, 345
101st Composite Gp, 197, 203, 224
103rd Composite Gp, 205, 226
306th Composite Gp, 224
Bomb Squadrons
353rd Sdn, 197
401st Sdn, 197, 202
422nd Sdn, 312–13
511th Sdn, 176, 197
525th Sdn, 205, 208
534th Sdn, 201
Fighter Groups
4th F. Gp, 188–91, 194, 196, 328
56th F. Gp, 56, 86–7, 111, 113, 118, 255–6, 258, 260–61, 263, 286, 328
78th F. Gp, 188–9, 329
353rd F. Gp, 86–7, 103, 111, 113, 261, 329
Fighter Squadrons
61st Sdn, 257, 259
62nd Sdn, 259
63rd Sdn, 257, 259–60
Airfields
Alconbury, 62–3, 325
Bassingbourn, 60, 174–5, 323
Boxted, 330
Bury St Edmunds, 66, 80, 319
Chelveston, 61, 326
Chipping Ongar, 245, 330
Debden, 328
Duxford, 329
Earls Colne, 330
Framlingham, 80–81, 322

Grafton Underwood, 61, 267–8, 328
Great Ashfield, 69, 80, 321
Halesworth, 328
Horham, 63, 80, 319
Kimbolton, 61, 326
Knettishall, 67, 80, 322
Martlesham Heath, 247
Metfield, 86, 329
Molesworth, 68, 325
Polebrook, 176, 326
Ridgewell, 175, 327
Snetterton Heath, 80, 319
Thorpe Abbots, 59, 63, 80, 321
Thurleigh, 326
United States Strategic Bombing Survey, 30, 291–2

Vance, Lt P. W., 278
Van Noy, Lt G. S., 81, 274–5
Van Pelt, S/Sgt A. W., 83, 104, 132
Vêche, L., 309
Verdun, S/Sgt F. L., 152
Vereinigte Kugellager factories (V.K.F. Nos. 1 and 2), 30–31, 224, 233, 235, 311
Vincent, F/O A. E. S., 171
Vollert, Obergef. H., 263, 265
Von Arb, Capt. G. W., 80–81, 276
Von Bonin, Hptm. E., 341–2
Von Der Heyde, 2/Lt D. S., 194

Wagner, Lt E. D., 206–7
Wallace, Gov. George, 316
Warsaw, 2/Lt E. E., 342, 345
Wasche, S/Sgt J. E., 211–12, 302
Washington Conference, 22, 294
Wehrmacht unit
36th Panzer Regt, 31, 236
Weiser, S/Sgt F. P., 67
Wentworth, 2/Lt W. L., 62, 301
Wenzel, 2/Lt J. E., 140
Werner, Lt T., 266
Wheeler, Capt. D. W., 248, 256
Wheeler, Lt W. H., 192–3, 202, 210
Wiener Neustadt raid, 22–7, 36, 272, 297
Wilhelmshaven raid, 18
Williams, Capt. D. M., 217
Williams, S/Sgt G. A., 114, 133
Williams, Brig. Gen. R. B., 47, 53–54, 76–7, 191, 202–3, 291, 315, 323
Wilson, Lt C., 200
Wilson, Lt C. R., 243–5
Wilson, Col R. A., 54
Wittan, Col E., 81–2, 149, 276
Witzke, Lt, 341
Wohlers, Hptm. H., 250
Woodbury, 2/Lt C. M., 177
Wurzbach, Lt Col C. K., 202, 221, 228, 266
Würzburg, 37, 141, 235, 249, 311

Yelle, 2/Lt E. J., 174, 209

Zemke, Col H., 255–6, 258–61
Zillmann, E., 235

MORE ABOUT PENGUINS, PELICANS AND PUFFINS

For further information about books available from Penguins please write to Dept EP, Penguin Books Ltd, Harmondsworth, Middlesex UB7 0DA.

In the U.S.A.: For a complete list of books available from Penguins in the United States write to Dept DG, Penguin Books, 299 Murray Hill Parkway, East Rutherford, New Jersey 07073.

In Canada: For a complete list of books available from Penguins in Canada write to Penguin Books Canada Ltd, 2801 John Street, Markham, Ontario L3R 1B4

In Australia: For a complete list of books available from Penguins in Australia write to the Marketing Department, Penguin Books Australia Ltd, P.O. Box 257, Ringwood, Victoria 3134.

In New Zealand: For a complete list of books available from Penguins in New Zealand write to the Marketing Department, Penguin Books (N.Z.) Ltd, P.O. Box 4019, Auckland 10.

In India: For a complete list of books available from Penguins in India write to Penguin Overseas Ltd, 706 Eros Apartments, 56 Nehru Place, New Delhi 110019.

A CHOICE OF PENGUINS

☐ ***The English House Through Seven Centuries***
Olive Cook £10.95

From Norman defensiveness and Tudor flourish to Georgian elegance and Victorian grandeur, this beautiful book records and describes the wealth of domestic architecture in Britain. With photographs by Edwin Smith.

☐ ***The Daughters of Karl Marx*** £4.95

The letters of Jenny, Laura and Eleanor Marx: 'An enlightening introduction to the preoccupations, political and personal, of the Marx family' – Lionel Kochan. 'The tale they tell is riveting' – *Standard*

☐ ***The First Day on the Somme***
Martin Middlebrook £3.95

1 July 1916 was the blackest day of slaughter in the history of the British Army. 'The soldiers receive the best service a historian can provide: their story told in their own words' – *Guardian*

☐ ***Lord Hervey's Memoirs*** £4.95

As an intimate of the Royal Court – and as a particularly witty and malicious raconteur – Lord Hervey was ideally equipped to write this sparkling account of royal personalities, politics and intrigues, 1727–37.

☐ ***Some Lovely Islands*** **Leslie Thomas** £5.95

The islands off the coast of Britain, and their islanders, are celebrated in this delightful book by well-known novelist Leslie Thomas. With photographs by Peter Chèze-Brown.

☐ ***Harold Nicolson: Diaries and Letters 1930–64*** £4.95

A selection of Nicolson's famous diaries and letters. 'A brilliant portrait of English society . . . a touching self-portrait of a highly intelligent and civilized man' – Kenneth Clark

A CHOICE OF PENGUINS

☐ ***A Colder Eye* Hugh Kenner** £4.95

A study of the modern Irish writers. 'Anyone interested in language, in theatre history, in, indeed, the great comic literature of Joyce, Beckett and O'Brien will find this a highly enjoyable read' – *Punch*

☐ ***The Europeans* Luigi Barzini** £2.95

Witty, stylish and provocative, this is a veteran journalist's-eye view of the past and present character of the British, French, Germans, Italians and Dutch. 'Fascinating . . . read it immediately' – *The New York Times*

☐ ***In Search of Ancient Astronomies* Ed. E. C. Krupp** £4.95

Forming an introduction to archaeo-astronomy, a series of new essays on the world's most spectacular ancient monuments, from Stonehenge to the pyramids. 'Outstanding . . . accessible even to the beginner' – Patrick Moore

☐ ***Clinging to the Wreckage* John Mortimer** £2.50

The bestselling autobiography by the creator of Rumpole and the playwright author of *A Voyage Round My Father*. 'Enchantingly witty . . . England would be a poor place without Mr Mortimer' – Auberon Waugh

☐ ***Chips: The Diaries of Sir Henry Channon*** £4.95

'Chips' Channon, M.P., knew everybody that was anybody. Here, from the abdication of Edward VIII to the coronation of Elizabeth II, he serves up history with an irresistible 'H.P.' sauce of gossip and glamour.

☐ ***The Miracle of Dunkirk* Walter Lord** £2.95

'This is contemporary history at its most readable' – *The New York Times*. 'It gives an effective new polish to the golden legend' – *The Times*